SECOND EDITION

Writing in the
Technical Fields

A PRACTICAL GUIDE

THORSTEN EWALD

OXFORD
UNIVERSITY PRESS

OXFORD
UNIVERSITY PRESS

Oxford University Press is a department of the University of Oxford.
It furthers the University's objective of excellence in research, scholarship,
and education by publishing worldwide. Oxford is a registered trade mark of
Oxford University Press in the UK and in certain other countries.

Published in Canada by
Oxford University Press
8 Sampson Mews, Suite 204,
Don Mills, Ontario M3C 0H5 Canada

www.oupcanada.com

Copyright © Oxford University Press Canada 2017

The moral rights of the author have been asserted

Database right Oxford University Press (maker)

First Edition published in 2014

Library and Archives Canada Cataloguing in Publication
Ewald, Thorsten, author
Writing in the technical fields: a practical guide/Thorsten
Ewald.—Second edition.

Includes bibliographical references and index.
ISBN 978–0–19–902149–9 (softcover)

1. Technical writing. I. Title.

T11.E83 2017   808'.066   C2016-907798-5

Cover image: © iStock/Varijanta

Oxford University Press is committed to our environment.
Wherever possible, our books are printed on paper which comes from
responsible sources.

Printed and bound in the United States of America

2 3 4 — 20 19 18 17

To my wife Caroline, for her patience and support during the writing of this text and during the many long, cranky evenings of marking.

Contents

Checklists

Acknowledgments

Many thanks to everyone at Oxford University Press for their help in putting together and polishing *Writing in the Technical Fields*: Cailen Swain, Peter Chambers, and Tara Tovell.

I've been teaching technical writing and business communication at the British Columbia Institute of Technology since 1997 and owe a huge debt to the many colleagues in multiple departments who have provided material, advice, aid, and comfort over the years; who have shared triumphs and frustrations; and who have served as inspirations and—in occasional, self-effacing, and amusing anecdotes—examples of what not to do. They have all contributed to my understanding of the field, to the development of my teaching methods, and to the creation of this text. Most especially, however, thanks are owed to Katherine Golder, David Hamilton, Deanna Levis, and Frank Schnurr for providing their own materials and suggesting student samples for use in this text.

Material, advice, and humour were also provided by my friend and occasional collaborator Andre Lanz. He has also generously allowed me to use in this text some of the fruits of our collaborations and a number of photos from his personal collection.

Similarly, I'd like to thank the professionals in the field who shared their experiences in the "In the Field" boxes. They have given the text a relevance to students that it might otherwise not have enjoyed: Heidi Carson, Gary Dean, Karin Garandza, Tom Gilchrist, Eric Hanson, Andre Lanz, and Behnaz Montazavi.

I also need to thank the legions of students over the years who have inspired me and challenged me to do better and for whose benefit this text is intended. It's incredibly rewarding to be in constant contact with such dedicated, hard-working, and energetic young people. It is also very comforting; the future of Canada is in good hands, it seems to me.

Of these many students, I'd especially like to thank the following for permitting me to use some of their assignments as samples: Scott Bird, Maxsim Opushnyev, Chang Zheng Michael Chen, Hamid Serti, and Monica Ip. I'm hoping that seeing the good work that these students have contributed will set a high, but clearly achievable, bar for future students.

Finally, of course, I need to thank my long-suffering wife and best friend, Caroline, for her patience and support, though in a candid moment she might admit that having some alone time while I immured myself in the study all those evenings was not altogether a bad thing.

Introduction

Rationale for This Text

The education marketplace is pretty crowded with technical writing textbooks, so you are right to question why you should choose this one. This text has been created because, despite the numerous textbooks extant for first-year survey courses on technical writing, none really suited my course. I started to develop my own modules to send out to students and have now bundled them into a text in case they suit your course as well. There are several reasons why most other technical writing books haven't worked well in my courses.

First, I have found that technical writing textbooks are generally too big and too expensive. They might make good desktop references to accompany students through their professional lives, but they contain too many chapters and too much information for a two-term introductory technical writing course. This text is pared down.

Second, students find the writing of many texts overly formal. This formal tone discourages them from reading and makes it hard for them to absorb the information they require. It also seems out of step with the much less formal style of writing generally used (and deemed perfectly appropriate) in the North American workplace. This text also employs a lot of labelled graphics in place of long explanations—for instance, to demonstrate the layout of letters. This is hardly a unique approach, but it is helpful.

Third, many technical writing textbooks don't show students how to actually achieve results on the page: for instance, how to use Word properly to format text, insert citations, and the like. It's always surprising how little facility some students have with word-processing software, despite their expertise with smartphones and their inventive use of the Internet to shortcut their homework.

This text does one more thing. You've probably found that students have little trouble copying the formatting of documents and can usually be taught how to select content and how to sequence it. What they consistently have trouble with is the writing itself. They struggle not so much with the macro-design of documents, but with clear expression. They are self-conscious about their writing, fearful of speaking incorrectly on the page, and end up writing strangulated, stilted, awkward sentences and choppy paragraphs—to a large extent because they think that writing needs to be difficult. But of course, it doesn't.

On the other hand, once we get beyond those grating "It was, like, OMGs" and "Oh shut ups!," you've probably discovered that many students are well able to construct clear sentences and fluid paragraphs—when they are speaking. This text attempts to harness that natural communication ability and transfer it to the students' writing. Given that goal, it contains two substantial chapters on writing (Chapter 2 on sentences and Chapter 3 on paragraphs). These can be incorporated into the course and lecture material or just assigned as home study. Instructors can access additional writing exercises for both chapters online. And throughout, as mentioned, the text models a casual yet clear and effective writing style that is less intimidating and easier to emulate than that of many other texts.

Technical writing is first and foremost practical writing, and it is a change agent. Its purpose is to convey information required by a specific reader in a specific situation as briefly, clearly, and simply as possible so that the reader can perform whatever follow-up task may be required. This text attempts to model that practicality. It is an introductory text for students in a technical field who are getting their first exposure to technical writing. It can't be all things to all people, especially considering its compact size and targeted price point, but I hope it will help you in the design of your technical writing course.

Thorsten Ewald
Pragmatist

Introduction to the Second Edition

Surprisingly and gratifyingly, this text has sold well enough to warrant a second edition. Unsurprisingly, but equally gratifyingly, instructors who have adopted the text and reviewers offered the opportunity by the Oxford University Press have provided suggestions for improvement. I have tried to please.

This second edition of *Writing in the Technical Fields* embraces two major improvements and a number of smaller ones. The first major improvement is that many of the chapters now contain more writing exercises that students can access directly without instructors having to print out and photocopy the materials from the website— or download and display them on screen. This will make classroom prep that much easier and will enable instructors to assign exercises as homework to accompany the reading. Dastardly, but effective.

To benefit instructors who have been using the exercises from the website, we have promoted many of those exercises to the textbook; this means that returning instructors will be familiar with them and won't have to do as much prep. However, we have also included a slew of additional exercises and answer keys on the new, improved, and expanded website. See for yourself whether I'm overpromising.

The second big change—or series of changes that add up to a big change—is that we've included subjects that instructors found missing in the first edition and were forced to teach without textual support; this includes a more thorough description of the use of headings, expanded information on copyright, and a sample functional résumé, to name but a few. I have tried to fill all the gaps in the original text.

In addition, I've made a large number of small textual changes to sharpen the clarity of the writing and to enhance the students' comprehension.

You will already have noted the new layout, colour scheme, and cover page.

I'm very pleased with the way things have turned out and hope that you will be too. I also sincerely hope, however, that if, or when, you find more things to improve, you will let us know. I want this text, perhaps by the third edition, to offer precisely the assistance that you would like in your classroom.

The Chapters in Detail

Chapter 1: Why Technical People Needn't Fear Writing

Chapter 1 introduces the notion that technical writing, though not easy, doesn't have to be hard. It stresses that we all have natural communication abilities that we can harness if we don't get too scared of the empty page and freeze up. It introduces the notion of a natural, flowing, conversational writing style and explains how the planning and editing cycles can help to achieve such a style. Many texts prefer to describe the planning and editing of documents in chapters dealing with formal reports. The point that this chapter makes is that all writing benefits from a bit of forethought and that all documents require some editing. However, when we are actually writing, we should imagine ourselves sitting across the desk from our readers and write more or less the way we'd speak to them—without the F-bombs, of course.

Chapter 2: Technical Sentences

Chapter 2 describes how to create concise, clear sentences by focusing on a short checklist of common errors. The point is not only to get students to look for and correct these errors—for example passive voice, weak expletives, nominalization, low-content expressions—but also to emphasize that writing well is a craft that can be mastered by technical people. Who better, after all, to apply checklists and work to a standard? The end of the chapter offers exercises with examples from multiple disciplines, the answer keys to which, as well as additional exercises, are on the companion website.

Chapter 3: Technical Paragraphs

Chapter 3 applies the same principles as Chapter 2, but to the marshalling of sentences into fluid and coherent paragraphs. It provides guidelines and a structured approach to building paragraphs, as technical students tend to respond to this approach. These rules obviously don't instantly create great writers, but if followed, they will instantly improve most students' writing. The end of the chapter offers exercises with examples from multiple disciplines, the answer keys to which, as well as additional exercises, are on the companion website.

Chapter 4: Parallelism, Lists, and Layout

Chapter 4 begins by describing parallelism in sentences before moving on to lists. It makes clear that lists are a convenience for the reader, not the writer, and that they are a way to draw attention to important information, not an excuse for sloppy point-form paragraph development. This chapter also describes how headings and lists function as navigation aids to help readers find key information.

Chapter 5: Routine Correspondence

Once students have learned the building blocks of technical writing—sentences, paragraphs, and lists—they are ready to put them together into technical documents. Chapter 5 covers routine letters, memos, and emails. It makes the point that correspondence takes our stead because we can't always be there to speak to the reader in person. However, as already noted, we should think of ourselves as sitting across the desk from the reader, and in most situations, we should write in that same tone—at least for our first draft. This will make the text flow more naturally and will make the writing much easier.

Chapter 6: Technical Reports and Documents

Chapter 6 is light on textual explanation, letting the examples with extensive labels and captions do the talking. The focus is on seeing reports as logical structures that help us achieve specific purposes and on understanding that form follows function, another notion that plays to the strengths of technically minded people.

Chapter 7: Formal Reports

Chapter 7 describes how any report, if it is sufficiently long, may be formally dressed. But the purpose of this formality is not primarily to impress with good manners, but to enable the reader to navigate a document easily and find necessary information quickly. This chapter explains the formal report from a reader's perspective. It also explains how to use Word to do some of the necessary formatting.

Chapter 8: Intercultural Communication, Collaborative Writing, and Document Control

Chapter 8 describes how to write in teams, from planning to group writing to creating a unified voice. One of the difficulties of working in groups is keeping track of all group members' input and making sure their writing and editing don't get confused. This is the essence of document control. Today's students have more intercultural experience than any previous generation; they are accepting, generous, and open. But a few points on intercultural communication are still worth making, particularly given the internationalization and localization of technical writing in an increasingly globalized economy and problem-solving environment.

Chapter 9: References and Citations

Chapter 9 is a pretty standard guide to providing references and citations, and it gives the standard explanation of why they're necessary. This chapter chooses as its focus the numerical citation method frequently used by engineering and scientific organizations. It explains that many different forms of citation are possible and that the one to use will depend on the preferences of instructors, bosses, professional organizations, and publishers. It also demonstrates how most citation methods assigned can be employed using Word's References tools or online citation engines.

Chapter 10: Technical Graphics

Chapter 10 is short, pithy, and, quite appropriately, graphic. It demonstrates what sort of graphics best convey what sort of information, and how to use Word to create, insert, and embed those graphics. It also describes some of the common ways in which graphics can misrepresent information, by accident or design.

Chapter 11: Job Application Packages

Chapter 11 describes how students should create the sort of résumés and application letters that will help them leave the academic nest successfully. To be effective, résumés must work for all three stages of the selection process: the glance, the scan, and the read. Application letters require more than just persuasive information; they require a persuasive style that helps potential employers visualize the student as the sort of hard-working, dependable, talented, long-term employee on whom they'll take a chance. Some samples demonstrate how to achieve this.

Chapter 12: Technical Definitions and Descriptions

Chapter 12 helps students write technical definitions in three lengths and levels of detail (parenthetical, formal, and extended) and to plan and craft audience- and context-appropriate mechanism and process descriptions. The focus, as ever in this text, is on plentiful examples with helpful annotations.

Chapter 13: Instructions, Procedures, and Manuals

Chapter 13 helps students keep their instruction steps concise, simple, and sequential. It also helps them remember to put the notes, cautions, warnings, and danger alerts in the right places. Because students are unlikely to have to write a full manual in a first-year technical writing course, this chapter provides only a brief discussion of how manuals combine a series of instructions and/or procedures into a comprehensive document.

Chapter 14: Oral Presentations

Chapter 14 was left to the end not so much because students hate it the most, but because oral presentations are often the last assignment in a technical writing course, in conjunction with the term-end formal report. This chapter provides practical information on how to organize oral presentations, how to sequence slides, and how to create proper transitions between sections. It shows how to use PowerPoint to create "progressive reveals" of text or graphics and provides easy-to-follow (or at least understand) tips on how to stand and deliver.

Appendix A: Punctuation and Grammar

Appendix A provides an overview of the most common grammatical mistakes made by students and uses examples and explanations to help students correct them. These errors are arranged alphabetically so that instructors can note them in the margins of students' papers and expect students to find the error and learn to correct it.

Appendix B: Mechanics and Conventions

Appendix B does the same as Appendix A, but for mechanics rather than grammar. It includes some technical mechanics, such as Latin numerical prefixes, the proper use of degree symbols for different temperature scales, and so on.

Appendix C: Ethics

Appendix C provides a brief overview of the importance of ethics in general, touches upon ethical requirements for students and professionals, and describes how ethics apply to technical writing. It's not intended that this appendix turn sinners into saints, but merely that it create a better understanding of the topic and stimulate some discussion.

Glossary

The glossary is an alphabetized collection of frequently confused or misused words, such as "affect" vs. "effect," "all ready" vs. "already," and "continual" vs. "continuous." It is intended as a place to which instructors can refer students when they encounter these common mistakes in the students' writing. As such, it should save instructors from having to write lengthy explanations in the margins. This section is also intended to be enjoyed if read on its own, believe it or not.

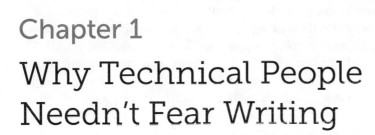

Chapter 1

Why Technical People Needn't Fear Writing

In this chapter we'll introduce the practice of writing in the technical workplace in four easy parts:

· Writing in the Technical Workplace
· Why Technical People Can Master Technical Writing
· Attributes of Technical Writing
· The Writing Process.

You probably chose a technical field because you want to make the world a better place in some small, practical, technical way. Perhaps you'd like to design buildings or mechanical systems; perhaps you're thinking of developing medical technologies or sustainable practices. Maybe you have a hunch about a better mousetrap. What appeals to you in any case is the idea of making real change in the real world and seeing the results of your labours. What you probably don't want to do is write about it.

Unfortunately, there's just no getting away from writing in the technical workplace because you'll never work in perfect isolation, and where there's a need to communicate, there's a need to write. But this needn't worry you. Writing is a technical skill, not a gift, and this means that as a technical person, you are actually in an enviable position when it comes to learning to write well, regardless of what your high school English teacher may have said about your writing.

Writing in the Technical Workplace

The Extent of Writing in the Technical Workplace

Writing is a constant in the technical workplace because nothing can happen without communication. Every project you work on—and you may be working on several at a time—involves teams of people, often dispersed across offices, cities, or even countries. And every step of every project requires documentation. For instance, the extension of one of the light rapid transit (LRT) lines for the City of Calgary required a request for proposals (RFP) of over 700 pages. A primary engineering firm in Vancouver produced the RFP in collaboration with a series of subcontractors.

If you had been a civil engineer working on the RFP, you would have been communicating constantly with peers in your group to coordinate activities and workflows and to verify or distribute information. You would also have been communicating with subcontractors responsible for writing different sections of the RFP, with surveyors in Calgary, with the City of Calgary Engineering Department, and with a host of other stakeholders, as they are called. At the same time, you might have had to write progress reports to management within your company and to the client, to write employee evaluations for team members, or to help with the selection of subcontractors, recording your deliberations and decisions in writing.

Before the RFP was awarded to your firm, you might have been involved in the process of securing the work, also mostly in writing because there always has to be a paper trail proving due diligence.

Once the RFP was posted, it drew competing proposals from a number of engineering companies vying to design and build the LRT extension according to the specifications laid out in the RFP. Those proposals all ran to several hundred, if not a thousand, pages, all written at great effort. When one proposal was selected, meaning that the rest were written in vain, the selection committee had to write a report to justify the choice, again to prove due diligence.

When construction started, the engineers overseeing the project kept a project log and wrote regular inspection reports, progress reports, quality test surveys, engineering change orders, traffic pattern alteration requests, environmental assessment reviews, and innumerable other documents required by the city, various ministries, managers, employees, and so on—probably enough documentation to fill the site office from top to bottom, front to back.

This is why technical professionals in all fields spend between 20 and 40 per cent of their time communicating in writing on the job. A couple of hours per day might be spent on email alone. And the higher up you move in your organization, the more time you'll spend writing and managing instead of designing and doing calculations. For a sampling of engineers' and software designers' discussions about the role and importance of written communication in their workday and the proportion of time it takes, go to http://www.embeddedinsights.com/channels/2010/08/04/how-much-of-an-engineer's-job-is-writing. You might be surprised. Hopefully, you won't be dismayed.

The Cost of Poor Communication in the Technical Workplace

Poor communication at any stage of a project is very costly. In fact, a proposal that took a team of engineers and support staff weeks to put together at great cost to their employer might fail not because it doesn't meet the specifications of the RFP, but because it is vaguely written and difficult to understand. In other words, it may fail not because of flaws in the engineering design, but because of the way it's written. Indeed, according to a web poll by the Computing Technology Industry Association (CompTIA), poor communication is the reason most IT (information technology) projects fail (1).

But aside from its role in the failure of whole projects, poor writing also wastes time and causes frustration in daily communication. Poorly worded emails require lengthy discussions or a chain of emails to clarify what should have been clear on first reading. Alternatively, a misunderstanding due to a badly written email may cause the reader to waste time going down the wrong trail and then later have to redo work.

Often an email's tone is incorrectly perceived, simply because body language cannot be analyzed and tone of voice cannot be perceived; this can cause hurt feelings, ill will, and inaction. That inaction, whether caused by an inappropriate tone or unclear meaning, means that your good ideas or requests for information or maybe even your dire warnings may be ignored (2). Corporate officials for BP have admitted, for instance, that the Deepwater Horizon catastrophe in 2006 occurred because emails warning of the impending problem were ignored (3). Eleven workers died in the subsequent explosion, the rig sank, and the environmental damage to the Gulf of Mexico and its coast is incalculable. Health effects may be felt for decades. All because of ignored emails.

Why Technical People Can Master Technical Writing

Technical Writing Isn't Like Literary Writing

However, if writing was not your strong suit in high school and if literature and romantic poetry are not among your passions, don't despair. What makes technical and business writing effective is not the same as what makes literary writing soar. Technical writing is a simple, stripped-down tool designed to get the job done, and that's to convey information to people who need it. It's not meant to be fancy. It's meant to be clear and effective.

This is not to suggest that writing well is easy. Like any craft, it requires discipline, conscious effort, and some practice. But it doesn't require a natural gift for wordplay or perfect linguistic pitch. Instead, learning to write well actually plays to the strengths of technical people. As a technical person, you should be good at working within structured systems that follow rules and guidelines. You are used to working to specification and to applying rules and best practices consistently.

Whether you are designing a building, an electrical system, a hydraulic system, or a septic field; whether you are coding software or websites or creating a user interface, you do not rely on inspiration or make sacrifices to the gods. Rather, you work according to a set procedure, following guidelines and rules, using previous designs as a launching point. You focus on usability and practicality; you don't add needless embellishments or take poetic licence. In fact, the most elegant engineering solutions are invariably the simplest.

IN THE FIELD

Tom Gilchrist, Subsea Technologist and Technical Writer

Technical communication has been a common theme through most of my career. Long before calling myself a technical writer, I worked in the subsea technology field with saturation diving systems, atmospheric diving suits, robotic vehicles, and deep-diving manned submersibles. This complex work required reference to a wide variety of technical documentation, and I was surprised at how much of it was inadequate and poorly produced. Manuals sometimes seemed to be an afterthought to the products themselves, even in that demanding environment. I spent considerable time updating documentation to reflect our actual hardware configurations. I did not have formal documentation training at the time; I just did what seemed to make sense, based on the need.

Following my subsea career, I was a customer-support engineer with an electrochemical fuel cell company. Technical communication was an essential and significant part of my role there as well, requiring report writing, technical specification development, business proposals, test procedures, data analysis, and much more. In many cases, English was a second language for my customers, which meant that conveying technical concepts clearly and simply was particularly important. I completed a technical writing program at a local university in order to establish a definitive foundation for my expanding communication role.

Understand the subject matter; a good writer with a strong technical background is a rare combination. Understand your audience; consider their perspective. Imagine doing their job and try to anticipate the information they need to perform the task or understand the data you are describing. Pay attention to technical accuracy and simplify the language. Use clear illustrations; ensure photographs print cleanly. Format consistently; make the document look good—people do in fact make judgments based on appearance.

Originally trained as an engineering technologist and commercial diver, I have been self-employed as a technical writer since 2002. I draw on my former experience to provide documentation services to the subsea engineering and fuel cell technology fields, among others.

Technical writing functions exactly the same way. This textbook will present a few rules that you need to follow and will introduce a number of guidelines and principles that you can adapt to specific writing situations. Initially, you may have to make a conscious effort to apply them. But with a little discipline, these rules and principles will become automatic and you'll find your writing improve not only in quality, but also in ease. You'll write more quickly, more confidently, and more clearly.

You Already Know How to Communicate Well

There's another reason you'll find it easy to learn to communicate well in writing: you already know how communication works; you speak to people much of the day; you read magazine articles, newspapers, blogs, and websites; you watch the news in the evening; and occasionally you even read assigned texts for school. You know what works; you know what sounds good and what doesn't, what creates clarity and what gets in the way. Now you just need to develop the habit of thinking like a reader and always asking yourself, "Would this be clear to me if I came across it for the first time and didn't already know what it meant to say?"

Attributes of Technical Writing

Documents are tools used to convey specific information. Like any tool, each technical document is fashioned uniquely to achieve its purpose. There are, however, a number of attributes that all technical writing shares.

Technical writing must be

clear: it must be understood by readers the first time they read it, without any ambiguity or possibility of misunderstanding.

complete: it must provide all the information the reader will need in order to understand the situation and the follow-up required.

concise: it must be as brief as possible while remaining clear and complete. The more words you take to say something, the longer it takes to read and the more verbiage there is in which readers may lose their way.

accessible: it must be organized and formatted so that readers can find the specific information they require without having to read the entire document.

In addition, of course, technical writing like all writing must be completely free of grammatical, mechanical, and factual errors. Grammatical errors can lead to misunderstandings and will, like mechanical errors, make you look unprofessional. Factual errors will make you look not just unprofessional, but incompetent.

Take a look at the examples of poor and good writing in Figures 1.1 and 1.2 and see how these attributes apply.

The main idea comes much too late in the first email, and the information is not clearly organized. The most important information in the document—the topics to be discussed at the meeting, for which Fred will have to prepare—is not easy to find. Some necessary information, such as the meeting time and place, are omitted completely.

The second email is far better. Even though, like the first, it takes the time to give Fred credit for work well done and has a friendly close, it is only 90 words long, compared to the first email's 174. In other words, the second email is virtually half as long, yet it contains more useful information, specifying, for example, a meeting time and place. This email has the virtues of conciseness and completeness.

It's also a far better work tool. It groups all the discussion topics for the meeting together and highlights them by creating a bulleted list. This list makes the key

Unclear subject line. Is this a proposal? No. It's about a proposal, but which one? Fred may be working on several.

Long, unnecessary ramble. Fred will be wondering when Jane will finally get to the point.

When is the meeting? Where? If Fred has to ask, then this email has failed. It needs to provide complete information.

Information isn't organized. The discussion topics for the meeting are in three separate paragraphs. Wastage is mentioned in two.

From: Jane Simms
To: Fred Nesbitt
Sent: October 09, 2017
Subject: Proposal

Let me first of all thank you for the draft proposal you submitted. I read it over the weekend with great interest and think that you've come up with some interesting ideas for improving the production line at Pinnacle Manufacturing. I had no idea that the materials wastage there was so significant. Shocking numbers.

We should probably talk about that and a couple of other things at a follow-up meeting of the project committee this week. Pinnacle will no doubt be surprised by the hidden wastage you found and we may have to develop that part of the proposal more. Also, Frank from accounting will be there and said he wants to go over your numbers so please bring a cost breakdown.

But don't worry. Everyone thinks you've done a really good job.

One more thing, can you bring your finalized production line schematic and your workflow charts? Wai-Lin wants to discuss them and maybe make some machine tool suggestions.

Looking forward to seeing you at the meeting. Let me know if you have any questions (ext. 4351).

FIGURE 1.1 Badly written and poorly organized email. Note how unhelpfully the information is structured. And when is the meeting? The email doesn't say. Read the subject line and ask yourself whether it accurately describes the contents of the email. Does the email actually contain a proposal?

information—the information that Fred will have to work on before the meeting—easy to find and easy to work with. In other words, this email makes information accessible.

Throughout this text and throughout the course, you will be exploring concepts and developing skills to enable you to write the second kind of document, the kind that helps your colleagues to quickly understand useful information and to use it to perform necessary tasks—no more, no less.

From: Jane Simms
To: Fred Nesbitt
Sent: October 09, 2017
Subject: Request for meeting about the Pinnacle Draft Proposal

I think we should have a follow-up meeting about the Pinnacle Manufacturing draft proposal this Wednesday at 3 p.m., in my office.

The feedback from the team has been really positive, but we'll need to discuss the following:

- Information on the hidden wastage you found. This part of the proposal needs more development.
- Finalized production line schematics and workflow charts. Wai-Lin may have machine tool suggestions.
- A breakdown of your cost calculations. Frank from Accounting asked to discuss them.

Looking forward to seeing you at the meeting. Let me know if you have questions (ext. 4351).

Clear, unambiguous subject line. Fred knows exactly what this email is about: a meeting. And he knows exactly about which proposal.

The opening statement identifies the purpose of the document. It immediately conveys the main idea.

The discussion topics are not just grouped, but also listed, forming a handy checklist that Fred can refer to and make notes against as he prepares for the meeting.

FIGURE 1.2 Properly written and well-formatted email. Note how easy it is to find relevant information. This email is half as long but contains more useful information, like a suggested time and place for the meeting. The list of discussion topics will help Fred prepare for the meeting. The clear subject line will help him find this email in his congested inbox every time he needs to check the list of discussion topics as he prepares for the meeting.

The Writing Process

So how do you go about crafting a concise, clear, and accessible professional document? In any writing situation, whether your document is short or long, formal or not, you should begin by thinking about what you hope to achieve with your document (its purpose) and to whom you are writing (the reader).

Determine the Purpose

If there's no reason to write, don't. But if you need to accomplish something by writing, be absolutely clear on what it is you hope to accomplish. Generally speaking,

> *"Perfection is finally attained not when there is nothing left to add, but when there is nothing left to take away."*
>
> —Antoine de Saint-Exupéry

you're trying to inform readers or trying to get them to do something. Often we combine these goals, as when you inform someone of an incident or circumstance and then ask them to perform or authorize an action in response. For instance, you may send your construction manager an email informing him or her that your pump broke and that you've purchased a new one, attaching a copy of the invoice. Or you may have to ask for approval to spend the money if it exceeds a certain amount. Your purpose in the latter case would be to obtain permission as quickly as possible to purchase a new pump.

Consider the Audience

The audience is the person or people to whom you're writing. If the audience is intimately familiar with the details of your project, you won't have to provide as much context. If the audience is a fellow techie, you won't have to define your terms. If your audience doesn't like to pinch pennies when it comes to necessary equipment, you don't have to do much persuading. However, if your audience is a penny-pinching accountant with no real understanding of construction practices, you may have to explain why replacing the pump is necessary given the hydrology of your site, even if it runs counter to the accounting department's every miserly instinct. Of course, you'll also have to explain hydrology in layperson's terms.

This is how audience and purpose define the content of documents. Ask yourself before you set pen to paper (or fingers to keyboard) what this particular reader will need to know and need to be told so that he or she understands what you're saying and will agree to what you're asking.

While every writing situation is unique, it is generally useful to think of audiences as falling into a few broad categories: decision makers, experts, agents, and general readers.

Decision Makers

Decision makers such as managers and supervisors, even if they come from a technical background, are often removed from the technical details of a project, their responsibilities being finance, policy, and administration. Managers are generally overwhelmed with correspondence, reports, and meetings, so they appreciate brief summaries to get the gist and clear context to figure out how your document fits into their business considerations as a whole. They may require definitions of technical terms. They will definitely want to know what you consider to be the most likely outcome of whatever you are recommending.

Inasmuch as managers tend to be the people who decide whether your document gets turned into action, it is their information needs that you need to consider most strongly.

Experts

Technical experts have a thorough understanding of the technical details of your report. They require detailed technical information and helpful tables and illustrative figures. Often they are the only ones who will look at the supporting information in the appendices. They are able to check your calculations and question your conclusions.

Busy managers often have their engineers, accountants, and other experts advise them on technical considerations, and thus experts often influence decisions even when they don't have decision-making responsibility.

Agents

Agents are the readers who will be directed to carry out the actions described in your document, such as machine operators, field technicians, office staff, laboratory workers, installers, or sales staff. They require clear organization so that they can find the directions they are to carry out, as well as clear instructions or procedures so that they can follow your directions without having your technical expertise. They will also always appreciate a clear explanation of why changes are necessary and how they will affect—and preferably improve—the agents' workdays.

General Readers

General readers, or lay people, have the least amount of technical expertise and are generally outside your organization: for example, citizens reading a report on the effects of an LRT extension on the environment, noise levels, traffic patterns, and so on in their neighbourhood. General readers need technical terms to be defined, they benefit from frequent graphics that illustrate basic technical concepts, and they appreciate descriptions of how the content of the document (the proposed LRT extension) will affect—and preferably benefit—them. They will need technical terms defined. On occasion, general readers can be decision makers, for instance, if they are clients or community members who have a chance to vote on your proposal.

Brainstorm the Content

With your purpose and audience clearly in mind, start brainstorming. At this stage, you're simply jotting down all the information that may be relevant and useful to the reader, in no particular order. Just put down ideas and elaborate on them a little.

You could use various worksheets available online, the back of an envelope, or, most efficiently, your word processor.

Organize the Content

Once you're satisfied that you've got all the information that you'll need to include in your document, begin to organize it. You don't need to rewrite it; save yourself some time by just numbering the items you've already written and drawing lines to

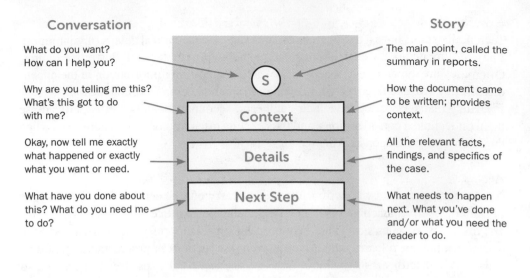

Conversation

What do you want?
How can I help you?

Why are you telling me this?
What's this got to do with me?

Okay, now tell me exactly what happened or exactly what you want or need.

What have you done about this? What do you need me to do?

Story

The main point, called the summary in reports.

How the document came to be written; provides context.

All the relevant facts, findings, and specifics of the case.

What needs to happen next. What you've done and/or what you need the reader to do.

S
Context
Details
Next Step

FIGURE 1.3 Standard document organization as a conversation or a story. Documents can be thought of either as stories or as one-way conversations with a reader unable to ask clarifying questions.

connect them. Or, if brainstorming on a word processor, rearrange your points with a few mouse clicks. In either case, what you're trying to do is group the information into a specific sequence of categories. And there are two ways of thinking about this. You can think of your documents as one-way conversations with your reader or as stories you tell your reader. In either case, documents follow the organizational structure shown in Figure 1.3. The questions to the left and the descriptions on the right indicate what sort of information goes into each section of the document.

Correspondence Is Like a One-Way Conversation

The first way to think of a document, particularly correspondence, is as a conversation with the reader—except that the reader isn't able to ask any clarifying questions, so you'll need to provide all the necessary details the first time around. Instead of poking your head into someone's office to tell them something, you send an email. It's as though you're there waiting for your reader when he or she gets back to the office.

So how does a conversation flow? Generally, the first thing someone asks (or waits politely for you to tell them) is something along the lines of "Why are you here?," "What do you want?," "What's up?," or more politely perhaps, "How can I help you?" This is where you have but a few seconds to state your case. This is the main idea, called a summary in longer documents where there's more than one main idea:

I think we should have a follow-up meeting about the Pinnacle Manufacturing draft proposal this Wednesday at 3 p.m., in my office.

Next the reader is going to wonder why you are making the request you are making or why the statement is important. The questions the reader will ask will be along the lines of "Why are you telling me this?," "What's this got to do with me?," or "How does this fit in with our business/project?" He or she will wonder, in other words, about the context of your request or statement. In this case, "Why do you want to have a meeting?"

> The feedback from the team has been really positive, but we'll need to discuss a few things.

Once readers understand the purpose of your email and how it fits into the conduct of business, they'll ask something along the lines of "What exactly happened?," "What exactly are you requesting?," or "What specific findings/deficiencies/parts list have you come up with?" In this case, the obvious question is "Well, what specific topics do you want to discuss at this meeting?"

> - Information on the hidden wastage you found. This part of the proposal needs more development.
> - Finalized production line schematics and workflow charts. Wai-Lin may have machine tool suggestions.
> - A breakdown of your cost calculations. Fred from Accounting asked to discuss them.

Generally, correspondence and reports require follow-up. You are writing because something has to get done. Writing is an integral part of getting things done in the workplace, so what specific action are you calling for? If you are reporting on an accident, you might make suggestions to improve safety protocols. If you are requesting something, you might urge the reader to grant the request and you might stipulate a deadline. In correspondence, if you have no specific request to make, or you've just made your request a few lines above, it's pretty standard to close with an offer to answer questions:

> Looking forward to seeing you at the meeting. Let me know if you have questions (ext. 4351).

Reports Tell Stories

The other way to think of documents, particularly reports, is as stories: they have a beginning, a middle, and an end. These parallels are obviously not perfect, but help the reader visualize the flow of information in a report or, perhaps, in longer correspondence. With that proviso, let's proceed.

In a story, we first introduce the context or set the scene:

> There once was a little girl called Little Red Riding Hood who lived on the edge of a deep dark forest with her mother. In that forest lived a big, bad wolf . . .

This is the background information, the context within which the events of the story make sense. We do the same in a technical report. We first describe the circumstances that led up to the writing of the report. We indicate how these circumstances relate to the conduct of business. We call this part the introduction in longer reports:

> On September 5, Pinnacle Manufacturing retained Johnson Engineering to investigate how the efficiency of Pinnacle's production line could be improved. From September 12 to 15, Fred Nesbitt, production engineer with Johnson Engineering, visited the Pinnacle plant to observe . . .

Then we tell the actual story. This is the part where Little Red Riding Hood goes into the woods to visit her grandmother and meets the big bad wolf. Alternatively, it's the part where Fred Nesbitt visits the production line, interviews union reps, researches company production metrics, and reads the company's ISO (International Organization for Standardization) documentation on their purchasing practices. In part, the body of the report might read like this:

> Another problem, according to Jim Malhotra, shop floor supervisor, is that the production line experiences gaps in production when the cutting press at the start of the line runs out of the properly sized sheet metal. He blames the staff in the materials warehouse for not delivering supplies as needed. Frank Chan, who runs the warehouse, however, has indicated that his staff is busy keeping the rest of the production line supplied and has little oversight of what happens at the cutting presses. He feels that the production staff should anticipate their own needs and communicate them. After observing the production line for several days, I came to the conclusion that . . .

At the end there is the moral of the story. It makes explicit the meaning of the events described in the story. This may be something along the lines that children shouldn't be given adult responsibilities and left unsupervised in a world of lurking dangers. But when they find themselves in such a danger, they can count on authority figures, like the hunter, to set things right. Admittedly, "Little Red Riding Hood" doesn't make this point quite so explicitly. A report, however, would:

> It seems clear from the investigation that production at Pinnacle Manufacturing suffers from three main challenges: production slowdowns, materials wastage, and inefficient use of staff. To overcome these problems, Johnson Engineering recommends . . .

In our report, we then do one more thing. We add a summary that condenses the whole report to roughly one-tenth the length of the original—more on that when we discuss formal reports in Chapter 7. We generally write the summary last, so we actually know what we are condensing, but we put it first in the report so that readers can get an overview at the start. If this overview proves sufficient, they may not even need to read the report for the details.

> At the request of Pinnacle Manufacturing, Johnson Engineering conducted a week-long on-site investigation of Pinnacle's production line and discovered three problems with its efficiency: . . .

> To solve these problems, Johnson Engineering recommends . . .

It may be useful to think of the summary as not being part of the report at all, but as a second, highly condensed version of the report for the reader's convenience. Its purpose is to enhance accessibility.

Determine the Correct Writing Style

You've analyzed your audience and, based on that analysis and the purpose of the document, you have decided what content should be included. Now go one step further. Different audiences require different writing styles. The box on pages 14–15, on audience, purpose, and tone, illustrates this.

Write the First Draft (in One Fell Swoop)

Once you have a clear outline, you already know what you're going to say and in what order you're going to say it—kind of like speech notes. And if we think of correspondence as a one-way conversation, then imagine yourself sitting across the desk from your reader, take a deep breath, and say what you would in person. But type.

Don't stop to second-guess yourself or you'll lose the thread. Do not bother to edit your sentences, to crack open a thesaurus, to tweak your grammar. Just write. You know how to speak. You make yourself understood in conversation all the time. So, just string together the ideas you already have on the screen in front of you: unselfconsciously, with no fear of judgment. This will give you a good, fluid first draft. Imagining yourself speaking to the reader should also help you set the proper tone.

Revise in Stages

When revising your first draft, do it in several easy stages, focusing on one type of revision at a time. Start with the large adjustments and make increasingly finer ones.

First, adjust and reorganize the content. If in reviewing your first draft you find it does not quite organize infor-

> Remember: Knowledge stuck in your head is no good to anyone else. Always think about how to make things perfectly clear to your reader.

mation as logically as it should or that it omits information necessary to craft a full argument, reorganize the content and fill in the holes. Conversely, if you find that some information doesn't advance the purpose of the document, delete it or put it into a

Audience, Purpose, and Tone

The purpose of your document is to get your reader to know something, to understand something, or to do something. This requires considerable understanding of who your audience actually is—their technical understanding, their role in a project or task, and their motivations. It also requires some consideration of the writing context.

BPA (bisphenol A) was widely used to harden plastics—for instance, in the manufacture of hard-plastic bottles, the reusable kind popular among hikers, runners, and cyclists. In 2008, Canada became the first country to declare BPA a toxic substance. Subsequently, Canada forbade its use in baby bottles and restricted its use in the liners of cans containing baby food. Since then, Canada and other nations have taken even stronger steps to limit the use and prevent the environmentally unsound disposal of BPA.

Let's imagine a lead chemist, back in the day, managing the materials laboratory for a company that produces, among other items, hard-plastic water bottles. Figure 1.4 shows what the chemist might write to a manager who holds the purse strings on the research budget. This manager is not a chemist, but she will be aware of the general debate around BPA because, though a scientifically untrained certified management accountant and an MBA, she works in the plastics industry.

Figure 1.5 shows what the chemist might have written to a colleague after obtaining permission to run some experiments. The colleague is an industrial chemist working in the lab, actively developing plastics. He is aware of the issues and of the chemistry and has discussed with the lead chemist the need to develop BPA-free plastics. Reader and writer work together closely.

Because this email addresses a superior at work and a decision maker, the tone is more polite and respectful than between colleagues who work together closely. If the writer worked with this manager closely and knew her well, he would have chosen a more familiar tone.

It seems increasingly likely that BPA (bisphenol A), which we use in the production of our hard-plastic water bottles, will be deemed a toxic substance. The rumour is that it will be made illegal in baby bottles, sippy cups, and the like to protect infants and toddlers. If that is the case, it is highly probable that many adult consumers will also want to avoid BPA-containing plastics. It would be prudent for us to begin investigating alternatives to BPA, of which there are several intriguing possibilities.

I'd like your permission to start a preliminary investigation into reformulating our plastics to use alternatives to BPA and am requesting an initial allocation of $50,000 for equipment (item list and costs attached). I would make this a Schedule A research project: bi-weekly cost accounting and monthly progress reports.

I fear that if we are not ready and consumers abandon BPA-containing bottles, we will be left without a marketable line of water bottles.

FIGURE 1.4 Email to a non-technical decision maker. The tone is somewhat formal because the reader is a work superior and a decision maker with whom the writer doesn't work closely. A bit of formality is called for in this situation. Also, because the reader comes from a business background, not a technical background, the writer takes pains to define terms with which the reader may not be familiar. Finally, because the writer has not discussed the scenario with the reader extensively, he also takes pains to clearly describe his reasoning.

It's obvious from the casual tone and the lack of explanation that reader and writer work together closely, have similar technical understanding, and are familiar with the subject matter.

Mike,

Danielle has given the go-ahead. Please start developing some protocols for alternative formulations for our plastics. Let's start with the copolymers we discussed. That still seems the most promising to me.

I've told Danielle that we'd work according to Schedule A. Please keep me in the loop with any developments.

FIGURE 1.5 Email to a familiar work colleague with a similar level of expertise on a topic familiar to both. This email is between two people who work together closely. Hence, even though one is the other's superior, the tone is informal. Because reader and writer share similar technical backgrounds, the writer doesn't need to define terms, and because this email is part of an ongoing discussion in the lab, the writer doesn't need to explain his reasoning.

Obviously this project will require many documents along the way, each ruled by the demands of purpose and audience. The lab reports on this project would be extremely technical; they'll be read by other chemists asked to duplicate or improve the results. The promised monthly progress reports to management would relate lab results in a manner that could be understood by management and would have content relevant to the business decisions for which management is responsible. The lab reports would likely include chemical formulae, possibly molecular diagrams; the progress reports would not—unless they were intended for a very technically sophisticated audience and then only if that information helped achieve the purpose of the document. A technically sophisticated reader could always be directed to the lab reports.

That's the thing about content and tone. Different audiences have different information needs based on their level of technical understanding and their role in the organization or in the project. Tone is a matter of how formal and how technical a document is. That, too, depends on the audience and situation. When speaking with technical audiences about technical content,

we use technical terminology without definition; we refer to procedures, processes, equipment, and componentry without explanation because we can (or as long as we can) be sure that that particular audience will understand. Don't insult a technical audience by baby-talking to it.

On the other hand, a non-technical audience will generally get the *Sesame Street* version of technical descriptions with all terms defined and all processes explained painstakingly and in layperson's terms. Of course, we have to ask ourselves in the first place whether the reader needs to know these terms or understand these processes at all. Don't frustrate a non-technical audience by writing something they can't understand or bore them by describing technical details that are of no interest or relevance to them.

When corresponding with colleagues, use a casual tone. When corresponding with a client, a superior, or a decision maker with whom you do not work closely and with whom you are not familiar, use a more formal tone. It's probably the kind of thing you would do automatically if you were speaking directly to your audience. You should be able to do it in writing, with a little forethought.

separate document with a different purpose. For instance, in an email calling people to a meeting, don't also remind them about the company picnic. Send a separate email under a separate subject line. However, if you often find yourself editing and moving content after your first draft, you may want to take more time at the planning stage.

Next, edit for style. Once you're sure you've got all the pieces in their proper place, focus on making your sentences flow well and on ensuring that they convey information clearly and succinctly. We'll discuss how to do this in chapters 2, 3, and 4. There's no point in agonizing about the precise phrasing of an idea or about the perfect transition between two sentences until you're sure that you won't be moving the information or sentences around later. What is moved generally has to be re-edited and you'll have wasted time.

Finally, edit for grammar, punctuation, and mechanics. Only once you've settled on exactly how your sentences will read should you worry about whether you've punctuated them correctly. There's no point in agonizing over the punctuation of a sentence that you are going to change for stylistic reasons later. We'll deal with grammar and punctuation in Appendix A.

Mechanics concern such things as consistent margins, parallel headings, capitalization, and so on (see Appendix B). These are important in signalling attention to detail and respect for form, and they enhance the accessibility of a document. However, unless the rest of the document works well, these elements are mere window dressing.

In a sense, you now know pretty much all the basic concepts of technical writing. All that remains is practice, specific examples, and the various applications. Congratulations: you're on your way to becoming a competent technical writer.

Exercises: Writing in the Workplace

Your instructor will assign which exercises to do, whether to do them singly or in groups, and whether to do them at home or in class.

Exercise 1.1: Understanding the Role of Writing in the Technical Workplace

Make contact with a professional in your field and ask how much time he or she spends writing in an average workday or workweek. Ask the person to list the different types of documents he or she produces, how these fit into his or her workflows, and why they are necessary.

Report to the class and write the list of documents on the whiteboard. Chances are that your contact will have forgotten some documents or that additional documents are produced in other niches of your field. Ask your classmates whether they can add to the list from their inquiries. With the help of your instructor, create a project timeline, flagging at what stage different documents are required. Some documents—such as emails, agendas and minutes for regular meetings, and periodic progress reports—will, of course, be produced throughout a project.

Exercise 1.2: Brainstorming and Sequencing Document Content

In class or at home, alone or in groups, organize the information in the brainstorming examples below into proper document sequence. Label and number them right on the page; for example, use "C" for context and then a number for the order in which you would place the information within the context section. Alternatively, retype the information in proper sequence, or, if your instructor provides copies as handouts, cut it out of the handouts and rearrange the pieces on your desk. But don't cut up the textbook, as tempting as that may be! Your instructor has answer keys to distribute and discuss.

Exercise 1.2.1: Scenario A

In this scenario, you are the head of production at Pinnacle Manufacturing announcing to your department heads that Johnson Production Engineering has been selected to investigate your production line problems. Your purpose is to get everyone to meet the consultant on Monday morning at 0900 and to get them to bring the documentation for which the consultant has asked. Hint: begin with the main idea or purpose of the document in brief. Then elaborate.

We have chosen a production consultant.

Meeting with their representative at 0900 Monday morning in my office.

Brian would like some documentation as well to familiarize himself with our operations

We have chosen Johnson Production Engineering of Markham, ON.

My extension is 214.

Brian Lee is the consultant who will be working with us.

Call me if you have questions or ideas.

Brian arrives on Monday morning and will stay for three days.

Brian needs to interview the production heads, observe procedures, and speak with workers.

Johnson PE has experience in the automotive industry: assembly and parts production

Looking forward to getting started.

Brian needs ISO documentation for purchasing procedures

Brian would like ISO documentation for production processes

Johnson PE is perfectly positioned to help us with our production of smart meters.

Brian is interested in org charts from the production departments

Brian would like to see the production line schematics

We have been looking for some time for someone to help identify and correct problems on our production line.

Brian requires production metrics.

Exercise 1.2.2: Scenario B

In this scenario, you the consultant that Johnson Production Engineering has sent to Pinnacle Manufacturing. You're waiting to get on the plane back to your office in Markham, ON, and are composing an email of your initial impression of the project for your supervisor, Jane, who has asked to be kept in the loop. But your real purpose is to ask for advice about a personnel issue at Pinnacle. Their production and warehouse managers have a personal conflict that is affecting productivity. You're not trained in conflict resolution, so you are asking Jane for advice. Again, lead with the main idea. In fact, this main idea is the first thing you wrote. Now sort the rest of your notes into proper document sequence.

Hi Jane,

Pinnacle Manufacturing has a personnel issue. I need advice.

So far I've taken a look at their documentation and observed their processes.

Please let me know so I can get started as soon as I land.

You assigned me to the project on Sept. 5.

There is a personnel issue as well as issues with the set-up of the production line.

The personal issue is affecting productivity, independent of the production setup.

I'm already seeing where some processes could be improved. I will look into things further and should be able to come up with some substantial recommendations.

Can someone on staff, perhaps from HR, advise me?

I visited their facility Sept. 12 through 15.

Pinnacle hired us to find out why their productivity is below industry average.

They have never come across this issue before.

In speaking with the supervisors of the production floor and the warehouse, I learned that these two people don't like one another.

Exercise 1.2.3: Scenario C

In this scenario, you are still the production engineer at Johnson Production Engineering who has been assigned to resolve the production problems at Pinnacle Manufacturing. This is the follow-up to your email to Jane in Exercise 1.2.2. Jane has put you in touch with someone from HR who, after you explained the personal issue between two supervisors at Pinnacle, advised you to simply pass the problem on to their boss. In this email, you will do so.

Pleasure to meet you and your staff. I'm looking forward to working on this project, but have a preliminary suggestion that I can make already.

Someone should be assigned to provide 50 pieces of precut sheet metal to the cutting press every hour.

The production line experiences gaps because the cutting press at the start of the line occasionally runs out of materials.

Jim Malhotra, production floor supervisor, blames the warehouse for not supplying materials on time.

I should have my report ready in two weeks. Please let me know if you have questions: 1-905-554-1234.

These gaps are costly, but easy to prevent.

Frank Chan, warehouse supervisor, says production should request materials when they run low. Says his staff is too busy and don't have a good line of sight to the cutting press.

You should impose a solution.

Your target is to produce 50 smart meters per hour.

Jim and Frank cannot agree and neither has authority over the other.

Exercise 1.3: From Sequenced Notes to First Draft (in One Fell Swoop)

In class, take your sequenced notes from Exercise 1.2 and read out a first draft. You have the notes in front of you, properly sequenced, so you know what you need to say and in what order. As explained in the chapter readings above, imagine yourself sitting across the desk from your reader, take a deep breath, and say what you would say to him or her in person. If you were taking dictation from yourself, or were dictating to Siri or Cortana, you'd already have your first draft written.

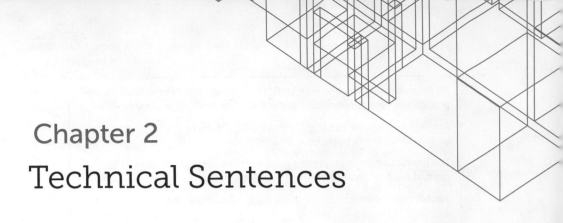

Chapter 2
Technical Sentences

In this chapter you will learn
- how to focus sentences on their real subjects and verbs
- how to rid your writing of meaningless words and expressions
- how to develop a confident, active, professional tone
- how to convey your meaning clearly and concisely.

Introduction

If we want our documents to be as direct, concise, and clear as possible, it stands to reason that our sentences—the basic building blocks of those documents—should be as well. Yet we frequently encounter examples like the following:

> Also reviewed was the root barrier installation on the upper roof decks, which was progressing during our inspection. It was observed that the root barrier was installed; however, correction of the irrigation scuppers and waterproofing of the anchor back plates were not carried out. (44 words)

If you knew the terms and were familiar with the processes, you might not have a problem figuring out what was meant. Even so, you'd have to agree that the following revision is a dramatic improvement:

> The root barrier on the upper roof decks was being installed during our inspection; however, the irrigation scuppers had not yet been corrected, nor had the anchor back plates been waterproofed. (31 words)

This second version is far clearer and easier to understand. It is also about a third shorter, which is no coincidence.

While the first example is decipherable with modest effort, ask yourself whether a reader would rather labour through a 44-page report written in this manner or breeze through a 31-page report written in the revised manner. Now consider that some of the documents you will produce in the workplace will run to hundreds of pages.

But take heart: the rest of this chapter provides a step-by-step strategy to make your writing clear, direct, simple, and effective. After writing your first draft in one fell swoop, as described in Chapter 1, revise your sentences in the following sequence.

- Find the real subject.
- Find the real verb.
- Edit for conciseness.
- Edit for clarity.
- Edit for gender-neutral language.
- Check the grammar and mechanics.

Eventually, of course, these techniques will become automatic and your first drafts will require less and less revision.

Find the Real Subject

The word "subject" has two meanings in relation to a sentence. The first is grammatical. The subject of a sentence is the thing that makes the action, the verb, happen. But the subject of the sentence also refers to the topic of a sentence, what the sentence is about. As a guideline, but not an absolute rule, sentences work best when the main grammatical subject also defines the topic of the sentence.

Sentences generally also work best if the subject appears at the start of the sentence, just as documents should begin with the summary, and paragraphs should begin with a topic sentence (Chapter 3). That way the reader knows right at the start what the sentence is about, making it easier to interpret.

The following subsections describe techniques for finding the real subjects of sentences.

Be as Direct as Possible

The secret to writing effective sentences is to be direct and to say what you mean. So as you are editing your sentences, ask yourself, "What is this sentence really about, what is its real subject, what is really driving the action?" Begin with that.

> The decision of the engineers was to double the chlorine concentration in the water treatment process.
> The engineers decided to double the chlorine concentration in the water treatment process.

> The drainage of runoff should be directed onto pervious ground.
> Runoff should be directed onto pervious ground.

Whenever possible, make the subject a real person or something concrete, not an abstraction, that is, an engineer instead of a decision, or runoff (water) instead of drainage (a concept).

Avoid Meaningless Sentence Starts (Weak Expletives)

Weak expletives are expressions such as "there are" and "it is" that take the place of the main noun and the main verb at the beginning of the sentence. Unless the "it" refers to a specific antecedent, these expressions are completely meaningless.

> There are eight hoisting points that need to be reinforced.
> Eight hoisting points need to be reinforced.

> It is not expected that we pay immediately.
> We are not expected to pay immediately.
> We don't need to pay immediately.

While it is not always wrong to use a weak expletive, try to avoid it. However, if the resulting sentence sounds worse, reinsert the weak expletive. Often, using a weak expletive is the best way to settle an is-there-or-isn't-there question.

> No reason exists to keep him on staff. (Ugh!)
> We have no reason to keep him on staff. (Correct, but the emphasis is weak)
> There's no reason to keep him on staff. (Better)

Use the Active Voice

In the active voice, the subject (agent) performs the action and precedes the verb:

> The engineer carefully calibrated the instrument.
> The tree shaded the room.
> The puppy licked my face.

In the passive voice, the subject (agent) is not performing the main action in the sentence and, if it appears at all, follows the verb:

> The instrument was carefully calibrated by the engineer.
> The room was shaded by the tree.
> My face was licked by the puppy.

Technical people overuse the passive voice because they think it makes them sound more objective. But the voice in which an opinion or fact is expressed doesn't alter its validity or the author's intent. What the passive voice will do, however, is make the writing faceless, frustrate the reader's desire to visualize an agent for an action, and force the writer into awkward, tangled sentence constructions.

> The investigation into the Johal noise complaint was conducted on May 15. Noise measurements were taken at 50 m intervals in a direct line from the wind turbine toward the Johal residence. This line was deviated from at the pond, at which point measurements had to be taken around the perimeter of the pond until the original line of travel was able to be resumed. (passive voice)

Here is the same report excerpt in the active voice:

> We investigated the Johal noise complaint on May 15, taking noise measurements at 50 m intervals in a line from the wind turbine toward the Johal residence. We had to deviate from this line at the pond, taking measurements around its perimeter until we were able to resume the original line of travel. (active voice)

Obviously the active voice is clearer and more concise. It also makes the writer sound more competent, forthright, confident, and professional. So, make the active voice your default, except when what you are writing about is, in fact, passive. For instance, if you are writing a description of a room, then as part of that description, you might write, "The room is shaded by the tree." The room is the subject of the sentence or paragraph, not the tree.

The other times you would use the passive voice are when you don't care who the agent is ("The building was erected in 1960"—in this sentence we're not at all concerned by whom), when you don't know who the agent is ("The report was sent to Wikileaks anonymously"), or when you have something to hide and don't want the reader to know who the agent is ("Mistakes were made . . . Papers were shredded . . . Relevant emails were deleted").

If you require more persuasion to use the active voice as your default, consider the following: if three of the four reasons for using the passive voice are that you don't know, don't care, or have something to hide, what sort of impression are you making on the reader when you use the passive voice unnecessarily?

Address the Reader Directly

One trick for writing actively is to address the reader directly as "you." Writers often go out of their way to avoid writing "you" and end up with convoluted, passive sentence structures.

> If a leak is detected . . .
> If you detect a leak . . .

> Do not open any fitting unless accompanied by qualified personnel and it has been ascertained that the component is not pressurized.
> Do not open any fitting unless you are qualified to do so and are certain that the component is not pressurized.

Don't refer to "one"; use "you."

> One must read all safety rules and instructions before beginning work.
> Read all safety rules and instructions before you begin work.

The second of these two sentences is written in the imperative mood, described in more detail below.

Use the Imperative Mood

Often as a professional you'll find yourself giving advice or providing instruction. Don't be shy about using the command voice, called the imperative mood by grammarians, or the "you-understood" voice by laypersons. The imperative mood complements the active voice.

> No tie-ins should be performed during summer months.
> Do not perform tie-ins during the summer months. ("you" understood)

> All efforts should be made to ensure that water is discharged onto landscaped or pervious areas.
> Discharge water onto landscaped or pervious areas. ("you" understood)

If this seems too curt or peremptory, feel free to preface your request with a "please." That's a perfectly polite way to tell people what to do:

> Please have that on my desk by 0800 tomorrow morning.

Find the Real Verb (Avoid Nominalizations)

Starting a sentence with the real subject is no guarantee that it will continue with the real verb.

> The programmers <u>made a modification to</u> the software after the technical writers had completed the documentation.
> The programmers <u>modified</u> the software after the technical writers had completed the documentation.

> The chemistry professor <u>gave a demonstration of</u> cold fusion.
> The chemistry professor <u>demonstrated</u> cold fusion.

When you turn a good, strong, clear verb like "modify" into a long, weak verb phrase like "made a modification to," you create a nominalization. The following table provides a short list of common nominalizations and their hidden verbs.[1]

---

1   Tables on the following pages are adapted from Otte, Michael. *Communication Manual*. British Columbia Institute of Technology. 1998/9.

REPLACE	WITH
are in agreement with	agree
conduct an investigation/inspection/ installation/review	investigate/inspect/install/review
carry out an analysis	analyze
come to a conclusion	conclude
give an indication of	indicate
give assistance to	assist
have a discussion about	discuss
make arrangements/decision	arrange/decide
perform a demonstration	demonstrate
place an order for	order
take into consideration	consider
take the measurement	measure
undertake a review	review

To check for nominalizations, look for broad, general-purpose verbs—such as "carry out," "perform," "conduct," "undertake," "give," or "make"—where specific actions are being described. Chances are you'll find a following noun that can be translated into the specific verb you need.

Edit for Conciseness

To be clear and easy to understand, sentences should be short. They should express one main thought only, with perhaps a couple of supporting thoughts.

As a rough guideline, make your sentences no more than 20 words long, at least on average, and make your paragraphs no more than 7 lines long, again, on average. Don't be afraid to use sentences that are much shorter, though if you use too many of them in a row, your paragraph will be choppy.

The following subsections describe techniques for creating concise, clear sentences.

Avoid Wordy Expressions

Replace long expressions with shorter ones if they express the same idea.

REPLACE	WITH
a decreased number of	fewer
a large number of	many
a long period of time	a long time
a majority of	most
adjacent to	near, next to
an increased number of	more

continued

as well as	and, also
at this point in time	at this point, now
at a rapid rate	rapidly
by means of	by
causal factor	cause
comply with	follow
due to the fact that	due to, because
during the month of April	during April, in April
during the period of	during
for the purpose of	for, to
gain access to	access, get, obtain
has a tendency to	tends to, may
in a timely manner	on time, promptly
in addition to	besides
in close proximity	near, next to
in connection with	about
in excess of	more than
in lieu of	instead
in most cases	usually
in order to	to
in regards to	as for, about
in short supply	scarce
in the absence of	without
in the course of	during
in the event of	if
in the event that	if
in the near future	soon
involves the use of	uses
is capable of	can
it can be seen that	—delete altogether—
it has been noted that	—delete altogether—
it is recognized that	—delete altogether—
it is necessary that we	we must
not later than	by, before
on a daily/weekly/regular basis	daily/weekly/regularly
on a timely basis	on time
on numerous occasions	often
prior to	before
pursuant to	by, following, as per, under
with reference to	about
with regard to	about, as to
years of age	years old

Avoid Redundancies

Avoid careless or useless repetition of the same idea or meaning:

> We used (already) existing technologies.

> We won't proceed at (the) present (time).

> We started (out) in the morning.

> If the symptoms (still) persist, call me.

> The transcripts are complete (and unabridged).

> The chemist mixed (together) the reagents.

Other common redundancies include:

(honest) opinion	(all time) record	(personal) friend	(falsely) misrepresent
(completely) destroy	(flatly) deny	(terrible) tragedy	(self-)confessed
glance (briefly)	(future) outlook	(personal) opinion	(final) outcome
(uniformly) consistent	(absolutely) essential	(past) history	(mutual) cooperation
(currently) available	(posted) sign	(in-depth) study	(very) unique
(new) innovation	(different) varieties	(true) facts	(pre-)planning
(advanced) planning	(near) proximity	(complete) stop	(meaningful) dialogue
(basic) essentials	(integral) part	(each and) every	estimated at (about)
(end) result	eliminate (completely)	(actual) experience	blue (in colour)
(close) proximity	(exactly) identical	severe (in nature)	(rate of) speed
small (in size)	a crisis (situation)	introduced a (new)	(private) industry
(separate) entities	triangular (in shape)	never (before)	
start (out)	period (of time)	none (at all)	

Edit for Clarity

Break up Chains of Nouns

Sometimes writers string nouns into long chains to come up with a name for something. But these chains can be difficult to understand, so break them up:

The deadline for the _municipal groundwater level investigation completion report_ is Monday morning.

The deadline for the completion report on the investigation into the municipal groundwater table is Monday morning. (revised)

The completion report on the investigation into the municipal groundwater table is due on Monday morning. (best)

Even though the revised sentence turned out to be longer, it is clearer, and clarity is always the first priority in a professional document.

Use Simple Language

Big words won't impress the reader, but they may puzzle the reader. Always use the simplest word that will convey your meaning.

On the other hand, always use the word that most accurately expresses what you need to say, even if the word may not be generally known. If it is a technical term, you may want to define it. If it is a general word, let your readers look it up in a dictionary. Just don't force them to do so unnecessarily.

REPLACE	WITH
accomplish	do
acknowledge	admit, concede
additional	more, extra, added
administer	manage, run
advocate	support, call for
alternative	other, choice
amendment	change
approximately	about
ascertain	determine, learn, find out
attempt	try
beneficial	good for, useful
bona fide	real
characteristic	trait, feature
commence	start, begin
communicate	tell, inform, write
complimentary	free
comprise	consist of, be made up of
conspicuous	obvious
constitute	make up
criterion	test, rule, standard
deem	consider

development	change, growth
duplicate	copy, repeat
endeavour	try
endorsement	support, backing
envisage	foresee
exonerate	clear, acquit
expenditure	cost, expense
expiration	end
facilitate	make easier, encourage, promote
forward	send
fundamental	basic, real
illumination	light, insight
illustration	example, picture
inaccuracy	mistake, error
inadvertent	careless, accidental
incorrect	wrong
indispensable	vital, essential, crucial
initial	first
injunction	ban, order
latitude	scope, range
locality	place, site
methodology	method
minuscule	tiny
mitigate	ease, temper
modification	change
necessitate	need, call for
nominal	small, token
notification	warning, notice
numerous	many
objective	aim, end, goal
obligation	duty
observation	remark, comment
obtain	get, gain
participate	take part, join in
perception	view
permission	consent
pertaining to	about, of, on
prerogative	right
presently	soon
prioritize	rank
probability	chance, likelihood

continued

procure	get, buy, order, find
prohibit	ban
proliferation	spread
purchase	buy
rationale	reason, theory
recuperate	recover
reiterate	repeat
render	make, give
require	need, ask for
restrain	stop
retain	keep
saturate	soak
stringent	strict
substantiate	prove, back up
sufficient	enough
systematic	orderly, regular
technicality	detail, minor point
terminate	end
therein	there
thereof	of it, of that
transform	alter, change
transmit	send
transparent	clear, lucid
unfavourable	poor
unmistakable	clear, plain, evident
unpretentious	modest, humble
unveil	announce
utilize	use
vacillate	waver, falter, hesitate
validity	truth, proof
velocity	speed
verbatim	exact, exactly, word for word
vicinity	area, region
visualize	see, picture
withstand	bear, endure, resist

Avoid Jargon

The terms and expressions unique to a discipline or profession are called jargon. Within those disciplines, jargon serves as technical shorthand and is extremely useful. But when jargon is misapplied outside of its specific technical application, it is inexact and irritating.

I've made some improvements to the user <u>interface</u>. (appropriate use of jargon)

We need to <u>interface</u> about that. (annoying use of jargon)

REPLACE	WITH
access (as a verb)	find, get, buy, obtain, get to
address (as a verb)	discuss, study, consider, deal with
aggregate	total, whole
characterize	describe, specify
concurrence	agreement
continuum	scale, series
dialogue	discussion, talk
elect	choose
enhance	improve, increase
expedite	hasten, speed up
facilitate	help, allow, permit, start, carry out
feedback	response, reaction, results
functionality	feature
impact (as a verb)	affect, increase, reduce
implement	begin, set up, do, carry out, start
input	information, figures, opinion (or be specific about what the input is)
interface (as a noun)	connection, contact
interface (as a verb)	meet, work with, talk to
liaise	meet, work with, talk to, coordinate
network (as a verb)	meet, work with, talk to
optimal	best
optimize	improve, increase
optimum	best, most, greatest
parameters	factors, guidelines, variables, limitations
posture	opinion, position
pursuant to	according to, following
regarding	about, as for
requisite	necessary
scenario	situation, events
source (as a verb)	find, locate
synergy	joint efforts, common goals, compatibility
thrust (as a verb)	project, move, attempt
upgrade	improve, better
utilization	use
value added	value
value proposition	business proposition
viable	possible, feasible, workable, practical
vis-à-vis	about, of

Check for Gender-Neutral Language

Use gender-neutral pronouns to refer to the subjects of your sentences, unless you can be sure of the subject's gender ("Please tell Mike that he must apply before the deadline"). But don't use those awful-sounding "he/she" "him/her" constructions.

> When the tax payer is filing his/her return by himself/herself, he/she should keep all of his/her receipts for seven years.

Instead, change the sentence to use a plural subject.

> When tax payers file their returns by themselves, they should keep all their documentation for seven years.

Or change the sentence to use "you" and "your":

> When you file your tax return, keep your documentation for seven years.

Alternatively, edit the sentence so that pronouns become unnecessary. This is easiest when you can refer to the subject by a title or designation.

> After filing a tax return, the taxpayer should keep all receipts for seven years.

Just be careful to make your titles and designation non-sexist. It's police officer, firefighter, letter carrier (not mailman), humankind, businessperson, actor (for both genders), supervisor (not foreman), and so on.

You have one more option with the personal pronouns, but you should use it sparingly: if the sentence cannot easily be edited to use one of the strategies employed above, you can use a plural pronoun to refer to a singular subject. Strictly speaking, this is ungrammatical, however it is becoming an increasingly acceptable way to avoid sexist language, but only as the lesser of two evils.

> Ask your technical writing instructor whether they consider using plural pronouns for singular subjects an acceptable strategy in exceptional cases.

In the example above, this strategy is acceptable. You have only one technical writing instructor, but this textbook has to acknowledge that your instructor could be of either gender.

Check the Grammar and Mechanics

If you are at all unsure about the grammar or the mechanics of what you've written, refer to Appendix A (Punctuation and Grammar) and Appendix B (Mechanics and Conventions). When your instructor labels grammatical and mechanical errors in the margins of your assignment, use these two appendices to correct those errors.

FIGURE 2.1 **Badly written message.** Obviously the writer meant that you can advertise your car for $20 in the newspaper. The phrasing suggests, however, that the sales price of the car is $20. Always make sure that what you've written can't possibly be misinterpreted, accidentally or even wilfully, by a lawyer for instance.

Editing Technical Sentences

When editing your sentences, check for the following:

Subjects and verbs

☐ Are your subjects and verbs focused on what the sentence is actually about?

☐ Are your subjects as concrete as they can be and your verbs as strong as possible?

☐ Are the weak expletives necessary to the sentence or just random thought starters?

☐ Is your voice active, unless required to be passive by the subject?

Wording

☐ Have you used the simplest words and shortest expressions that best convey your intended meaning?

☐ Have you ruthlessly eliminated redundancies, expressions of the obvious, and otherwise unnecessary words?

☐ Have you consistently used gender-neutral language except where you can be sure of the gender of your reader or subject?

Grammar and mechanics

☐ Have you checked Appendices A and B whenever you're unsure of the punctuation, capitalization, or other fussy correctness of your sentences?

Exercises: Editing Technical Sentences

Please edit the sentences in the following exercises to make them as clear and concise as possible, without changing their meaning. Do so singly, in pairs, or in groups, as determined by your instructor.

Your instructor has access to the answer keys online, as well as to additional exercises.

Exercise 2.1: Shorter Sentences on No Particular Topic

1. In many instances the lead engineer failed to submit the personnel evaluations in a timely manner.
2. A decreasing number of students are studying the sciences, while an increasing number of students are studying business and economics.
3. Municipal wastewater has a tendency to concentrate phosphorus and nitrogen.
4. The engineers will make modifications to the wastewater treatment process so that a decreased amount of phosphorus will be released into the river.
5. There are three water pumps at the mine whose purpose it is to clear groundwater out of the shafts.
6. It is possible that the retained-fill structure may cause interference with existing drainage patterns.
7. Run-of-the-river power plants have a need to be built in close proximity to rivers in order that they can take advantage of the spring freshets, that is to say, the snow melt.
8. Incorporation of subdrains into the structure may have to be undertaken at these points.
9. There will be no requirement for water quality enhancement methods assuming the provision that runoff water does not become contaminated.
10. There is a likelihood that the elevated structure will be cross-sloped so that runoff will be directed toward the gutters.

Exercise 2.2: Longer Sentences on No Particular Topic

1. There are some new safety protocols we need to have a discussion about, following the incident of the fire in the processing lab.
2. It is absolutely essential that your report's formatting be uniformly consistent in order to make the best impression on the client that it is possible for us to make.
3. The engineer has made predictions that the roadway changes will create an increase in general traffic and that this will inevitably create an increase in accidents.
4. It is difficult to establish a general area cost per square foot of installation for this system due to the fact that each installation is quite unique and depends on many different factors.
5. While it is true that many international consumer electronics manufacturers will add Netflix buttons to their remote controls for the North American market, it is a

fact that there may be severe monthly bandwidth limitations imposed on Canadian consumers.

6. It is a matter of logic that these sorts of industrial facilities are also likely targets for cyber-terrorists as it is a known fact that an attack on these facilities would cause widespread disruptions in terms of the economy, as well as to the environment.

7. There is a limitation to the effectiveness of on-site computer backups in the home or in the office because thieves may steal the back-up device at the very same time they steal a person's computer.

8. It is an oft-told and generally accepted axiom that a 10,000-square-metre data centre has the capacity to release as much carbon dioxide as to be the equivalent of 100,000 SUVs on the road getting 25 litres per 100 kilometres.

9. Given the fact that more and more employees are using and sharing confidential information on mobile devices such as tablets and smartphones, there is a growing trend that proprietary information is increasingly compromised due to lost or stolen mobile devices than there is to any actual hacking.

10. Malware in the form of Trojan horse viruses for stealing corporate information are increasingly being distributed through free games for children because it is well known that when employees bring home their work laptops, their children will oftentimes download games onto them to play.

Exercise 2.3: Keystone Species

1. There is a type of species called a keystone species that is one that has a disproportionately large effect on its host environment when compared to its relatively small numbers.

2. Such species are described as playing a critical role in helping in the maintenance of the structure of an ecological community.

3. It is said that they have an effect on many other organisms in an ecosystem and help to determine the types and numbers of various other species in the community.

4. To give just one example, when wolves were reintroduced to the famous Yellowstone National Park they immediately began to hunt and prey on the elk that had been the only other major mammalian species in the area.

5. As an immediate consequence, the number of the elk population began to dwindle and as the elk began to learn to stay on the high ground to better see their predators and thereby stay safe, there were a number of startling changes that began to take place in the park.

6. In the valleys, all the various young saplings that the elk had been eating up to that point were now able to grow into full trees.

7. This had the consequent effect of attracting many species of bird that had been up to then missing from the area.

8. What happened also is that because the streams and the rivers were once again shaded by trees, their temperature dropped and this had the resultant effect of allowing trout to return and indeed to thrive.

9. With the abundance of trees, beavers once again found a home in the area, where they built the dams for which they are so known, and this created ponds that attracted frogs, as well as the predators of frogs such as snakes.

10. It was in this way that wolves even despite their small number were nonetheless able to affect the restoration of the balance and also of the diversity of the ecosystem in Yellowstone National Park.

Exercise 2.4: Photosynthesis

1. It is a known fact that plants are not able to make use of the whole entirety of the light spectrum of visible light for the process of photosynthesis.

2. The part of the light that can be utilized for the process of photosynthesis is what is called the photosynthetically active radiation (PAR).

3. The PAR range has been determined to lie between the wavelength values of at least 400 to at most 700 nanometres (billionth of a metre).

4. Even in this range, not all wavelengths are equally effective.

5. Green light, that would be the light of between 500 and 600 nm, is not well able to be absorbed by chlorophyll.

6. This is precisely why it is the green light that is partially reflected back by the chlorophyll, making plants look green.

7. The main absorption peaks most effective for chlorophyll actually happen to lie in the red and blue light bands.

8. What is generally not well known is the fact that leaves don't just automatically conduct photosynthesis whenever they are exposed to sunlight.

9. If it is the case that the plant cannot store the starches that are being produced or that it cannot do so quickly enough, then the chloroplasts will stop the process of photosynthesis.

10. The quantity of photosynthesis carried out will always be dependent on precisely three properties of the light striking the leaf, the first of which is the quality of the light, the second of which is the intensity of the light, and the third of which is the duration of the light shining on the leaf.

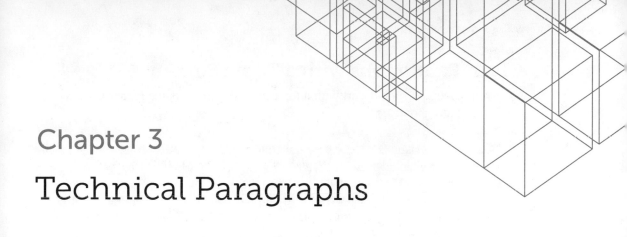

Chapter 3

Technical Paragraphs

In this chapter you will learn

· how to keep paragraphs short and to the point
· how to use topic sentences to orient the reader and enable scanning
· how to tie sentences together to make paragraphs flow and easy to understand.

Like technical sentences, technical paragraphs should be short, to the point, simple, and unadorned. Technical information can be very complex, even for a technical audience, so make your documents as easy to understand as possible. Create this clarity by breaking complex information into small, clear, easily digested paragraphs.

Apply the following guidelines for constructing effective paragraphs:

- Keep paragraphs short.
- Begin paragraphs with a topic sentence.
- Make paragraphs unified.
- Make paragraphs complete.
- Make paragraphs cohesive.

Keep Paragraphs Short

We try to keep paragraphs short for the same reasons we keep sentences short. Smaller bits of information are easier to process. Therefore, every sentence should express only a single thought and every paragraph should express only a single idea.

In general, paragraphs should be no more than 7 lines long, on average. If they are longer than that, check that the writing is concise. If it is, check that you've discussed only a single idea in the paragraph. Some paragraphs may well have to be more than 7 lines long to cover their topic. Generally, though, if you've written clear, tight sentences and your paragraphs are still more than 10 lines long, chances are that you are trying to do too much in a single paragraph; in those cases, break the paragraph in two.

However, despite what you may have been told in high school, paragraphs have no minimum length: one-sentence paragraphs are perfectly legitimate.

Begin Paragraphs with a Topic Sentence

Ideally, a paragraph should start with a topic sentence that lets the reader know what the paragraph is about:

> To optimize a building for passive solar thermal control, the first consideration is the building's orientation on the site and its design. Obviously, the longer side of the building should face due south, to expose the walls and, especially, the glazing to the sun for as much of the day as possible. In general the ideal length-to-width ratio is between 1.3 and 1.5 to 1. This ratio creates liveable proportions for the interior arrangements of the building, while permitting the sun's rays to penetrate deep into the interior. For this reason, the larger rooms are usually placed on the south side, providing more natural light and exposing more floor area to the sun.
>
> Aside from orientation and layout, thermal mass also plays a vital role in managing and stabilizing temperature in a passive solar house. Thermal mass captures and stores solar radiation in the form of heat until the mass reaches ambient temperature. Only when the mass's temperature exceeds the ambient temperature will it begin to release the stored heat. In this manner, thermal mass stabilizes indoor temperature throughout the 24-hour sun cycle. For this reason, the walls and floors of passive solar homes are often made of particularly thick materials that can absorb and store a lot of heat.
>
> However, much of the effort to capture and regulate thermal energy can be undone by furnishings. Carpet, for instance, can reduce a floor's solar gain by up to 70%; linoleum by up to 50%. The former insulates the floor; the latter reflects solar radiation. Bare concrete floors and ceramic tiling work best to ensure that the UV radiation striking the interior surfaces of the building is stored as heat within the surface, rather than heating the indoor air.
>
> Another consideration is the landscaping surrounding the structure. For instance, trees planted too close to south-facing windows will prevent heat gain in the winter, especially if evergreens were planted. Because both the interior and the exterior of passive solar homes have to be carefully designed to take the solar path into consideration, changes to landscaping made by owners can easily cause homes to overheat in the summer or to fail to capture sufficient heat in the winter.

You'll notice that in each paragraph, the topic sentence lets the reader know immediately what the paragraph is about.

The first topic sentence informs the reader that this paragraph is about how to orient and lay out a house for optimal passive solar thermal control. The topic sentence also hints that subsequent paragraphs will describe other factors that affect solar thermal control: "the first consideration is . . ." Presumably there will be others.

The second topic sentence informs the reader that the second paragraph describes the effect of thermal mass on passive solar thermal control. The rest of the paragraph then describes this effect in more detail.

IN THE FIELD

Gary Dean, P.Eng., AMIMechE, Graduated Queen's University of Belfast 1996

When I embarked on my career in mechanical engineering, I expected to develop and use a skill-set heavily biased towards technical abilities but away from an extensive use of text. I imagined I would undertake research, analysis, calculations, collation of data, and presentation of that data in a logical, graphical manner, with little use of the English language. This naive notion was quickly dispelled.

From university, I landed a job at Ford Motor Company in Essex, Great Britain, and was charged with overseeing the design of base engine and lubrication components for a new family of small diesel engines. This task involved my having to describe the function of each component, all the possible ways a component could fail to meet that function, the reason for the failure, and the effect on the engine system as experienced by the customer (e.g., the assembly plant worker, the vehicle mechanic, or the owner of the vehicle). Essentially, my job devolved to writing.

I quickly learned that an ability to describe a situation clearly, so as to be understood by readers with both technical and non-technical backgrounds, was a critical skill in engineering.

As my career progressed within Ford, from design engineering through to a supervisory role, I discovered that strong writing skills were also required in many other areas related to engineering work—chairing meetings and issuing minutes; reporting on design testing and development; resolution of issues; tracking of cost, weight, and schedule targets; and staff appraisals.

Engineers may also be approached to lead extracurricular activities and studies. In this vein, I was asked to head a team of engineers in implementing a process of "kitting" high-complexity engine parts to travel along the assembly line with the engine, thereby reducing the space required for parts storage at line-side.

After a series of meetings, I summarized the opinions of my team and wrote a justification document. The recommendation was accepted and the system installed. Writing skills had thus helped to illustrate and implement a solution.

Prospective engineers should understand that writing skills are independent of any technical knowledge or experience gained and thus never become obsolete or irrelevant because of technical changes in an industry.

If engineering is the practice of turning ideas into reality, then technical writing is one of the primary means by which engineers communicate their visions to others. It is absolutely central to the professional practice of engineering.

The third topic sentence introduces the fact that furnishings can undo much of the benefit of thermal mass; the rest of the paragraph provides examples to develop and support this assertion.

The fourth topic sentence informs the reader that landscaping also plays a role; the rest of the paragraph describes how.

This is precisely how a paragraph should work: the topic sentence orients the reader and the rest of the paragraph provides the details.

Now reread just the four topic sentences:

> To optimize a building for passive solar thermal control, the first consideration is the building's orientation on the site and its design.

> Aside from orientation and layout, thermal mass also plays a vital role in managing and stabilizing temperature in a passive solar house.

> However, much of the effort to capture and regulate thermal energy can be undone by furnishings.

> Another consideration is the landscaping surrounding the structure.

Do you get a sense of how this description of passive solar housing and thermal mass is organized? Note also that the topic sentences provide transition between the ideas in the paragraphs. This is why the topic sentences read so well together. More on transition below.

By beginning every paragraph with a proper topic sentence, we don't just orient the reader about the paragraph: we also enable the reader to skim the document effectively. Readers should be able to read just the topic sentences of a document and get a very good idea of what it is about. If they want more detail about a particular point, they can read the rest of the paragraph.

In effect, then, topic sentences function a bit like headings. Headings identify the topic of a report section consisting of multiple paragraphs; topic sentences identify the topics of individual paragraphs within sections (see Figure 3.1).

Make Every Paragraph Unified

A unified paragraph is one that contains only details relevant to the central idea introduced by the topic sentence.

The fourth paragraph in the example on page 38 is about how landscaping can affect thermal gain. Any information about factors other than landscaping that affect thermal gain has no business in this paragraph. If relevant to the article or report, it should be moved to a different paragraph or developed in an entirely new paragraph. If not relevant, it should be removed from the document entirely.

Make Every Paragraph Complete

A complete paragraph is one that presents all the information the reader will need to understand the idea developed in the paragraph. Whether it turns up in instructions or in reports, one of the most common mistakes in professional writing is to omit information or steps in logic that the reader will need to make sense of the document.

In these cases, the writer has assumed that the reader is as familiar with the situation or as technically versed as the writer. However, by definition, readers read

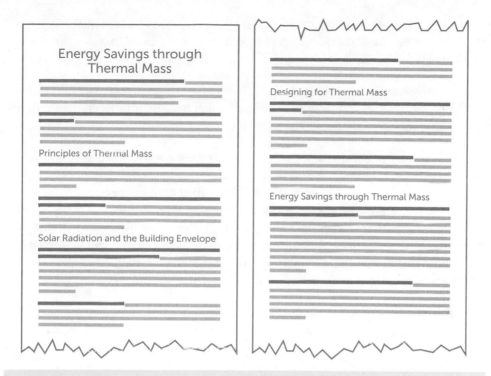

FIGURE 3.1 Paragraph topic sentences help the reader skim for main ideas and content. Every paragraph is a box of information labelled by the topic sentence. A series of paragraphs on the same topic form a section, labelled by a heading. This makes the organization of a document easy to comprehend and the main ideas easy to find.

documents to get the information they require but don't yet have, so the writer almost always knows more than the reader.

Remember that you must consider the needs of your audience and that it's better to provide a little too much information than too little. As we've said before, no one will ever complain that a document (or a paragraph) is too easy to understand.

Make Every Paragraph Cohesive

It's not good enough to put all the right information into grammatically correct sentences and lump them into a paragraph. The paragraph must also provide clear logical connections between sentences and ideas. Without the signposts provided by transitional devices, readers have a difficult time understanding complex information, as in the following example.

Thermal mass is one of the ways in which passive solar houses use the sun's energy to maintain a comfortable, constant indoor temperature. By requiring a lot of heat to warm up, thermal mass warms up slowly when ambient temperature is higher, drawing heat from the house, and releases heat energy slowly when the ambient temperature is lower, heating the house. Thermal capacitance, denoted with the symbol C_{th}, is the name given to the ability of a material to store heat. Concrete, gypsum board, and ceramic tiles are examples of materials with high thermal capacitance.

All the sentences in this passage are grammatically correct. The paragraph is unified and complete. However, this is a terrible paragraph because it lacks cohesion. Instead we want to read something like the following:

One of the ways in which passive solar houses use the sun's energy to maintain a comfortable, constant indoor temperature is through thermal mass. Essentially, thermal mass is material (mass) that requires a lot of energy to warm up. It therefore warms up slowly when ambient temperature is higher, drawing heat from the house, and releases heat energy slowly when the ambient temperature is lower, heating the house. This ability to store a lot of heat is called the thermal capacitance, denoted by the symbol C_{th}. Examples of materials with high thermal capacitance are concrete, gypsum board, and ceramic tiles.

This paragraph coheres. As you read it, you can follow the development of ideas easily and everything makes sense the first time through. Writers have three tools for creating cohesive paragraphs:

- given-new repetition
- transition words
- variegated sentence patterns.

Given-New Repetition

To help the reader transition from the information "given" in a previous sentence to the "new" information in the next, it's often a good idea to repeat information from that previous sentence. This "given-new" rule can take the form of key-word repetition or of a restatement of ideas, which helps to stitch sentences together logically.

One of the ways in which passive solar houses use the sun's energy to maintain a comfortable, constant indoor temperature is through <u>thermal mass</u>. Essentially, <u>thermal mass</u> is material (mass) that requires a lot of energy to warm up. <u>It</u> therefore warms up slowly when ambient temperature is higher, drawing heat from the house, and releases heat energy slowly when the ambient temperature is lower, heating the house. <u>This ability to store a lot of heat</u> is called the thermal capacitance, denoted by the symbol Cth. Examples of materials with <u>high thermal capacitance</u> are concrete, gypsum board, and ceramic tiles.

By referring readers back to what they already know, before introducing new material, the given-new repetition guides the reader step by step through the development of a logical argument. It ties new sentences into a framework of information with which the reader has already become familiar.

Transition Words

English abounds in transition words, some of which have been grouped by function below:

addition:	also, and, besides, furthermore, in addition, next, moreover; first, second, third
causation:	accordingly, as a result, because, consequently, hence, so, then, therefore, thus
clarification:	because, for example, for instance, in fact, so, specifically, such as, this means
comparison:	also, in like manner, likewise, similarly, too
concession:	admittedly, although, granted that, in spite of, naturally, of course, while it is true that
conclusion:	in brief, in conclusion, in short, in summation, to conclude
contradiction:	although, anyway, but, conversely, despite, however, in contrast, instead, nevertheless, on the other hand, rather, yet
emphasis:	above all, chiefly, furthermore, indeed, in particular, most important(ly)
illustration:	for example, for instance, in other words, such as, to illustrate
place:	behind, beyond, elsewhere, everywhere, here, in the background, on the other side, opposite, straight ahead, there, to the right
time:	afterward, as, at the same time, before, concurrently, during, gradually, in the afternoon, later, meanwhile, now, soon, until, while

Let's take a look at the transitional words in the revised paragraph:

One of the ways in which passive solar houses use the sun's energy to maintain a comfortable, constant indoor temperature is through thermal mass. Essentially, thermal mass is material (mass) that requires a lot of energy to warm up. It therefore warms up slowly when ambient temperature is higher, drawing heat from the house, and releases heat energy slowly when the ambient temperature is lower, heating the house. This ability to store a lot of heat is called the thermal capacitance, denoted by the symbol Cth. Examples of materials with high thermal capacitance are concrete, gypsum board, and ceramic tiles.

In the following paragraph the transition words establish a sequence in time and clarify why an engineer with certain experience can move between fields.

Dave is a mechanical engineer who for many years designed heavy lifting equipment such as harbour cranes. Gradually, he came to do less and less engineering and more and more project management. Eventually his company was bought out and he was downsized. There was no work in his field, but because he had good project management skills, he was able to find work supervising the development of a processing facility at a mine.

One more example should suffice. Below are the topic sentences we saw at the beginning of the chapter. Note how the transitional devices—both transition words and the given-new repetition—indicate how the content of each paragraph relates to the material that has come before:

> To optimize a building for passive solar thermal control, <u>the first consideration</u> is the building's orientation on the site and its design.

> <u>Aside from orientation and layout</u>, thermal mass also plays a vital role in managing and stabilizing temperature in a passive solar house.

> <u>However,</u> much of the effort to capture and regulate thermal energy can be undone by furnishings.

> <u>Another consideration</u> is the landscaping surrounding the structure.

This is how transitional devices stitch together sentences and ideas; they continually establish how new material relates to what has come before, creating a logical framework into which to fit each new sentence.

Variegated Sentence Patterns

Simple sentences contain only one independent clause and when strung together sound choppy and lack coherence. However, multiple simple sentences—and their ideas—can be combined into more complex sentences that flow better and more clearly establish the relationship between ideas.

Simple sentences:

> We are experiencing an early spring. Rain is combining with melting snow. Extensive flooding is likely.

Coordination:

When you coordinate sentences, place a comma before the coordinating conjunction: and, or, for, so, yet, but, nor.

> We are experiencing an early spring, so rain is combining with melting snow. Extensive flooding is likely.

> We are experiencing an early spring, so rain is combining with melting snow, making extensive flooding likely. (coordination and embedding)

Subordination:

> <u>Because the early spring is combining rains with melting snow</u>, extensive flooding is likely.

Embedding:

> <u>Combining rain with melting snow</u>, the early spring makes extensive flooding likely.

Editing Technical Paragraphs

When editing your paragraphs, check for the following:

☐ Does each paragraph contain a topic sentence, ideally at the start?

☐ Does each paragraph develop that topic fully and exclusively; that is, is each paragraph complete and unified?

☐ Does every paragraph cohere; that is, have you used sufficient transitional devices to clarify how the ideas in the individual sentences relate to one another?

☐ Have you used a good mix of

    ☐ transitional words and phrases

    ☐ key-word repetition, including pronouns

    ☐ the given-new rule

    ☐ sentence coordination, subordination, and embedding?

☐ Have you provided logical transitions between paragraphs to signal how the argument is structured and where sections start and end?

Exercises: Editing Technical Paragraphs and Reports

Exercise 3.1: Examining Paragraph Structure

Find a technical article in a journal or online or use one provided by your instructor. In a pinch, you could look at sections of this textbook or sample documents within the textbook. Individually, in pairs, or in groups, scan the first lines of the paragraphs and see if you can get a feel for the content and organization of the article. Select a few paragraphs, find the topic sentences (generally but not always the first sentence), and see how the paragraphs develop the material introduced in their respective topic sentences. Look for the transition between paragraphs that indicates that a longer argument or description is being made. Underline the topic sentences, circle the transitional devices, and draw arrows from the transitional devices to the paragraph or sentence to which they refer the reader. When done, you'll have a diagram illustrating the logical connections between the ideas in the article.

Exercise 3.2: Applying the Given-New Rule to Construction and Green Roof Sentences

Improve the coherence between each sentence pair by using the given-new rule. This exercise is probably a good warm-up for Exercise 3.4, in which you will improve the coherence of entire paragraphs. Your instructor has access to the answer key and to additional sentence-pair exercises online.

1. One panel of the exterior concrete at the southwest corner of level 01/02 lacks eyebrow protection. This section of the wall will be subject to increased runoff, causing the silicone elastomeric coating to stain heavily, without the eyebrow ledge.

2. We recommend that Johnson Engineering provide project specific shop drawings that specify the parts installation sequence at the interfaces and penetrations. Fastener type, corrosion resistance and spacing for attachment of the base plate should also be indicated in the drawings.

3. The remainder of this section of the LRT between the retained fill structures will be an elevated guideway set on piers. To direct runoff to curb walls along the edges of the deck, it is likely that the deck of the guideway will be cross sloped.

4. The city of Toronto is the first in North America to have a by-law requiring green roofs. New residential, commercial and institutional developments with a gross area of more than 2,000 m^2 are covered by this by-law.

5. Green roofs are multi-layered and have a top layer of soil and plants. "Extensive" is the term for roofs that have a thin layer of soil planted with grasses and ground cover plants, while intensive roofs have deeper soil planted with larger plants, bushes, and even trees.

6. Green roofs are becoming increasingly popular across the country. Energy efficiency, greater durability, and functionality are some of the reasons for this popularity.

7. The layer of soil and living plants provide excellent insulation and protect green roofs from damaging ultraviolet rays. That green roofs can be turned into garden space for staff or residents or even into kitchen gardens or urban farms is another potential benefit.

8. In fact, some supermarkets now have urban farms on their rooftops, with rows of green houses. Zero food miles and ultra freshness are two obvious advantages of such an arrangement.

9. Vancouver does not yet have a green-roof by-law, but it does have a number of green roofs on both public and private buildings. In fact, at 2.5 hectares, the green roof covering the Vancouver Convention Centre is the largest in Canada.

10. The roof is covered in coastal grasses and plants that are well suited to the environment and provide habitat for insects and birds. Over 45 kilograms of wildflower honey were harvested from the roof last year, even though it was primarily intended as a thermally efficient building feature and wildlife refuge in the heart of the city, not as a producing garden.

Exercise 3.3: Applying the Given-New Rule to Fish and Wildlife Lore

As in Exercise 3.2, improve the coherence between each sentence pair by using the given-new rule. Your instructor has access to the answer key and to additional sentence-pair exercises online.

1. Brook trout generally do best at water temperatures between roughly 10°C and 20°C. Trout reproduction, susceptibility to parasites, vulnerability to predation, feeding patterns, and many other factors affecting the survival of trout can all be negatively affected by temperatures outside this narrow range.

2. Temperatures outside the most suitable range cause trout stress and they will move to and hang out in more suitable areas. "Behavioural thermoregulation" is the term for migration in order to find waters with an ideal temperature.

3. Stream temperatures are affected by many factors, but primarily sunlight, the riparian flora, and the stream cross-section. The rate of flow and the depth of a stream, for instance, are determined by its cross-section.

4. A wider, shallower stream will be slow moving and sunshine will penetrate and warm the water to a greater extent than in a narrower, deeper, faster-moving stream. Riparian flora, such as trees with overhangs, however, can shade even wide, shallow streams to cool them sufficiently.

5. Shade or pools of deeper water can create pockets of cooler temperature where trout will hang out on hot days. Fly fishers cast their flies most successfully by knowing where these pockets are located.

6. Colony collapse disease (CCD) is the name given to the sudden dying out of an entire bee colony. With worrying frequency, throughout the Western world, these die-offs are occurring.

7. In North America, about a third of our food crops are pollinated by bees. Crops of almonds, apples, peaches, broccoli, squashes, berries, melons, and so on would be in jeopardy, so some experts claim, without these pollination services.

8. What most people think of when they hear the word "bee" is the type with the yellow and black striped abdomen. The European honeybee, which was originally brought over by the pilgrims, is what this species of bee is actually called.

9. The European honeybee is the only bee species used commercially, but there are approximately four thousand species of bees native to North America. Generally not straying far from their native habitats and favoured plants, these native species only pollinate gardens and the edges of fields and orchards.

10. It's quite likely that most city gardeners do not recognize that they have native bees buzzing about their flowers because some native bees look too much like European honeybees and others don't look like bees at all, at least to the untrained eye. Probably most of the pollination services in city and suburban gardens is provided by these native bees, however.

Exercise 3.4: Revising Paragraphs: Wind Farms

Improve the coherence of the following paragraphs by using transitional devices and combining sentences.

Obviously, when you are editing whole paragraphs, the choices you make in the first sentence will cascade into subsequent sentences. This means that your revision, no matter how good, may not look like someone else's and is unlikely to look exactly like the answer key. However, as long as your paragraphs flow well and your instructor doesn't find too many additional things to correct, your version will be fine.

The key to these exercises, however, is not to stop after your first revision. You should be going through several drafts, each increasingly more brief and increasingly clear and professional.

Good luck and have fun.[1]

1. A wind farm may be a single machine. It may consist of a large number of machines. It could even possibly consist of hundreds of wind turbines. The design approach will be the same. The construction method will be almost identical also. This is true regardless of the size of the project.

2. People tend to think of a wind farm as a power station. There are differences between these two types of power generation. These differences are important. A conventional power station is one large machine. It will not generate power until the completion of its construction. It will often need a substantial and complicated civil structure. Construction risk will be an important part of the project assessment.

3. The construction of a wind farm is more like purchasing of a fleet of trucks than constructing a power station. The turbines will be purchased at a fixed cost. These costs are agreed in advance. A delivery schedule will be established in advance as well. This is exactly as it would be for a fleet of trucks. This is a modular approach. Few wind farms are delivered late. Few farms are finished over budget.

---

1   Adapted from http://www.wind-energy-the-facts.org/en/part-i-technology/chapter-4-wind-farm-design/construction-issues.html

Chapter 4

Parallelism, Lists, and Layout

In this chapter you will learn
- how to recognize and create parallel structures
- how to create proper lists
- how to format and phrase clear, scannable headings.

The formatting of a document determines its visual appeal and directs the reader's eye to important information. Hence, formatting and organization determine a document's accessibility and, to a large extent, its usefulness.

When readers encounter a document, whether it be a brief email or a lengthy feasibility study, they don't actually want to read it; they just want to get from it the information they need at that moment.

The writer, however, has to write a thorough document that will remain clear well into the future and for many different readers. The document has to provide sufficient context so that even a future reader unfamiliar with the circumstances of the report can figure out why it was written. And the document has to provide all the information that different potential readers may require, whether they are from the engineering, finance, or marketing department. Each will look for different information.

However, to prevent readers who are looking for specific information from getting lost in the totality of information required by due diligence but not relevant to them, the document has to be made accessible. It has to be formatted in such a way that any given reader can quickly figure out how the report is organized and where specific information can be found.

Writers do this with bulleted lists and with headings.

Before we describe how to use these, however, we need to talk about parallelism. Lists and headings need to be grammatically parallel so that they can be understood more easily and scanned more quickly. Sentences benefit from the same dynamic; we'll look at them first.

Parallelism in Sentences

Human beings love symmetry, both visual and verbal. In sentences, we refer to symmetry as parallelism because two phrases or clauses will have an identical (or parallel) grammatical structure. For instance, which of the following two sentences sounds better?

> By logic we prove, but it is intuition that makes us discover.
> By logic we prove, but by intuition we discover. (Leonardo da Vinci)

Obviously, the second. It is easier to understand and easier to remember. Why? Because it requires less effort to interpret the grammar. If two clauses that express similar information have similar grammatical structures, the reader has to interpret the grammar only once. Read the following pairs of sentences and, again, take note of your reaction to them. In each case the first sentence is not parallel, and the second is.

> When you are right, you cannot be too radical. But when you are wrong, it is best to be as conservative as possible.
>
> When you are right, you cannot be too radical; when you are wrong, you cannot be too conservative. (Martin Luther King, Jr.)

> The inherent vice of capitalism is the unequal sharing of blessing; in socialism, equal sharing of miseries is the inherent vice.
>
> The inherent vice of capitalism is the unequal sharing of blessing; the inherent virtue of socialism is the equal sharing of miseries. (Winston Churchill)

In each case the second expression, the parallel one, is both shorter and easier to understand. The same holds true of technical sentences.

> Runoff that is not subject to contamination can be discharged directly into the storm sewer system. When the possibility of contamination does exist, the runoff should be treated before entering the storm sewer system.
>
> Runoff that is not subject to contamination can be discharged directly into the storm sewer system. Runoff that is subject to contamination should be treated before being discharged into the storm sewer system.

Consider the example given in Figure 4.1. Read the sign and note the striking lack of parallelism in the three-part description of the delights offered by this well-known social house located in Vancouver, B.C. The problem, of course, is that there is no good noun to describe a location where one socializes, other than "social house," but that had already been used. But how about "Eat. Drink. Socialize"?

FIGURE 4.1 Lack of parallelism. A proper parallel description of the delights of the social house would read either "Eat. Drink. Socialize" or "Restaurant. Bar. Meeting Place."

Source: Courtesy of Andre Lanz

Similar errors in parallelism are often found in technical writing.

Writing and submitting proposals is time consuming, expensive, and it involves an element of risk.

Writing and submitting proposals is <u>time consuming, expensive, and risky</u>.

Wind turbines, for all their environmental advantages, have several drawbacks, such as the amount of embodied energy, the visual impact, and <u>they have the potential of killing birds</u>.

Wind turbines, for all their environmental advantages, have several drawbacks, such as the amount of embodied energy, the visual impact, and the potential for killing birds.

One of the advantages of parallelism is that we can simply omit the repeated words or phrases and know that the reader will fill them in based on the pattern.

Susan prefers wine with dinner, but Bob ~~prefers~~ beer.
Linda likes writing user documentation more than I ~~like writing user documentation~~.
Linda likes writing user documentation more than ~~she likes~~ me.

Parallel sentences are clearer, shorter, and more elegant. The rule of parallelism, then, is that if you are expressing similar information, do so in a similar manner. Repetition and predictability are strengths in technical writing. Flights of fancy and experiments with form usually aren't.

Lists

A list is a series of items. These can either be run into a sentence horizontally and separated with commas or be stacked vertically and preceded by bullets. Generally speaking, we stack lists vertically for two reasons, either to clarify the list or to draw attention to the list.

Clarifying, Not Brainstorming

Lists are not brainstorming tools or shortcuts for writers. They are work tools, carefully crafted to aid the reader's comprehension. They itemize discrete points that would otherwise be difficult to follow if, for instance, the individual items are long and complex.

The following series doesn't work in sentence form:

> The design-build contractor shall provide written notice to property owners informing them of the extent and type of work that will be performed on their property, meet with owners to explain what work will take place on their property, and obtain written permission of private property owners prior to proceeding with work on their property; obtain all permits and approvals from municipal, provincial, and federal authorities, when and where required; verify the location of all buried and overhead utilities prior to commencement of subsurface investigations; notify the city of the dates and times that field investigations will be carried out; and provide copies of all reports to the city as soon as they are available.

These items are logically parallel (they are about the same thing) and grammatically parallel (they share the same grammatical pattern). But they are very difficult to follow.

But as a list, this sentence is much easier to follow:

The design-build contractor shall
- provide written notice to property owners informing them of the extent and type of work that will be performed on their property, meet with owners to explain what work will take place on their property, and obtain written permission of private property owners prior to proceeding with work on their property
- obtain all permits and approvals from municipal, provincial, and federal authorities, when and where required
- verify the location of all buried and overhead utilities prior to commencement of subsurface investigations
- notify the city of the dates and times that field investigations will be carried out
- provide copies of all reports to the city as soon as they are available.

Too often, however, writers create something like the following, which is really no more than brainstorming notes. It's very difficult for a reader to follow the writer's intent, and after a few weeks, even the writer might have trouble remembering exactly what was intended:

The tunnel ventilation shall:

- Satisfy tenability and comfort criteria detailed below in the Market Street Tunnel and Market Street Station in the following functional modes:
  - Normal operations
  - Congested operations
  - Fire emergency operations
- Passive and active systems shall include
  - Train movement
  - Fan systems
- Provide controls to operate the fans remotely from the operation control centre:
  - Operations shall be integrated with the Market Street Station's two-stage fire alarm system
  - Allow for manual operation during emergencies
- Provide the following:
  - Fan details
  - All associated plant design drawings and specifications
- Plant room requirements
  - Plant room layouts if required
  - All components shall be CSA or ULC tested; if not, an exemption must be sought from the city.
  - The tunnel ventilation system shall include but is not limited to fans, silencers, dampers, ducts, grilles, ventilation shafts, and all electrical components including electrical infrastructure with two separate sources of power.

> *Caution: The list on this page is an example of an improper list. Never include something like this in your writing.*

The above is not a proper list; rather it is a stack of point-form thoughts. These items are neither logically nor grammatically parallel. They are separate ideas that need to be developed in separate paragraphs that anyone can understand on first reading:

> *"Shall" is often used to spell out requirements, as in specifications and requests for proposals (RFP).*

The tunnel ventilation shall satisfy tenability, comfort, and smoke-extraction criteria within the Westbrook Mall east tunnel, Market Street Tunnel, and Market Street Station.

Tunnel ventilation shall consist of passive and/or active air movement during normal, congested, and fire emergency operations. Passive air movement shall derive from train movement through the tunnel sections. Active air movement shall derive from ventilation fan systems installed in each tunnel section.

The ventilation fan system components shall include fans, silencers, dampers, ducts, grilles, ventilation shafts, controls, and all electrical components including electrical infrastructure linked to two separate sources of power. The control system shall permit remote operation from the operations control centre and localized manual operation by emergency responders. Fan operations shall be integrated with the two-phase fire alarm system at Market Street Station.

The contractor shall provide fan system details and all associated plant design drawings and specifications (including plant room requirements and plant room layouts if required) to the city for review and approval. All components shall be CSA or ULC labelled; if not, the contractor shall seek an exemption from the city.[1]

So, use lists to enhance clarity. Don't use them when they muddy it.

Drawing Attention and Creating Work Tools

The second function of lists is to draw the reader's attention to key information and thereby to create work tools.

Just like headings, bulleted lists are formatted to stand out. They are indented to create a border of white space and feature large black graphical elements called bullets to direct the reader's attention. In effect, bulleted lists are graphics and, like headings, are one of the first things a reader notices on the page.

Check your own response as you look at the illustration below.

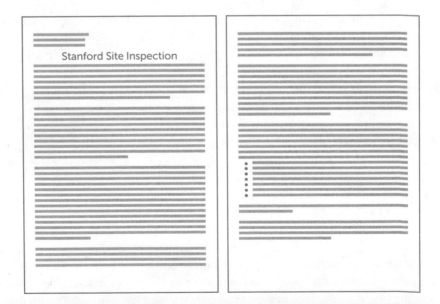

Stanford Site Inspection

FIGURE 4.2 Proper bulleting draws attention to key information in a report. Quite predictably, the first thing every reader will look at is the heading. The next is the list. This is how we help readers identify and find key information.

---

1   Thanks to Andre Lanz for these examples.

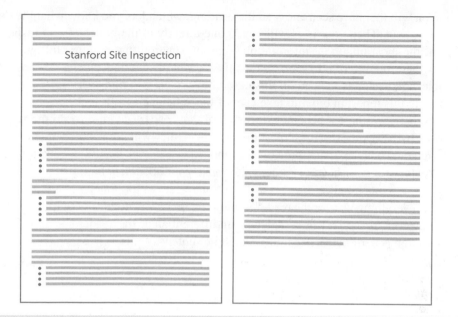

FIGURE 4.3 **If you emphasize too much with bullets,** everything seems to be attempting to stand out. In that case, you're not really helping readers so much as shouting at them.

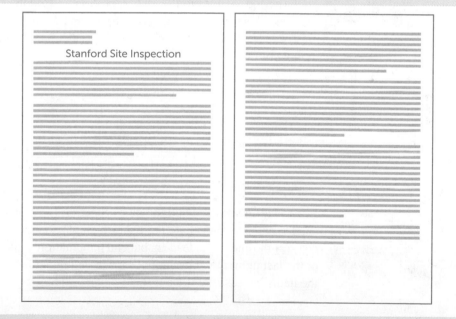

FIGURE 4.4 **This is just an unrelieved wash of grey.** There's nothing here to direct the reader's attention to important information or to help the reader understand how the document is structured.[2]

---

2   Page graphics adapted from Kipling, David. Comm 1145 lecture. BCIT, BC: 1997/8.

You will first have seen and read the heading, which lets you know what the document is about. Then your eyes will have gone directly to the bullets. In an inspection report, the most important information—the information that requires follow-up and that is therefore referred to most frequently—concerns the deficiencies. If those deficiencies are listed, as they are in this case, they are easy to find every time the reader returns to this report in order to take care of the deficiencies.

In that way, the list becomes a work tool that readers can use to do the required follow-up. Every time readers look at the document, they will immediately find the list of tasks required of them. If they print out the report, they can even make notes against the list.

You can, of course, go overboard and make your document look like a huge shopping list; too much bulleted text is as hard to navigate as too much paragraph text because if everything vies for the reader's attention, in the end nothing actually stands out.

However, if the text is completely undifferentiated, the reader's search for key information is undirected, except for the topic sentences.

Punctuating Lists

Full Sentence Lists

Hint: If the lead-in ends in "the following" or "as follows," it is most likely a full sentence lead-in.

If the items are full sentences, punctuate them as full sentences, with an initial capital letter and end punctuation (period, or question mark if appropriate). End the full-sentence lead-in with a colon (:). Strictly speaking, you can also end a full sentence lead-in with a period, but it's much more common to use a colon.

Criticisms levelled at wind turbines include the following:
- They contain a high level of embodied energy.
- They have been alleged to kill birds when placed in flight paths.
- They are considered unsightly by many.
- They produce energy at a relatively high cost.

Partial Sentence Lists

If the list and lead-in form a single sentence, punctuate it as one—more or less.

If the lead-in sentence and the items function to complete a single sentence, punctuate the list as a single sentence—no colon at the end of the lead-in, but end punctuation at the end of the last item. Don't use initial caps or end punctuation for the items because they're not stand-alone sentences.

Criticisms levelled at wind turbines include
- a high level of embodied energy
- potential bird strikes
- poor aesthetics
- the relatively high cost of energy production.

You could put a comma after every item but the last, but then you would have to add an "and" at the end of the penultimate (second to last) item. If you choose this style, use it consistently throughout the document, and if the items are long and contain commas of their own, use semi-colons (;) instead of commas at the ends of the items. See the corrected list under "Clarifying, Not Brainstorming," above.

Criticisms levelled at wind turbines include
- a high level of embodied energy,
- potential bird strikes,
- poor aesthetics, and
- relatively high energy-generation cost.

Shopping Lists

If the items are nouns or noun phrases instead of sentences but don't complete the lead-in to form a single grammatical sentence, use a colon at the end of the lead-in, but don't punctuate the items. These are your standard shopping or laundry lists, and they are considered to be fairly informal. Officially, these are called fragment lists.

Site issues that are of particular concern:
- the lack of temporary banisters on stairways and upper-level window openings
- the burning of waste vinyl siding on-site
- the lack of temporary toilets
- the consumption of alcohol and the smoking of illicit substances during work hours.

Don't capitalize the items unless, of course, you are listing proper names.

Requirements for completion of these instructions:
- Robertson #3 screwdriver
- 4 mm Allen wrench
- standard hammer
- pinking shears.

Numbered Lists, Lettered Lists, and Nested Lists

Lists may be formed using bullets, numbers, or letters. However, bullets do not imply sequence or order, whereas numbers and letters do.

Bullets indicate that this information can be collected in any order.

In preparation for obtaining a copyright clearance, collect the following information:
- author's or editor's full name
- exact title, including journal title if applicable
- edition, or volume and issue if in a journal

- publisher
- city of publication
- year of publication
- specific page numbers.

Always use numbered lists for sequential instructions.

> *Numbers or letters indicate that these actions must be carried out in a specific order. If the listed items are not actions, the numbers indicate a specific ranking, like a top ten list.*

To remove the motor, follow these steps:

1. Remove the six gearbox socket cap screws.
2. Slide the blower with attached gearbox mechanism out of the gearbox housing.
3. Remove the coupling access screw.
4. Rotate the coupling until the coupling setscrew is visible through the opening left by the coupling access screw.
5. Loosen the coupling setscrew.
6. Remove the four retaining screws.
7. Slide the coupling off the motor shaft.
8. Remove the four motor socket cap screws.
9. Remove the motor.

Use bulleted lists for secondary (nested) non-sequential lists beneath a numbered- or lettered-list item. Use lettered lists for a secondary (nested) sequential list beneath a numbered-list item.

To remove the motor, follow these steps:

1. Remove the six gearbox socket cap screws:
   - Remove the two bottom screws.
   - Remove the two middle screws.
   - Remove the two top screws.
2. Slide the blower with attached gearbox mechanism out of the gearbox housing.
3. Remove the coupling:
   a) Remove the coupling access screw.
   b) Rotate the coupling until the coupling setscrew is visible through the opening left by the coupling access screw.
   c) Loosen the coupling setscrew.
   d) Remove the four retaining screws:
      - Remove the two bottom screws.
      - Remove the two top screws.
   e) Slide the coupling off the motor shaft.
4. Remove the four motor socket cap screws.
5. Remove the motor.[3]

---

3   Thanks to Andre Lanz for these examples.

Don't use more than three levels of hierarchy in a list or it will become too difficult to follow.

Although not technically incorrect, it's bad form to place bullets under bullets. Usually, a little rewriting will solve the problem. For example,

Provide a digital alarm status signal for the following devices:
- rectifier
  - diode
  - temperature
  - DC control
  - reverse current
- transformer
- pilot wire
- winding temperature.

can become

Provide a digital alarm status signal for the following devices:
- rectifier diode, temperature, DC control, and reverse current
- transformer
- pilot wire
- winding temperature.

or

Provide a digital alarm status signal for the following devices:
- rectifier diode
- rectifier temperature
- rectifler DC control
- rectifier reverse current
- transformer
- pilot wire
- winding temperature.

If you write numbered or lettered lists in sentence form, use parentheses instead of periods to set off the numbers or letters so that it won't look as though you're using end punctuation. Do not use bullets in a sentence-form list:

A passive thermal home design requires careful consideration of four factors: (1) the structure's orlentation in relation to the sun, (2) the area of glazing in relation to the structure's square footage, (3) the thermal mass of the structure, and (4) shading by the structure (eaves) and by the landscaping (trees).

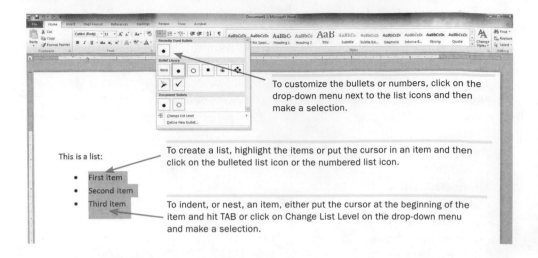

To customize the bullets or numbers, click on the drop-down menu next to the list icons and then make a selection.

This is a list:

To create a list, highlight the items or put the cursor in an item and then click on the bulleted list icon or the numbered list icon.

- First item
- Second item
- Third item

To indent, or nest, an item, either put the cursor at the beginning of the item and hit TAB or click on Change List Level on the drop-down menu and make a selection.

FIGURE 4.5 List customization options in Word. Word-processing software makes it easy to customize lists with a few mouse clicks. The next list you start will automatically use the formatting of the list you last customized in the document.

Source: Used with permission from Microsoft.

Using Word to Create Lists

Word allows you to create and customize lists with a few mouse clicks, as shown in Figure 4.5.

Headings

The first order of organization in a document is actually the paragraph, which we discussed in Chapter 3. As you now know, paragraphs break reports up into discrete ideas or discrete steps in an argument or a description. Each new idea goes into a separate paragraph, with a clear topic sentence. When several paragraphs elaborate a single idea (or make up a full description), those paragraphs form a section. And these sections should be clearly labelled and separated from other sections by headings.

The purpose of headings, then, is to label sections or categories of information. And by doing so, headings permit vertical scanning. Generally readers will skim a page vertically, scanning only the headings, to get a sense of how the report is organized and where to find specific information. When they find the section in which they're interested, then and only then, do they read with attention.

Creating Effective Headings

To help readers scan headings more easily, make headings parallel and word them as descriptive phrases.

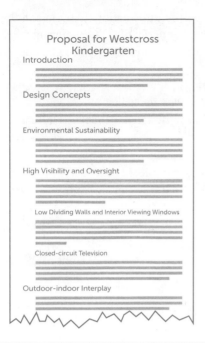
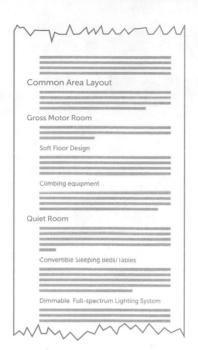

FIGURE 4.6 **Headings are signposts for the reader.** They permit the reader to quickly scan a document to find out how it's organized and where to find specific information.

By creating grammatically parallel headings, you are in effect creating an easily scannable list of report topics.

And by framing headings as phrases rather than full sentences you make them easier to understand. Phrases are also shorter than full sentences and therefore take up less space, which at larger point sizes means that a heading is less likely to break across a line. There's no absolute rule restricting headings to a single line, but they do look better and scan more easily that way.

However, don't stint on information. In fact, because phrases are shorter than sentences, we can provide more information in fewer words than we could if we were writing full sentences. Take advantage of this to make your headings as helpful as possible; think of the readers' reaction to receiving your document. The first thing they'll ask is something along the lines of "What is this (document)?" So make sure your subject line or title tells them clearly. Consider including a tag that describes the function of the document:

Proposal to change the tunnel lighting system to LED

Invoice for lighting installation at . . .

Reminder about start of lighting installation

Request for reimbursement for purchase of . . .

When the readers move to the body of the document, they'll ask of each heading and subheading something like, "What's this section about?" Again, make sure you

> *Just like buttons and links on a website, headings help readers navigate a document. Always provide the clearest road map you can.*

provide the most specific information that you can. Instead of saying something generic like "Dewatering," provide something clear, complete, and descriptive such as

Successful Dewatering of Tunnel 3G

Need for a Dewatering Plan for Tunnel 3G

Anticipated Delays Due to Dewatering Problems in Tunnel 3G

Dewatering is a very large issue in a mine. The three descriptive headings listed above clarify whether the section is about a successfully completed past task, a call to prepare for a potential future problem, or an admission that dewatering attempts have failed and that delays are now inevitable.

Another way to make headings more effective is to think of them as being completely separate from the report itself. Treat them like labels inserted after the report has been written. That way you don't end up making headings the starting thought of the section.

Need for a Dewatering Plan

We need one because the hydrology of the site suggests that . . .

Need for a Dewatering Plan

This is because the hydrology of the site suggests that . . .

In the examples above, the sentences following the headings make sense only in conjunction with those headings. However, readers often find this confusing because they scan vertically to find their place and then take a breath and begin reading closely and horizontally for specific information. When they do so, a sentence that begins without context can confuse. Instead, the opening sentence of a section should repeat the key information or key word from the heading:

Need for a Dewatering Plan

We need a dewatering plan because the hydrology of the site suggests that . . .

Levels of Headings

Often sections in a report are broken into multiple subsections, some of which may even be broken into sub-subsections. These levels of headings are referred to as first-level, second-level, and third-level headings, or primary, secondary, and tertiary headings.

It's generally better to create more sections than longer sections to more effectively signal the report's organization and to make information easier to find. Look at the structure of any table of contents, including the one for this textbook, to see this concept in action. The following is another example. Notice how even if you know nothing about mining, you immediately get a sense of what this report is about and how it's organized. The same holds true for the report outline in Figure 4.6.

Progress in Tunnel 3G
  Exploratory drilling
  Initial assay results
  Hydrology
    Water seepage investigation
    Potential dewatering strategies
      Straight pumping
      Drainage and reservoir system
    Cost comparison of dewatering strategies

Formatting Headings

Format headings so that readers are never unsure what level of heading they are look-ing at. Make primary headings noticeably more emphatic than secondary headings, and make secondary headings noticeably more emphatic than tertiary headings (see Figure 4.6). You can do this by increasing the point size for each higher-level heading or by indenting lower-level headings. However, it's generally not a good idea to indent the text for lower-level sections as that will create narrower columns of text.

Additional ways to distinguish headings from body text, useful for lower-level headings whose point size and left margin may be the same as that of the body text, are to use colour, and to use a different typeface.

However, be careful with the use of colour if you are not in control of the output. For instance, if you email your report, the colour will pop off the screen and instantly identify your headings. But if your reader then prints out the report on a black-and-white printer, those headings will come out a shade of grey and lose some of their impact. Consider doing a test print of one of your pages containing the lower-level headings to check that they remain sufficiently distinct from the body text to be identified instantly.

In terms of font changes, consider using a sans serif font (Arial, Verdana, or the like) for the headings and a serif font (Times Roman, Schoolbook, or the like) for the body text. Serifs are the little extra strokes found at the ends of the main vertical and horizontal strokes of letters (see Figure 4.7). These serifs actually guide the eye from one letter to the next, making text easier to read at small point sizes. Times Roman, for instance, was specifically designed for *The New York Times*, so they could squeeze

Text in Verdana (sans serifs)

Text in Times Roman (serifs)

FIGURE 4.7 Serifs guide the readers' eyes helpfully at smaller point sizes but don't enhance legibility at larger point sizes. Consider using a serif font for body text and a sans serif font for headings to increase the contrast between headings and body text.

more words on the page but keep the text legible. "Roman" is another way typographers say "serif."

Be sure to avoid two common formatting mistakes: do not use all caps and do not underline your headings. These two formatting conventions went out with the typewriter, which offered only those two methods for setting headings apart from body

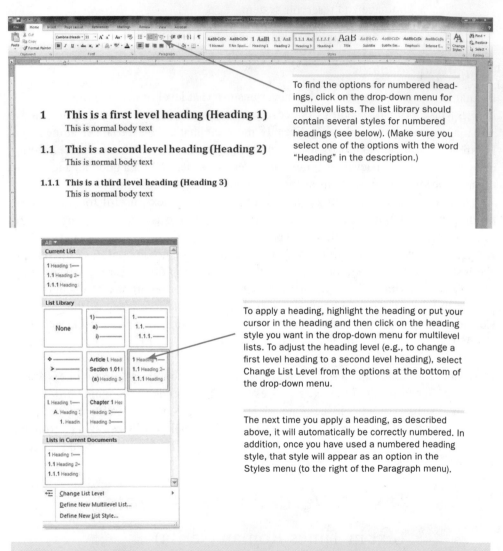

To find the options for numbered headings, click on the drop-down menu for multilevel lists. The list library should contain several styles for numbered headings (see below). (Make sure you select one of the options with the word "Heading" in the description.)

To apply a heading, highlight the heading or put your cursor in the heading and then click on the heading style you want in the drop-down menu for multilevel lists. To adjust the heading level (e.g., to change a first level heading to a second level heading), select Change List Level from the options at the bottom of the drop-down menu.

The next time you apply a heading, as described above, it will automatically be correctly numbered. In addition, once you have used a numbered heading style, that style will appear as an option in the Styles menu (to the right of the Paragraph menu).

FIGURE 4.8 Applying numbered headings in Word. Word-processing software makes it easy both to apply heading styles consistently and to use numbered headings. The software will keep track of heading numbers and correct them when sections or subsections get moved around.

Source: Used with permission from Microsoft

text. All caps and underlining make headings harder to read, look a little dated and amateurish, and are considered a bit of an eyesore.

Numbering Headings

Another way to signal the different levels of headings is to number them. This also dramatically increases ease of reference; it is far easier to refer colleagues to something that has been labelled alphanumerically ("Let's take a look at section 3.2.2") than it is to refer them to a section by a name that might occur anywhere in the document ("Let's take a look at the section on the drainage and reservoir system"). This is why numbered headings are particularly common in works of reference, such as bodies of law, codes of conduct, specifications documents, standard operating procedures, ISO certification, and the like.

Most word-processing software will automatically number headings for you as illustrated in Figure 4.8.

Using Word to Create Headings

Word provides a number of templates with pre-set heading styles. Simply choose one you like and apply it. Most organizations have a preferred look for their headings and issue a template designed according to a corporate style guide to ensure that all their documents are formatted consistently. Only occasionally will you have to design your own look for headings.

Parallelism, Lists, and Layout

When you edit your documents, check for the following:

Lists and parallelism

- [ ] Have you expressed similar information in a similar manner?
- [ ] When information is presented in series, is it presented in parallel, whether in list or paragraph form?
- [ ] When you have listed information (stacked it vertically with bullets), have you done so because the information is important and deserves attention?
- [ ] Have you punctuated your lists correctly?

Headings

- [ ] Are your headings parallel, descriptive phrases?
- [ ] Does the text that follows the headings work independently of the headings?
- [ ] Are your headings formatted to clearly distinguish them from body text and to clearly distinguish between the different levels of headings?

Exercises: Creating Parallel Sentences and Lists

Complete these exercises singly, in pairs, or in groups as determined by your instructor. Either submit them for marks or discuss them in groups or with the whole class, again, as determined by your instructor. Answer keys and additional exercises are available to your instructor online.

Exercise 4.1: Creating a Parallel List

Please revise the following list to make it grammatically parallel. Check the punctuation.

> The design-build contractor shall undertake a detailed storm water drainage analysis for. . . . The analysis shall include:
> - Appropriate delineation of catchment areas, imperviousness, and drainage patterns for both the pre- and post-construction conditions to verify runoff characteristics and determine which catchment areas are subject to an increase in runoff.
> - also computer simulations to determine pre- and post-construction discharge rates, volumes, and storage requirements for up to a 1-in-100-year rain event.
> - Detailed overland flow assessment of water depths, velocities, escape routes, trap low storage, and spill elevations. And
> - There should be other measures to confirm that the design of the minor and major drainage system components meet the design criteria.

Exercise 4.2: Editing an Email

Please revise the following email so that it is grammatically and logically parallel. If some items don't fit logically, take them out of the list and find a new place for them.

> Hi Dave,
>
> When you return from Calgary, please bring the following for our meeting.
> - The City of Calgary Wastewater & Drainage Storm Water Management & Design Manual (Dec. 2013)
> - The City of Calgary Water Resources Standard Specifications Sewer Construction 2015.
> - Parks Development Guidelines, Province of Alberta 2013;
> - read the minutes from the last meeting. Some interesting stuff there.
> - Also, Waterworks Standard Specifications Waterworks Construction 2011, City of Calgary.
> - See if you can take some photos of the Bow Trail corridor east of 26th Street SW towards the Crowchild Interchange. They'll help us discuss some of the details.
>
> Have fun on the red eye. Looking forward to seeing you at the meeting at 9 a.m., sharp.

Exercise 4.3: Correcting Faulty Parallelism in a Public Place

Correct the following sign (adapted from one posted at a public park in Canada).

Garibaldi Provincial Park

Notice:

PLEASE DON'T LEAVE YOUR MARK!

- No Campfires
- Keep Water Clean
- Carry Out Your Garbage
- Stay On Trails
- Leave Wild Plants for Others to See and Enjoy
- Dogs are prohibited in Garibaldi Park.
- Garibaldi Park is a user maintain park throughout the year.

BE A MINIMUM IMPACT HIKER
HELP US PRESERVE OUR PARKS AND WILDERNESS
Take only pictures and leave only footprints.

www.bcparks.ca    BCParks

Source: Courtesy of Andre Lanz

Exercise 4.4: Deficiency list

The following paragraph describes a series of WorkSafe BC infractions carried out by a framer on a construction site. Change this series into a proper, parallel list.

Dave,

As I've mentioned to you a couple of times, your crew is breaking a bunch of Work-Safe BC regulations. We ought to follow those regulations, not just because they have the force of law in the province, but also because we want to keep everyone on site safe. Please make sure that your crew from now on lowers waste wood from the upper storey frames safely. Then they have to collect that waste wood, they have to remove all the nails and should deposit the wood in the wood recycle bins. Also make sure that your framers trap sawdust in containers at the cutting stations. Alternatively they could wet the sawdust down.

Make sure you erect temporary railings on all stairs and across the low window openings in the upper storeys.

One more thing, neighbours have complained about acrid smoke when your guys burn their vinyl siding waste on site. This is a serious health hazard, so please follow the WorkSafe regulation and truck your vinyl waste off site for environmentally safe disposal.

Thanks for your help on this.

Exercise 4.5: Expanded Deficiency List

This exercise expands on the list from Exercise 4.4 by adding explanations in each bullet. Use either the "to prevent," or the "so that no one" formulation, or some other, consistently. The entire bullet item needs to be as parallel as possible, not just the opening.

Hi Dave,

As I've mentioned to you a couple of times, your crew is breaking a bunch of Work-Safe BC regulations. We ought to follow those regulations, not just because they have the force of law in the province, but also because we want to keep everyone on site safe. Please make sure that your crew from now on lowers waste wood from the upper storey frames safely, to prevent passersby being hit by dropping lumber. Then they have to collect that waste wood, avoiding tripping hazards. They have to remove all the nails so that no one receives a puncture wound. Also they should deposit the wood in the wood recycle bins to prevent tripping hazards. Furthermore, please make sure that your framers trap sawdust in containers at the cutting stations; otherwise it will blow around the site and get in people's eyes and lungs. Alternatively they could wet the sawdust down.

Make sure you erect temporary railings on all stairs and across the low window openings in the upper storeys, so people don't fall off stairs or out of windows.

Thanks for your help on this.

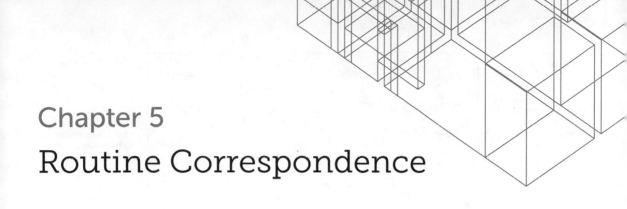

Chapter 5

Routine Correspondence

In this chapter you will learn
- how to format letters, memos, and emails properly
- how to apply proper netiquette to prevent email faux pas
- how to write in a professional, friendly, and tactful tone.

Much of the on-the-job writing you will do as a professional will be correspondence, not reports; that is, much of your writing will be only one to two pages long and in the form of letters, memos, and, mostly, emails.

Broadly speaking, you'll write to inform, to remind, to request, or to record. You may, for instance, make routine requests for information, set meeting times, confirm test results, ask for technical details, and so on. Occasionally, however, you will write letters with possible legal ramifications, such as complaints about poorly performed services or about improperly functioning equipment. In all cases, your correspondence must be clear and unambiguous.

Letter Format

Letters have a standard format. By observing a uniform letter format, writers can ensure that readers always know where to look for specific information. Uniform formatting speeds up the reading process and allows readers to concentrate on the content of the letter.

Readers expect professionally formatted and professionally written letters. If you fall short of their expectations, you create an unprofessional impression not just of yourself, but also of the organization that allows you to represent them.

Figures 5.1 and 5.2 depict proper letter format. Use them as models for your own letters.

Your return address: No name, title, phone number or email address. But do put the postal code on the same line as the city and the province code.

Full mailing address: Include the title, if there is one, but no phone number or email address. Leave at least two spaces between the provincial and postal codes; no comma.

Salutation: No one wants to be addressed as "Dear Sir or Madam" or some such generic formulation. If you cannot make a personal appeal because you don't know the reader's name, omit the salutation. If it's too awkward to call someone "Dear" but you don't know them well enough to say "Hi, David," you can also omit the salutation.

Date: Don't write something ambiguous like 03/08/12.

Clear, descriptive title: it's generally better when a reader can immediately identify the purpose of a document, but not every letter has to have a title.

Full block paragraphs: left justified, no first-line indent, double-space in between. Don't use full justification; it creates odd spacing between letters and words and makes text harder to read.

Continued line: This information is optional. If the page ends mid-sentence, the reader knows to expect another page.

---

123 Nonsuch St., Unit 13
Vancouver, BC V4E 1A2

September 12, 2017

Dr. David Thompson
City Manager
800 Macleod Trail SE
Calgary, AB T2P 1M4

Dear Dr. Thompson,

Proposal Submission: Westcross Kindergarten

We are pleased to present our design for the Westcross Kindergarten for the City of Calgary design competition #CoG-WCK-2017-32A. The following are some highlights from the design rationale (enclosed).

You will note from our plans (enclosed) that we have created a somewhat larger footprint for this building than initially discussed, but that we have kept this footprint within the property setbacks stipulated by the by-laws and the costs within the limits set by the City of Calgary Planning Department.

Our decision was guided by the idea that children would benefit from a larger indoor grossmotor play area to run around in and get exercise when opportunities to play outdoors may be limited, for instance during particularly cold spells in the winter or sudden cold snaps in spring or fall. This did reduce the outdoor play area a little bit, but seemed a reasonable compromise.

Also, while the design specification stated a preference for easy-clean and aseptic surfaces, we have used as many natural materials inside the kindergarten as possible to bring the outdoors in and to give the interior space a more comfortable feel. For instance, we have created a post and beam structure using wooden glu-lam beams and have paneled parts of the interior with beetle-killed pine. However, we would treat these natural materials with organic, low-VOC stains that will meet the City's requirement for an easy-to-clean and aseptic public space.

We are particularly pleased with the high insulation values we've been able to maintain, despite the large window surfaces, by using triple-glazed windows (R-value 24), by designing extra thick walls (R-value 32), by including a green roof (R-value 45), and by specifying a very tightly sealed building envelope.

... 2

FIGURE 5.1 **Full block letter format, first page.** Some slight variations that put the return address and signature block toward the right margin, for instance, are still in use, but less and less. Just adopt the format illustrated here and you can't go wrong.

Memo and Email Formats

These days emails are used even in many formal situations that used to demand letters. They're obviously much quicker, save postage and stationery, and, if securely backed up, still constitute a legally binding record of what you and your reader discussed and agreed to.

Signature: Don't forget to sign your letters. If you're sending your letter as a PDF, you can omit the signature (and move up the signature block), or insert an electronic signature (a scan of your signature).

Copy line: Just like in an email, list the people to whom the letter is not directly addressed but whom you are sending copies for their records or for information.

Enclosure line: What you'd call an attachment in an email, but it's enclosed in an envelope. It's a good idea to list the enclosed items. Alternatively, just indicate how many were included. Note that a twenty-page report constitutes a single enclosure.

Dr. Thompson
September 12, 2017   2

The green roof will be accessible to staff and students and would make a great place for a kitchen garden. We do not intend for this area to be used for play, but feel that it will partially compensate for the reduced outdoor play area caused by our increased building footprint.

We would like to thank the city planning team for answering our continual questions about the design requirements, in particular Mr. Dan Paisevic, Planning Director, and Dr. Jean Schmidt, City Health Officer. Their patience and ability to explain complex material in layperson's terms were invaluable.

Please let me know if you have any questions about our design; I would be delighted to show how our design decisions were motivated by the well being of the children and staff who will occupy the space.

Sincerely,

T. Comford

Theodore Comford
President, Streamline Architects
tcomford@streamlinearch.ca
778-822-1111

cc: Bing Thom

encl: design rationale
drawing package

Header: All professional documents need a header on every page after the first. In correspondence, include the page number, the addressee and the date. This will make the document easy to identify and sort in case the pages become separated.

Complimentary close: "Sincerely" is standard. "Cheers," or "Thanks," or similar are acceptable in less formal correspondence. Reserve "Truly" for deeply personal correspondence. As with the salutation, feel free to drop the close entirely.

Signature block: Leave enough room for the actual signature (about four lines); then provide your name, title, and contact information. Omit the contact information if you have already put it in the last paragraph.

FIGURE 5.2 Letter format, last page. This is the letter that would have accompanied the submission package sent to the City of Calgary. Its purpose and tone are quite formal.

In fact, these days there's very little difference between letters, memos, and emails, except for the addressing information that reflects their different delivery methods. Obviously, some email is quite informal, more so than a letter ever would be, but only because no one ever mails a letter to a colleague three cubicles over.

Emails with significant content sent to an important client, sponsor, or researcher with whom you are not on familiar terms will obviously have a more formal tone and diction than a quick email to your colleagues down the hall announcing you're meeting up for lunch. But overall the bodies of letters, memos, and emails are largely indistinguishable.

Figure 5.3 illustrates a quick informal email. Figures 5.4 and 5.5 illustrate an official memo. Emails are, of course, formatted for you by the software. Because emails are personal correspondence, they always include salutations and closes.

A more formal email would probably include a signature block, though generally without a signature. However, some writers do include a scanned, digital copy of their signature.

To: tcomford@streamlinearch.ca
From: david_thompson@cog.gov.ab
Date: September 13, 2017
Subject: Submission of Streamline's Westcross Kindergarten design

Hi Theo,

Thanks for the design for the Westcross Kindergarten. I've forwarded the plans and the design rationale to the selection committee. I'll let you know their decision as soon as they give it to me, but, unfortunately, they are not allowed to ask clarifying questions after the submission deadline, which is when they start looking at the designs. The designs remain sealed until then.

Rest assured, though, that small deviations from our initial requests won't disqualify your design, as long the design meets our overall criteria and remains within budget, of course. Thanks for all the hard work that you and your team have put into this project.

Best,
David

Emails format themselves, though in longer emails, writers may choose to include headings and subheadings. Those they'll have to format for themselves.

FIGURE 5.3 Email format. This is a quick, informal email to let Theodore at Streamline know that John has received his proposal and what happens next. However, it's no longer necessarily true that emails are less formal than letters. It all depends on context.

Addressing block: in this order. It's considered tidy to line up the names and date to a common margin. To provide more identifying information, you can include people's titles and departments (internal) or companies (external)

Generally speaking, memos do not use salutations ("Hi John,") or friendly closes. This is largely because they are more generally addressed and not considered personal correspondence.

To: Selection Committee
From: Dr. David Thompson DT
Date: Sept. 15, 2017
Subject: Evaluation of Westcross Kindergarten Submissions

The attached are the four proposals for the Westcross Kindergarten. Each consists of a design rationale and a drawing package. I've also attached the evaluation forms for you to fill out.

This officially closes the competition and requires us to cease all communication with the proponents.

We'll hold our preliminary assessment meeting on the 24th, as discussed. As always, I'm available for questions at john_johnstone@cog.gov.ab or local 213.

attach: 4 design submissions (1 design rationale and 1 drawing pkg each)
          4 evaluation forms

You can put more than one name in the To: line if the memo is intended for more than one reader. Add a Copy: line (or cc: or c: line) for secondary readers who are receiving copies for their information only.

Initial (don't sign) the memo next to the From: line. Alternatively, initial or sign at the end of the memo. Hard copy correspondence must be initialled or signed so the readers know that it actually came from you.

FIGURE 5.4 Standard memo format. This is a hard copy placed atop the pile of hard-copy proposals to make sure that everyone on the selection committee gets a copy and has their instructions before they begin assessing the proposals. Often, of course, this information would be sent by email as well or instead.

Because word processors make it so easy we are increasingly using properly formatted titles on memos, so readers can instantly identify the purpose and content of the document.

To: Selection Committee

From: Dr. David Thompson DT

Date: Sept. 15, 2017

Evaluation of Westcross Kindergarten Submissions

The attached are the four proposals for the Westcross Kindergarten. Each consists of a design rationale and a drawing package. I've also attached the evaluation forms for you to fill out.

This officially closes the competition and requires us to cease all communication with the proponents.

We'll hold our preliminary assessment meeting on the 24th, as discussed. As always, I'm available for questions at john_johnstone@cog.gov.ab or local 213.

attch: 4 design submissions (1 design rationale and 1 drawing pkg each)
   4 evaluation forms

FIGURE 5.5 Variation of memo format. Instead of a subject line, this email uses a heading, or title. This makes the document and its purpose easier to find and identify in a pile of papers, as we've discussed in Chapter 4.

However, memos are generally addressed more widely and are often posted somewhere for wider consumption, usually as hard copies; in these instances personal salutations and friendly closes are omitted.

Email Etiquette ("Netiquette")

Absolute rules for email etiquette do not exist; like everything else on the Internet and when it comes to manners, netiquette is in flux. However, some core guidelines are unlikely to change because they've proven to prevent embarrassment, hostile reactions, and wasted time.

Netiquette calls for a modicum of forbearance and a bit of effort. Good manners and good practices always do; it's a form of paying forward.

Guideline 1: Remember that you're creating a permanent record

Any email you write at work is the property of your employer. And that employer will archive your emails and is free to read them at any time. This means that your correspondence forms a permanent, and public, record of your work, your attitude, your professionalism, and your opinions. Think of yourself as being under constant

IN THE FIELD

Karin Garandza, P.Eng.—Electrical Engineer and Technical Writer

I worked as an electrical engineer for over 20 years, first in SCADA systems and later in fuel cells. Writing was always a part of the job. When I was employed as a control systems programmer, the writing I did ranged from documenting my programs to writing user guides. Being able to write clearly and accurately was vital to the success of the products I worked on. As my career developed, I learned that it was important to get to know the customers and understand their technical abilities and communication styles so that I could write user guides that worked for them.

Later in my career, I became an engineering manager and found that writing constituted most of the job. In the era of the Internet, much of my work as a manager involved writing emails—to provide detailed directions to my team, to communicate with other departments, to communicate with customers, to track project progress, and to provide status updates to project stakeholders. There is a real art to writing a good email—clear, consistent language, short sentences, bullet points or numbered lists, and direct and specific questions. It takes skill and practice, and an understanding of your audience, to write a good email that gets results. Some days, I spent most of the day crafting emails, particularly when collaborating on developing specifications with the customer.

Other writing I did as a manager included technical specifications and reports, system requirements, user guides, and numerous other documents. As well as writing my own documents, I also contributed to other people's documents, where I needed to pay attention to the original author's writing style in order to integrate my contributions smoothly. The keys to writing good technical documents are very much the same as those for writing good emails—clear, consistent language, short paragraphs, organized sections, and an understanding of your audience.

I've been working full-time as a technical writer for the past two years, doing manuals, user guides, technical reports, government claims, and technical proposals. It's very satisfying to combine my technical background with my ability to write. It's still rare to find people who can write clearly in the engineering field, but a good writer is made, not born—all it takes is practice and an interest in being a good communicator.

surveillance. You are responsible for what you say and do online, and there have been plenty of examples of email exchanges on company computers, which the writers assumed to be private, leading to disciplinary action. To some extent, most of the other rules follow from this one.

Guideline 2: It isn't casual

An email written in a professional setting is never casual and should be treated like a business document: don't use slang, don't get pally or cute, and don't write in fragments—what we call telegram English. Don't use emoticons and cute Internet abbreviations; they may make your BFF LOL, but they won't impress a boss or client, especially if the boss or client doesn't understand the abbreviation.

Guideline 3: Don't be hasty

Always take the time to reread your emails before sending them out. At the very least, this will prevent the embarrassment of spelling or factual errors, lack of clarity, or incomplete information. If your reader has to reply asking for clarification, your email has failed. Just as importantly, however, a reread of your email will give you an opportunity to check your tone. See Guideline 4 below.

Guideline 4: Do unto others

You're not a saint. You don't suffer fools gladly. The trick is not to let on. Instead, write the sort of email that you yourself would like to receive, in the sort of tone in which you would like to be addressed. Don't be sarcastic; don't respond in anger. Flaming people only inflames situations, so maintain a professional calm.

Always remember that though you're looking at a computer screen, you are communicating with a human being, fragile ego and all. And bruised egos tend to hold grudges and try to repay you in kind down the road.

Guideline 5: Target your emails

Before you copy everyone you can think of, ask yourself who really needs to see the email. The technology makes it easy to add whole mailing lists to an email's "To:" box, or to click automatically on "Reply to All," but unsolicited emails with irrelevant information are a bane to everyone. You don't like them; don't inflict them on others.

Guideline 6: Set aside time; respond promptly

Assuming all senders target their emails appropriately, you'll have more time for the remaining, relevant emails. Use that time to provide prompt, thorough responses to your colleagues and clients. If they've turned to you for information, it's only courteous that you respond promptly.

However, it's bad practice to jump to your email inbox, like Pavlov's dog, every time it chirps to let you know that you've got mail. Instead, turn off the alert and do your other work in concentrated blocks of time. Then, at designated times, such as the first 15 minutes of every hour or every second hour, check to see what email has come in and deal with it. It's been shown again and again that a one-minute interruption to answer an email creates a much longer loss of productivity as your distracted mind tries to reassemble all the facts and figures it was sifting through before the interruption.

This practice will improve your email responses because they won't be as rushed, and it will improve the rest of your work because it won't be subject to constant interruption. Multi-tasking is mostly myth, especially if you're doing work that requires concentration or creativity.

Guideline 7: Don't overemphasize

It's always tempting to vie for the reader's attention by flagging your email as urgent or by using all caps in the subject line. Use the former only in extremely urgent cases—in which case you should probably take a walk to someone's cubicle or make a call.

Never use all caps in any context. All-caps formatting is textual shouting and rude. It's also a sure-fire way to get your email consigned to a spam folder. On the other hand, don't write all in lower-case; neglecting to use capital letters at the beginnings of sentences will make text harder to read and will be interpreted as a sign of laziness. Use proper punctuation for the same reason. An email is not a tweet.

Guideline 8: Don't omit the email thread

While you want your own response to be concise, it's generally not a good idea to strip off the email chain. If your reader gets a lot of email, he or she may not remember the precise context of yours and may have difficulty making sense of it. If the email is forwarded to a new reader, that new reader will be completely lost without the email thread. Admittedly, some professionals disagree with this advice and prefer to receive emails without the chain. Ask around at your firm to see whether they have a policy on this topic.

Guideline 9: Don't use recall requests

Some software and internal communication systems allow you to recall a sent email from the server if it hasn't yet been downloaded by the reader. However, if your email has already been downloaded, your request for the recall usually shows up, which is a bit embarrassing. It's far better not to send emails that aren't ready to be sent (see Guideline 3 above). If you do make an error, just admit it and send a correction (or apology).

Guideline 10: Use a descriptive subject line

Always provide a clear and descriptive subject line that defines the contents of the document. Say something like "Inquiry about picnic attendance" instead of "picnic" or "Request for reimbursement (of picnic expenses)" instead of "picnic." That way readers will know exactly what the email is about and will be able to find it easily when looking for it in an inbox stacked hundreds deep. This rule applies to every document you write, not just to emails. (See Chapter 4.)

By extension, this means that when you are sending an email on a new topic, send a new email with a new subject line. Don't just open an old email, hit reply, and start on a new subject. Otherwise, the Re: tag will not match the content and purpose of the new email.

Guideline 11: Never reply to spam

When you reply to spam, you are simply alerting the spammer that your email account is active. Flagging the email address for your spam filter is not particularly effective either, because spammers switch their emails often, precisely to get around this defence. As galling as spam is, it's best to simply ignore it.

Guideline 12: Don't forward chain letters; use judgment with jokes

Chain letters are annoying hoaxes. Even when they're of the feel-good, puppy-cuddling thought of the day kind, they are a waste of time, and most people would rather not receive them. If you get one, don't get caught; delete it without opening it.

A joke appropriate to forward has to be inoffensive not just to the person to whom you've sent it, but also to anyone looking over that person's shoulder or reading your emails at some point in the future; recall Guideline 1. Large punitive payments have been awarded to people offended by jokes that were never intended for their eyes or ears.

It's really best to send jokes only from your private email address, only to someone else's private email address, and only on your own time. This makes for a safe, if dull, day at work.

Professional Correspondence: Style and Tone

Don't waste your reader's time. Always start with the main point and the standard organization discussed in Chapter 1 and illustrated again below. Chapter 1 also contains some sample routine correspondence that demonstrates this pattern in action.

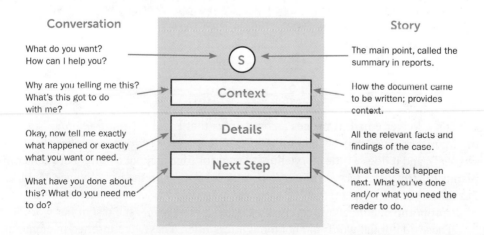

On the other hand, never forget that correspondence goes back and forth between two people and is, in effect, a conversation on the instalment plan. This is the key difference between correspondence and reports. In correspondence you are speaking directly to a particular person, generally addressing that person by name. Therefore your reader will take what you say very personally. With that in mind, read the following:

Harb,

You've met the deadline, but your interface still doesn't do what I asked and there are glitches with the coding.

See me in my office tomorrow at 0800.

Mai Ling

Ouch! You wouldn't speak to someone like this face to face, unless, of course, you were really angry and didn't care about the consequences. An email like this will fester in someone's mind and make that person plot revenge. However, it's quite likely that the writer never intended to sound so curt and irritated. She was probably just in a hurry and wasn't sufficiently aware of how she came across.

Please read the alternative below. It contains essentially the same information and will get exactly the same result, but no one gets hurt, and no flame wars get started.

Harb,

Thanks for getting the app to me yesterday.

I've been playing with it and have noticed a couple of functions that don't quite work yet the way we'd discussed. Also, when I took a closer look at the coding, I found some areas that I felt we could improve.

Can we have a chat about this tomorrow at, say, 8 a.m. in my office? I've got a busy schedule and want to clear this up first thing so you can get going on the changes.

Thanks,

Mai Ling

It's a longer email. It hedges ("*some areas* that I feel *we could improve*" instead of "*there are some errors*") and it qualifies ("*don't quite work yet the way we'd discussed*"), and it does a little storytelling to stall for time and put a buffer between complaints ("*Also, when I took a closer look at the coding*"). In the last sentence Mai Ling has taken pains to explain that the early meeting time has not been set out of a sense of disproportionate urgency, merely to fit it conveniently into the rest of her workday.

These additional words are not thoughtless filler. They were inserted to create the proper tone and, as such, are necessary to the email. When it comes to correspondence, it is doubly important that you imagine yourself sitting across the desk from the reader and that you take the time not only to get the bare information across, but also to make a personal connection and convey the proper attitude: friendly, helpful, personable. Being professional doesn't mean pulling rank and acting peevish. Official writing shouldn't be officious.

Largely, of course, this boils down to interpersonal skills. But there are a couple of guidelines.

Avoid language that sounds negative, angry, or condescending.

REPLACE	WITH
Surely you understand that …	I hope you'll agree that …
I simply can't understand why you would think that …	Perhaps you were under the impression …
You are wrong.	Have you considered …
Your report is wrong about …	I've redone your calculation and found …
I'm shocked/upset/angry about what you said.	I am surprised that you feel …
	You say that …, but when I looked into … I found that …
Why is this happening again?	As you may recall, this issue has come up before.
We trust that you will …	Please …

Avoid archaic and overly formal language. As a rule, if you wouldn't use an expression in normal conversation, don't use it in your correspondence. Try to sound natural in both contexts.

REPLACE	WITH
Enclosed please find	Enclosed is, here is, I've enclosed
It has come to my attention that	— delete altogether —
Please be advised	— delete altogether —
If any questions should arise, do not hesitate to contact the undersigned	Please call me if you have any questions
It would be appreciated if you would	Please
We acknowledge receipt of your letter	Thank you for your letter
Pursuant to your request	As you requested
At your earliest convenience	Soon, as soon as possible, by (a specific date)
Contingent upon receipt of	As soon as we receive

The exact wording will depend on the context, but your wording should stick with neutral facts and should take the reader's feelings into consideration. Always ask yourself how you would like to be spoken to in a situation, and then write that kind of letter. This is called the You-attitude.

Strive for a positive tone. Don't complain about problems; suggest solutions. If criticism is warranted, don't get personal; remain professional.

Editing Routine Correspondence

When you edit your correspondence, check for the following:

Format and organization

☐ Have you provided a clear and descriptive title or subject line?

☐ Have you begun with the main idea instead of making the reader wait for you to get to the point?

☐ Have you crafted a clear and complete document so the reader doesn't have to request clarification or necessary information?

☐ Have you closed in a friendly and encouraging manner, inviting the reader to continue the conversation, if necessary? (See Chapter 1.)

☐ Have you taken care to use proper letter or memo format to convey a sense of professionalism? (Emails format themselves.)

Tone

☐ Have you adopted a friendly, conversational, personable tone?

☐ Have you checked your writing for anything that might be misinterpreted as peevish?

☐ If you are writing about something that has gone wrong, have you remained professional and positive? Have you focused on getting things done rather than venting your feelings?

Exercises: Standard Correspondence

Exercise 5.1: Discovering the Role of Correspondence in the Workplace

Research online or discuss with professionals in your field the amount of correspondence they have to write daily. Ask whether they get any secretarial assistance or have opportunities to get colleagues to check their work. Find out how much of their writing is to non-technical audiences and whether their companies encourage face-to-face interactions over emails in some situations.

Exercise 5.2: Discussing Correspondence in the Workplace

Consider and discuss the following, either in pairs or in groups, and report your findings to the class:

1. Though it is important to send out professional documents, what might stop technical professionals from running their writing past their colleagues, either occasionally or as a matter of habit?

2.   What drawbacks, if any, are there to conducting business via email as opposed to via hardcopy documents such as letters and memos?

3.   When is it preferable to speak to someone on the phone or in person rather than sending an email?

4.   If you conduct business in person or over the phone, should you create a permanent record? How should you do so?

Exercise 5.3: Examining Successful Correspondence

Find a few examples of successful professional correspondence. You may draw on your own experience or the experience of someone you know, or you may search for examples online. Discuss in groups or as a class what makes this correspondence effective. To get you started, consider sample correspondence in this chapter.

Exercise 5.4: Inquiring about a Hybrid HVAC System

Your instructor has access to assignments online. Complete one or a series of these assignments to practise your letter-writing skills. Do so individually, in pairs, or in groups, either in class or at home, as determined by your instructor. Answer keys for discussion are also available online.

The following scenario is here just to get you started.

You are working for No-Leak Construction Ltd., a medium-sized builder operating primarily in the Lower Mainland. You've recently shown your team an article in *Construction Canada* (March 2010) about hybrid heating systems and everyone agreed that incorporating such a heating system into some of the proposals that you are working on, may help you win the contract. The technology is new enough that not every company will be aware of it, so you could give yourselves an edge.

Currently, you are putting together a hotly contested proposal for an administrative facility of about 80,000 square feet as part of the expansion of the dock facilities at the Canadian Navy Base Esquimalt.[1] You're wondering what sort of savings a hybrid HVAC system might generate. The author won't be able to tell you specifically, but perhaps, so you hope, he can tell you about some of the factors that affect payback so you can do some rough calculations yourself to see whether it's worth pursuing the idea.

Your boss has raised the issue of the potential difficulty of integrating the installation of such a system with the construction processes that he is comfortable with and, being a cynic and skeptic in general, would like to have more information (he called it proof) of the kinds of savings that such systems can generate in Esquimalt's temperate climate. After all, the article specifies that hybrid heating systems work best in cold climates.

Also, the military services generally specify systems that are foolproof. The article referred to equipment failure. Your boss wants to have some stats on the likelihood of such failure and on the service and maintenance contracts that are offered.

---

1   Esquimalt is located just west of the City of Victoria, BC, on Vancouver Island.

Michael Metcalf's (author) contact information is at the end of the article, so you poke around his website a bit, but find that it doesn't provide a lot of useful technical specifications. Luckily, the article (and website) also provides contact information so you can email Michael directly. Do so now: michael.metcalf@hybridheatingconsult.com

Note that this scenario is deliberately badly written so that you won't be tempted to copy from it too much. Use your own language; employ a conversational tone.

Exercise 5.5: Requesting Permission to Include a Green Roof in a Design

Use the same instructions as in Exercise 5.4.

You are employed by Welbilt Construction Ltd., of Vancouver. The project you are currently working on is nearing completion and you will next be moved on to the proposal team for a research facility being built in Nanaimo for the Ministry of Fisheries and Oceans. It's going to be a low-rise structure of at most two storeys, with tanks and labs in the first storey and administrative offices in the second. It will sit on a spit[2] sticking out into the ocean so that trenches can be dug that will direct tidal water under the building to refresh tanks and holding ponds conveniently and frequently. Because of the location, a high-rise would look out of place and also take up too much of the sightlines of pleasure craft rounding the spit. As this will be a 4,000 m[2] facility, the roof will comprise about 2,000 m[2].

You've been thinking that your proposal should include a green roof. Sure, it would add an additional 10 per cent to the cost of the structure, but it would save money in the long run. The green roof at the MEC outlet in Toronto, for instance, has an R-value of 45, saving considerably on the heating costs. Since the client would stay in the building for a long time—the structure is purpose-built and occupant owned—that extra money would repay itself you estimate in about 12 years. You'd have to do a more exact calculation once design details are firmed up.

As green roofs are only going to become more popular, getting into this technology early could help to build your company's reputation in the field here on the West Coast and give you early experience. If a client in future specifically wants a green roof, they are likely to come to your firm first. This could be good for business.

A green roof, you think, would also look quite esthetic. On that lonely spit would be a low-slung, modest structure topped with native grasses and shore plants. If the government is worried about sightlines, looks, and public perception, a green roof may be part of the answer.

In addition to generating savings on the cost of heating in the colder seasons, a green roof would also generate savings on the cooling costs in the heat of summer.

You've spoken with Matt Mahoney, the ministry contact for the design phase of the project. He has indicated that environmental values should be incorporated into the structure because the ministry is eager to be seen as a steward of the future and as a champion in

---

2   A narrow point of land projecting into the sea.

the fight against global warming. Your firm is already planning to include a number of other green features, such as an ocean-water run geothermal HVAC system, superior insulation values, water conservation measures, and various other things to achieve at least a LEED[3] Gold standard.

Another benefit of a green roof is that it reduces the cost of roof maintenance because it protects the roof membranes from UV radiation, which is the main cause of material breakdown on most multi-ply roofs. A green roof can easily last 50 years before requiring repair. A standard roof might need repair in as little as 15 years. This actually would reduce the ROI[4] by a couple of years.

You think that including a green roof in your proposal might give your company a bit of an edge in winning the contract because green roofs are functional and look good.

Green roofs are also an up and coming technology. The recently completed Vancouver Convention Centre has Western Canada's largest green roof (at 2.4 hectares), proving the concept. Many jurisdictions are actually making green roofs part of the building code. Toronto, for instance, now requires that all flat roofs of 2,000 m² or more incorporate green roofs. Can Vancouver be far behind?

Write an email to your boss, Jane Smolenskova, broaching the subject and asking for permission to include a green roof in your design. Obviously this email will only be the start of a discussion on the matter, but you should present a pretty clear argument and lay out your reasons for her. Jane is the one who assigned you to the proposal team and is the person to whom the proposal team reports.

Please note that this scenario is badly written, so you would do well to rewrite the information in your own words and then take some time to edit those words. Also consider the sequencing of the information.

Have fun.

---

3 Leadership in Energy and Environmental Design is a private initiative to rate buildings for their environmental sustainability. LEED offers four levels of certification: certified, silver, gold, and platinum.

4 Return on investment: the time it takes for an expense or investment to repay itself, in the case of a green roof through savings in HVAC costs, maintenance, and repairs.

Chapter 6

Technical Reports and Documents

In this chapter you will learn
· about the most common types of reports written in the technical workplace
· how to select and sequence information for these kinds of reports
· the proper tone and level of detail to include, depending on the knowledge level of your readers.

There is a key difference between correspondence and reports.

Correspondence is personal: you are writing to another individual. You may be writing as a representative of your organization to someone else representing his or her organization, but you are still an individual speaking directly to another individual. So correspondence doesn't just convey information, it also expresses a relationship.

Reports, however, are more widely distributed. They have more readers because they tend to be about more general, wider issues and are specifically written to help create a permanent record, a resource intended to be accessible to multiple people. It follows that the tone will be somewhat more formal.

Short, informal reports can be written in either memo or letter format, depending on the situation; you can review the formatting and the organization of memos and letters in Chapter 5. Alternatively, they can be formatted as free-standing reports, that is, without the addressing information found on letters and memos. If you submit these latter types of reports via email or in hard copy, they'll be accompanied by a transmittal email or letter, as is the case for a formal report. See Chapter 7 for details. Reports are generally not written as emails because they are intended for separate filing and are permanently stored, often in project folders, for future reference.

If reports exceed seven or eight pages, it becomes inconvenient for a reader to flip through the document, scanning for specific information. So we add a table of contents as an aid to navigation, which forces us to create a title page, which means we've got a formal report. It's not quite that simple, of course, because formal reports have some additional requirements, but we will deal with those in Chapter 7.

In this chapter, we are going to discuss five categories of technical documents—not all of them, strictly speaking, are reports:

- documents that report on past events or completed tasks
- documents that report on ongoing tasks
- documents that recommend a future action
- documents that record technical or performance standards
- lab reports.

Report Structure

Regardless of their purpose, reports tend to share a similar structure, one with which, in fact, you are already familiar. They begin with a summary, establish the context, follow with the details, then end with a conclusion or next step. After a bit more information on each of these components, we'll go straight into the examples.

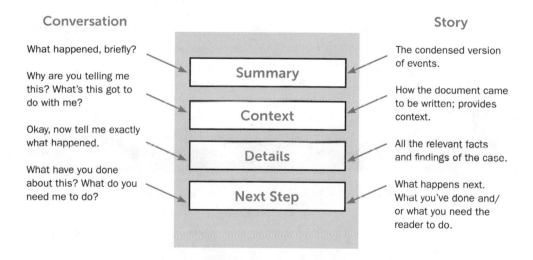

Summaries

Generally written last, but read first, the summary is a condensed version of the report, containing the main ideas of the report and reflecting the emphases of the report. It's really as though you were submitting each report twice: a full version for those who have time and interest and a condensed version for those in the know or in a rush.

Context

The context section is sometimes referred to as the background or, in longer documents, the introduction. A report has to make sense even to readers not already familiar with how the report came to be written, such as secondary readers to whom the report may be passed, even years down the road. Without context, a report will not make sense. Therefore, place in the context paragraph(s) all the information a reader will require to figure out why the report was written and how it fits into the conduct of business. If a report were a movie, this would be the opening, or establishing, shot. Among other things, it establishes audience and purpose.

Details

The details are the meat of the report, where the report fulfills its purpose, so the details section is generally, but not always, the longest part of a report. We'll learn more about this section in the annotated samples below, but obviously every type of report has a slightly different purpose and the context and purpose will determine the content and structure of the details section.

Next Step

Generally speaking, a report does not just record information; it's a change agent that provides information that will be used to make decisions about future action. The next step section anticipates this by describing what actions have been taken as a result of the investigation or by suggesting what future actions should be taken.

IN THE FIELD

Andre Lanz, P.Eng., Vancouver, British Columbia

Andre Lanz is a professional engineer with a wide-ranging career that spans program management, project financing, government relations, research and development, systems engineering, product development, mechanical design, customer support, and training. He has worked on a variety of technology development and infrastructure projects, owned a specialized engineering company, and taught at a technical college. Now a consultant to the engineering industry, he holds that "all engineering boils down to creating documents—proposals, specifications, plans, drawings, reports, etc.—which is all that's left after a project has been delivered. Clear, succinct, and accurate technical writing is an essential part of every project and can be the fundamental difference between success and failure. Others judge our capabilities by the way we present information, and poor writing signals incompetence."

Documents that Report on Past Events or Completed Tasks

Throughout your career, in fact throughout your workday, you will be assigned to perform specific tasks and to respond to specific events. When you have done so, you will be asked to produce a report to prove due diligence to a client and justify billing them, to provide a record of your work and abilities, to create a permanent storehouse of information as a resource for colleagues, and to meet any number of other requirements.

We are going to highlight three major types of task reports: inspection reports, trip reports, and incident reports. But these are broad categories; they frequently overlap in the field (as when you take a trip to carry out an inspection or when something unusual and unexpected happens during an inspection). They can range from simple half-pagers to full formal reports, depending on the complexity of the situation.

Let's take a look.

Inspection/Assessment Reports

Inspection reports are written to create a permanent record any time you're examining something in order to

- determine its suitability for a purpose
- measure or ascertain how close something comes to specs or expectations (legal, contractual, or standard practice)
- check for the correct quality, quantity, or item.

Inspection reports employ the following structure.

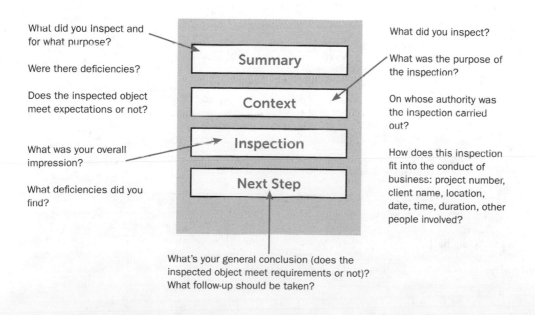

What did you inspect and for what purpose?

Were there deficiencies?

Does the inspected object meet expectations or not?

What was your overall impression?

What deficiencies did you find?

Summary

Context

Inspection

Next Step

What did you inspect?

What was the purpose of the inspection?

On whose authority was the inspection carried out?

How does this inspection fit into the conduct of business: project number, client name, location, date, time, duration, other people involved?

What's your general conclusion (does the inspected object meet requirements or not)? What follow-up should be taken?

The summary provides the gist: the results of the inspection and the recommendation.

Two paragraphs of context: how this report came to be written.

General overview of the object being inspected to help to make sense of the inspection process and findings.

Most often deficiencies are listed, assuming there's more than one, of course. However, this table functions essentially like a list.

The conclusion provides an overall assessment of the inspected object. In this case the writer recommends a specific action.

Indicate all attachments where the materials are first mentioned. Add an attachment line at the end of the document.

Describing the methodology gives credibility to the results. The details about the hazards of decks, dormers, and bays are there for the non-technical audience.

A technical reader would know what these values mean and wouldn't require this explanation.

To: Mike M. Abdullah, President, Ash Street Mews Strata Council
From: Alaine Gaspardi, Senior Building Technologist, Bender Harris Building   AG
        Science Inc.
Date: February 27, 2017

Inspection of Pennington Mews (LMS 2714) for Water Ingress

The Ash Street Mews has high moisture content in all four elevations, suggesting flourishing fungal growth and potential compromise of the structure. The strata council should contract a more thorough survey of the structural integrity as soon as possible.

On February 12, 1017, the strata council of the Pennington Mews (LMS 2714), 620 Ash Street, Burnaby, contacted Bender Harris Building Sciences Inc. to conduct an envelope inspection to determine whether the structure has suffered water ingress.

I was assigned the inspection on February 15th and conducted the inspection on February 30th, accompanied by Junior Building Technologist Sven Olufson. The inspection took 7 hours.

The Pennington is a three-storey wood-frame structure clad with face-sealed stucco. It has minimal roof overhangs, which exposes the lower storeys to wind-driven rain. In places, particularly under windows and dormers, the stucco is discoloured, indicating prolonged exposure to moisture and probable mold growth (photos attached).

We drilled holes in 80 locations, focusing on areas around the decks, dormers, and bays, places where interfaces, penetrations, and poor workmanship most often permit water ingress.

We inserted the probes from a moisture meter into each hole and recorded the moisture content (MC). The test locations and the test values for each location are indicated on the attached drawing. Average values are listed in the table below.

Elevation	Average MC
North	36%
East	25%
South	28%
West	38%

These values represent annual maximums because the measurements were taken toward the end of the Lower Mainland's wet season. Though these values will drop somewhat over the summer as the structure dries out, they are unlikely to drop below 19%, which is where fungal growth occurs.

I recommend that the strata council of the Pennington Mews conduct a more thorough investigation of the extent of fungal growth within the structure and the structural damage that may already have taken place. It's quite clear that remediation work will be required.

Attach: Photos of building exterior
         Drawings of elevations with test locations and readings

---

FIGURE 6.1 Simple inspection report. What makes this a simple inspection report is that only one thing, the building envelope, was inspected. If the team had been tasked to check the building foundation as well, the report would have split the inspection section into two separate, complete mini-inspections with subheadings for the building envelope and the foundation.

The length and complexity of the inspection will determine how the inspection section is organized. For simple inspections, write a very brief paragraph description of your overall impression of the object being inspected or assessed. Then list your specific findings. For complex inspections, break the findings into logical sections so that you are in effect writing a series of simple inspections or assessments. The sample occasional progress report further on in this chapter (Figure 6.5) illustrates this strategy.

Trip Reports

It probably goes without saying that trip reports are written whenever someone is sent on a business trip. The report justifies the employee's time away from the office and records what the employee was sent to do and what the employee actually accomplished—not always the same thing. It guides the billing for the work done and describes any follow-up that may be required.

Note, however, that being sent across town does not constitute a trip, but a commute. A trip is overnight or outside of your home city, though you'll have to use some judgment. When you commute to a site within your normal reach of business, just record the location and mileage, if applicable, in the context section.

If, in fact, you haven't travelled anywhere to do a job but still need to report on having completed the job, we call it a completion report: a trip report without the trip, as it were.

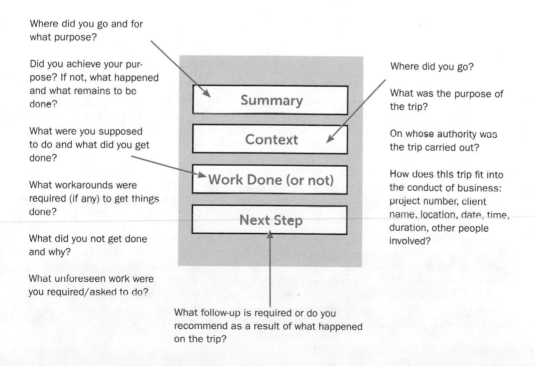

Where did you go and for what purpose?

Did you achieve your purpose? If not, what happened and what remains to be done?

What were you supposed to do and what did you get done?

What workarounds were required (if any) to get things done?

What did you not get done and why?

What unforeseen work were you required/asked to do?

Summary

Context

Work Done (or not)

Next Step

Where did you go?

What was the purpose of the trip?

On whose authority was the trip carried out?

How does this trip fit into the conduct of business: project number, client name, location, date, time, duration, other people involved?

What follow-up is required or do you recommend as a result of what happened on the trip?

CHP stands for combined heat and power, but Ha-Joon hardly needs to define that for his technical, insider audience.

Context: Where, what for, how long, with whom, and so on. Aside from including the filing information, this section sets up exactly what the scope of work was on this trip: the service connections, for instance, had already been prepped.

To: Mike Terrestre, Operations Manager
From: Ha-Joon Kim, Installations & Maintenance Technician   HJK
Date: November 11, 2017

CHP Installation at Regina General Hospital (2017-027 CHP RGH1)

Our CHP unit has been successfully installed at the Regina General Hospital (RGH). A problem with the absorption chiller has been repaired, but the system will have to be charged by a local contractor and will be tested by the RGH facility manager. Her report is expected within the week.

The summary provides the highlights, with an emphasis on what will happen next: the job is not yet done, after all.

From November 04 to November 10, 2017, I was in Regina to oversee the installation of our 3 MW CHP unit at the Regina General Hospital (project code 2017-027 CHP RGH1). The equipment had been delivered the week before but remained crated in the facility warehouse. My responsibility was to do a complete install with the help of local contractors. These contractors had already prepped the services connections (natural gas, electrical, and mechanical), according to the plans and specifications we sent on October 15.

The work done section answers the following questions, generally in this order:

Following uncrating and inspection, we moved all the components into the facility utility room in the basement. The assembly took four days, as expected. All the services connections had been properly set up and required no changes or workarounds. The contractors have been asked to submit their bills directly to accounting using our project code for identification.

The work done section begins here. It tells a more or less chronological story to make it easier to follow what you did and why you did it that way.

What did you get done according to plan?

However, when we tested the assembled unit, we discovered one problem. The absorption chiller for the a/c did not work. After a number of mechanical tests that revealed no problem but took most of a day, I thought it might be a problem with the fluid. When I tried to get a pressure reading at the bleed valve, I got a reading of zero.

I called Carl (Struthers) in fabrication; he assured me that records indicate that the unit had been fully charged and sealed prior to shipment. He suspected a leak. Visual examination didn't show any problems, so I soaped the condensation coil and condenser, charged the system with air (invoice for air compressor rental attached), and discovered a crack in the lower joint between the condenser coil and the condenser unit. We used the facility soldering equipment to seal the leak.

What workarounds did you have to employ to get things done?

What remains to be done? The next step is to see whether the system will work to RGH's satisfaction once the absorption chiller has been charged. Sandra will make that report within a week.

I have engaged a local refrigeration specialist, Steve Horolochuck (Steve@prairiecoolrefrigeration.com), to recharge the system, but I was unable to stay in Regina to oversee the process because I had to return to headquarters to start assembly on another project.

The RGH facility manager, Sandra LeBaron (slebaron@rgh.sk.ca), will test the system within the week and report directly to you.

Attch: Rona invoice (air compressor rental)

What didn't you get done and why not?

FIGURE 6.2 Sample trip report. Note that contact information has been provided for all parties involved. This means that even those reading the report after the fact can follow up with, for instance, Steve the refrigeration guy. Also, if Mike Terrestre hasn't received confirmation from Sandra LeBaron within one week that all is in order, he can follow up easily. Always anticipate what follow-up might be necessary and enable it.

Incident/Accident Reports

An incident could be a workplace or traffic accident, a strike, an electrical or equipment failure, or anything unexpected, unusual, and generally negative that, perhaps dramatically, affects the project or job at hand. It usually constitutes a pain in the butt and requires follow-up. For these reasons, it also needs to be recorded, to justify project delays, materials costs, billable time, and requests for whatever follow-up action is necessary. (See Figure 6.3 for a sample incident report.)

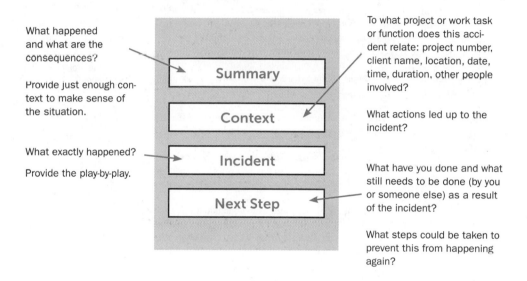

What happened and what are the consequences?

Provide just enough context to make sense of the situation.

What exactly happened?

Provide the play-by-play.

Summary

Context

Incident

Next Step

To what project or work task or function does this accident relate: project number, client name, location, date, time, duration, other people involved?

What actions led up to the incident?

What have you done and what still needs to be done (by you or someone else) as a result of the incident?

What steps could be taken to prevent this from happening again?

Documents that Report on Ongoing Tasks: Progress Reports

Organizations run on the free, timely, and accurate flow of information. A large part of that information is provided by progress reports. As the person in the field, in the lab, or on the job, you will be responsible for keeping management and colleagues informed about progress on projects.

Management and the client need to know as soon as possible if delays and cost overruns are likely. Any problems that arise, or are likely to arise, may require the coordination of various departments and resources at your organization over which you have no control and may require additional external experts or resources that you are not authorized to deploy.

For any number of reasons, you will have to write progress reports to keep everyone informed of what is going on and to create a permanent record of what happened.

You may be asked to write one of two kinds of progress reports: occasional progress reports and periodic progress reports. Both employ the structure illustrated below.

The summary answers the most important questions: what happened and how does this affect the project?

The context section describes the project or situation that the incident disrupted. Note the usual filing information.

The next step section is also generally chronological. It tells the story of what you did as a result of the incident and/or what still needs to be done and by whom.

Copper and rare earth elements: a knowledgeable audience won't need these terms defined. They just need a reminder of what the project is about.

The incident section tells the story of what happened and why. It usually also follows your investigation chronologically.

To: Mike Smith, Exploration Manager
From: David John, Lead Geologist
Date: August 02, 2017

Damage to work truck 017

Work truck 017 has been damaged by a bear and can no longer be operated safely. We have arranged for a rental replacement and for a repair estimate. Work progress will not be affected.

My crew and I are doing preliminary exploration for Cu and REE potential of the Cascade Falls area near Stewart, B.C.: project BC-13.011. On August 01, we were working an area near the Premier Mine (Lot 4) and were able to use the work truck (vehicle no. 017) rather than helicopter to get on location. We parked the truck on Granduc Road about 2.5 km short of the mine, approximately 20 km from Stewart (location is marked on the attached map), and went into the bush for the day.

When we returned at dusk, we found the truck badly damaged. The back passenger side window was smashed and the door had been pulled open by brute force. The door is badly deformed and the top hinge is loose. Also, the door frame has been damaged at the back edge, where the lock was pulled apart. The upholstery of the back bench is torn in places and dirty (photos attached).

Tracks at the site (and the back bench) lead us to conclude it was a grizzly bear. However, neither of the two crew members who were sitting in the back on the way up have admitted to having left food in the truck and neither had mentioned that they were short of food over the course of the day.

We roped the door closed on the way back to town, but it leaves a five-inch gap; the truck is not safe for the occupant of the right rear seat and admits a lot of road dust. I have arranged for a rental from Terrace for the three weeks of work we have left (invoice from Off-Road Rentals attached). One of their employees will drive the rental up to us and take our work truck back to Terrace and will drop it off at Joe's Reliable Autobody (1-250-335-2221). I've asked Joe's Autobody to forward their repair estimate to you directly for approval. Please let us know what you decide.

Attach: Google Map
        Photos of damage
        Off-Road Rentals invoice

FIGURE 6.3 Sample incident report. Incidents cause inconvenience, unexpected costs, and unwelcome delays. We record them to explain why we are behind schedule or why we have undergone unbudgeted expenses, and to show how we cope when the unexpected happens. In many cases, of course, incident reports may also be used to change standard operating procedures to prevent future problems.

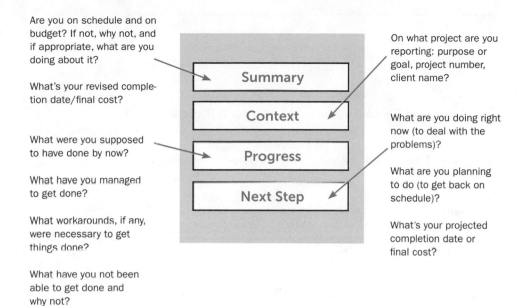

Are you on schedule and on budget? If not, why not, and if appropriate, what are you doing about it?

What's your revised completion date/final cost?

What were you supposed to have done by now?

What have you managed to get done?

What workarounds, if any, were necessary to get things done?

What have you not been able to get done and why not?

On what project are you reporting: purpose or goal, project number, client name?

What are you doing right now (to deal with the problems)?

What are you planning to do (to get back on schedule)?

What's your projected completion date or final cost?

Note how closely the structure of the progress section matches that of the work done section of a trip report. In both cases, you are reporting on a task that you've been assigned. However, in a trip report, you are reporting on a task that was to have been completed during the trip, whereas in a progress report you are reporting on an ongoing project.

Note also that if everything is on schedule and on budget and no problems have occurred, progress reports are extremely short and easy to write. It's only the untoward and unusual that requires extensive description.

Occasional Progress Report

An occasional progress report is generally the only type of progress report written if the project is of modest duration, generally at the midpoint to confirm that everything is on schedule and budget. Alternatively, as soon as the writer discovers or begins to anticipate a problem that is likely to cause a delay or a cost overrun (see Figure 6.4), he or she will write an occasional progress report to alert those who might be affected (also known as stakeholders).

Periodic Progress Report

Periodic progress reports are written regularly (periodically) on longer projects. For such projects, often spanning years, progress reports are submitted weekly, biweekly, or monthly, depending on what the client and the management team demand (see Figure 6.5). In fact, you may find yourself keeping a daily project log, writing a weekly progress report to your management, and presenting a monthly or quarterly progress report to the client.

The heading doesn't have to have the word "progress" in it. This title is more descriptive.

To: Mike Smith, Exploration Manager
From: David John, Lead Geologist D
Date: August 21, 2017

Delay in Cascade Falls Area Exploration Program

Our preliminary prospecting of the Cascade Falls Area has been delayed four days so far by a forest fire. We are not sure when we can resume our work, but we should still be able to finish the project by the end of the season.

The context section identifies the project on which you are reporting and gives those in the know an idea of how far the project should have progressed by now.

My crew and I are doing preliminary exploration for Cu and REE potential of the Cascade Falls area near Stewart, B.C.: project BC-17.011. By the end of this season we were to have determined whether it was worth pursuing a core drilling program and to have mapped out such a drill program.

What have you done so far?

Work had been progressing on schedule. We have so far mapped out the road-accessible terrain for the entire property (Lots 4–6, 9–11). Two weeks ago (Aug. 07) we began exploring areas accessible only from the air, for which we'd booked Hummingbird Helicopters August 7th–September 19th. We have to date completed the surveys of Lots 4 and 5 and half of 6.

What has not been done is the rest of the lots. You don't need to state the obvious, as long as the information is clear. The "why not" does need to be explained, however.

In this case, no workaround is possible.

Unfortunately, a forest fire that started approximately 50 km northeast of Stewart five days ago (August 16th) is blanketing the valley with smoke. Because the fire is likely to travel quickly if winds pick up, the Forest Service has forbidden all work in the valley for safety reasons. The area has been in drought for months. We will be unable to continue our exploration until the fire has been brought under control or burned itself out.

This is the next step section: what you have done and/or will do to complete the project.

Because we've worked the past 23 days straight, I've given the crew time off to visit their families; all three flew out this morning. I will stay in town to monitor the situation so I can call the crew back in good time as the fire is brought under control; I'll use the down time to get a start on the final report to the client, using the assay results we've obtained so far.

If you have an estimated completion date or revised final cost, state it here as well.

Unless the fire burns for more than three weeks, we should still easily be able to finish the project by the end of the season. I've checked with Hummingbird, and their helicopter is not booked again until the start of the heli-skiing season. I've provisionally booked it until the end of September.

FIGURE 6.4 Sample occasional progress report. The occasion in an occasional progress report is often an incident that has caused a delay. In that regard these reports are not unlike incident reports. Notice that you don't have to answer all the questions from the schematic in lock-step. The information can be slightly out of sequence if it flows better that way. Some information can be omitted altogether if it is strongly implied and you're sure your reader will comprehend.

The summary answers the most important questions in about one-tenth the length of the rest of the report.

In complex (as opposed to simple) progress reports, each separate task is described in a separate mini progress report. In the case of the fuel cage, there's not much to say because everything has gone according to plan and schedule.

Note, however, that each mini progress report answers all the questions indicated in the schematic: what was done, what required workarounds, what did not get done and why, and what you have done or are going to do about the problems.

Periodic progress reports have a double focus in their next step sections—one is on how to catch up on the work for the current reporting period; the other is a projection for the project as a whole.

Progress Report #5: January 2017
Flyer F40 Fuel Cell Conversion (MTA)

All components for the conversion are ready except for the fuel cell stack, which is not producing the power that it should. We are redesigning the gas channels on the separator plates to increase the output, but we suspect that fabrication and testing will take at least a month, putting us three weeks behind schedule.

Progress

Fuel Cage
The fuel cage was delivered by Westcoast Fabrication on January 4th and installed, after inspection, on the 8th and 9th. The natural gas tanks were installed on the 15th and connected to the supply hoses to the converter location at the back of the bus. The whole system was tested on the 16th and proved free of leaks. This part of the project has been completed.

Catalytic Gas Converter
The converter can't be installed until after the stack has been put in place because of the geometry of the engine compartment, but all bench tests show the converter to be ready for installation. We found a 98% CH4 to H2 conversion rate, which is at the high end of our expectations and it is unlikely that we will get better efficiency out of this generation of converter.

We will need only about five hours to install the converter after installing the stack. This part of the project is also on schedule.

Fuel Cell Stack
We had hoped to have the fuel cell stack fully operational by the end of January, but we encountered a problem. Our bench test registered a power output 15% lower than expected—despite the fact that we'd resolved the problem with the gas leakage between the cell plates (see progress report for December 2016).

The actual output is too far below the theoretical to be accounted for by friction or flow rates. We engaged Dr. Weisz at U of T to design a different channel configuration to increase surface area for the reaction. He provided his design on January 27, but we'll need about a month to machine the plates. This puts us three weeks behind schedule for this part of the project.

Electrical Converter
The Canadex DC to AC inverter was delivered at the end of December and installed January 12th to 14th.

Plans
The fuel cell stack with the new plates should be ready for testing by March 03. If all goes well, we will be able to install the stack and converter and make all the connections on the 4th and 5th and conduct the actual driving tests on the 6th through 8th. Barring any problems, we can load the bus for delivery on the 10th. Delivery should take approximately three days by truck (March 13th).

I've spoken with Bill Chan at the MTA and he is okay with those dates. They are eager to drive and test the fuel cell bus and he has suggested that we could begin with the operational testing the following Monday, March 17th.

I have also prepared him that March 13th is not a firm delivery date. He has indicated that he understands that delays are an unfortunate part of prototype commercialization.

Reza Shahidi
Reza Shahidi
Design & Prototyping Team Lead
February 1, 2017

Because periodic reports are often filed together in a project log they may be written as standard reports, rather than correspondence reports. Hence, this progress report does not have any addressing information.

In periodic progress reports, the context section describing the project is often omitted after the first installment, as was done here. It would be too repetitive otherwise. If readers need the project description, they can always flip back to the first report in the binder or open the first file in the folder.

This is a semi-formal report—it is neither informal (memo or letter) nor formal. The signature block at the bottom could have been omitted, but then the report would have to be accompanied by a cover document. The provenance of a report has to be indicated somewhere, after all.

FIGURE 6.5 Sample of a semi-formal periodic progress report. This is a monthly update on a project to convert a transit bus to run off a fuel-cell power stack as part of a test program to commercialize the technology. Note that the progress section has been broken up into several mini progress reports, each of which maintains proper progress report content. This is the way to deal with complex reports (inspections, progress, and the like): break them into series of simpler and more manageable sections.

Documents that Recommend Future Actions

The reports we've looked at so far have all projected some action into the future—but always to finish up some task or incident that took place in the past. In a sense, these are documents that react to something.

However, organizations thrive only to the extent that they are able to anticipate and plan. That's what the following group of documents does. They are entirely forward looking. They help organizations chart a path into the future.

Proposals

Proposals report on a situation or problem and suggest a solution to be implemented. They are the main way for organizations to obtain contracts or projects and for researchers to obtain funding. (See the following schematic and Figure 6.6.)

Proposals can be internal or external to an organization, and they can be either solicited or unsolicited. Their length will be determined by the complexity of what is being proposed; if they are long enough, they may be written as formal reports (Chapter 7).

An **internal proposal** is addressed to someone within your organization. This means that the reader is aware of your abilities and qualifications and of the context surrounding the writing of the report. Much of this information, then, doesn't have to be included. An internal proposal is likely to be presented in memo format.

An **external proposal** is written for another (external) organization. This means that you have to do more to prove that you actually understand the problem, and in addition to providing a solution, you may have to persuade the reader that you are qualified to implement it. Therefore, external proposals have longer introductions and more thorough descriptions of problems. They are also more likely to include a qualification and references section, less likely to be in memo format, and more likely to be semi-formal or formal.

A **solicited proposal** is one for which the recipient has asked, either personally or by releasing an RFP (request for proposals) in order to stimulate a little competition. This means that the recipient has described a problem for you and set out the requirements for a suitable solution. You'll need to acknowledge both, but you don't have to develop them yourself or convince the reader of them.

An **unsolicited proposal** is one the recipient has not asked for and is not expecting; yet you have seen a way to improve their operations through a service, product, or change in procedures. To make readers receptive to your solution, you will first have to convince them that they have a problem and that a solution is worth pursuing.

Investigation Reports/Recommendation Reports/Feasibility Studies

With some justification, the terms "investigation report" and "recommendation report," and "feasibility study" and "proposal" are often used interchangeably: all of them look at a situation and make a recommendation. However, there are some useful distinctions between them.

A **proposal**, as you saw above, seeks approval to make a change or pursue a project. Writers of proposals have a clear understanding of a problem and a detailed solution. The purpose of the proposal is to describe and sell that solution.

An **investigation report** attempts to identify and define a problem in the first place. For instance, if the causes of the shutdowns of the conveyor belt in the sample proposal (Figure 6.6) had been unknown, someone might have been tasked to investigate the cause. That person would have written an investigation report clearly describing the investigative methodology and its outcomes.

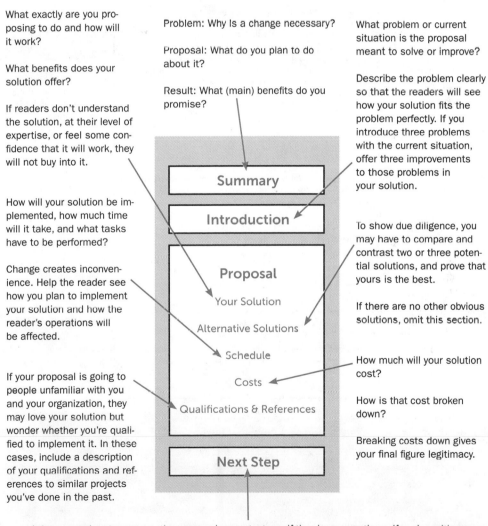

What exactly are you proposing to do and how will it work?

What benefits does your solution offer?

If readers don't understand the solution, at their level of expertise, or feel some confidence that it will work, they will not buy into it.

How will your solution be implemented, how much time will it take, and what tasks have to be performed?

Change creates inconvenience. Help the reader see how you plan to implement your solution and how the reader's operations will be affected.

If your proposal is going to people unfamiliar with you and your organization, they may love your solution but wonder whether you're qualified to implement it. In these cases, include a description of your qualifications and references to similar projects you've done in the past.

Problem: Why is a change necessary?

Proposal: What do you plan to do about it?

Result: What (main) benefits do you promise?

Summary

Introduction

Proposal

Your Solution

Alternative Solutions

Schedule

Costs

Qualifications & References

Next Step

What problem or current situation is the proposal meant to solve or improve?

Describe the problem clearly so that the readers will see how your solution fits the problem perfectly. If you introduce three problems with the current situation, offer three improvements to those problems in your solution.

To show due diligence, you may have to compare and contrast two or three potential solutions, and prove that yours is the best.

If there are no other obvious solutions, omit this section.

How much will your solution cost?

How is that cost broken down?

Breaking costs down gives your final figure legitimacy.

Ask your readers to approve the proposal or contact you if they have questions. If you're writing a semi-formal proposal, that is, neither a memo nor a letter proposal, put the next step in the transmittal document: the email to which the proposal is attached or the letter with which it is enclosed.

This is the problem.

Because this proposed solution is already in circulation, it's actually part of the problem. Otherwise it wouldn't be mentioned in the introduction.

Readers will make their decision about your proposal based on benefits and costs. Benefits will make them want your solution; costs may deter them. You must, of course, be scrupulously honest about both.

To: Jeff Oehlson, Operation Director
From: Hamid Serti and Chang Zheng Chen, Technical Group   HS CZC
Date: March 19, 2017

Proposal to install a PLC-based control system on the conveyor

Summary

The cross-feed conveyor M-100 control system has been having problems and has even caused several shutdowns. We strongly recommend replacing it with a PLC-based system at a one-time cost of $7940.80, instead of exchanging all the contactors periodically at a cost of $6960.80, each time.

Introduction

Our cross-feed conveyor, which transfers wood chips selectively to one of our two silos, has broken down seven times over the past four years. Each breakdown causes a two-day work stoppage because we have to troubleshoot the problem and order the faulty parts. These work stoppages are obviously very expensive.

The problem is that the M-100 control system for the conveyor belt relies on 15 relay contactors and these contactors are aging prematurely because of their location near the silos, which exposes them to dust and humidity.

To prevent any more sudden work stoppages, Production Director Sarah Mitchells suggested at the last review meeting that we simply replace all the contactors prophylactically. However, this solution is quite expensive and only temporary. If we were to replace the contactors regularly to prevent all future shutdowns, the solution would be even more expensive.

A better solution may be to replace our out-dated M-100 contactor-based control systems with a PLC-based one.

Technical details

Mechanical contactor-based control systems are out-dated, expensive, and relatively unreliable. Because they rely on physical controls, they are subject to physical deterioration and breakdown (as our system has proven). They are also very inflexible. Any additional control functions or any desired changes have to be built into the system physically, meaning more contactors and considerable time. It would also mean shutting the system down to make the changes.

Modern PLC-based control systems, on the other hand, offer a number of advantages. For our system specifically, a PLC-based system would do everything that our current system does, as well as provide the following:

- Protection against overheating the motor. The system would automatically stop the conveyor when it is overloaded.
- Warning indicators when the conveyor starts.
- A time delay when the conveyor direction is changed.
- Safety pull cords to stop the conveyor in cases of emergency.

These are just the additional functions that we've thought of so far. A PLC solution will provide flexibility to add additional control functions simply by modifying the software: no work stoppages required.

In addition, a PLC control system would be operated from our control room, using the HMI console. This will provide the operators with a better working environment (less dust and noise).

continued

The solution is named in the intro to induce the reader to keep reading.

Identifying the problems really makes readers wish for a solution and see the advantages you're offering through your solution. It's tough to get people to change unless they see a problem with the way things are.

FIGURE 6.6 Sample informal proposal. Note that the content of the proposal doesn't have to follow the sequence in the schematic perfectly, as long as the information is complete and flows well.

FIGURE 6.6 continued

Cost comparison

The cost of sticking with the old system and replacing all the relay contactors is detailed in the table below.

	QTY.	PRICE
Relay contactors	15	$350.00
Wiring cable		$90.00
Labour for wiring and testing (35 hrs)		$25/hr
TOTAL		$6215.00
HST		$745.80
FINAL COST		$6960.80

Itemizing costs proves that you've included everything (due diligence) and that your number isn't an over-the-thumb estimate (legitimacy).

Please note that when replacing the relay contactors a shutdown of the conveyor for about four days would be required because the wiring and the relays are close to the conveyor, constituting a safety hazard. And please note also that this procedure would have to be repeated at least bi-annually to prevent the next round of unexpected shutdowns.

The one-time cost of implementing a PLC-based solution is detailed in the table below.

	QTY.	PRICE
PLC GE Fanuc 90-30	1	$1500.00
Profiecy software which includes HMI	1	$2500.00
Computer	1	$800.00
Warning horn GE YA-102	1	$75.00
Conveyer speed sensor (GE SSL-103)	1	$155.00
Safety pull cord GE HSS-105	1	$110.00
Training and installation cost		$1950.00
TOTAL		$7090.00
HST		$850.80
FINAL COST		$7940.80

Describing the implementation process and timeline helps readers to see the solution as achievable and helps them to visualize how to arrange the conduct of their business around the required implementation tasks.

Please note that the PLC-based solution requires a shutdown of the conveyor for one day only.

Schedule

We would keep the relay system in place until the PLC installation and test simulation are completed. Once the program is ready and sensors are put in place, we can switch the conveyor to run from the PLC control system. Finally we will proceed to the last step of disconnecting the old control relay system. These last two steps should be done in one day.

I have received an email from GE confirming that they have all the equipment in stock and that their delivery time is three weeks; we would require two weeks for training and installation. Therefore we can get this project completed five to six weeks after your approval.

This last sentence is a sly, indirect next step statement, asking the reader to approve the proposal.

Once a problem has been identified, a solution will often present itself, so investigation reports may include recommendations for a solution. If not, they might recommend further study. Quite often, however, a recommendation report will do something in between—it will establish the criteria for a suitable solution. In the conveyor case example, for instance, an investigation report might have spelled out that a suitable solution to the problem would have to provide greater reliability, should cost less than current maintenance and repair expenses, and should be easily scalable and upgradable to meet future demands. Someone else could then be tasked to find a suitable solution and propose it.

In this way, investigation reports often precede proposals or RFPs.

A **recommendation report** compares several options and recommends one. It may, for instance, compare and contrast several types of cellphones and service providers for organization-wide adoption. It may assess a number of competing proposals that have been submitted in response to an RFP and recommend which one should be adopted. In each case, clear evaluation criteria have to be established and all options have to be assessed in relation to those criteria. Recommendation reports prove due diligence before major decisions.

A **feasibility study** assesses a previously proposed solution, project, or idea to see if it can or should in fact be pursued. In a sense, it's like a recommendation report that assesses a single option and makes a yes-or-no recommendation. For instance, it might establish whether an organization should or should not develop a certain property, pursue development of a new software program, establish a branch office in another country, or take on some other new project. It answers the question, "Should we do this?" So, like a recommendation report, it proves due diligence before a major decision; it justifies a new course of action or new direction in the conduct of business.

In all of these reports, writers must describe their criteria and their methodology thoroughly. Readers won't just take the writer's recommendations at face value. They need to understand exactly why that recommendation was made, and for that to happen, they need to be able to follow the writer's line of reasoning and understand the selection process every step along the way.

Documents that Define Standards: Specifications

Specifications detail specific (yes, that's where the term "specification" comes from) and binding requirements for objects, tools, systems, processes, documents, or just about anything else that requires consistency, reliability, and minimum standards in order to function, meet codes and requirements, or be interoperable. As you can imagine, this includes just about every single technical thing or service for which someone is willing to pay. In fact, when an organization puts out a request for proposals (RFP), that RFP will frequently include specs or consist largely of specs outlining the organization's requirements and expectations for a successful solution to its technical needs.

Generally, specs use the structure illustrated below.

Describe the object, process, and system to which the specifications apply. Include, where appropriate, the scope, costs, start and end dates, an overall definition, a definition of terms, and anything else that does not fit into the technical part-by-part specifications but is necessary to fully identify, limit, and define the purpose of the specifications

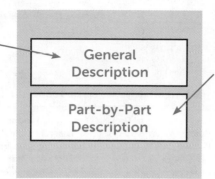

Note that specifications do not have summaries or next step sections. They are reference documents, not addressed to any particular reader and not urging any particular action. They are full of irreducible information that cannot really be summarized.

Use headings and subheadings to create a clear and logical structure for the specific technical requirements with which the reader must comply. Convey the information as clearly, briefly, and accessibly as possible.

Specifications can be either open or closed.

Open specifications specify what something should do or what it should be capable of. They define performance, not components, permitting suppliers or contractors to meet those performance requirements any way they choose. Open specifications are also known as functional or performance specs.

Closed specifications detail exactly how something should be made, what it should be like, or what components must be used. For the sake of interoperability, for instance, a supplier might be required to use specific operating software or a standard connection system. Closed specifications are also known as restrictive specs.

Specifications can be presented in sentences (see Figures 6.7 and 6.8) or in tabular, numeric style (see Figure 6.9).

These two styles can be mixed within a set of specifications.

Readers of specifications put a premium on accessibility, so feel free to write quite tersely, but make sure that omitted articles or prepositions never lead to misunderstanding. You will be liable for any inadvertent misunderstanding that costs readers time or money or any wilful misunderstanding that readers could potentially exploit as a loophole enabling them to take shortcuts.

Naturally, a spec document must be complete and accurate. It must provide all specifications that a reader might need in order to fulfil the requirements, and all of that information—every single number—must be accurate. Again, you're liable for any confusion, error, or cost incurred if you've written something inaccurate. Perhaps for this reason, spec documents often refer the reader to other, prior spec documents rather than repeat information from prior documentation word for word. This keeps documents short and prevents transcription errors.

It is general practice to use the verb "shall" to denote requirements, not "must," and to use "should" for preferences, where the reader is given some leeway.

1   GENERAL INFORMATION

1.1   SCOPE

1.1.1   These Engineering Specifications and Standard Drawings shall apply to the design and installation of Waterworks connected to the Juan de Fuca Water Distribution System owned by the Capital Regional District (CRD) and operated by the **Capital Regional District Water Services (CRD Water Services)** as defined in CRD Bylaw 2538. The CRD Water Services Engineering Specifications and Standard Drawings apply to the design and installation of water mains, together with their respective connections and appurtenances and any other associated works such as pump houses, reservoirs, vaults, etc. which are required to be designed and/or installed.

1.2   DOCUMENTS

1.2.1   The following specifications and conditions shall apply to all or any of the respective services:

Section 1	General Information
Section 2	Water Main Connection/Extension Policies and Procedures
Section 3	Drawings
Section 4	Design of Water Mains and Water Services
Section 5	Installation
Section 6	Water Utility Excavation, Backfill, Restoration and Cleanup
Appendix A	Approved Materials
Appendix B	Standards Forms
Appendix C	Standard Drawings

1.2.2   All services shall be designed and installed as detailed in the specifications and according to the procedures set out in this specification.

1.2.3   Where strict compliance with these specifications is impractical or unreasonable, the General Manager, CRD Water Services may permit a minor variance to the specifications provided prior approval is obtained. Once approved a record of these changes shall be sent to CRD Water Services.

Page 1

FIGURE 6.7 General description from the specifications of the Capital Regional District Water Services Department in B.C. Note that this description defines exactly to what these specifications apply and sets out the parameters of their use. Note: The specifications presented in this document may not reflect current standards.

Source: www.crd.bc.ca/water/engineering/documents/engineering_specs2009.pdf

4.5 FIRE HYDRANTS

4.5.1   Hydrants shall be located in the boulevard and should preferably be located at or near a street intersection; otherwise they may be located on the projection of the property line dividing two lots. Consult with the local Fire Department and CRD Water Services to confirm proposed hydrant locations.

4.5.2   Hydrants shall be located a minimum of 1.2 m from face of curb and a maximum of 2.5 m.

4.5.3   All hydrants shall be installed with a Mueller Hydrant Defender Security Device or approved equal, where required by CRD Water Services.

4.5.4   Provide hydrant spacing in accordance with the following table:

ZONING	MAXIMUM HYDRANT SPACING
Single family residential areas with more than 3m separation between houses.	150 m
Single family residential areas with less than 3 m separation between houses.	90 m
Townhouses or multi-family	90 m
Institutional, commercial, industrial, apartments or other high density areas.	90 m

4.5.5   Generally, a hydrant shall not be located within 3 m of a utility pole or light standard or within 1 m of underground utility or open ditches. Where the hydrant must be located in the ditch, it shall be installed as per Drawing 4.14.

4.5.6   All hydrants shall be installed in accordance with Standard Drawing 1.3 or 1.14.

4.5.7   Hydrants shall conform to the latest version of AWWA C502, Dry Barrel Fire Hydrants and shall be rated for a minimum working pressure of 1225 kPa (175 psi).

4.5.8   Inlet connections shall be for 150 mm (6") or 200 mm (8") I.D. pipe.

4.5.9   Inlet joints shall conform to the latest version of AWWA C111.

FIGURE 6.8 Sentence-style specifications. Note the numbering system for easy reference and the use of the verb "shall" to identify requirements. Note also in items 4.5.5 and 4.5.6 that the reader is directed to drawings and in items 4.5.7 and 4.5.9 that the reader is directed to other sets of specifications without further explanation. Note: The specifications presented in this document may not reflect current standards.

Source: www.crd.bc.ca/water/engineering/documents/engineering_specs2009.pdf

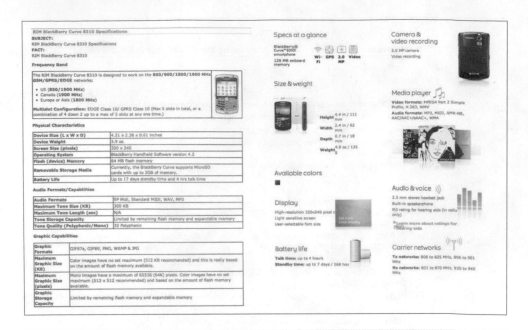

FIGURE 6.9 Table-type specifications (excerpts). Both of these samples do the same thing—provide specifications for BlackBerry smartphones. The one on the right is highly graphical and colourful (in the original); it came off the web and is intended to make it easy for consumers to check out features. The one on the left is intended for technical types (such as IT specialists who make organization-wide acquisition decisions). In both cases, note the minimal use of text to convey information.

Graphics are frequently used in spec documents because they convey some information more clearly and succinctly than words. Graphics are either placed on the pages of the document or, if too large to fit on the page, such as AutoCAD drawings or schematics, included in an appendix. When specifications are available online, links to separate graphics files are often provided.

The two samples in Figure 6.9 show tabular specifications, which are more suited for displaying technical data.

Lab Reports

Lab reports can vary greatly from discipline to discipline. In addition, academic lab reports and real-world lab reports have different purposes, which alter their presentation. In school, laboratory experiments test theories to teach basic principles—for example, testing the constant of gravity or showing that the temperature at which a liquid boils varies with atmospheric pressure. In a professional setting, on the other hand, you will test very practical applications—for example, assaying the content of metals in a core sample or destructively testing the crash worthiness of a bicycle helmet. In the real world, your experiments will discover new information on which people will act.

However, all lab reports will follow the organizational pattern described below, with some variation. Generally, your instructor or supervisor will define the precise requirements.

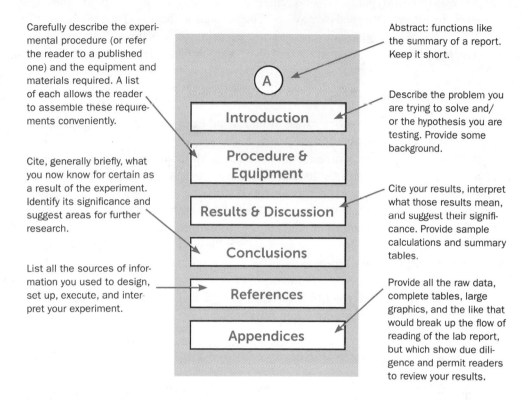

Carefully describe the experimental procedure (or refer the reader to a published one) and the equipment and materials required. A list of each allows the reader to assemble these requirements conveniently.

Abstract: functions like the summary of a report. Keep it short.

Describe the problem you are trying to solve and/or the hypothesis you are testing. Provide some background.

Cite, generally briefly, what you now know for certain as a result of the experiment. Identify its significance and suggest areas for further research.

Cite your results, interpret what those results mean, and suggest their significance. Provide sample calculations and summary tables.

List all the sources of information you used to design, set up, execute, and interpret your experiment.

Provide all the raw data, complete tables, large graphics, and the like that would break up the flow of reading of the lab report, but which show due diligence and permit readers to review your results.

A

Introduction

Procedure & Equipment

Results & Discussion

Conclusions

References

Appendices

Abstracts

Abstracts function like summaries in reports. They provide a highly condensed version of the whole lab report, focusing on the purpose of the experiment, its key findings, their significance, and the major conclusions you've reached. Often abstracts include a brief mention of the methodology.

The abstract should be fewer than 200 words, most sources agree—even fewer for short lab reports. Short, unpublished lab reports, such as those written in school, may omit the abstract altogether, with your instructor's permission, of course.

Unlike summaries, abstracts begin quite self-consciously: "This experiment examined the relationship between . . ."

Introduction

The introduction should describe the problem or issue your experiment intends to resolve and provide sufficient background information for the reader to understand how the experiment fits into the larger technical/scientific background. It may refer to previous research or experiments on the problem and indicate how your experiment will clarify or expand the knowledge in the field.

The introduction should end with a purpose statement (sometimes in the form of a hypothesis or null hypothesis): one sentence which specifically states the question your experiment was designed to answer: "The purpose of this experiment was to . . ."

If the introduction gets quite long, consider using subheadings. In physics, for instance, Introductions are frequently broken into Problem and Hypothesis, or Theory.

Procedure and Equipment

This section may alternatively be called Methods and Equipment or Methods and Materials, whichever is most appropriate.

By describing your experimental procedure you allow the reader to see its merit and hence the merit of your results and you allow the reader, quite critically to the scientific method, to replicate the experiment. If you are following a well-established, published procedure, you can refer to it ("We used the standard ASME 123 procedure" or "We followed the procedure in the Physics 101 Lab Manual, pp. 12–14"), unless your instructor says otherwise. However, always indicate how you've strayed from the referenced procedure. ("We repeated the titration in Step 11 only twice instead of three times because we ran out of phenolphthalein.")

When you are not referring to a standard procedure, describe your procedure in full sentences and paragraphs, providing full detail.

Results and Discussion

This section can alternatively be called Data and Discussion. Sometimes, depending on length, this section is broken into two. However, if you have a choice, consider how effective it is to list a bunch of results and then, much later, discuss their significance in a separate section. Sometimes it's better to interpret data as it comes in.

The Results and Discussion section will contain sample calculations and summary tables. Full calculations and complete data sets are often left for the appendices where they won't interrupt the flow of reading, just as in other reports.

The discussion is the most important part of the lab report, in a sense, because this is where you analyze and interpret the results. In an academic setting, this is where you prove your understanding of the concepts you were meant to learn. In a professional setting, this is where you answer the question you are being paid to explore. Your discussion should compare the actual results to the expected results, to the results of similar experiments, and to the experiment's objectives. It should consider experimental error and may analyze the strengths and limitations of the experimental design. Note that you do not have to do all of these things all of the time.

Conclusions

The Conclusion section is often very short, summarizing what you know for sure now that you've completed your experiment. Back that up with a brief supporting statement. You may also want to indicate the significance of your conclusions and suggest ideas for further research.

References

List all the sources to which you referred to define, design, set up, execute, and interpret your experiment. Refer to these sources in the body of the lab report.

Appendices

The appendices compile raw data, long tables, graphs, series of calculations, and other supporting material that would break up the flow of reading in the body of the lab report. Create a separate appendix for each discrete type of information and refer your reader to the appendices within the lab report: "See Appendix A for the complete table of results."

Informal Report Checklist

☐ Have you clearly identified the purpose of the report and chosen the correct report type: incident, trip, inspection, proposal, and so on?

☐ Have you chosen the proper report format given the formality of the situation and the length of the report: memo or letter (informal), semi-formal, or formal?

☐ Have you analyzed your readers and determined what information they will require and what terminology they will understand?

☐ Have you provided sufficient subheadings on longer reports to help readers find the information they are looking for?

☐ Have you provided full information so that readers will understand what has happened or what is going on and also understand what you have done or what you are asking them to do?

☐ Have you provided all the information that readers need to carry out the necessary follow-up actions: clear instructions and third-party contact information, for instance?

Because this is a very short lab report, it does not require an abstract—unless your instructor disagrees, of course.

Introduction

Transpiration is the evaporation of water from plant surfaces. This takes place both directly through the surfaces of the epidermal cells of the leaves, but mostly through the stomata, the surface openings on the undersides of leaves.

Rates of transpiration are determined by environmental conditions such as sunlight, humidity, air movement, and temperature.

The purpose of this experiment is to determine the relative effects of temperature, wind, and humidity on rates of transpiration. It does not test the effects of sunlight or its absence.

The introduction introduces the topic and its significance and ends with a statement of the experiment's intent and scope.

Materials and Methods

Materials:

2 rubber tubes

2 measuring pipettes

2 one-hole stoppers the same gauge as the tubes

2 sweet pea plants of equal size and development

2 lab stands with two clamp arms each

Distilled water

A list of equipment and materials is not always necessary, but it helps those who want to repeat your experiment pull together what they'll need.

Provide clear descriptions of what you did. Note that these are not instructions, though you can proceed step by step or even use subheadings to improve clarity.

I built two potometers by clamping a rubber tube in a U-shape to each lab stand. I fitted a rubber stopper into one end of each tube and a measuring pipette into the other. I then poured distilled water into the tubes, through the pipettes, until the tubes were filled to the top, that is, until the water formed a meniscus above the stopper to ensure that no air was trapped in the system.

I cut two sweet pea plants of equal size and inserted one into each of the stoppers, forming a good seal and ensuring that each cutting was submersed at least 2 cm into the water.

I used one cutting as a control, leaving it on the test bench, at a room temperature of 20 °C throughout the experiment.

For the first part of the experiment, I left the test cutting on the bench next to the control cutting for half an hour. Then I placed the test cutting in the room next door, which was measured to have a temperature of 25 °C for half an hour. After that I returned it to the original room, but placed it under the hood and set the fan to high. Finally, I took the test cutting out from under the hood, wrapped it in clear plastic, which I taped sealed, leaving the measuring pipette exposed.

The test cutting was subjected to each environmental condition for exactly 30 minutes and I took measurements of the meniscus on the measuring pipette every three minutes, for both cuttings.

The 80 measurements (40 per plant cutting) would break up the flow of reading too much and have been tabulated in the appendix (not shown).

Results and Discussion

Table 1 summarizes the volume of water transpired by each cutting. Precise measurements at three-minute intervals are provided in the tables in the appendix.

Table 1: Total transpiration under different conditions

Stage	Control	Test cutting
1	1.5 mL (20 °C, still air)	1.5 mL (20 °C, still air)
2	1.5 mL (20 °C, still air)	2.1 mL (25 °C, still air)
3	1.5 mL (20 °C, still air)	2.9 mL (20 °C, strong breeze)
4	1.5 mL (20 °C, still air)	0.3 mL (20 °C , 100% humidity)

FIGURE 6.10 Simple lab report. For the sake of brevity, this sample lab report omits the References section and the appendix. Short lab reports like this, especially when performed for school and not destined to be published, tend not to include an abstract.

Graphs and summary tables are, of course, excellent ways to make complex data comprehensible at a glance.

Graph 1 provides this same information visually.

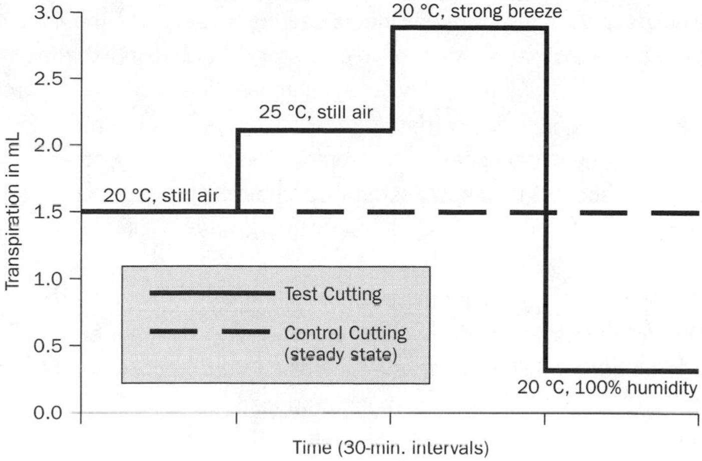

Graph 1: Relative transpiration under different conditions

The discussion interprets the results for the reader.

The results show that air movement has a stronger effect on transpiration than temperature, at least at the temperature tested. Normally I would have expected that at 100% humidity, there would have been no transpiration at all, which is actually what happened after 12 minutes. It took those first 12 minutes for transpiration to fill the plastic wrap container to 100 % humidity, after which transpiration ceased, as can be seen in Table 4: Transpiration in Plastic Wrap, in the appendix.

Where appropriate, the discussion includes a statement about potential experimental error.

Note that transpiration at the top end (the strong-breeze set-up) may have been limited by how much water the cutting was able to absorb because it lacked a root system. It is, therefore, possible that a plant under similar conditions would have transpired more water than the cutting was able to. If that is the case, then part of the 0.3 mL of water used up in the final stage (100% humidity) may have rehydrated the plant rather been transpired.

The conclusion indicates what you know for sure as a result of your experiment.

Conclusion

This experiment seems to prove that strong air currents create more transpiration than increases in temperature, at least in the ranges tested.

The conclusion may also suggest improvements to future experiments or, more broadly, areas of further research.

Future experiments might make two improvements. The first would be to use small plants with intact root systems rather than cuttings. This would ensure that the plants are able to absorb more water and may yield higher transpiration at higher temperatures and stronger air currents.

A future experiment might also test plants at higher temperatures than the 25 °C at which this experiment peaked because in summers, even in our climate, plants regularly experience temperatures as high as 35 °C. This would help determine to what extent transpiration increases exponentially with temperature.

The References section (not shown) would list all the resources to which you referred in order to set up, perform, and interpret your experiment.

Exercises: Writing Different Kinds of Reports

You are working as team lead at Canada Motion Cinema, a Calgary-based start-up that designs, builds, and installs motion cinema seating. Essentially, the audience gets a simulator effect in which the rows of seats move on a stage—tilting and shifting—and on which seats also move and vibrate individually, all synchronized perfectly to the actions on the screen. It's a rapidly growing industry that dramatically enhances the movie-going experience.

These motion stages are very complex assemblages of about 10,000 parts, put together into about 3,000 sub-assemblies, that are put together into roughly 500 assemblies that can be shipped in containers to the install locations for final assembly and installation.

Motion cinema combines the work of mechanical engineers, robotics specialists, computer programmers, millwrights, electricians, and many other areas of expertise, and each install is uniquely engineered to the dimensions and technical requirements of the installation site. Because they are not mass produced, each motion cinema install must be assembled and tested at your production facility to make sure that all the 500 assemblies fit and work together. Then the entire system is disassembled and packaged into about 100 containers and shipped to the install location, where your team will reassemble it.

Your job is to lead the design, manufacturing, testing, shipping, and installation of each custom install.

Incident Report

Your team is working on a motion cinema installation for a cinema that is being included in an extension of the Royal Newfoundland Museum of History in St. John's, which will feature action-packed simulation films including Viking sea voyages and helicopter flights to offshore oil rigs. This is, in fact, the first commercial sale that Canada Motion Cinema has made.

You are assembling the components in the assembly shed, which is connected to the production floor. To assemble the components, you use the same lifts and other equipment that you will use on location. This equipment also needs to be shipped.

Today, after assembling the flooring platform onto which the rows of seats will be bolted, your job was to raise the platform to a vertical position so that you could attach the telescoping hydraulic cylinders that will move the stage.

Your team had attached two spreader bars to the end of the stage that was to be hoisted and attached the bars by chains to the hoisting engines mounted on the portable hoisting rig which was located at the end of the stage that was to remain grounded. In other words, the chains and lifting force, were directed across the width of the stage from the lifting end upward to the hoist on the stationary end.

When everything was in place, you called out the safety checks and everyone at their stations answered in the affirmative. You gave the all clear to power the hoisting lifts. The chains tightened and then the stage began to lift.

Suddenly there was a terrible noise from the stationary end of the stage. As you looked over there, your heart sank and you shouted out a warning to everyone in the vicinity, though they were already shouting warnings of their own and scrambling to safety.

What happened was that the end of the stage that was meant to remain stationary and act as a pivot point for the lift had broken loose and was sliding rapidly toward the hoist, accelerating along the way. As the stage hit the hoist, the bolts on the hoist held (the hoist is temporarily bolted into the floor for each lift to provide the necessary stability), the stage slid up the inclined braces of the hoist, scraping off the paint, and came to a rest against the tubular pillar, which was dented.

One of the workers, Steve Chan, was not able to get out of the way quickly enough and was clipped by the stage at the ankle. He was taken to hospital by ambulance, which was called immediately. Thanks to his safety boots, his ankle was badly bruised, but unbroken. He will take several days off work.

The dent in the tubular pillar of the hoist means that the hoist's structural integrity has been compromised and the hoist will need to be replaced. Your best estimate, after calling Industrial Hoist and Lift, your supplier, will be that the replacement parts will arrive in about three days (delivery has to be made from Toronto) and will take most of a day to install. The cost will be, excluding labour, approximately $4,500.

As soon as the stage stopped moving, you took charge of the situation. You called out to see whether everyone was okay. When Steve indicated that he'd been hurt, you assigned two workers to see to him (Jane Smith, Raj Ghataura; Raj called the ambulance).

Then you and Phil Orneston reversed the hoist lifts to lower the stage to release the pressure on the chains and the damaged pillar. Those lifts had automatically stopped when the operators released the controls to run for safety.

Later, after the ambulance had left, you pulled the stage away from the hoist to investigate the cause of the accident. It appears that the block that was intended to hold the stationary end of the stage in place, had been placed correctly, that the bolt holes to secure it had been drilled through the block and into the concrete, but that only four of the twelve bolts had actually been placed. Those four broke under pressure, allowing the stage to break free.

Use today's date and the current time to record this incident. Make up any reasonable information that you would add to this report, but which has not been included in this write-up.

Occasional Progress Report

You have accompanied your installation team (names above) to St. John's to install the motion cinema equipment at the Royal Newfoundland Museum of History. Not including the delays caused by the stage-hoisting incident, the assembly in Calgary took your four-person team just under four weeks. You have scheduled the install for four weeks.

Progress has generally been good. However, today you unloaded container #37, which contained strut assemblies for the motion stage. These assemblies, consisting of tubular steel trusses, are connected using flanges and bolts. The bolts are not in the container.

The containers have all been numbered, but you don't have a complete manifest of what's in each container. You've opened a couple of other containers containing similar assemblies, but those don't contain any bolts either. You have no idea where the bolts might be.

You call head office in Calgary, but they can't locate them either. The bolts have either gone missing in Calgary or have been placed in some other container, possibly one that hasn't been delivered yet.

You have no choice. Because these bolts are specifically manufactured for you by a small plant in Saskatchewan and are not available at your local hardware store, you call your supplier and ask them to air ship the required four dozen bolts. The bolts cost $25 each and air freight, given that this will be a rush order and that the weight will be considerable, will cost, according to Canpar's website, $758.23, plus GST. However, you cannot proceed until you have those bolts. Nor can you start on another part of the assembly because the necessary containers have not yet arrived. It's Monday today. The bolts won't arrive until Wednesday, possibly quite late.

You are now looking at a three-day delay. For those three days your crew will accrue per diems and costs for accommodations. It also seems likely that similar delays will plague the rest of the install, so it's difficult to estimate a final completion date.

Write a quick (occasional) progress report to your CEO, Greg Smithson, and copy the head of the museum, Dr. Caroline Sauder. Make up any reasonable information that you would add to this report, but which has not been included in this write-up.

Trip Report (Completion Report)

You have just returned from completing the install at the Royal Newfoundland Museum of History. As you had feared, the install was plagued by several delays. On three separate occasions, simple assembly pieces had not been packed or had been mis-packed. It turned out, for instance, that all the bolts had been placed in container #79, which you only opened a full ten days after you had received and used the air-shipped replacement bolts.

You had also not been shipped a required chain for the hoists, nor a sledgehammer, a crowbar, and replacement pairs of work gloves. Each of these you were easily able to find at local hardware stores, but each caused delays while crew were waiting for the necessary equipment and while one of your crew was deputized to pick up the necessary supplies by cab. A car rental was not part of the planned cost item for the St. John's install because your Motel 6 was right across the street from the museum.

Your crew arrived home two days ago, but you had stayed behind to train the staff at the museum in the proper operation of the motion cinema stage and to guide their technical staff in some minor maintenance and inspection procedures that they are expected to perform. Your firm has a maintenance contract with the museum and remotely monitors the system for faults and warning triggers, but the locals still have to perform some functions and seemed a little helpless with the technology. You think that Canada Motion Cinema should produce some training materials to send ahead to customers so that staff have a head start. You think that account manager Jane Choi should follow up with Phil Doman, who runs the maintenance department at the museum to see how it's going. You are handing this project over to her for follow-up.

But the real problem, of course, was that the missing parts cost a total of $2,400 of air freight, $3,254 in tools and materials, and eight days of delay; per diems of $65/day per staff member; and hotel costs of $120 per day per staff member. You are anticipating about four installs per year (there are two production teams), so the annual cost could be considerable.

You would like to recommend that Canada Motion Cinema produce disassembly drawings as well as assembly drawings and manifests with checklists for each assembly, to ensure that all the required parts and tools are shipped with each assembly. Each container load should be inspected before it is placed in the containers and the containers are sealed.

Please write the required trip report, now that you have completed the project.

Inspection Report (Packaging/Shipping)

Almost immediately after completing your install at the Royal Newfoundland Museum of History, Jane Choi, account manager, handed you the next approved contract, a considerably larger install at Disney World in Bay Lake, Florida, near Orlando.

You immediately flew down to Orlando, discussed the client's requirements, and established the dimensions of the facility. Then you set to work with your team to design and build the install. This process took four months. Everything works perfectly.

You have now disassembled the tested install and have placed all the sub-assemblies and their parts into groups for loading into the shipping containers. Your job is to inspect these groups of materials to make sure they are complete, before they are placed in the containers and the containers are sealed for shipping. On the St. John's install, missing components and tools cost the company dearly (see Trip Report above).

You expect that this install will require 117 containers in total. You are writing inspection reports for every 20 containers. You have already inspected the contents for containers 1 through 40. You are now inspecting the contents of containers 41 to 60.

The contents for containers 41 through 47 were complete. In the assembled materials for Container 48, you discovered that seven bolts (CMC-9-03) with which two sub-assemblies are connected are missing. The rest of the containers are fine, but for Container 55, you notice that a required spanner is not among the contents (Husky Brand #17-34-SP3). It's required for the assembly of the sub-assemblies in this container. You suspect that because it's a specialized tool, someone has taken it back to the fabrication floor. It's not your responsibility, however, at this point, to go get it. Also, Container 51 seems to be missing a specially shaped heat-shield for a weld that you will have to make during the assembly. It's made in-house (CMC-HS-01).

Please write the required inspection report. Make up any reasonable information that you would add to this report, but which has not been included in this write-up.

Chapter 7

Formal Reports

In this chapter you will learn

- the purpose of formal report formatting
- the parts of a formal report, their functions, sequencing, content, and layout
- how to use your word processor to set up some formal report formatting conventions.

The longer the report, the greater the need for tables of contents and lists of tables and figures so that readers can navigate the document and find the specific information they need. These aids to navigation are unique to the formal report.

Longer reports also contain numerous conclusions and recommendations scattered throughout tens or hundreds of pages. A reader needs quick access to this information but shouldn't have to spend many hours, highlighter poised, reading a long report in order to get the gist. So, we pull all this key information into conclusions and recommendations sections at the end of the report.

We also add a summary at the very beginning that very highly condenses the report, generally to a single page or so, but more on that later.

What a formal report does, then, is provide multiple points of access and multiple levels of detail to readers of long, complex documents. The purpose of a formal report is not just to impress with pomp and circumstance, though that is part of it; it's also to help readers find information they need at whatever level of detail they require in order to act on the report.

There is no firm rule about the minimum length at which a report should be made formal, but 10 pages is a good guideline. At that point the reader begins to find it a hassle to flip through the pages, scanning headings to find specific information. Often, however, even slightly shorter reports are dressed up formally if the occasion is important and the writer wants to make a good impression. Anything less than six pages, however, should probably not be formatted formally, but this, too, is just a guideline.

Parts of a Formal Report

The following are the parts of a formal report, from front to back:

- letter of transmittal
- title page
- acknowledgements (if used)
- disclaimers (if used)
- summary
- table of contents
- list of tables and figures
- introduction
- discussion
- conclusions
- recommendations
- glossary
- references
- appendices.

We'll describe these parts of the formal report more thoroughly in the following sections.

Letter of Transmittal

The letter of transmittal isn't part of the report, but a courtesy exclusive to the person receiving the report, usually the person who commissioned or authorized it. We say in it the sort of things that we would tell the recipient if we were handing over (transmitting) the report in person.

Include the following information, generally in the following order:

- purpose of the report
- authorization of the report
- main conclusion(s) of the report
- comments that do not belong in the report but may interest the reader
- acknowledgments to people and organizations who assisted you in the writing of the report
- friendly close.

Use a standard business letter format (Chapter 5).

Because the letter isn't part of the report, don't bind it into the report. Instead, paperclip it to the front of the report or slip it inside the cover. The idea is that the recipient reads it, sets it aside, and then reads the report. The report may be passed on to other readers or even duplicated many times for numerous readers, but the letter is read only once and only by the person to whom it is addressed.

This gives the writer a chance to speak with the addressee personally, a chance to include information that the addressee may find useful or even important, but which does not belong in the report itself.

Correct letter format. Attention to detail is necessary and considered a sign of professionalism.

1289 Westweld Cr., Suite 204
Markham, ON L3P 2N8

Jan. 06, 2017

Mr. Jeff Gould
President
Pinnacle Manufacturing
15349 Xetra Place, Unit 112
Richmond, BC V4E 1A6

Transmittal of Report on the Investigation of the
Production Line at Pinnacle Manufacturing

Dear Jeff,

Thanks and acknowledgments, where appropriate.

I have enclosed the report (PM17-01) on the investigation you asked us to conduct on the production problems at Pinnacle Manufacturing.

Report context: purpose and authorization.

We particularly want to thank your staff members Janet Woo and Brendan Smith-Jones for helping us put together the metrics for your production department. Their help was invaluable.

Chief results or outcomes, briefly.

Our recommendations focus on small changes to the material flow, but we don't feel that it will be necessary to reorganize the production machine layout. Please see page 73 of the report for our specific recommendations.

Information useful to the reader but not appropriate in the report.

However, we also found that part of the problem with the production actually stems from a personality conflict between two employees, Frank Chan and Jim Malhotra. Obviously we do not specialize in advising on personnel issues, but we are concerned that this may become an ongoing and worsening problem if these two employees continue to have contact during work. If they cannot be reassigned, you might think about engaging consultants or counselors who specialize in helping firms overcome such personal conflicts in the workplace.

We've enjoyed working with your firm and thank you for the opportunity. If you need any help interpreting parts of the report, or if there is ever anything else that we can do for you, we would be very glad to hear from you.

Standard friendly close, generally an offer to help interpret the report and to do more work in future.

Sincerely,

Fred Nesbitt

Fred Nesbitt, P. Eng., MBA
Senior Production Engineer
Johnson Engineering
fnesbitt@jpengineering.com
406-231-9856

FIGURE 7.1 Sample letter of transmittal. Note that we are looking at the final report submitted by Johnson Engineering for Pinnacle Manufacturing, a scenario we first looked at in Chapter 1. Note also the use of standard letter format. Of course, in a less formal environment, such as an in-house report, you could write a memo of transmittal.

Title Page

The title page should include the following information:

- title of the report, worded very specifically to indicate the main purpose of the report
- name and title of the primary reader (usually the one who commissioned the report)
- name and title of the author(s)
- date of completion.

Set these elements up attractively on the page to make a good first impression. Make sure that the title of the report is, by far, the largest and most visible thing on the page. A little modesty when scaling your own name would not be out of place.

Consider including a picture or other graphic, as long as it helps the reader identify the project or context. Don't use random clip art or people shots because those are likely to confuse or distract a reader expecting the graphic to be relevant.

Though the title page is the first page of the report, it should not be paginated.

Acknowledgements and Disclaimers

Acknowledgements are a polite way to give credit to individuals or organizations that have been instrumental in the production of the document, generally in a supportive role such as organizing access or authorizing resources. These are usually not a legal requirement and are usually expressed in the letter of transmittal, as in Figure 7.1 and in the letter of transmittal for the sample formal report below.

Specific information provided by individuals should be acknowledged in the text through citations and references (Chapter 9) and not in an acknowledgement page.

If you do feel the need to include acknowledgements in the report, place them on a page by themselves in the orientation section; they are not a part of the report proper. Generally, acknowledgements are placed immediately after the title page.

Legal disclaimers, on the other hand, are increasingly common, regrettably. Usually, however, they consist of boilerplate text provided by your organization's legal counsel—or pulled off the Internet after having been written by someone else's legal counsel. Not only are you not required to write it; you will be forbidden to go near it. Some typical examples include the following.

This report may identify some products by proprietary or trade names to help readers identify specific types of products. However, this is not, and is not intended to be, an endorsement or recommendation of any product or manufacturer. Readers are responsible for verifying the . . .

> This report has been prepared in good faith on the basis of information available at the date of publication and provided by vendors without independent verification. XYZ Engineering cannot guarantee the accuracy of . . .

You get the idea. As with acknowledgements, legal disclaimers go on a page of their own in the orientation section, generally right after the title page, as in the sample formal report below.

Summary

The summary should be no more than one-tenth the length of the report—not including the conclusion and recommendation sections—up to a maximum of one page. This means that a 20-page report should have a one-page summary. Reports running to hundreds of pages can break this rule and some organizations have slightly different rules on summary lengths, so if you're in doubt, ask.

Summaries are sufficiently important—and sufficiently challenging to many writers—that the topic merits some development. Please read the following three subsections if you're unsure of how summaries function, what they should contain, and how to go about writing them.

Function of Summaries

The summary is in some ways the most important part of a report because every single reader will read it. Indeed, many readers will selectively read only certain parts of the rest of the report. This is particularly relevant when readers are evaluating competing proposals, for instance. A selection committee may, on first reading, simply review the summaries before eliminating some proposals from consideration. For these reasons some writers claim that they spend as much time writing the summary as they do the whole rest of the report. This is, of course, more likely in a 20-page report than, say, a 200-page report.

However, at any length, summaries are difficult to get right. They must not only contain all the right information, but also be written very concisely (to fit as much information in as possible) and clearly—otherwise, what's the point?

It's actually very useful to think of yourself as always submitting two versions of the same report. One is for those in a hurry who merely want the gist; this is the summary. The other provides full details, describes your methodology, explains your findings, exhibits your evidence, and follows your line of reasoning—thereby proving due diligence. This is the report itself.

Content and Tone of Summaries

It's important to distinguish between descriptive summaries and executive summaries. Descriptive summaries, also known as abstracts, describe articles, theses, lab reports, and other documents intended for publishing, research, and/or academic purposes. They begin with "This article . . . ," "This experiment . . . ," or "This report . . . ." As

Abstract

This article describes current trends in production line automation in the window manufacturing industry in North America supported with statistics from industry bodies. It details production line improvements made by Acme Window Systems Ltd. of Mississauga, Ontario, to provide an example, and lists a sampling of equipment currently available to the industry. This equipment is compared on the basis of the manufacturer's specifications, not on field tests or metrics.

FIGURE 7.2 Sample abstract. An abstract describes the contents of a document almost like a prose table of contents. It is primarily a tool for researchers to figure out what sort of information a document contains.

such, they are useful for researchers reading their way into a topic, verifying that a document contains the kind of information they're looking for. We use abstracts for documents that contain pure information or pure research that is not applied in a business situation and is not intended to propose a course of action.

The vast majority of the time, however, when working in a professional capacity, you will be writing executive summaries, the purpose of which is to provide a highly condensed overview of the most important information in the report. The idea is that readers should be able to make some (executive) decisions based on the summary alone. If they feel they don't have quite enough information, they will read selectively from the report.

It is important therefore to answer the reader's most important questions and to do so in the same order and tone and with the same emphasis as in the report. An executive summary will focus on the following information:

- Report context: how it came to be written, its purpose, and its scope. What problem is the report intended to resolve?
- Report methodology: briefly, how the writer investigated the issue or how the report is organized. This is usually accorded only a single sentence because the results are more important, but it does add credibility to your findings. What did you do?
- Report findings and recommendations: only briefly, so that they fit within the length restriction. The details are in the report, after all. What did you find out? What do you think we should do about it?

Everything in the summary must also be mentioned in the report. There should never be any new information in a summary.

Writing Summaries

Though the summary is placed first in the report, it should be the last thing you write. It's only once you've finished the report that you'll have a clear idea of the content and its relative weighting and importance. You can't summarize what hasn't been written.

When pulling together the information for the summary, think of yourself as highlighting the most important information in the report, then putting it together in one location (the summary) and editing it for cohesion. Focus on the introduction, which describes the problem the report is attempting to resolve, and on the conclusions and recommendations sections, which have already pulled together the report findings and the actions to be taken based on those findings. Include just a very quick description of the method of investigation. Leave the information in the same order in which you pulled it from the report.

When you find yourself summarizing a report too short to merit separate conclusions and recommendations sections, focus on the topic sentences of each paragraph to establish the main ideas for the summary.

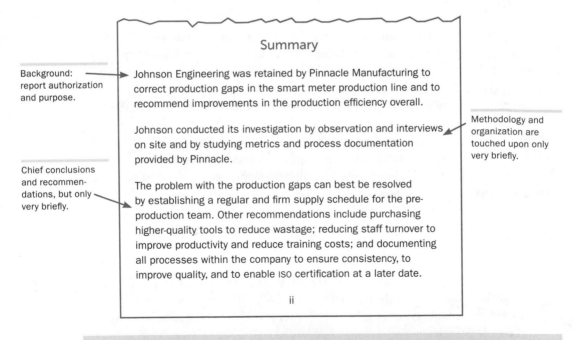

Background: report authorization and purpose.

Summary

Johnson Engineering was retained by Pinnacle Manufacturing to correct production gaps in the smart meter production line and to recommend improvements in the production efficiency overall.

Johnson conducted its investigation by observation and interviews on site and by studying metrics and process documentation provided by Pinnacle.

Methodology and organization are touched upon only very briefly.

Chief conclusions and recommendations, but only very briefly.

The problem with the production gaps can best be resolved by establishing a regular and firm supply schedule for the pre-production team. Other recommendations include purchasing higher-quality tools to reduce wastage; reducing staff turnover to improve productivity and reduce training costs; and documenting all processes within the company to ensure consistency, to improve quality, and to enable ISO certification at a later date.

ii

FIGURE 7.3 Sample report summary. This is an exceptionally short summary for demonstration purposes. A summary is set on a page by itself in a formal report, for easy reference, duplication, and distribution. Note that it summarizes primarily the information from the introduction (the context) and from the conclusions and recommendations sections. Consider this a shortcut to summary writing. Start on the summary only after you've completed the report; then focus on summarizing those three sections.

At this point you'll have the key relevant information in your summary and in the proper order. Now take your first cut at editing the summary for conciseness and cohesion (chapters 2 and 3). If you're less than 20 per cent over your word limit after this first edit, you can probably get down to your word limit through editing.

If you find that you're more than 20 per cent over the word limit, you'll need to eliminate some material. When you do so, check first that you've provided a consistent level of detail for all sections covered in the summary. If one of the ideas is presented in more detail than the rest, eliminate the extra, unbalancing detail. What is often to blame in these instances is the inclusion of an example for one of the ideas where the others are not clarified by examples.

If balance and consistency are not the problem, you've probably provided too much detail in general. You'll have to rewrite, providing a lower level of detail, then re-edit. Don't worry, the details will still be in the conclusions and recommendations sections for those who need more information, and in the report itself for those who want the full information.

Table of Contents (TOC)

A table of contents (TOC) lets readers see the report organization at a glance and find specific sections that interest them. The alternative would be to force readers to flip through potentially hundreds of pages to figure out how a report is organized.

Place the TOC after the title page and summary (though the summary may also be placed just before the introduction).

Word automates tables of contents for you. Simply assign heading styles to all the headings and subheadings in your document, place your cursor where you want the TOC to appear, and then go to the References ribbon and click on the Table of Contents icon on the left end of the ribbon.

The sample formal report at the end of this chapter shows what a table of contents should look like.

List of Tables and Figures (LTF)

A list of tables and figures (LTF) lets the reader know that you have included informative tables, graphs, and illustrations (figures) in the document, and where to find them.

Place the LTF on a new page immediately after the TOC. The LTF can be put on the same page as the TOC, as long as it is short enough to finish on the same page.

In Word, insert a caption by highlighting the table or figure and selecting the Insert Caption icon from the References ribbon. Word will automatically number these captions.

To insert a list of tables and figures in Word, simply put your cursor where you want the list of tables and figures to appear, then go to the References ribbon and click on the Insert Table of Figures icon at the centre of the ribbon.

The sample formal report at the end of this chapter shows what a list of tables and figures should look like.

Introduction

The introduction of a formal report functions like the context section of informal reports, but supplies some additional information in that it forecasts the organization of the report. The introduction should include the following information:

- purpose of the report
- scope of the project
- context (anything about the report and project that will make its reading and comprehension easier for the reader and an explanation of how the report fits into the conduct of your business or how it came to be written)
- methodology or organization.

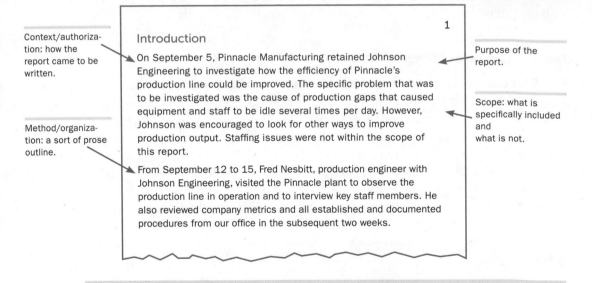

Context/authorization: how the report came to be written.

Method/organization: a sort of prose outline.

1

Introduction

On September 5, Pinnacle Manufacturing retained Johnson Engineering to investigate how the efficiency of Pinnacle's production line could be improved. The specific problem that was to be investigated was the cause of production gaps that caused equipment and staff to be idle several times per day. However, Johnson was encouraged to look for other ways to improve production output. Staffing issues were not within the scope of this report.

From September 12 to 15, Fred Nesbitt, production engineer with Johnson Engineering, visited the Pinnacle plant to observe the production line in operation and to interview key staff members. He also reviewed company metrics and all established and documented procedures from our office in the subsequent two weeks.

Purpose of the report.

Scope: what is specifically included and what is not.

FIGURE 7.4 Sample introduction. Note that the introduction establishes the circumstances of the writing of the report without giving away any of the details. It describes the context (how the report came to be written), its purpose, the scope (parameters and limitations), and the method of investigation. It absolutely does not give away any of the findings.

Discussion

The discussion section is the body of the report; that is, it will constitute the majority of the word count. Its content and organization will be determined by its purpose and audience. Because formal reports are just long versions of the types of reports discussed in Chapter 6, look there for the organizational logic that best suits your purpose.

Conclusions

The discussion section may be hundreds of pages long describing the steps in your investigation. Your findings, the facts that you discovered during your investigation, will be presented chronologically—at those parts of the story, where you discovered them.

Readers don't necessarily want to read the whole report, but they will want to know all the relevant findings. So, the conclusions section lists these findings in a

---

71

Conclusions

Our investigation established the following:

- The production machine layout is optimized. It would need to be rearranged only if increased demand required the addition of another line within the same space. We feel that the current shop is large enough to accommodate future growth.
- The production line is generally well run and well organized. The only cause of the production gaps appears to be the inability of the pre-production team to anticipate the materials needs of the cutting press at the start of the production line.
- The pre-production team does not use materials as efficiently as it could, due to high staff turnover, which means that the staff there is relatively inexperienced and untrained.
- The cutting templates and dyes supplied to Pinnacle are not the highest quality and their relatively short duty life may be costing money. Toward the end of their duty cycles, these templates and dyes also cause inaccuracies and materials wastage.
- The metrics indicate that Pinnacle is running its operations efficiently otherwise. All metrics are within industry norms.
- A number of processes have not been documented. For example, Pinnacle has no standardized process documented for purchasing of materials or equipment, or for training personnel. This leads to inconsistencies that may stray from best practices. As no record exists, however, it is difficult to assess Pinnacle's performance in these regards.

FIGURE 7.5 Sample conclusions section. In the discussion section, writers document their methods for credibility and to prove due diligence. In the conclusions section, they bring together, in one convenient location and without additional detail, everything that they discovered during the research or investigation phase. Note that bullets are a convenient and accessible way to present findings, but they aren't always appropriate or feasible, depending on the report. Conclusions are facts, not subject to opinion.

single convenient location. Think of the conclusions section as an end-summary of findings. It lists incontrovertible facts. Its function is to list all the findings, so it is not limited in length. However, do remember to be concise.

Recommendations

The recommendations section lists specific actions you want your reader to take to resolve the problems investigated in the report. The recommendation(s) should develop logically from the findings, that is, from the conclusions. The recommendations section lists your professional opinions about what should happen next.

73

Recommendations

Based on our findings, we recommend the following:

- Establish a regular schedule to deliver 50 pre-dimensioned sheet metal plates to the cutting press at the stroke of every hour. If this schedule is maintained, the pre-production department will not have to communicate with the production line about this issue and the cutting press will not run out of supplies.

- Conduct interviews with the staff or engage a personnel consultant to determine the causes of the high staff turnover. Untrained and inexperienced staff is causing a considerable number of errors and wastage of materials.

- Purchase higher-quality templates and dyes to save money in the long run. Some recommendations with product codes are found in Appendix C: Comparative Tool Performance.

- Standardize and document all procedures within the operation to ensure consistent high standards in all processes and to make it easier to train new staff. This documentation does not necessarily need to be to ISO standards, but it should be. That could pave the way for ISO certification in the future.

FIGURE 7.6 **Sample recommendations section.** The recommendations are the writer's opinions about what should be done as a response to the facts presented in the conclusions section. This is a key difference. At the risk of being repetitive, the conclusions section lists facts unearthed during an investigation. The recommendations section recommends actions. Often, these actions will be bulleted, even numbered if the actions should be carried out in a particular sequence.

Everything you say in your conclusions and recommendations sections must have been mentioned or implied in the discussion section. These two sections are, in effect, summaries, so they should contain nothing that isn't also mentioned in the report.

Glossary

When you use technical terms with which your audience may not be familiar, provide a parenthetical reference.

> Our tests showed high levels of rBGH (recombinant bovine growth hormone) in the samples.

However, if the definitions are too long and would break up the flow of the reading too much or if you think that not all readers will require the definition and you want to save the knowledgeable readers some time and inconvenience, place your definitions in a glossary.

When you do this, you can use a number of formatting conventions as long as you use one consistently and explain that convention to the reader the first time you use it, usually in a footnote. In a longer document, explain the convention the first time you use it in each section or chapter.

> Our tests showed high levels of rBGH,* which is a known carcinogen* and a suspected teratogen.*

or

> Our tests showed high levels of **rBGH**,* which is a known **carcinogen** and a suspected **teratogen**.

Then at the foot of the page, define the convention:

> _____
>
> * Asterisked words are defined in the glossary at the end of the report.

or

> _____
>
> * Bolded words are defined in the glossary at the end of the report.

In a report, the glossary section is placed either before the start of the report, between the table of contents and the summary, or, more commonly, at the end, between the recommendations and references sections. Its contents should be alphabetical and formatted for easy scanning.

Glossary

carcinogen	a chemical cancer-causing agent
rGBH	recombinant bovine growth hormone
teratogen	a chemical birth-defect-causing agent
vitamin A	a vitamin said to be good for eyesight, unfortunately not found in red meat

---

References

See Chapter 9, "References and Citations," for details.

Appendices

Appendices are end sections that contain additional information to which a reader may refer, but which would break up the flow of reading too much: corroborating reports, manufacturer's specifications sheets, MSDS documents, site plans or elevations, extended calculations, and so on. Appendices provide support for your conclusions and prove due diligence.

Use a separate appendix for each item of information. Label the appendices in capital letters, not with numbers. Identify each appendix with its own title so that the separate appendices will appear in the table of contents for the reader to find and refer to:

Appendix A: Detailed Calculation of Stresses on Load Bearing Walls

Place these titles on separate title pages. If the material is less than one page in length, you can place the title at the top of that page.

Do not number the pages in appendices. They are not really part of the report and may already have been paginated by their source—for instance, if you are including a copy of a published journal article, pages of by-laws, or something like that.

See Formal Report Pagination below for more detailed pagination instructions.

The appendices section is the last section of the report, appearing immediately after the references section.

Formal Report Pagination

What makes a formal report formal are the title page, the table of contents, the list of tables and figures, the conclusions and recommendations sections, and so on. These elements are primarily aids to navigation that allow the reader to find information quickly. We call the formal elements up to and including the list of tables and figures the orientation section, or more recently, the navigation section thanks to the influence of the Internet. The elements in it orient the reader as to what the report is about, how it is organized, and where specific information can be found.

Because this orientation section is not part of the report proper, we paginate it differently than the rest of the report, as shown in the sample report below.

All the pages up to the end of the list of tables and figures are paginated in lower-case Roman numerals (i, ii, iii, iv, v, vi, vii, viii, ix, x, etc.). Lower-case Roman page numbers are usually centred at the bottom of the page.

The report proper is paginated in normal Arabic numerals (1, 2, 3, 4, 5, 6, etc.). Arabic page numbers are usually placed in the top right corner of the page, where they are easiest to find when readers thumb through a report looking for specific pages.

Though the title page usually counts in the numbering scheme, it is not paginated; that is, no page number appears on the title page.

The summary will be either page ii, if it comes directly after the title page, or page 1, if it comes directly before the introduction (i.e., after the list of tables and figures).

To paginate different sections of the report differently in MS Word, you'll first have to insert a section break and then create separate headers and footers for each section.

To insert a section break:

1. Place your cursor where you want to insert the break.
2. Go to the Page Layout ribbon.
3. Click on Breaks.
4. Choose Section Breaks Next Page in the scroll-down menu.

To insert a page number with proper headers and footers:

1. Go to the Insert ribbon.
2. Click on the Header (or Footer) icon, centre-right.
3. Select a look from the preformatted headers/footers or click on Edit Header/Footer to create your own look.
4. Put your cursor in Section 2. The bottom status bar indicates what section and page you are on.
5. Double-click on the header or footer to activate it. The Header/Footer ribbon will appear automatically.
6. Click on the Link to Previous icon in the Header & Footer Tools ribbon to deactivate this feature.
7. Then click on the Page Number icon to customize the page numbers in both sections.

If you don't deactivate the Link to Previous feature, whatever change you make in one section will be mirrored in the other.

The following pages contain an investigation report written by a student on an industry project. Names and some of the details have been changed to maintain privacy and confidentiality.

This is a formal letter of transmittal with proper letter format to honour the occasion.

102 - 57 Glenlyon Court
Burnaby, BC V57 4M2

April 23, 2012

Mr. John Michael, EIT
NorthWest Consultants Limited
215 - 5590 Franklin Avenue
Yellowknife, NT   X1A 4E6

**Submission of Final Report on the Redesign of a Steel Spreader Bar
and Its Detail Connections**

Dear Mr. Michael:

Report purpose

I am pleased to present my project report for the redesign of a steel spreader bar and its detail connections for the Deh Cho Bridge Project in the Northwest Territories.

Main findings and conclusions of the report

I redesigned a spreader bar using different types of hollow structural sections (HSS): square, rectangular, and round. The beam members determined for the redesign consist of HSS 305x305x13, HSS 356x254x13, and HSS 324x13. Through performance and cost analysis, I determined that the round HSS member is most efficient for this project. However, I produced shop drawings for the square member since site conditions favour flat surfaces.

Comments on the report or process not appropriate in the report itself

During the spreader beam design, I gained insight on approaching new projects. For instance, free-body diagrams should be drawn from the start to clarify the design. Moreover, I learned steel detailing for connections and fabrication drawings. I have also become more familiar with the *Handbook of Steel Construction* due to the design calculations.

Thanks and acknowledgments

Thank you and my advisor, Martin Bollo, for the time and willingness to guide me through the design of this project, and to Pamela Barbarosa, my project advisor, who explained connection calculations with examples used in practice. I would also like to thank Jim Billiken for allowing me to work with NorthWest. Please feel free to contact me at ibs.monika09@gmail.com or at 604.603.1597 for further information.

Standard friendly close: an offer to help interpret the report or answer any questions and, often, an expression of gratitude for the opportunity to have worked on the project.

Sincerely,

Monika Ibsen
Monika Ibsen

cc: Martin Bollo, Project Advisor
     Projects Committee
     Deanna Levis, Communication Instructor

Normally, of course, letters have enclosures, but if the report wasn't enclosed in an envelope, it was, in fact, an attachment.

attachment: project report

Source: Monika Ip, Department of Civil Engineering, British Columbia Institute of Technology.

12-16

REDESIGN OF A STEEL SPREADER BAR & ITS DETAIL CONNECTIONS

Photo by Michael Owen. Used with permission.

Prepared For
John Michael, EIT, NorthWest Consultants Limited
Projects Committee, Department of Civil Engineering, BCIT
Martin Bollo, Department of Civil Engineering, BCIT
Deanna Levis, Communication Instructor, BCIT

Prepared By
Monika Ibsen
Submitted on April 23, 2012

Department of Civil Engineering
British Columbia Institute of Technology
Burnaby, BC

A large clear title, the project identification number, and a relevant photo all help with the filing, retrieval, and instant recognition of the report content.

Title pages must also identify the authors, audience, and date of submission.

Note that the title page is not paginated; title pages never are.

Legal disclaimer page. This report does not have offer acknowledgments because those have already been covered in the letter of transmittal and aren't required in the report for legal reasons.

DISCLAIMER

The work represented in this client report is the result of a student project at the British Columbia Institute of Technology. Any analysis or solution presented in this report must be reviewed by a professional engineer before implementation. While the student's performance in the completion of this report may have been reviewed by a faculty advisor, such review and any advice obtained therefrom does not constitute professional certification of the work. This report is made available without any representation as to its use in any particular situation and on the strict understanding that each reader accepts full liability for the application of its contents.

In addition:
- All design calculations for the spreader bar were referenced from the Handbook of Steel Construction.
- My sponsor provided drawings of truss No. 23 and specifications for Crosby Bolt Type Shackles. (Refer to Appendix B.)

Note that the orientation section that precedes the report itself is paginated in lower-case Roman numerals at the bottom of the page. In this case, the title page has been counted. You could elect not to and start the numbering here at page i.

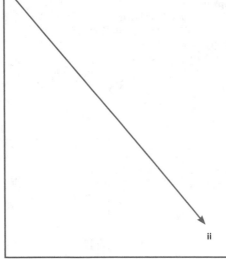

ii

SUMMARY

In response to a request by NorthWest Consultants Ltd., I have redesigned the steel spreader to hoist Truss Segment 23 of the Deh Cho Bridge in the Northwest Territories. The purpose of the project was to determine which shape of spreader bar was most efficient and to produce working drawings for it: round, square, or rectangular hollow structural sections (HSS).

Working for a safety factor of at least three, the following dimensions are required for the spreader to bear the load of Truss Segment 23. They are listed in order from least to most expensive (most to least efficient):

- HSS 324x13 (round) $1,894.86
- HSS 305x305x13 (square) $1,975.69
- HSS 356x254x13 (rectangular) $1,984.54

Although the round member is marginally more economical, site conditions and ease of reuse favour flat surfaces. Therefore, I chose to perform detail connection design on the square beam. I also created both a fabrication drawing and a general arrangement drawing for the square spreader (Appendix E). The fabrication drawing contains only piece information, while the general arrangement drawing outlines the spreader bar set up to the crane above and truss below it.

Purpose and authorization of the report and enough context to identify the writing situation.

The chief findings of the investigation. The drawings would be called a deliverable, rather than a finding.

The decision to work up drawings for the square HSS spreader instead of the round one functions as a recommendation.

This summary is approximately 200 words for a report of about 2,000 words.

This is a standard table of contents. Note the tab leaders to make it easier for the reader's eye to get from the end of the heading to the correct page number.

Large AutoCAD drawings clearly aren't part of the report body and belong in appendices. Appendices should not be paginated for a number of reasons: they are tabbed, so they don't need numbers; some appendices have page numbers of their own (such as copies of articles or other reports) or cannot be paginated (such as glossy brochures or manufacturer's specifications).

REDESIGN OF A STEEL SPREADER BAR & ITS DETAIL CONNECTIONS   12-16

TABLE OF CONTENTS

LIST OF TABLES AND FIGURES

TABLES

FIGURES

The header usually carries project identification information as well as the page number. In this case, the organization's format prefers the project identification code in the top-right margin; the page number appears in the bottom-right. Note the switch to Arabic numerals for the report body.

Purpose/authorization: this is an industry project carried out by a student for her sponsor.

Context: this section clearly establishes how the report fits into the conduct of NorthWest's business. NorthWest wants to find efficiencies in one part of its operations in the building of the Deh Cho Bridge.

Methodology/ organization: in this case, the report is organized in the sequence of the bulleted list, which also states very clearly the purposes of the report.

1.0 INTRODUCTION

This industry project involved the redesign of a steel spreader bar and its detail connections and was prepared for John Michael, EIT, at NorthWest Consultants Limited.

NorthWest is providing engineering services for the Deh Cho Bridge Project located on Yellowknife Highway No. 3 by Fort Providence, Northwest Territories. The cable-stayed bridge will span approximately 1 kilometre across the MacKenzie River.

The bridge deck will sit on an assembly of steel truss segments, varying from 15 metres to 27 metres in length. After fabrication, the trusses are to be shipped vertically by train to the Hay River Rail Yard. Once there, two mobile cranes each use a spreader bar, composed of two steel channels, bolted back to back, to hoist the truss and place it horizontally on a flat-bed truck (Figure 1). The truck then transports the truss to the Deh Cho Bridge site. Thus, the loading and transport of truss segments is one aspect of the Deh Cho Bridge Project for NorthWest Consultants.

NorthWest wanted to compare the performance and material cost of alternative spreader bar designs using round, rectangular, and square hollow structural sections.

Figure 1: Photo of a spreader bar and truss segment at the Hay River rail yard, NWT
(Photo by Michael Owen. Used with permission.)

There were three major objectives for this project:

- Redesign a steel spreader bar using round, rectangular, and square hollow structural sections
- Compare performance and cost of different HSS members
- Prepare shop drawings for fabrication and general arrangement.

2.0   SPREADER BAR DESIGN PROCESS

The design of this project is based on loading from Deh Cho Bridge truss segment No. 23, which is referenced in Appendix A. As shown in Figure 2, the truss has two pick points that are each rigged to slings attached to the lifting lugs.

The reader is referred to the graphic in the preceding text.

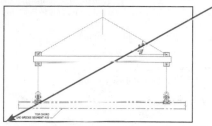

Figure 2: Profile of a spreader bar configuration (Ibsen, 2012)

The writer has chosen to credit herself for creating the graphic. This is unnecessary, but not inappropriate. It is generally assumed that if no credit is given, the report writer created the graphic.

The spreader bar has a sling attached to a shackle at the top of a lifting lug to the crane shackle at a 30° angle, minimum. And, as the spreader bar is symmetrical, the bar's components are equally spaced from the centre line.

The design process is broken down into four sections: loading, crane attachments, HSS beam sizing, and detail connection design.

Note the mini-introductions to the subsections.

2.1 Loading

Figure 3 shows a design sketch of the forces acting on the HSS beam.

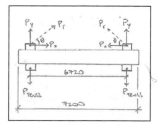

Figure 3: Design sketch showing spreader bar loading summary (Ibsen, 2012)

The calculations are included in appendices, should the reader wish to check on them or verify them. This, too, proves due diligence and builds confidence in the report's findings.

Note the detailed description of the writer's methodical approach to achieving the project purpose. This proves due diligence and allows the reader to follow along to verify that everything was done correctly.

Using the principles of statics, I determined all the loads acting on the spreader bar (refer to Appendix B). Loads on one end of the beam are equivalent to the other end due to truss symmetry. The vertical force Py counteracts Ptruss acting downwards on the spreader bar, thus Py is equal to Ptruss. I then determined the horizontal forces Px. The resultant load Pr, caused by the angle from the lifting lug to the crane shackle, was also calculated.

By calculating forces Px and Pr with an angle of 30°, I found that the reaction forces determined are maximums. When using maximum loads to determine other components of the spreader bar, the results produce ultimate values, which will be compared to resistance values. Therefore, the arrangement in Figure 2 is conservative.

2.2   Crane Attachments: Shackles & Slings

In addition to designing the spreader bar, I sized the shackles and slings used to connect the bar to the crane at the top and truss at the bottom in Appendix B.

With the slings at an angle of 30° upwards from the horizontal, I considered several factors to size the shackles on the lifting lug:

- Work Safe BC Clause 15.6(1) states that 20 per cent of the breaking strength, or resultant angled load, is the working load limit (WLL) of the shackle.
- Crosby Bolt Type Shackles specification states that minimum ultimate strength is six times the working load limit.
- Factor of safety is limited to a minimum of 3 for the whole project.

I compared the working load limit of failure to the shackle working load limits. The failure load is resultant load, or breaking strength, in tons. Then, I chose a 2-1/2" shackle since it has a reasonable strength over the failure load. I also calculated the factor of safety by multiplying six into the specification WLL, and divided that value by the breaking strength. The resulting safety factor exceeded 3; therefore, the 2-1/2" shackle is sufficient.

For the sling's connecting the spreader bar to the crane, I decided to use Surelift wire rope by Wire Rope Industries. By comparing the failure load of the spreader bar, with the safety factor included, to the wire rope's breaking strength, I chose a 63 mm diameter 6x41 EIPS IWRC wire rope. I considered Work Safe BC Clause 15.34, which reduces the WLL of slings with angles 45° to 60° from the vertical. This increases the safety factor to 5. Moreover, I checked that the wire rope would have acceptable space through the shackle after taking into account the lug plate.

2.3   HSS Beam Sizing

I designed three types of HSS beams for the spreader bar using the *Handbook of Steel Construction*: square, rectangular, and round (refer to Appendix C). First, I determined minimum edge distances from shackle bolt centre to a sheared edge and to a cut edge as per Clause 22.3.2; these dimensions governed the lifting lug plate size and moment acting between the beam centre and bolt centre. I then used the largest HSS size in the Handbook to calculate factored moment, Mf, for the beam members,

Page 3

and I found minimum moment resistance by multiplying Mf by the safety factor. Next, I classified the members to determine the moment resistance, Mr, as per Section 13.5. In addition, I compared the resulting moment resistance to the minimum, and I sized down to check if smaller members were possible.

As per Clause 13.8.3, I calculated the capacity of a beam member as a beam-column, which resists bending moments and axial compressive forces. Reviewing cross-sectional strength is not considered since the spreader bar is unbraced. I checked that overall member strength and lateral torsional buckling strength met the code. However, the beams did not satisfy the safety factor even though they met the code requirements.

For the beams to meet safety criteria, I modified the angle of slings from 30° to 45°. Generally, slings are angled at 45° or greater for contractor comfort or possible errors in rigging on site. The increased angle reduces the forces acting on the spreader bar. Consequently, I found the reduction ratio of the changed angle and multiplied that by the governing beam-column strength before I took the inverse of the product. The inverse outcome is the factor of safety, which is met for all the chosen beams using 45° slings.

After meeting all revised requirements, the HSS members used for the spreader beam are

- HSS 305 x 305 x 13 (square)
- HSS 356 x 254 x 13 (rectangular)
- HSS 324 x 13 (round).

2.4 Detail Connection Design

Calculations were completed for the connections between the shackle and lifting lugs and between the lifting lugs and the spreader bar in Appendix D:

- Shear along the area between the length of the lug plate and beam
- Shear at the shackle hole tearing through the plate (block tear-out)
- Bearing in plate for force applied at the shackle hole
- Shear along the weld between the length of the plate and beam.

The first three considerations of the above list meet safety requirements. However, the shear along the weld does not meet the required safety factor. I am assuming that by combining the shear along the weld and the bearing against the plate width (not determined), the safety factor is met.

The lug plate is 50 mm wide and the shackle has an opening of 105 mm. I added boss plates on each side of the lug plate where the shackle bolt is located to act as spacers.

Welds between the perimeter of the plate and beam are 10 mm E49XX. And, since the boss plate does not take any loading, welds between the perimeter of the boss plate and lug plate are 6 mm E49XX.

Note again how the topics are introduced and then detailed in the order in which they were introduced. Always try to signpost your report organization to your readers. It helps them to keep track of the discussion.

3.0   COMPARISON OF HSS TYPES

To evaluate member efficiency, I compared the square, rectangular, and round HSS beams selected. Table 1 shows beam values for area, volume, and mass.

Table 1: Beam comparison of HSS types

Pipe	Square HSS 305 x 305 x 13	Rectangular HSS 356 x 254 x 13	Round HSS 324 x 13
Length (mm)	7,200	7,200	7,200
Surface Area (mm2)	14,400	14,400	12,400
Volume (m3)	0.10368	0.10368	0.08928
Mass (kg)	797	797	687

Tables, like other graphics, should be introduced in the preceding text. Table titles are properly placed above the table, where they are closer to the column headers, making it quicker for readers to understand the table's architecture.

The data for the square and rectangular beams are the same since their cross-sectional area is equal. The round beam has a smaller area, which means this beam uses approximately 14 per cent less steel. Therefore, the performance of the round beam is most efficient.

I also completed a brief cost analysis between the members by referring to 2011 National Construction Estimator. Table 2 presents costs for material, labour, and equipment based on unit prices per ton (p. 383).

Table 2: Cost analysis of HSS types

Pipe	Square HSS 305 x 305 x 13	Rectangular HSS 356 x 254 x 13	Round HSS 324 x 13
American Ton (1 ton = 900 kg)	0.885	0.885	0.764
Material Cost ($)	1,584.45	1,593.30	1,489.31
Labour Cost ($)	269.09	269.09	278.77
Equipment Cost ($)	122.15	122.15	126.78
Total Cost	$1,975.69	$1,984.54	$1,894.86

Table 2 shows that the rectangular beam costs the most, then the square beam, while the round member costs the least. The cost difference between the square and rectangular beams is minimal. However, the change in cost between the round and the square members is 4.3 per cent. Moreover, the percentage difference in cost between the round and the rectangular members is 4.7 per cent. As a result, the round beam provides minimal cost to support the spreader bar loads.

Page 5

4.0   SHOP DRAWINGS

I prepared fabrication and general arrangement drawings for the square HSS spreader bar using AutoCAD 2012. Due to site conditions and the common reuse of spreader bars, I produced drawings for the square beam instead of the round HSS (refer to Appendix E). I did not prepare drawings for the rectangular as the square member costs less to fabricate.

4.1   Fabrication Drawing

The fabrication drawing contains only the information necessary for the spreader bar to be manufactured. All components are located in a "Bill of Materials" labeled Shop Drawing S01 in Appendix E. Shackles were not included because they will be installed by the contractor on site.

4.2   General Arrangement Drawing

Consultants produce general arrangement drawings for the contractor to provide an overview of the design and to guide installation of miscellaneous pieces to fabricated products.

Refer to Appendix E for the spreader bar drawing to view overall design and details. Figure 4 includes shackle placement on the lifting lug plates that are not drawn for the fabrication drawings.

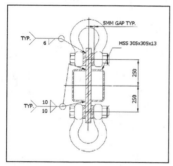

Figure 4: Spreader bar section at lifting lug (Ibsen, 2012)

The section above shows the contractor the locations of shackles. While one side is flush between the boss plate and shackle interior, the other side has a 5 mm gap to ensure ease of shackle installation.

This report does not have a series of conclusions, nor a series of recommendations, so the writer chose to create a "Conclusion" section.

This conclusion forms an end-summary of what the writer considers most important in the report. Conclusions and recommendations sections don't have length limits, unlike the summary, though writers need to work within reason.

The idea is that readers will read the summary; if that doesn't provide enough information, they will read the concluding section(s). If, after reading the concluding section(s), there's still something specific they wonder about, they will look it up in specific sections of the report and in very precise detail.

In effect, then, formal reports present the same information in three levels of detail: a highly condensed summary, a condensed conclusion, and a highly detailed report.

REDESIGN OF A STEEL SPREADER BAR & ITS DETAIL CONNECTIONS   12-16

5.0   CONCLUSION

To be conservative while redesigning the spreader bar for Deh Cho Bridge Truss Segment 23, I determined forces acting on the spreader bar at a 30° angle. I also determined the size of shackles and slings attaching the beam to the crane and truss by comparing the working load limit of the shackles and slings to the ultimate strength of the beam. Loading on the spreader bar specified that 2-1/2" shackles and 63 mm wire rope be used.

After determining compression and bending moments of the spreader bar, I found the capacity of the beam to act as a beam-column as per Clause 13.8.3 in the Handbook of Steel Construction. The resulting safety factor for all beams did not meet the safety factor of 3 with an angle of 30°. However, due to contractor safety, sling angles are usually 45° from the horizontal. I changed my design angle from 30° to 45,° which increased the safety factors of the beams I selected to exceed 3 and satisfy requirements.

I have provided a detail connection design for a square HSS beam. I considered the following to obtain a 10 mm weld, E49XX around the lug plate of dimensions 720 mm x 305 mm x 50 mm:

- Bearing in plate for force applied at the shackle hole
- Shear at the shackle hole tearing through the plate (block tear-out)
- Shear along the area between the length of the lug plate and beam
- Shear along the weld between the length of the plate and beam.

I included boss plates to act as spacers around the area where the shackle bolt would pass through the lifting lug. This provides support to the shackle to stop any movement when airborne.

By comparing the cross-sectional areas of the different types of HSS selected, I determined that round HSS was most efficient in performance and cost, then the square HSS, and finally the rectangular HSS. However, square members are preferred for this project due to ease of reuse, so I prepared fabrication and general arrangement shop drawings (Appendix E) for the square spreader, not the round.

Page 7

REDESIGN OF A STEEL SPREADER BAR & ITS DETAIL CONNECTIONS 12-16

REFERENCES

Cal Pacific Estimators. (2010). *2011 National Construction Estimator* (59th ed.). Carlsbad, California: Craftsman Book Company.

Canadian Institute of Steel Construction. (2011). *Handbook of Steel Construction* (10th ed.). Mississauga, Ontario: Canadian Standards Association.

Northwest Territories Transportation. (2011). Retrieved November 19, 2011, from The Deh Cho Bridge Project: http://www.dehchobridge.info/index.html

Steel Tube Institute of North America. (2012). *Hollow Structural Sections: Dimensions & Section Properties*. Retrieved April 2, 2012, from HSS Steel Tubing: http://www.hss-steeltubing.org/pdf/brochures/dimension_brochure.pdf

Wire Rope Industries. (2012). *Performance Series 630 Specifications*. Retrieved March 17, 2012, from Cranes – Overhead: http://wirerope.com/PDF/surelift_ps_630.pdf

WorkSafe BC. (2012). Part 15 Rigging. Retrieved February 25, 2012, from WorkSafeBC.com: http://www2.worksafebc.com/Publications/OHSRegulation/Part15.asp

Formal Report Checklist

Formatting

☐ Does the title page clearly identify the report?

☐ Is the summary on its own page?

☐ Is everything up to and including the list of tables and figures (except for the title page) paginated in lower-case Roman numerals?

☐ Is the report paginated in standard Arabic numerals?

☐ Do the page numbers stop at the end of the report; that is, are the appendices left unpaginated?

☐ Does every appendix start on a new page with a title?

Content

☐ Does the introduction describe how the report came to be written, what the purpose of the report is, and how the report is organized or how the writer went about finding the information for the report (background, purpose/scope, methodology/organization)?

☐ Does the introduction absolutely not contain any of the information that was discovered during the information-gathering or research phase of the report; that is, does the introduction not contain any findings, any conclusions, any opinions?

☐ Does the conclusions section bring together ALL the relevant facts and findings from the report in one convenient, accessible location, but does it exclude any recommendations or opinions based on those findings?

☐ Does the recommendations section convey the writer's opinions about a course of action that the reader should take and are these recommendations clearly based on the conclusions in the previous section?

☐ Does the summary bring together the most important information from the introduction, conclusions, and recommendations, faithfully reflecting the importance and weighting of the report? The summary should add a brief statement about the research methodology or report organization.

Exercises: Formal Reports

Exercise 7.1: Formal Reports in Professional Settings

Research online or discuss with engineers in the field the situations that require formal, as opposed to informal, reports in technical environments. Bring your findings to the class and present or discuss them.

Exercise 7.2: The Function of Formal Formatting

Consider and discuss the following, either as a class or in groups, and then report your findings to the class:

1. When faced with a report 100 pages long or more, how would you go about finding specific information? How would you go about getting the gist of the report, an overview? How would you refer colleagues to specific information in or specific parts of the report? What features of formal report formatting help you to do all these things?
2. Assume that you have been tasked with shortlisting three proposals from a total of 10 that have been submitted in response to a request for proposals (RFP) that your firm has issued. Each proposal is several hundred pages long and you have about a week—and of course you also have all your usual duties to attend to and you have to keep up with your daily emails from colleagues. What features of the formal report format would help you to make your selection? What importance would writing style (clarity and conciseness, for instance) play in your decision?

Exercise 7.3: Writing a Formal Report

Your instructor will ask you to write a report of a type described in Chapter 6 and submit it as a formal report. Alternatively, your instructor may ask you to research a technique, innovation, piece of equipment, a legal or environmental requirement, a historical development, or a similar topic in your field and submit it as a formal report. You may also be asked to do an oral presentation on your topic so that your classmates can benefit from your research.

Chapter 8

Intercultural Communication, Collaborative Writing, and Document Control

In this chapter you will learn

- how the workplace and documentation requirements are changing as a result of technology and globalization
- how to communicate with greater consideration for the needs of non-native speakers of English
- how to work collaboratively on longer documentation
- how to keep track of documentation when multiple people are working on it simultaneously.

It's a given that you will work in an increasingly multicultural environment and that you will increasingly be working in teams. These two happenstances require special consideration in the creation of effective technical communication.

Intercultural Communication

Canada is becoming increasingly multicultural, and so, quite naturally, is the Canadian workplace. In addition, of course, the economy is becoming increasingly global because technology enables increasing international trade, cooperation, and interaction. This is a boon to efficiency and innovation, as worldwide resources can be brought to bear on the many issues facing humanity. However, communicating in this environment requires a certain finesse. Luckily, as Canada's most multicultural generation ever, you have a bit of a head start.

Write for Translatability

Your first advantage is that you already speak English, which is rapidly becoming the common language of the business world. English is not the world's most spoken language. That would be Mandarin. But English is the world's most frequently adopted second language and the most widespread and has become the language of choice for the world's business and scientific communities. When Chinese and Latin American business people meet, for example, they are quite likely to negotiate in English. Symposia and conferences around the world are held in English to encourage international participation. Some universities in non-English-speaking countries are adopting English as the language of instruction. The idea is to steep students in the language they will increasingly use in the workplace and to attract more foreign students and thereby help with the cross-pollination of ideas, the growth of intercultural understanding, and the development of international connections.

Some continental European businesses use English as their at-work language because their workforce is so international. For the same reason, cross-border projects and collaborations in European countries are often conducted in English, even if English isn't the official language within either border.

It's an exciting time. And, as stated before, you have the advantage of already being fluent in the language that others are struggling to master. However, with that advantage comes some responsibility. You need to be aware that much of the material you produce will be read by people who do not speak English as a first language, perhaps even within your own firm. You may be submitting bids internationally, writing reports that will be made available internationally, or creating documentation that people abroad will use without the benefit of translation. Technology is changing so quickly that the delay imposed by formal translation and reprinting processes would handicap foreign adopters. Programming languages generally use English in the command structure. Books written on those programming languages will generally be written in English and read in English by programmers all around the world. Scientific and engineering journals and texts are increasingly written and read exclusively in English. The list is almost inexhaustible.

So much for the pep talk and moral harangue. Let's take a look at some practical tips.

Write Simply

The first injunctions of this textbook—to write as simply as possible, to write concisely and concretely, to focus on real subjects and real verbs, and to use the simplest words to express what you mean (chapters 1, 2, and 3)—are a good first step to helping non-native speakers of English understand your writing.

If you've ever attempted to learn another language, you will be keenly aware that erudite vocabulary (look it up to get the point) and complex sentence structures can confuse. In fact, they may even confuse native speakers.

Write Unidiomatically

Another injunction is not to use culturally dependent expressions. An idiom is a phrase whose meaning cannot be derived from the meaning of the words. An idiomatic expression relies on cultural freight and common usage to make sense, severely handicapping those who haven't grown up in the culture. For example, just what does "and Bob's your uncle" mean? How likely are readers in New Delhi, Shanghai, or Helsinki to have an uncle named Bob? How would they be helped if they did?

So, when you write, try to avoid untranslatable expressions, a few examples of which are listed below.

REPLACE	WITH
Run it up the flagpole and see who salutes.	Let's suggest it to them and find out what they think.
above board	legal, nothing hidden, honest
Is this your bottom line?	Is this your final offer?
Please just cut to the chase.	Please state your point.
The early bird gets the worm.	We might be more successful if we submit/apply/ enter the market soon/first/early.
The squeaky wheel gets the grease.	If we complain/explain/speak up, we might succeed/get a positive response.
where the rubber meets the road	in a practical application
Here's my two cents' worth.	In my (humble) opinion
A bird in the hand (is worth two in the bush)	It's better to secure a smaller gain or advantage than to take a large risk for a potentially bigger gain, but end up with nothing.
blowing smoke	deceiving
elbow grease	effort
I have seen the light.	I've been persuaded.
I don't have the bandwidth for that right now.	I'm too busy/don't have time for that right now.

Write Politely

This tip is more relevant in correspondence than in reports. North Americans are notoriously informal and direct. We immediately get on a first-name basis, even between people with considerable differences in age, social position, or company rank. In some countries, on the other hand, you might work side by side with someone for years and never know his or her first name.

In Canada, even junior people feel free to question people in authority, to offer suggestions, and to speak up at meetings, albeit politely and respectfully. Other cultures would view an underling who dared to question a superior or to raise a doubt about a manager's idea as shockingly aggressive and a threat to company cohesion (1).

So, when you send correspondence abroad, understand that most cultures are more formal than ours and that directness may be translated as abruptness and rudeness and that a friendly first-name salutation may be seen as disrespectful. Find out something about the norms of the culture of the person with whom you are corresponding.

In fact, if your firm has a major client or expects to do business in a specific country, it may well engage someone to teach you how to behave and communicate appropriately. There's quite an industry in books and courses to teach people how to behave in other cultures. Do some research.

If you are responding to an email from abroad, take note of the tone, particularly the formality of address. Try to mirror it, to some extent, in your response. In fact, do that if you receive an email from within Canada as well. This is the sort of basic inter personal skill that will also work well interculturally.

As a first step, however, when corresponding with someone from another culture, put your best foot forward. Be more polite, respectful, and formal than you might normally be. Then, try to find someone within your organization who is from or has knowledge of that culture and ask that person to read your draft. Someone with cultural knowledge will be able to help you set a proper tone and prevent giving offence unintentionally (1).

Practise Mindfulness, Openness, and Engagement

A few pages ago we mentioned your mastery of English as your first advantage in a globalizing world. Your second advantage is that you are part of Canada's most multicultural generation ever. Never before have we had so many cultures mingling, heard so many languages, worked and played with so many different peoples. In a sense, and without wanting to applaud ourselves too much or ignore problems that still exist, Canada is a model of what the world is becoming. And you've experienced it first-hand. You have grown more comfortable with difference, more tolerant of otherness, and more accepting of the changing face of society than previous generations.

We make this work in Canada because of our traditional virtues of politeness, openness, inclusiveness, and tolerance. This is not to say that our history is unblemished by their opposites. But your generation more than any other embraces these values and has made them work for a larger and larger proportion of our cultural mosaic.

Going forward, you must continue to be mindful of and actively curious about other cultures and other ways of viewing and doing things (2), as well as attuned to personal differences. It's really a matter of listening properly.

For instance, let's say you are having a discussion about a technical problem with your project team and you suggest a solution. Others may disagree with you, which is actually a good thing; you should always encourage refinements on solutions. But there are a number of different approaches that they might take.

One person might say, for example, "Oh, there's no way that'll ever work!" This person obviously has a rather direct manner of speaking, either because of a family history or cultural predilection. It's the sort of utterance more common in Australia perhaps than in, say, Japan. It doesn't mean that the intention is to insult. It may only sound that way to those used to and expecting greater circumspection.

Another might say, "That sounds pretty good, [insert your name here], but I'm wondering whether you've considered that [insert technical qualification here]." This would probably be the ideal response in a Canadian milieu: polite and encouraging without being overly reticent.

Yet another person might simply knit their eyebrows and say something mild like, "Hmm."

In all three cases, they are saying exactly the same thing; they don't feel that your suggested solution will work, at least not without some changes. The proper response in all three cases is, "Okay, so what would you suggest?"

Your job, in the first example, is not to take insult and not to let the situation get personal. In the last example, your job is, in the first place, to listen (and look) carefully for such mild responses and to acknowledge them: "[insert person's name], you looked a little puzzled just now. What are your thoughts about the suggestion?"

Understand that different people and different cultures have different communication styles, and assume in the first instance that people are trying to work towards the same goal as you and intend no disrespect. Don't judge utterances (or written communication) by their style, but try to divine the intended meaning. React calmly to those who seem to communicate more flamboyantly than you do; pay close attention to those who communicate more mildly.

It's always your job to take note of these differences and work within them to draw out the best in everyone. This is a hallmark of leadership. Anyone can give orders; that's a boss. A leader brings out the best in people and helps them to achieve their potential. Unfortunately, it's not within the purview of this textbook to delve into leadership skills. It is, however, something you will want to pay attention to in your career.

By the way, the above is not to suggest that you should put up with genuinely rude behaviour or bullying.

Writing in Teams

Large documentation projects often require teams of writers because of the sheer volume of work and the need to provide specialized knowledge. However, writing teams can easily descend into chaos and recriminations. For one thing, each team member may have his or her own writing style and tone, but the final document has to have a single voice; for another, information and files have to be shared back and forth, but if the team isn't disciplined about version control, this sharing can lead to confusion, duplication, and rework.

The following procedure will explain how to work in teams with the greatest efficiency and the least personal friction.

IN THE FIELD

Intercultural Communication in Practice

A Canadian engineering firm that had ordered measuring instruments from a German supplier received a letter reminding the Canadian firm that they had not settled the account within 30 days and that their supplier was now free to consider legal action. The letter's officious tone caused some consternation here in Canada; the Canadians felt insulted. Once tempers calmed, someone wrote a polite letter explaining that the Canadian firm had every intention of paying, but that it is customary in North America to allow up to 90 days for payment, though a modest interest charge was appropriate after 30 days, if agreed to beforehand. The Germans wrote back, though still in formal and somewhat curt language, stating that 90 days would be fine.

Obviously, no insult had been intended. Such a reminder letter, stating that full recourse to the law was allowable, was simply the way this German company did business. They considered it a standard reminder letter, no insult intended and no grudge held. Both sides wanted to continue the business relationship but had approached the situation through different norms. The situation was salvaged by clear and polite communication of expectations, made possible because, in the end, both parties were able to make cultural allowances.[1]

---

1 This example comes from the author's personal experience.

GROUP WRITING PROCESS	ACCOMPANYING PRESENTATION
1. Plan the report.	1. Plan the presentation.
2. Assign tasks and set timelines.	2. Decide who presents on what.
3. Select arbiters.	
4. Agree on format and style.	
5. Create performance contracts.	
6. Write draft sections.	3. Create speech notes and visuals.
7. Edit draft sections.	4. Prepare to answer questions.
8. Combine sections and perform final edit.	5. Practise delivery.
9. Submit the report.	6. Deliver the presentation.
10. Debrief. ◄———	

FIGURE 8.1 **Group writing procedure.** The steps are described in greater detail below. The procedure on the right is a concurrent procedure if the report is to be accompanied by a presentation, as is often the case.

1. Plan the Report

The planning of documents, through the stages of purpose and audience analysis, content selection, and sequencing, has been covered in chapters 1, 6, and 7. If you are writing an instruction or procedure document, please refer to chapters 12 and 13 as well. This part is the same, whether you are writing alone or with a team. When with a team, you just have to get everyone to agree.

2. Assign Tasks and Set Timelines

Once you have a list of sections and an idea of their relative lengths, assign specific sections and tasks to individuals in the group based on interest and expertise. Be sure to assign an equal workload for everyone, taking into account, for instance, that one person will have responsibility for the final edit and should perhaps enjoy a lighter workload at the beginning.

Set realistic timelines, working backward from the deadline. It's usually a good idea to give yourself a team deadline several days ahead of the formal deadline, to allow some time for contingencies. Build in sufficient time for research, graphics creation, and the editing stages.

If the report is accompanied by a presentation, it's most likely that individuals will present on the section that they've written, assuming it's a group presentation. Be sure to factor in sufficient time for the concurrent requirements of the presentation, including time for practising your delivery.

3. Select Arbiters

Group work, with group consultation, is efficient and improves results only as long as the group can agree or, if there is a failure to agree, as long as the group has a process for making final decisions. This can be either by vote or, much more likely, by deferring to an arbiter, such as a final editor, final layout designer, or the team lead, depending on the issue.

Often the final editor is the team lead, the person ultimately responsible for presenting the report and the person with the most experience writing such reports. Sometimes, while the team lead retains final authority on report content and the like, a separate final editor is assigned to decide on matters of wording and style. Yet another person may be assigned responsibility for the final look of the document, the formatting. Always give ultimate responsibility, and hence authority, to people best able to do the job.

The purpose of assigning final authority for such decisions is not to introduce hierarchy into a group, but to limit debate and argument. Assuming the arbiters chosen are reasonable and competent, they will listen to the opinions of group members and then make a reasonable decision. Once that decision is made, the debate ends and everyone gets on with the next task. This prevents deadlock and endless debate, which is the bane of committee work.

So, if you really like your phrasing but the final editor decides to change it, just shrug it off. It's not that important. Let it go for the sake of team cohesion, and assume that the arbiter has been chosen because he or she is qualified. Also, if you're writing a, say, 30-page report for your class or a 300-page proposal for your organization, compromising on a single phrase or a single formatting decision probably won't make or break your submission.

4. Agree on Format and Style

To prevent rework during the editing process, it's best to agree on how the report should look and sound before people start writing their first drafts. Often organizations will have a corporate style guide and use report templates to make their documentation consistent and consistently professional. In a school project, you may have to decide on these things for yourselves. Consider the following:

1. **Formatting**. Choose one of Word's default style groups or create your own. Decide on whether to number the headings, what sort of numbering system to use for the report graphics, what sort of bullets to use, and the like. While formatting can be changed fairly quickly in the final editing stages, it's a fussy detail that the final editor shouldn't have to worry about. It adds unnecessary work and distraction.

   You'll also want to decide whether to work in colour or black and white, depending on what you know about the final output.

2. **Wording and mechanics**. Decide on the level of formality required of the document and on whether to stray from the Canadian dictionary, something you would do only if the report were destined for the US market, for instance.

   Furthermore, decide on a reference book that defines the rules of grammar, capitalization, hyphenation, when to use numerals or words for numbers, whether to use decimals or fractions, and the like. That way you will all submit mechanically consistent sections and there's no need for argument or discussion about these conventions at a later stage. Appendix B of this textbook provides some useful guidelines in that regard, but is not exhaustive.

   Also decide on technical terms and references to use consistently and what abbreviations to use for them. For instance, in a request for proposals, decide whether you will consistently refer to the bidders as the contractor, the design builder, the DB contractor, the D/B, or something else. Referring to the same thing in different ways creates confusion.

   Also use the same word for specific actions. For example, if you write "affix" for one part and "screw on" for the second, even though both parts are threaded, the reader may wonder what the difference is.

   Obviously it's difficult to come up with all contingencies at a single meeting. You'll probably have to fine-tune your list as the project proceeds.

3. **Graphics**. Decide whether to use three-dimensional graphics as much as possible—for instance, pie charts and bar graphs—or to make do with two dimensions. Decide whether to use colour graphics or stick with black and white. A document looks odd if the graphics are inconsistent, and it's always harder to make the adjustments later—and unfair to the final editor.

Setting all this up may seem daunting, as it's impossible to anticipate all contingencies and potential points of argument at the outset. This is why organizations set up (or adopt) corporate style guides. Obviously, as things come up, you'll have to make decisions on the fly; having a competent arbiter will speed up that process.

5. Create a Performance Contract

In steps 1 through 4, you've made a lot of decisions. It would be a mistake to rely on everyone's correct recollection of those decisions as the project proceeds. It is always best to record decisions so they can't be contested later, either out of crafty self-interest or genuine misunderstanding.

So set down a detailed list of the group's decisions: document plan, assigned tasks, deadlines, times and dates for future meetings, formatting and style guidelines, and who has been assigned what authority to make final decisions. Do so in a set of meeting minutes, in a full performance contract, or just on the back of an envelope if there is room. The key is to generate the document quickly (generally within 24 hours) and to get everyone to sign it as an acknowledgement that they've read it, agree with its accuracy, and will abide by it.

Often groups object to creating a paper trail. They see it as unnecessary, as a sign of distrust, perhaps even as an insult to their professionalism and good will. It is anything but. A paper trail is a device to ensure that everyone remembers what was decided, has a document for reliable future reference, and has a mediation tool should conflict arise. Consider it an insurance policy that dramatically reduces the chances of a group's cohesion falling apart over silly disagreements about when people thought things were due or about niggling little points of formatting and phrasing. In the former case, it's been recorded in black and white; in the latter, the final arbiter decides and the discussion ends.

This allows everyone to concentrate on what's really important, the success of the project.

6. Write Draft Sections

Try to complete your draft a few days before the stipulated deadline so that you have a bit of time to get away from it and then edit it with a fresh and more detached eye. Writers are often too close to their work right after having written it to see their errors.

7. Edit Draft Sections

Editing draft sections really means peer editing; you are responsible for submitting as good a draft as you are able to create in Stage 6. So hand your draft to someone on your team to give it the once-over to see how what you have written will strike a new, first-time reader. Remember that writing must always be clear on first reading.

The feedback will help you improve your writing, so accept it gracefully.

8. Combine Sections and Do the Final Edit

The final editor will take all the sections and put them into a single file to edit them for consistency and clarity. This editor may also make final layout and formatting adjustments or pass the document on to a different editor for design decisions, depending on what has been decided by the group.

When pasting someone else's file into the master file, it's a good idea to use the Paste Special or Keep Text Only function to insert the text without formatting (in Word, right-click where you want to insert the text; then click on the Keep Text Only paste icon in the pop-up menu). That way you don't end up overwriting the styles and importing a whole bunch of additional, random styles into the master document.

9. Submit the Report

Pay very close attention to the submission requirements because failing to do so could result in your submission being rejected. Aside from the deadline, pay attention to such things as length restrictions, formatting requirements, requirements for supplementary materials or for accompanying submission forms or references, or any other requirement that the receiving company, client, instructor, government body, or what have you has chosen to set.

If the receiving organization requested a PDF and you submit a DOCX file, that could be enough for them to reject your submission, whether it be a competitive bid, an application for university research grants, a government Scientific Research and Experimental Development (SRED) tax exemption, a conference paper, an article for publication in a professional journal, or what have you. This is especially true whenever you submit something in a competitive environment. Adjudicators are always eager to thin the field of applicants by eliminating a few for failure to comply with submission requirements.

In terms of formality and professionalism, consider whether an email submission is good enough or whether you ought to courier over a hard copy—perhaps both. If you intend to courier a printed and bound version of a proposal, for instance, make sure you know precisely how many copies will be required. If the recipients of the report are forced to make their own photocopies, spiral spine and all, those copies will look terrible and present a considerable inconvenience. That will not make you look good.

For your own sake, practise careful version control so you'll always know exactly what version of the project you did submit, for future reference (see the subsequent section).

10. Debrief

Get the group together to discuss what improvements could be made to the process, style guide, or any other part of the project. The time to do so is now, while the project is still fresh in everyone's mind, not three months from now when you're starting the next project.

As always, record your decisions, and adjust your guides and procedure documents to reflect the improvements you've come up with.

Document Sharing and Control

When multiple people work on a report, they have to find a way to keep track of who is making changes to what version and to make sure that people are always working on the latest version, not reworking an older, already corrected file. With group work, different versions of a single document can proliferate very quickly.

No one but the final editor should be able to make changes to the final document that you intend to submit to the instructor or send to the client.

Luckily, technology and some discipline make this possible.

Track Changes Function

When you ask a colleague to look at a draft for you, you can either give that person a hard copy to scribble on and then enter the changes yourself, or you can send that person a file and ask him or her to use the Track Changes and the Comments functions. Figure 8.2 shows how to do so in MS Word, but other word-processing software has the same functions.

Make it absolutely clear, however, that no one but the final editor, the person with the ultimate authority and responsibility, may make changes to a document without using Track Changes. Otherwise, if edits without revision marks introduce errors or vagueness into a report, these errors are unlikely to be caught.

Also, as soon as you open a document to edit, save it under a different name (see Document Version Control below) before you make any changes. This will help keep track of who made what changes to the document.

Document Version Control

Track Changes will keep track of who made what changes, indicating different editors' changes in a different colour and tagging their changes with their initials. However, once those changes have been accepted or rejected, the new edited document is a different document from the initial one. It should have a different file name. This prevents new files from overwriting old files, causing the old files to be lost, and makes it easier to track which is the most up-to-date and authoritative version of a draft. This in turn prevents people from editing or working with an earlier, already corrected version of a document.

Version control really exists in two stages. The first is internal as you go through various versions to create the final release document for the client or instructor. This is

Deleted words are crossed out, inserted words are underlined; both are presented in a different colour, coded to different editors, so more than one editor can comment (consecutively) on a draft.

In the Review ribbon, click on Track Changes to activate the function and on New Comment whenever you want to insert a comment.

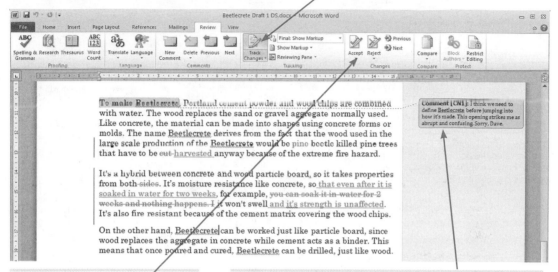

When reviewing an edited document, use these buttons to accept changes or to reject them. Word will either adopt the changes or revert to the original version.

This comment was made by CN on a file created by DS (see file name above ribbon). CN really should have saved this file with a new name (Beetlecrete Draft 2 CN.docx) as soon as he started making changes, to prevent an accidental save under the original name.

FIGURE 8.2 Using Track Changes and Comments to edit a draft. All word processors have these functions; you just have to look for them.

the stage you'll be most concerned with now. In industry, however, you might release different versions of documents to different clients or to the same client as you make ongoing changes, improvements, or customizations to equipment or software that you deliver. This is the second step of version control.

The file-naming convention for version control consists of three parts:

1. **The document name**. In industry you usually use a unique document number; it generally coincides with a project number.

2. **A revision identification**. A revision is a major release. Since you will get to "release" your assignment only once to an instructor, you may omit this part while still in school.

3. **The draft identification**. If you're allowed to work concurrently, you might just identify the person responsible for the changes to the draft with initials. If the changes are consecutive, you'll want to add a draft number.

It's a good idea to include the file name in the footers of the document. That way, even on a hard copy, readers will always know whose draft they are looking at and how recent it is.

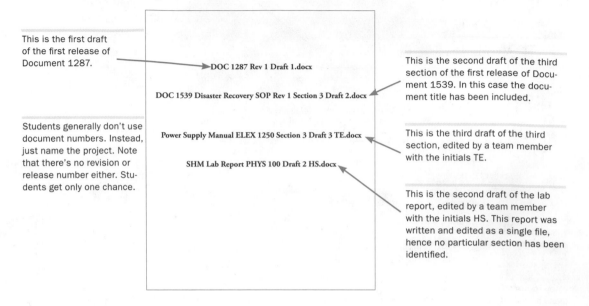

This is the first draft of the first release of Document 1287.

DOC 1287 Rev 1 Draft 1.docx

This is the second draft of the third section of the first release of Document 1539. In this case the document title has been included.

DOC 1539 Disaster Recovery SOP Rev 1 Section 3 Draft 2.docx

Students generally don't use document numbers. Instead, just name the project. Note that there's no revision or release number either. Students get only one chance.

Power Supply Manual ELEX 1250 Section 3 Draft 3 TE.docx

This is the third draft of the third section, edited by a team member with the initials TE.

SHM Lab Report PHYS 100 Draft 2 HS.docx

This is the second draft of the lab report, edited by a team member with the initials HS. This report was written and edited as a single file, hence no particular section has been identified.

Dropbox/OneDrive/Google Docs

A better way to keep track of files and to avoid the hassle of emailing attachments back and forth, each of which becomes a new file floating around and needing to be tracked, is to keep all the project files in a central location, a cloud, accessible by all. Utilities such as Dropbox, OneDrive, and Google Docs offer these services for free.

Dropbox/OneDrive

Dropbox (dropbox.com) and Microsoft's OneDrive permit you to mirror your files on a server. When you save your files on your hard drive, a copy is sent to the server and the server updates these files on all your devices linked to the Dropbox or OneDrive service. That way, instead of moving files about via email or a memory stick, your files are always updated on all your devices. As an added service, they are also securely backed up on the server.

Because this seems magical and is entirely effortless, we call this server and its services the cloud. In the past, the Internet was sometimes referred to as the ether (you may be familiar with "ethernets"), particularly when files went missing.

What makes cloud services interesting to workgroups is that you can make some of your folders public and give the rest of your workgroup access to that folder. This means that everyone works on the same files from one central location, making file sharing and tracking a snap. However, you do have to make absolutely sure that everyone uses the proper file-naming conventions (described above) so that files don't get confused and so that changes don't get lost or overwritten.

Microsoft's 2016 version of Office makes sharing even easier. It features a Share icon in the top right corner of Word. When working on a file you want others to have access to, simply click on this button, select a OneDrive or SharePoint folder into which to save it (the file can't be shared if it isn't in the cloud), and then follow the prompts to permit team members access to the file.

When those team members work on the file, their changes will be recorded using the Track Changes function (see above) and, just as in Google Docs, multiple people can work on the file at the same time; their changes will be made and flagged in real time on everyone else's document and screen. It's a fantastic way to collaborate and, at the time of writing, by far the easiest.

In Dropbox, if two people work on a file simultaneously and save those files, they will generate conflicting copies—unless, of course, they do what they're supposed to and save those files under new names.

Google Docs

Google Docs also offers online storage of files with access to an entire workgroup and allows multiple people to work on a file simultaneously, just like MS Word 2016; they can even use a chat function while doing so.

However, the disadvantage of Google Docs is in formatting and output. At the time of writing, Google's formatting abilities are not yet as sophisticated as those of other word-processing software, so you may be disappointed with the way your document looks, with some navigation features, and with cross-referencing features such as changing section headers, linked references to graphics and the like.

Wikis

Firms are increasingly using Wikis to create not only internal documentation (such as standard operating procedures and company policies), but also documentation made available to clients or the public. Wikis are great ways to collaborate on information and keep it continually up to date.

Wikis offer many document-control functions, such as limiting who is able to make changes, and various administrative functions, such as notifying an email list whenever a page has been updated. Though increasingly used for documents that are to be made widely available, Wikis don't yet (at least at time of writing) do a good job of page layout and document print control. If you are creating a document whose final submission is meant to be printed or printable, you might find yourself cutting and pasting a lot of information into a word-processor file and therefore wishing you'd just worked in the word processor to begin with.

If you do decide that a Wiki is a good medium for your purposes, check out the various free Wiki software packages available online.

Collaborative Writing, Document Control, and Intercultural Communication

When you edit your documents, check for the following:

Writing for translatability

☐ Have you presented information as simply as possible?

☐ Have you avoided untranslatable (idiomatic) expressions?

☐ Have you adopted a tone and a level of politeness and formality appropriate to your reader's culture (or preference)?

Writing in teams

☐ Have you established clear timelines and assigned tasks to specific individuals?

☐ Do you have a clear team structure indicating who has the ultimate responsibility and authority for the various functions and tasks of the project?

☐ Have you set all this information down, had everyone read it and agree to it, and gotten everyone to sign off on it?

Controlling file proliferation and confusion

☐ Have you created a consistent, clear naming convention for the document and all its component files?

☐ Have you consistently created new file names for each new version of a file?

Exercises: Intercultural Considerations

Exercise 8.1: Discussing Cultural Differences

Take advantage of your resources. Get together in groups or pairs, making sure that each pair or group contains people from or with exposure to other cultures or countries. Discuss some of the cultural differences and differences in social behaviour between those countries and Canada.

Report some of these differences back to the class.

Exercise 8.2: Advising on Cultural Differences

Form groups or pairs as in Exercise 8.1. Pretend that your company is sending representatives to a client, conference, or technical training session in a country with which one of you is familiar. If you wish, if there is time, or if your instructor assigns it, do some additional research. Then write a brief memo explaining to your company representatives how to behave while on their trip in order to represent the company well and prevent intercultural miscommunication.

Exercise 8.3: Improving Intercultural Communication

This is a follow-up exercise to either of the two above. Take some correspondence that you've written as part of this course, find some correspondence online, or refer to a sample document in this text. In pairs or groups, discuss how tone and wording of the correspondence might be perceived in the culture you've discussed above. Rewrite the letter to make it more successful in that culture.

Present your before-and-after pieces to the class, explaining why you chose to make the changes that you did.

Chapter 9

References and Citations

> **In this chapter you will learn**
> - the purpose and importance of providing references and citations
> - a little about the different citation styles
> - how to create in-text citations and references sections.

When you use someone else's ideas, facts, and figures, or draw information from a textbook, journal article, report, letter, the Internet, or even private conversation, you must acknowledge the source of that information.

While it is completely normal, in fact, expected, that you will draw information and ideas from other sources—after all, you can't know everything or derive everything yourself—it is dishonest not to acknowledge that you did so. By default, you would be claiming that the information or idea is your own.

It really boils down to this: the fruits of someone else's efforts belong to them—or to their employer or the client who paid for it. When someone has invested their time, effort or money into creating or acquiring something, they own it. This is true of intellectual property, such as published articles, test results, experimental designs, and the like, as it is of physical property, such as cars and furniture; and you are not free to use other people's property without permission—that's called theft or, in the case of intellectual property, intellectual property theft. It is, in fact, a crime.

But, of course, the point of material published on the Internet and in professional journals, newspapers, and the like, is at least in part so that the public may derive benefit from it. So, there is something called the fair use provision, which means that you can make use of intellectual property without first getting express permission to do so, but only within certain limits, that is, if the use is considered fair: you must acknowledge the source of this information, you can only quote or use parts of the information (not reproduce large parts of it), and you are not permitted to make money off it, at least directly. This means that you can use information from print journals or the Internet to prove a point in your proposal even though the proposal is intended to win business for your employer. But you are not permitted to show clips from a movie and charge admission.

Since this is a fairly important field in law, these preceding paragraphs are obviously a seriously condensed version of a difficult topic that keeps hordes of lawyers busy and well fed. Your program, for instance if you're destined to become an engineer, will probably ask you to take ethics courses that include copyright issues; your professional association almost certainly will. But for the purposes of this text, and of your technical writing course, it may suffice to repeat that if you didn't dream it up yourself, if you didn't derive it, if you didn't invest time, effort, and ingenuity into coming up with something entirely original and if there is clearly an outside source of the information that you are including in your writing, then you absolutely must let your reader know where you got that information from.

But don't just think of this as an odious task imposed for form's sake and out of obeisance to the law. References actually have a threefold purpose and are, in fact, a benefit to you as a writer:

1. They give your report credibility when you cite information that is not common knowledge; having an expert back up your points for you can't really be a bad thing, after all.
2. They help readers find your source if they want more information; this is a courtesy and a convenience a reader can't help but appreciate.
3. They give credit to the originator of the idea or information, which keeps you out of trouble.

In school, failure to acknowledge sources is considered academic dishonesty and can cause you to fail the assignment, be kicked out of your course, or even be dismissed from your institution. In the professional world, it is punishable by heavy fines and punitive damages.

Don't do it. Ever. No one will think less of you for doing research and being honest about it.

The Common Knowledge Exception

So, broadly speaking anything that you didn't know before you read it or heard it should be referenced. However, common knowledge, even if new to you, does not need to be referenced. When you say that 2 + 2 = 4, you obviously don't have to cite your grade 2 teacher. It's common knowledge and your teacher didn't come up with it either.

It's the same with common knowledge in your field, at least once you're out in the field and using this knowledge regularly. So there's a bit of a judgment call to be made. It is wise, however, to provide reputable sources even for facts considered common knowledge in your field if those facts are likely to be unknown to your reader but provide particularly strong support for your position in an argument—just to make sure your reader will believe your surprising, convenient facts.

While in school, it is best if you provide references for all information that you research, even if it is common knowledge in the field in which you aspire to be active. Simply put, you haven't paid your dues yet, don't have enough experience, and don't have enough credibility to claim that you have mastered the concepts that your seniors work with as a matter of course. Sorry, but your time will come.

So, while in school, if you didn't know it before you read it and your instructor didn't mention it in a lecture, provide a reference.

Terminology

Before we discuss citation methods, let's establish some vocabulary.

A **citation** is an in-text indication that you are using someone else's ideas or words. Citations go right in the sentences at the locations where you use the borrowed information.

A **reference** is the source of that information, be it a printed or an electronic text, a video, a podcast, or even a personal conversation.

A **reference list** or **reference section** goes at the end of the document and lists all the references that you cited in the document. Every report must have a references section. Depending on the citation method you use, the references section will be in numerical or alphabetical order.

A **bibliography** is a list of all the sources that you have consulted—a sort of reading list—whether you have referred to those sources in your report or not. This means that bibliographies are generally longer than references sections. Bibliographies are always in alphabetical order, but they are not always required; ask your instructor, boss, or publisher for their preference.

Types: MLA, APA, Turabian, Chicago, IEEE, ACS, Vancouver

Different disciplines and professional organizations use different citation formats, all of which work well, with small advantages for each in their specific fields. The point is to provide all the information readers will need in order to find your sources and check those sources out for themselves.

Broadly speaking, however, there are two categories of citation methods, those that use name citations (MLA, APA, Turabian) and those that use number citations (IEEE, ACS, Vancouver).

The name version is more common in, but not exclusive to, the humanities (MLA: Modern Language Association) and the social sciences (APA: American Psychological

Association). This makes sense because these disciplines have schools of thought: Jungian versus Freudian psychologists, right- versus left-wing economists, postcolonial versus deconstructionist critics, and the like. Schools of thought are associated with specific people and personalities, and thus naming a source right in the text tells the reader something about the source's point of view or even politics:

> Some say that taxes on the wealthy must be lowered to stimulate trickle-down benefits (Jameson, 2014), while other say that it is the middle-class consumer who requires the greatest tax breaks in order to stimulate consumption, a sort of trickle-up benefit (Chan, 2016).

In the sciences and the technical disciplines, number-citation methods are more commonly used: the IEEE (Institute of Electrical and Electronics Engineers), the ACS (American Chemical Society), and the Vancouver (used in the biochemistry and pharmaceutical fields) formats, among others. These formats, instead of inserting the names of sources, simply insert numbers to represent the sources.

> Most of the Western world's nuclear power stations are already over 30 years old [2]. This is part of the problem with . . .

> Earlier studies [2; 3; 5; 9–11] have claimed that . . . , but lately a few have contradicted these findings [8; 13; 21].

If you've ever looked anything up in Wikipedia, you'll be familiar with the concept. The use of numbers is an advantage for two reasons. First, numbers are discrete and don't break up the flow of the reading as much as lengthy names. Second, in the technical fields, where data is verifiable and schools of thought less frequent, the names of sources add little useful information.

For the sake of illustration, we will work with the IEEE method in this chapter, which is used in both the electronics and the electrical fields, as well as in computer science. The differences between it and the other number-citation methods are slight, and the IEEE method is supported by MS Word's citation engine (see below).

However, if your instructor or boss prefers a different format, use that. As mentioned, all formats work. Just adapt the principles described below. You'll also find excellent explanations online.

Citing Sources

When you alert the reader that you are using information gleaned elsewhere than from your own fertile mind, you need to distinguish between two types of borrowing: paraphrasing and quoting.

Paraphrasing

When you are paraphrasing—that is, using someone else's facts or ideas but putting them in your own words—simply cite the source's number from the references section, as we've already seen above:

> Wood, by weight, not volume, is actually stronger than steel [4]. However, the strength requirements of most structural members in this type of construction preclude the use of wood, because the amount of wood required would . . .

Readers can simply skip over the number or, if they're curious or doubtful about the information, can turn to your references section, find the numbered source, and check it out for themselves.

Quoting

Sometimes, however, the author's words cannot be improved upon and fit perfectly into your paragraph. In that case, feel free to use the author's original words—do so verbatim, that is, word for word—and surround them in quotation marks to indicate that the words are not your own.

Because quotes refer to very specific parts of the author's text, not to broader ideas or concepts, provide the specific page number on which you found the quote, to make it easier for the reader to find.

> "Pound for pound, wood is considerably stronger than steel" [4, p. 35]. However, the strength requirements of most structural members in this type of construction preclude the use of wood, because the amount of wood required would . . .

Because the page numbers of ebooks change with the selected size of the typeface, ebooks now offer location counts; use those instead of page numbers when quoting.

If you are quoting from a source that does not have numbered pages or location counts, you'll have to omit them. However, if the source document is short, you can narrow down the location by offering a paragraph count, as in the sample long quote below. But you must always use quotation marks when you've used the author's exact wording.

Short Quotes vs. Long Quotes

You should incorporate quotes of less than two lines or so into your sentence, enclosed in quotation marks. With quotes longer than approximately two lines, you don't need to add quotation marks if you indent them as a "block quotation."

"Pound for pound, wood is considerably stronger than steel" [4, p. 35]. However, the strength requirements of most structural members in this type of construction preclude the use of wood in structures over six storeys tall. At the same time,

> Austria and Germany have been experimenting with building office and apartment structures up to 14 storeys tall, using advanced glu-lam technology. Essentially massed wood post-and-beam structures, they rely on new advances in glue technology that give these members considerable additional strength over standard glu-lams currently in use. [3, para. 8]

The Brock Commons student residence at the University of British Columbia is slated to be an 18-storey . . .

Number Sequencing

Citations in your report will be sequential—they will start at [1] and work their way up. However, every time you refer to the same document, continue to refer to it by

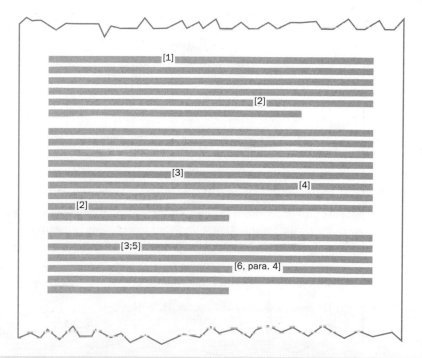

FIGURE 9.1 Sample citation sequence. Note that the first instance of each reference number appears in ascending order. A larger number never appears before a smaller number has appeared. All subsequent references to the same text use the same number. Normally, you probably wouldn't cite quite as often as on this page, which is for illustration purposes only. No pressure.

the same number. This is an easy way to keep track of how often you use a particular source and how many sources you've used overall. It also means that the source has to be listed only once in the references section.

In this system, then, a larger number never appears for the first time before a smaller number, but the smaller number will be reused if the writer returns to a previously cited source.

Creating References Sections

References are compiled in a separate references section at the end of the report. The references section follows the conclusions and recommendations sections (formal reports), but precedes the appendices.

In the number-citation systems, list the references in the order in which you first referred to them in the report. This means that the references are not in alphabetical order, as you'll note in the sample references section (Figure 9.2).

References

[1] C. L. Summakindt, Ed., *Marketing Wood Products in Pacific Rim Countries.* Vancouver, BC: Dover Books Inc., 2007.

[2] J. Doman, "Getting Students Past the Fear in Technical Presentations," in *Proc. 9th Annual IATTW Conference on Integrating Engineering and Education Needs.* T. Nogh and M. Smythe, Eds. Winnipeg, MB, June 21–23, 2012. Available: http://www.iattwc.com/confproc/2013.

[3] City of Calgary Engineering Department, "Waterworks Standard Specifications Waterworks Construction 2011," City of Calgary, Calgary, AB, Rep., 2011.

[4] G. LeBouef, "Teaching Engineers Not to Over-rely on the Passive Voice," presented at 9th Annual IATTW Conference on Integrating Engineering and Education Needs, Winnipeg, MB, 2012.

[5] _____, "What I've Learned the Hard Way," *Personal DIY Disasters*, Oct. 14, 2011. Available: http://www.pdiydisasters.com. [Accessed: Apr. 09, 2014]

[7] D. Ainslie, private conversation, Jan. 11, 2016.

When you list works by the same author consecutively, replace the name with an underscore line. Obviously, use the name if works by the same author are not listed consecutively.

FIGURE 9.2 Sample references section. Note that the sources are listed in the order in which they were first referred to in the text, not in alphabetical order. This makes it possible for the reader to match an in-text citation to the reference source. All subsequent citations of the same text will use the same number.

Autogenerating Reference Entries

Online Citation Engines and Word Processors

Whichever method you end up using, you'll find excellent explanations online. In fact, you'll also find excellent citation machines online that will create the reference entries for you. Just select the citation method, select the type of source, fill in the dialogue box, and let the machine create the entry for you. Then just cut and paste.

Makecitation.com and easybib.com are excellent resources. Other citation machines are just a Google search away.

If the citation method you are using is supported by your word processor, don't bother with the online citation machines. That way, you don't have to cut and paste; when your report is done, your word processor will even generate the references section, much like it does a table of contents.

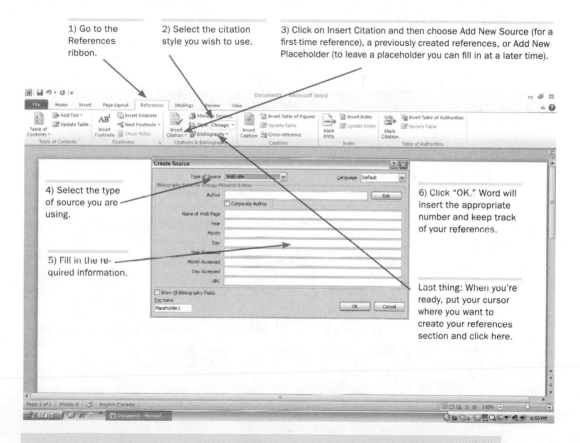

FIGURE 9.3 **MS Word's References function.** This is a handy in-document way to insert citations and have Word generate a references section. Sadly, the Vancouver method is not represented.

Google Scholar

Principally, Google Scholar (scholar.google.ca) is an online research tool that links to your university or college's library, giving you access to all the professional journals and other resources to which the library has subscribed—on top of all the usual resources available for free online. As with all online research, you will need to verify the credibility of your sources; not everything you find online has equal research value and decisions or recommendation based on poor information will lead to poor results, and poor grades. For a quick introduction on how to evaluate the credibility of a source, check out the following three-minute video: www.lib.ncsu.edu/tutorials/evaluating-sources.

However, Google Scholar also has a very useful citation function that allows you to link your research sources to RefWorks (refworks.com) to create a personal database of online sources. You can then use RefWorks to generate citations, reference lists, and bibliographies in a variety of citation methods. The Google Scholar and RefWorks websites provide useful instructions on how to use Google Scholar as a research and citation tool.

Sample IEEE Reference Entries

The examples below show what the reference entries in the references section should look like for different sources. Not all possible sources are listed here, so you may have to refer to IEEE citation guidelines (available in various forms online) or the style guide for whatever other system you are tasked with using.

The purpose of these entries, in all systems, is to supply readers with all the information they need to find the original sources. The information you provide must therefore be as complete as possible.

Most of the sources listed below are entirely made up. Don't bother looking for them.

Note that the IEEE system uses just the initial of an author's given names.

Print Sources

Believe it or not, some people still read hard copies. Some professional journals are still available only in print, and older volumes of many journals remain available only in print.

Book by One Author

[1] M. Gerbrant, *Neural and Fibreoptic Networks*, 3rd ed. Montreal, QC: Technical Publications Associates Inc., 2013.

If a book is a second or subsequent edition, the words "2nd ed." or "3rd ed." should be entered immediately after the book title, as above.

Ebook

> [1] M. Gerbrant, *Neural and Fibreoptic Networks*, 3rd ed. Montreal, QC: Technical Publication Associates Inc.; 2013 [ebook]. Available: TPA electronic collection: http://www.tpa.com/ecollection

As this example illustrates, ebooks have the same reference entries as hard-copy books, but they include two additional pieces of information: the fact that it is an ebook and where the ebook is available. Of course, if the book is widely available at ebook resellers, like Chapters/Indigo's Kobo website, you don't need to mention where it's available. This is a judgment call.

Book by Two or Three Authors

> [2] D. Jackson, R. S. Singh, and L. Leong, *Gestalt Experiments on Sequential Machines*, 7th ed. Scarborough, ON: Prentice Hall Canada Inc., 2014.

Book by Four or More Authors

> [3] P. L. Gneiss et al., *Introducing New Technology to Developing Nations*. Toronto, ON: Scientific and Technical Press, 2009.

Book without Author or Editor

> [4] *The Oxford Chinese Dictionary*. Toronto, Oxford, UK: Oxford University Press, 2013.

Book by Organization (Private, Gov't, NGO, etc.)

> [5] Canadian Mortgage and Housing Corporation, *Canadian Wood-frame House Construction*. Ottawa, ON: Canadian Mortgage and Housing Corporation, 2010.

Note that the authoring organization is listed twice: as author and as publisher.

Books by Editors: Anthologies

An anthology is a book containing sections written by different authors, with the whole book edited by another person. If your reference is to the whole book, the editor's name is used and his or her editorial role is identified by the abbreviation "Ed." immediately after the name:

> [6] C. L. Summakindt, Ed., *Marketing Wood Products in Pacific Rim Countries*. Vancouver, BC: Dover Books Inc., 2007.

If the book has multiple editors, use the same rule as for multiple authors in [2–3] above.

Article in an Anthology

[7] J. Ng, "Strong Enough? Perception of Western Stick Framing in Asian Markets," in *Marketing Wood Products in Pacific Rim Countries*, C. L. Summakindt, Ed. Vancouver, BC: Dover Books Inc., 2007, pp. 24–57.

Article from a Journal, Newspaper, or Magazine

[8] H. Weston, "Surviving the Greek Crisis," *Business Up Here*, vol. 12, no. 6, pp. 18–25, June 2014.

If the author of the article is not identified, begin the reference with the title of the article. Omit whatever information is not provided in the source; not all publications identify volumes, for instance.

Treat published interviews like published articles.

Entry from a Reference Work

[9] "Amniocentesis," *The Oxford Canadian Dictionary*, 2nd ed. Toronto, ON: Oxford University Press, 2011.

If the listings are alphabetical, the page number is unnecessary.

Report Written by You or Another Person

[10] D. Freeman and S. Woo, "Reducing Vibration of the Propeller Shaft in the BC Ferries Fast Ferries," Halifax Marine Engineering Group, Halifax, NS, Rep. 2007/23/23A-2, Oct. 15, 2009.

If no document number is provided, omit the number, but still include "Rep." so the reader knows what sort of document it is.

Report Written by an Organization

Professional organization and government departments or ministries often author reports without ascribing an individual author's name. However, because they are taking responsibility for the accuracy of the document, use the organization's name as the author. Restate the organization's name as the publisher.

[11] City of Calgary Engineering Department, *"Waterworks Standard Specifications Waterworks Construction 2011," City of Calgary, Calgary, AB, Rep., 2011.*

Conference Proceedings

Conference proceedings are anthologized conference papers. Treat them like any other anthology, but add the date(s) on which the conference took place.

[12] T. Nogh and M. Smythe, Eds., *Proc. 9th Annual IATTW Conference on Integrating Engineering and Education Needs*. Winnipeg, MB, June 21–23, 2009. Toronto, ON: Oxford University Press. 2013.

Conference Paper (Published)

[13] W. Sung, "Granularity and Information Density in Technical Reports by EITs," in *Proc. 9th Annual IATTW Conference on Integrating Engineering and Education Needs*, T. Nogh and M. Smythe, Eds. Winnipeg, MB, June 21–23, 2009. Toronto, ON: Oxford University Press, 2013, pp. 121–154.

Conference Paper (Published on Internet)

[14] J. Doman, "Getting Students Past the Fear in Technical Presentations," in *Proc. 9th Annual IATTW Conference on Integrating Engineering and Education Needs*, T. Nogh and M. Smythe, Eds. Winnipeg, MB, June 21–23, 2009. Available: http://www.iattw.com/confproc/2013

Conference Paper (Unpublished)

[15] G. LeBouef, "Teaching Engineers Not to Over-rely on the Passive Voice," presented at 9th Annual *IATTW Conference on Integrating Engineering and Education Needs*, Winnipeg, MB, June 21–23, 2012.

Pamphlets, Brochures, or Promotional Material

[16] Canadian Coast Guard Safe Boating Practices. Brochure, 2011.

Face-to-Face and Private Sources

Even ideas or information that has never made its way into print or online must still be acknowledged. This is not only a requirement of law and every notion of fair play, but also allows you to avoid the awkwardness and potential hostility of being found out by the colleague whose ideas you've, essentially, stolen.

However, if the sources are not published, you don't have to have a reference number for them or list them in the references list. After all, the reader cannot go looking for them. But you must then name your sources in the document so that you are fulfilling your legal requirement to acknowledge intellectual debts:

In a speech to the IEEE Conference on SCADA Security, Sanjay Gupta stated that . . .

In a personal conversation with the author, Linda Ainslie said that . . .

Speech

[17] P. Sanghera, Ryerson Engineering Group, Kingston, Ontario, speaking to the IEEE Conference on SCADA Security, Montreal, QC, Mar. 21, 2013.

Lecture

[18] J. Smith, Lecturer, Topic: "Computer Forensics," Southern Alberta Institute of Technology, Calgary, AB, Oct. 22, 2015.

Private Conversation, Private Correspondence, Unpublished Interview

[19] D. Ainslie, private conversation, Jan. 11, 2016.

[20] J. Tsing, "RE: Inquiry about frequency fluctuations," personal email, Jan. 15, 2015.

Internet Sources

As with the sources listed above, provide complete information about your Internet sources. Be sure to include the date on which the information was posted or on which the site was last updated. If that information is not provided on the site, list the date on which you accessed the site. We recommend including these dates so that readers can check the website's archives for the version to which you actually referred.

Website

[21] "Governance Review and Transformation," Canadian Green Building Council. Available: http://www.cagbc.org/AM/Template.cfm?Section= The_CaGBC [Cited: Apr. 18, 2014].

Of course, if the article is ascribed to a specific writer, begin with the writer's name. If the page or article doesn't have a title, omit it. As always, provide all the information available. Omit what isn't available. What choice do you have, after all?

Online Journal, Newspaper, or Magazine Article

[22] H. Weston, "Surviving the Greek Crisis," *Business Up Here*, vol. 12, no. 6, June 2014 [online]. Available: http://www.businessuphere.com/news/ intl/europe/article4398732/ [Accessed: July 23, 2014].

If the site is searchable, you don't need to provide the full URL (see Wiki below). If no author is identified, you can't provide the name.

[23] "Human and Environmental Factors for Scaling HVAC Systems," *Canadian Civil Eng.*, vol. 23, no. 10, pp. 11–18, Oct. 2015 [online]. Available: http://www.cce.org/archives [Accessed: Jan. 12, 2017].

If the document has a DOI (Digital Object Identifier) or HDL (Handle System Identifier), use that instead of the URL, but do identify the database.

[24] "Thorium Reactor Update," *NPCC Bulletin*, vol. 42, no. 4, p. 12, Sept. 2013 [online]. Available: NPCC Digital Library, DOI: 12.2547/695412.695387 [Accessed: July 14, 2014].

Wiki

[25] "Green Roofs," *Wikipedia.org* [modified Dec. 15, 2013]. Available: http://en.wikipedia.org

Blog

[26] J. Zeeman, "What I've Learned the Hard Way," *Personal DIY Disasters*, Oct. 14, 2011 [online]. Available: http://www.pdiydisasters.com [Accessed: Apr. 09, 2014].

URLs can become quite unwieldy. For convenience, if the website, blog, or Wiki is searchable by author or article, you can just cite the root URL, as in the two examples immediately above.

Audiovisual Sources

DVDs

[27] L. Clark, presenter, *Passive House Building Standards and Techniques* [DVD]. Toronto, ON: Stern, Wallace, and Wong, 2014.

Radio Program (Broadcast)

[28] T. Dobson, interviewer, J. Tsang, interviewee, and R. J. Santos, producer, "The Wind-noise and Bird-kill Myths with Wind Turbines," *Environmental Briefs* [radio broadcast]. Vancouver, BC: CKNX Radio, Jan. 23, 2013.

Radio Program (Podcast)

[29] T. Dobson, interviewer, J. Tsang, interviewee, and R. J. Santos, producer, "The Wind-noise and Bird-kill Myths with Wind Turbines," *Environmental Briefs* [podcast]. Vancouver, BC: CKNX Radio, Jan. 23, 2013. Available: http://cknx.ca/programs/podcasts/environmentalbriefs.xml

Because a radio program podcast is not edited after being posted, dates of access are not relevant.

Sound Recording

[30] M. Wong, writer, and Q. Warner, presenter, *Healing the Soul after Heartache* [sound recording]. Regina, SK: Part Time Productions, Feb. 10, 2011.

Program

[31] H. Owatsky, reporter, "Environmental Building By-laws," *Community Corner* [television broadcast]. St. John's, NL: XTV Atlantic, Aug. 21, 2008.

Television Program (Podcast)

[32] H. Owatsky, reporter, "Environmental Building By-laws," *Community Corner*. St. John's, NL: XTV Atlantic, Aug. 21, 2008 [podcast]. Available: http://btv.net.ca/tv/communitycorner/podcasts/envirobldgbylaws.xml

Podcast

[33] P. Vukovicz, speaker, *Chemical Bonding Explained* [podcast]. Exeter, UK: Camberleigh University, 2011. Available: http://www.cu.edu.uk/chem/podcasts/

Video Recording

[34] H. Kahn, writer and director, *Environmental Performance on the Tar Sands Projects* [video recording]. Edmonton, AB: Educational Products Ltd., 2012.

Graphic, Map, or Other Visual

[35] Radiation Exposure by Medical Procedure [graph], *The Sciences*, vol. 3, p. 24, Summer 2011.

Note in this case as well that if you access these sources online, you don't include the date on which you downloaded them, because they aren't updated or altered once made available.

Secondary Sources

A primary source is the article that you are reading. A secondary source is a source that is being referenced in the article that you are reading. The IEEE system doesn't permit the citing of secondary sources. You'll have to find and refer to the primary source. If you cannot, then you cannot use the reference—presumably because you cannot verify that it was used correctly in the source you have accessed.

Editing References and Citations

- ☐ Have you verified which method of referencing and citing you should be using? Ask your instructor, boss, or publisher.

- ☐ Have you verified whether you are required to provide a bibliography as well as a reference list?

- ☐ Have you indicated in the text of your report, in every case, the source of information that you are using?

- ☐ Have you done so every single time you've used that source; that is, if you use a reference source more than once, have you cited it each time?

- ☐ Have you consistently used quotation marks when you have used the actual wording from your source?

- ☐ Is every source listed in your references section, either in alphabetical order or in numerical sequence, depending on the method you are using?

Exercises: References and Citations

This chapter is intended primarily as a reference chapter for students required to provide proper citations and references while working on report or research assignments. Practice citation assignments hardly seem relevant, particularly given the prevalence of online citation engines and in-software citation tools. However, some discussion of principles, as a follow-up to the reading, may be useful.

Exercise 9.1: In-Office Citation

Imagine that a colleague has won an award, garnered a promotion, or simply been widely lauded for an idea he or she presented in a report. Imagine that as you hear this colleague's praises sung and are being told over and over that this colleague will probably run the company one day, you realize that the brilliant idea for which this person is getting credit is something that you suggested to him or her at a meeting or over coffee. How would you feel? What should your colleague have done?

What will your colleague's failure to give credit where credit is due do to your, and potentially to company, morale? How might it affect company performance?

What are the consequences to the company for promoting individuals on the strength of ideas that are not their own?

Exercise 9.2: The Consequences of Failing to Provide Proper Citations

Imagine that your work team has submitted a proposal or a funding request or a research tax grant application. Imagine that one of the reviewers has noticed that your submission contains ideas or information that others have come up with first, but for which your team did not provide proper citations and references. This is not just embarrassing; it's potentially career ending. Consider why.

What will be the reaction of the reviewers? Are they likely to consider your application? Can they do so without compromising the integrity of their own selection process?

Your team will have been found guilty of intellectual property theft. Are the consequences likely to be a one-time thing; that is, is your next submission likely to be viewed without suspicion or read without prejudice?

How will the rest of your organization feel about what you've done? What are the possible consequences to your organization and how are your colleagues and managers likely to try to correct the damage to the organization's reputation? What will happen to you?

Similarly, what will happen to you if you are found guilty of academic dishonesty in school? Your school's online policies will hold some of the official answers. But what will happen to your standing in the eyes of your peers and instructors? What will happen to your chances of getting letters of reference or personal recommendations? If your peers find out about your transgressions and some of them turn into colleagues or competitors in the future, for how long do you think your transgression will follow you? Are the potential costs worth the modest benefits? What, after all, is really gained by failing to cite a source?

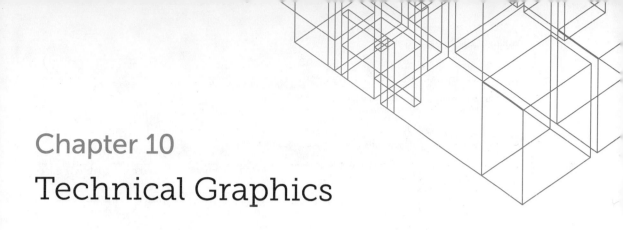

Chapter 10
Technical Graphics

In this chapter you will learn

- the purpose of graphics in reports
- what types of graphics are best suited to convey what sort of information
- how to create graphics in Word
- how to include graphics in reports for best effect.

Graphics are highly concise, easy-to-understand representations of complex informa-tion whose power is derived by providing information in the way we prefer to process it: visually. We are visual animals. When we read, we attempt to form pictures of what we are reading, which is why strong, direct verbs and concrete nouns are so much easier to comprehend than weak or abstract ones. Graphics don't force us to search for a way to interpret text visually; they provide the information visually in the first place.

In fact, some information can only be processed visually because it has to be seen to be understood.

In addition to being more easily understood, visually presented information is also more easily remembered because it provides a snapshot. Images are, after scents, our strongest triggers of memory.

Types and Uses

Like your writing, your illustrations should be simple, clear, and accurate to ensure reader comprehension.

Tables

You may not think of tables as graphics; however, they present information not in sen-tence syntax, but in a visual syntax, aligning information in a matrix of columns and rows for easy reference (see Figure 10.1). They provide a snapshot of information in

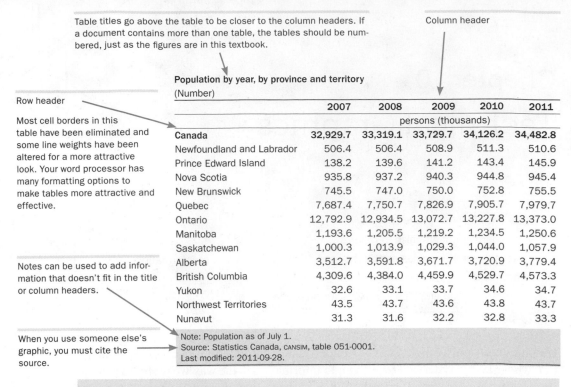

Table titles go above the table to be closer to the column headers. If a document contains more than one table, the tables should be numbered, just as the figures are in this textbook.

Column header

Row header

Most cell borders in this table have been eliminated and some line weights have been altered for a more attractive look. Your word processor has many formatting options to make tables more attractive and effective.

Notes can be used to add information that doesn't fit in the title or column headers.

When you use someone else's graphic, you must cite the source.

Population by year, by province and territory
(Number)

	2007	2008	2009	2010	2011
	persons (thousands)				
Canada	32,929.7	33,319.1	33,729.7	34,126.2	34,482.8
Newfoundland and Labrador	506.4	506.4	508.9	511.3	510.6
Prince Edward Island	138.2	139.6	141.2	143.4	145.9
Nova Scotia	935.8	937.2	940.3	944.8	945.4
New Brunswick	745.5	747.0	750.0	752.8	755.5
Quebec	7,687.4	7,750.7	7,826.9	7,905.7	7,979.7
Ontario	12,792.9	12,934.5	13,072.7	13,227.8	13,373.0
Manitoba	1,193.6	1,205.5	1,219.2	1,234.5	1,250.6
Saskatchewan	1,000.3	1,013.9	1,029.3	1,044.0	1,057.9
Alberta	3,512.7	3,591.8	3,671.7	3,720.9	3,779.4
British Columbia	4,309.6	4,384.0	4,459.9	4,529.7	4,573.3
Yukon	32.6	33.1	33.7	34.6	34.7
Northwest Territories	43.5	43.7	43.6	43.8	43.7
Nunavut	31.3	31.6	32.2	32.8	33.3

Note: Population as of July 1.
Source: Statistics Canada, CANSIM, table 051-0001.
Last modified: 2011-09-28.

FIGURE 10.1 Sample table. This information could not possibly be presented clearly or accessibly in sentences and paragraphs. Tables are an excellent way to present detailed and plentiful information, particularly numerical information. But tables can also be used to align text, for instance, in spec sheets (Chapter 6) or troubleshooting guides (Chapter 13).

Source: Statistics Canada, CANSIM, table 051-0001.

tabular form when that information cannot be expressed clearly or accessibly in sentence form. How, for instance, would you record the population of Canada's provinces over a five-year span in a paragraph?

Pie Charts

Pie charts are excellent tools to show proportions of a whole. The graphic itself provides a quick visual overview. Add specific numbers or details in the pie pieces themselves or in call-outs. You can also pull out one piece of the pie to draw attention to it.

Bar Graphs/Column Graphs

Bar graphs and column graphs provide quick visual comparisons of quantity. It's easy to see, for instance, that one bar is roughly half the length or height of another. Again, the graphic provides a rough overview. Specific numbers can be added either within the bar, in a call-out, or on the axes.

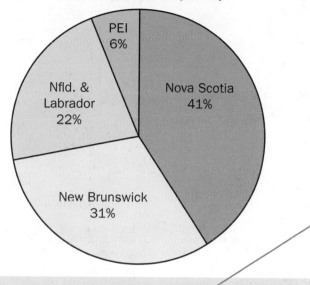

Relative population of the Atlantic provinces (2011)

When you create your graphic using someone else's information, acknowledge that source as the source of your data, not of the graphic.

FIGURE 10.2 Sample pie chart showing the relative population of the Atlantic provinces (2011). To draw attention to a particular variable (province), you could pull that piece out of the pie; Word has an option for exploded pie charts.

Data Source: Statistics Canada, CANSIM, Table 051-001.

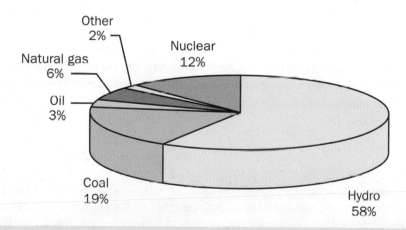

FIGURE 10.3 3-D pie chart showing net electricity generation in Canada (2003). 3-D graphics are more visually interesting because they add depth and technical sophistication. But they don't make information more accessible or credible. Generally, 3-D graphics work best when reproduced in colour. In black and white, the individual pieces don't stand out sufficiently and the proportions are harder to discern.

Source: Canadian Electricity Association. Used with permission.

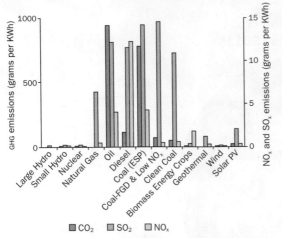

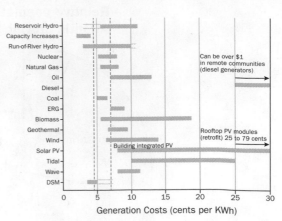

EPS: Electrostatic precipitators (dust control only)
FGD: Flue gas desulphurization

ERG: Energy recovery generation
Dotted lines: Range of current wholesale prices in Canada

FIGURE 10.4 Column graph showing emission values of CO_2, SO_2, and NO_x for different electricity generation methods. The column graph makes it easier to compare relative values against one another, whereas pie charts make it easier to see proportions of a whole.

Source: Canadian Electricity Association. Used with permission.

FIGURE 10.5 Bar graph showing relative electricity generation costs. The note at the bottom explains the significance of the dotted lines. Use notes (as at the bottom of the graph) to provide information that helps the reader interpret the graph correctly.

Source: Canadian Electricity Association. Used with permission.

In a bar graph, the bars originate on the *y*-axis (the vertical axis), but in a column graph, they originate on the *x*-axis (the horizontal axis). The advantage of the bar graph is that it is easier to stack long bar labels on the *y*-axis than to place them side by side on the *x*-axis.

A pictogram is generally a bar or column graph in which the bars have been replaced with pictorial representations, for instance, stacked human forms for population bars or stacked coins for costs. This is visually interesting and draws the reader's attention, but it is unnecessary in technical writing. Leave that for the glossy magazines and fancy annual reports.

Line Graphs

Line graphs track dependent values on the *y* or vertical axis against an independent value on the *x* or horizontal axis. Examples might be CO_2 emissions over time, wind resistance in response to rising speeds, or federal deficits budget-year by budget-year. If these changing values show a particular direction or pattern, they are called trends.

Line graphs are your typical stock-price trackers. They allow readers to see trends at a glance or give a quick visual comparison of two or more values over time. Sometimes we can extrapolate from line graphs, but we have to be careful when we do so. How can we be sure that the trends will continue, after all?

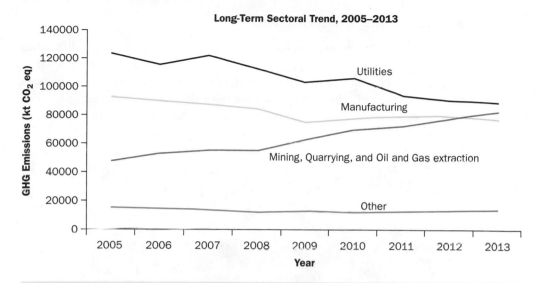

FIGURE 10.6 Line graph showing long-term Canadian GHG emissions by industrial sector. Line graphs are good at showing trends, in this case the trend of generally decreasing GHG emissions by the manufacturing and utilities sectors, but increasing emissions in the mining, quarrying, and oil and gas extraction sector. Of course, what accounts for these trends cannot be determined from the graphs. For instance, the decline in emissions in the manufacturing sector could be due to increasing efficiency, declining production, or a combination of the two.

Source: Environment Canada (2015, April), *Facility Greenhouse Gas Emissions Reporting Program: Overview of Reported Emissions 2013* (Gatineau, QC: Environment Canada): p. 13, Fig. 11.

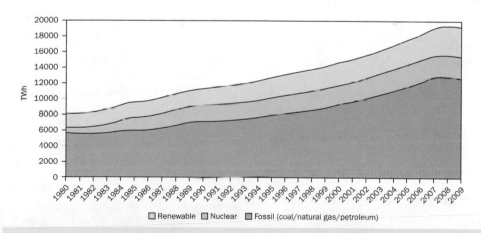

FIGURE 10.7 Line graph showing net generation of electricity (global). This line graph shows cumulative values, adding up the volumes under each line. It shows the overall growth of energy consumption as well as the proportions of the various kinds of energy being consumed. Note that you could use the same data to create a cumulative bar graph, with one layered bar for each year.

Source: http://en.wikipedia.org/wiki/File:Annual_electricity_net_generation_in_the_world.svg

Photos, Line Drawings, and Diagrams

Photos depict objects very accurately, but sometimes they provide too much distracting detail. Line drawings and diagrams provide simplified images that draw readers' attention to the most important details. Exploded illustrations show assembly sequences, component layering, or internal components not normally visible, and cutaways reveal inner working or locations of internal components normally hidden from view.

FIGURE 10.8 ATLAS detector, CERN. This is one of several detector experiments at the Large Hadron Collider particle accelerator at CERN, Geneva, Switzerland. Photos provide an excellent sense of scale and level of detail. Note the person standing down in front and the many structures on display. It would be very difficult, however, to point out any particular detail to a reader.

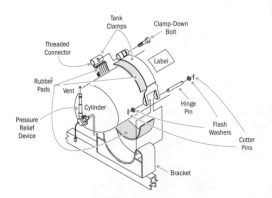

FIGURE 10.9 An exploded line drawing detailing the mounting procedure for a high-pressure cylinder. The line drawing removes unnecessary detail, focuses on surfaces and components, and can thereby direct the reader's attention to what's really important, which in this case are the assembly components. This illustration would make an excellent addition to the cylinder's mounting instructions.

Source: Andre Lanz

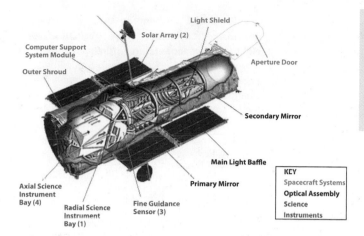

FIGURE 10.10 Cutaway diagram of the Hubble telescope. Diagrams are essentially line drawings with shading to show surfaces. Cutaways provide an internal glimpse of how things work or are put together.

Source: NASA

Flowcharts and Schematics

Schematics are conceptual graphical representations of processes; organization; flows of work, traffic, data, ideas, or money; or any number of other things that may or may not exist physically. They are visual representations of complex interrelationships and processes. Examples include decision trees, process descriptions, org charts, and flowcharts, but also highly technical systems such as circuit diagrams, control systems, and so on. They are conceptual because they often don't correlate with physical objects and, when they do, they aren't to scale.

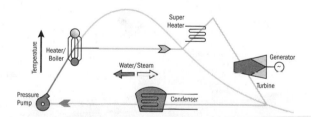

FIGURE 10.11 A flowchart showing the process(es) by which electricity is generated from steam. Because it shows flows (or movements), "flowchart" is the preferable term for this type of graphic. Strictly speaking, however, it could also be called a schematic. It shows, very roughly (or schematically), how such a steam-driven power plant is laid out.

Source: Canadian Electricity Association, Used with permission.

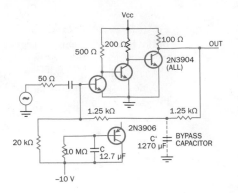

FIGURE 10.12 Schematic of a capacitance multiplier. Obviously these symbols for electrical components are entirely conceptual. A resistor doesn't actually look like a jagged zigzag, for instance. However, the figure does clearly show the components of this system and their relationships, the input and the outputs. Congratulations: it's a schematic!

Source: Schmutz, L.E. Transistor gain boosts capacitor value. Electronics. July 25, 1974. Available at www.schematicsforfree.com

Putting Graphics into Reports

To insert a graphic in your report, begin by putting your cursor in an empty paragraph in the location on the page where you want the graphic to go. If you don't put the cursor in an empty paragraph, your graphic will turn into art in the middle of a sentence, which you don't want. Then follow the procedure described in the illustrations below. The screen captures have been taken from MS Word. Other word-processing software and future versions of MS Word will have the same features, but you may have to adjust the procedure a bit.

Alternatively, of course, you can create graphics in Excel and then import them into your Word file.

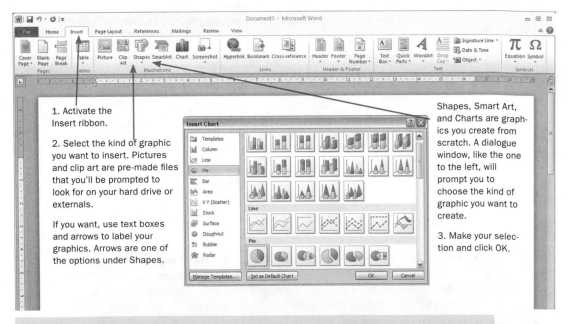

1. Activate the Insert ribbon.

2. Select the kind of graphic you want to insert. Pictures and clip art are pre-made files that you'll be prompted to look for on your hard drive or externals.

If you want, use text boxes and arrows to label your graphics. Arrows are one of the options under Shapes.

Shapes, Smart Art, and Charts are graphics you create from scratch. A dialogue window, like the one to the left, will prompt you to choose the kind of graphic you want to create.

3. Make your selection and click OK.

FIGURE 10.13 Inserting graphics into your report. Once you get the hang of it, it's quite easy to include graphics in reports. The hard part will be making sure you don't get carried away.

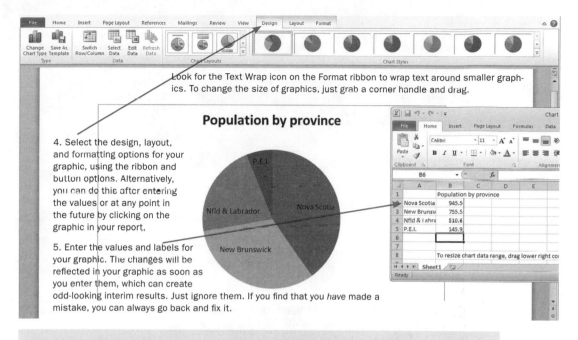

Look for the Text Wrap icon on the Format ribbon to wrap text around smaller graphics. To change the size of graphics, just grab a corner handle and drag.

4. Select the design, layout, and formatting options for your graphic, using the ribbon and button options. Alternatively, you can do this after entering the values or at any point in the future by clicking on the graphic in your report.

5. Enter the values and labels for your graphic. The changes will be reflected in your graphic as soon as you enter them, which can create odd-looking interim results. Just ignore them. If you find that you *have* made a mistake, you can always go back and fix it.

FIGURE 10.14 Entering values for charts and graphs. When you select the chart type, an Excel spreadsheet will open, with some default values. Change these values to reflect your requirements. Initially, it can be a bit tricky to understand how to fill in your values. Fortunately, the program is quite forgiving; you can always go back and make changes.

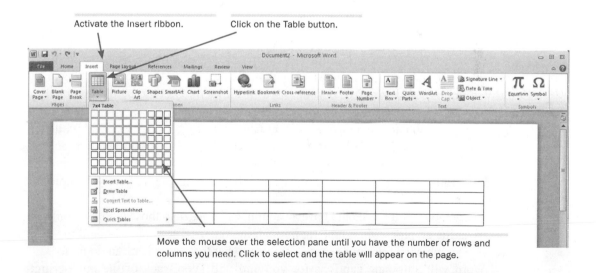

Activate the Insert ribbon.

Click on the Table button.

Move the mouse over the selection pane until you have the number of rows and columns you need. Click to select and the table will appear on the page.

FIGURE 10.15 Inserting tables into Word. You'll have to plan ahead a bit to select the correct number of columns and rows for your table, but if you make a mistake, you can always correct it later. Word's table functions are very flexible.

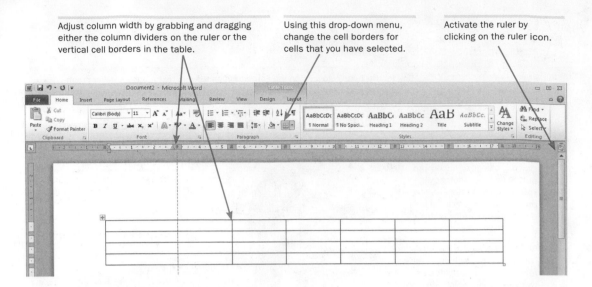

Adjust column width by grabbing and dragging either the column dividers on the ruler or the vertical cell borders in the table.

Using this drop-down menu, change the cell borders for cells that you have selected.

Activate the ruler by clicking on the ruler icon.

FIGURE 10.16 Formatting tables in Word. Once inserted, tables can be almost endlessly customized. Spec sheets (Chapter 6), for example, are generally created as tables, as are résumés with a parallel structure (Chapter 11), but once the borders are eliminated, to name just one potential change, readers can no longer see the underlying table structure. All they see is attractively aligned, easily accessible text.

Rules for Incorporating Report Graphics

While colour graphics may look wonderful on the monitor, if the report is going to be printed in black and white, or if your colour print job is likely to be photocopied in black and white, those colours could all come out as virtually the same shade of grey. Therefore, if you cannot control output, create your graphics in black and white. If you really want to use colour, print out your graphics in black and white to ensure that the shades of grey into which the colours you have chosen will be interpreted have enough contrast that the graphics are still recognizable. Adjust your colours if necessary.

Every report graphic should have a caption. Captions help those who look only or mostly at the graphics while flipping through the report. The caption should indicate what the graphic is of or, in the case of a photo, what the reader is meant to notice.

Word will automate captions for you and will keep track of the numbering; when you move sections of the document around, Word will automatically re-number the captions. To insert a Word caption, follow the procedure illustrated in Figure 10.17.

IN THE FIELD

Eric Hanson, Exploration Geologist

You might not think that writing skills would be that important to an exploration geologist. You would be wrong. I have worked in 11 countries on 4 continents. Usually the people I report to, the exploration manager or vice president of exploration, aren't even in the same country. So these people depend on, and insist on, clearly written reports to keep them informed. Exploration geology is about ideas. If you can't explain your ideas about the project you are working on, you are going to have problems.

The type and size of reports an exploration geologist is expected to write will vary greatly from one employer to another. Typically, I have to write a budget proposal for a project. What do I plan to do and how much do I plan to spend? If I can't justify the spending on my project, I won't get the money. The money could go to another geologist's project with less potential simply because the other geologist wrote a better proposal. Once a project is started, progress reports are normally required. This will include small maps and photos, but I still have to explain in words how well the work is going and how my ideas on the project are changing as the work progresses. At the end of a field campaign, a complete report with all the results is normally required. Included in this will be recommendations. Should the company drop the project and move on or should the company spend more money on the project? Whatever my recommendations, I have to be able to explain and justify them.

Also keep in mind that an exploration geologist has to write reports for people with various levels of technical knowledge. The exploration manager or VP of exploration will normally be another geologist or perhaps a geophysicist or a mining engineer. However, company presidents, board-of-director members, and investors may have little technical knowledge. The exploration geologist will have to explain to these people what is going on with the project. Good writing skills are essential.

Please note that while figure titles (captions) go below the figure, table titles (captions) go above the table where they are closer to the column headers and help the reader make sense of the table's organization more quickly. When you click on Insert Caption in the References Ribbon, select the proper type of caption in the dialogue box that opens and, if necessary, the appropriate location for the caption.

Every graphic should be introduced or at least referred to in the preceding text. That way, readers will know at what point they should look at the graphic and what the graphic is intended to illustrate or clarify. These references can be right in the sentence—*follow the procedure illustrated below*—or parenthetical: for instance, *(see figure below)* or *(Figure 10.17 below)*. If you use parenthetical references, try to keep them consistent.

Chapter 7 describes how to get Word to autogenerate a list of tables and figures for your report.

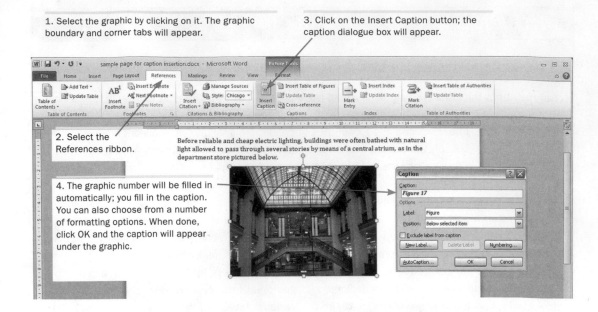

FIGURE 10.17 Inserting figure captions in Word. In a report, every graphic should have a caption so that casual browsers will know what the graphic is intended to show.

Avoiding Graphical Misrepresentation

The great strength of graphics, that they convey a lot of information at a glance, can also be their downfall. A glance affords only an impression, and impressions can be deceiving. The following are some common errors made with graphs, either inadvertently or with the intent to deceive. They all have to do with scaling.

Though we generally advise against using pictograms, if you do choose to use them, do so accurately. Figure 10.18 might be a pictogram comparing the populations of two provinces or countries, but note what happens to the area of a pictogram when you increase its height: it grows exponentially.

Sometimes, when differences are slight, it's hard for readers to actually see a difference (Figure 10.19, left). The temptation in these cases is to alter the scale on the y-axis (Figure 10.19, right), but the result can be deceiving. It exaggerates the difference, in this case making the 2 per cent difference look like a 100 per cent difference.

There are two correct ways to deal with this problem. First, you can begin the y-axis at a number other than zero and use a scale that shows the difference without exaggerating it (Figure 10.20, left). Second, you can add a jagged (broken) line to signal that the y-axis is not continuous (Figure 10.20, right).

FIGURE 10.18 Improper (left) vs. proper (right) use of pictograms. When you scale two-dimensional graphics, you end up scaling both vertically and horizontally, not just vertically. The difference in populations looks much more dramatic on the graph on the left.

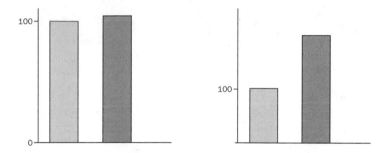

FIGURE 10.19 Altering the scale to show differences (right) can often exaggerate those differences. The graph on the left uses a continuous scale from 0 to 100, which makes the 2 per cent difference between the two bars virtually disappear. The graph on the right exaggerates that difference considerably. What's the starting value on the y-axis?

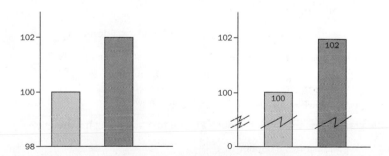

FIGURE 10.20 These graphs clearly indicate the scale on the y-axis and leave no doubt about the absolute values being represented. The graph on the left indicates clearly that the y-axis starts at 98, not at 0. The y-axis on the right starts at 0, but the broken lines clearly indicate that the scale is not continuous.

Scaling also affects line graphs, as shown in Figure 10.21.

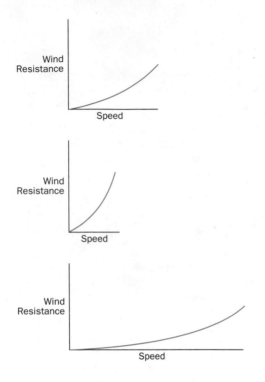

FIGURE 10.21 **Scaling issues affect line graphs as drastically as bar graphs.** By changing the scale on either axis, you dramatically alter the plotted curve. In these examples, the effect was achieved by changing the lengths of the axes. The same effect would be achieved by changing the scale represented on the axes.

Editing Technical Graphics

For each of your graphics,

☐ have you used the best possible graphic to present the information?

☐ are the axes, column headers, legends, and other conventions clear?

☐ is the graphic accurate and easy to understand?

☐ have you chosen colours that take into account how the report will be reproduced?

☐ is the graphic referred to or introduced in the text preceding the graphic?

☐ does the graphic have a caption?

☐ does the graphic have a source attributed where required?

Exercises: Technical Graphics

Exercise 10.1: Seeing How Graphics and Formatting Function in Reports

Find a report online or in hard copy or look at one given to you by your instructor. Singly, in pairs, or in groups, take a look at the report, and as you turn pages, take note of the sequence in which you look at the graphics, their captions, the headings, and the text.

Having flipped through the report and looked at the graphics, do you feel that you have a good overview of what the report is about? Read the summary to see whether it confirms your impression. Once you've read the report or skimmed it, do you feel that your initial impression of the contents of the report was accurate? So, if you read the summary of a report and then looked through the graphics, would that give you a pretty good idea of the report's contents? This is, in fact, how many readers "read" reports, particularly long ones. They read with close attention only those parts of the body of a report that directly pertain to their job. They skim, or ignore, the rest and look at the graphics.

Exercise 10.2: Using Graphics Ethically

Mark Twain, America's Stephen Leacock, once famously said: "There are three kinds of lies: lies, damned lies, and statistics." Graphics can be just as deceptive as statistics.

For instance, if you look at the bar graph below, you'll note a good distribution of values along the *y*-axis, starting at zero and going up to one million. Now imagine that we were comparing only the populations of Nova Scotia and New Brunswick. What if, to save space or enhance the difference between the bars, we started the values on the *y*-axis not at zero, but at 600,000. To get a sense of what that might look like, use your hand or a piece of paper to block off the *y*-axis at that value. If someone wasn't paying attention to the values on the *y*-axis, what conclusion might he or she come to about the relative populations of those two provinces?

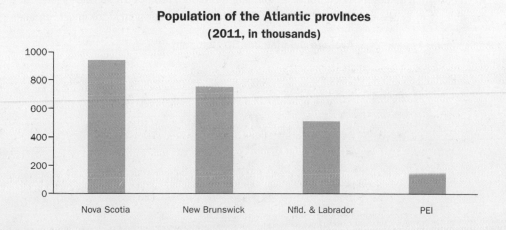

Population of the Atlantic provinces
(2011, in thousands)

The two bar graphs below chart the prices of cable and Internet subscriptions over time. The prices in both are the same; both *x*-axes start and end at the same values. Why is your impression of the rate of the price increases so different for each?

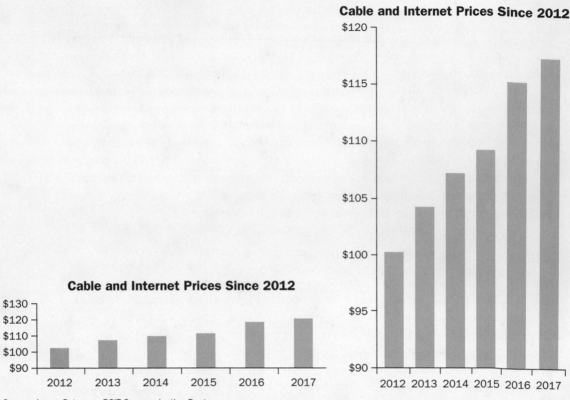

Cable and Internet Prices Since 2012

Source: James Peterson, BCIT Communication Dept.

Take a look at the graphic below indicating the salary differences between managers, office workers, and labourers at ABC Company and take note of your first reaction to the magnitude of those differences. Then take a look at the actual dollar values of the salaries. Do you notice a discrepancy? If not, try sketching out a bar graph of those values (or create one quickly in Excel) and see if the salary differences don't suddenly look much smaller.

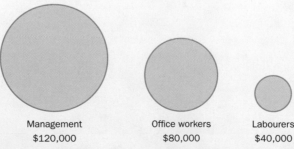

Average Salaries in ABC Company

Management	Office workers	Labourers
$120,000	$80,000	$40,000

Source: James Peterson, BCIT Communication Dept.

What accounts for this difference? Who might want to use the graph to illustrate salary differences? Who would benefit from this presentation?

Take a look at the line graph below. Back in 2006 one of your friends invested $1,000 in ABC Company and another an equal amount in XYZ Company. Who made the better investment?

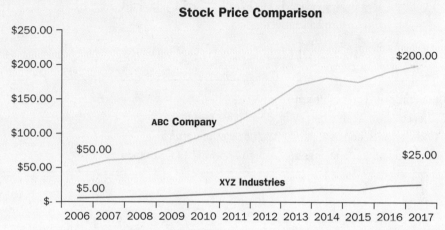

Stock Price Comparison

Source: James Peterson, BCIT Communication Dept.

Now do the math and figure out for how much money your friends sold their respective stocks in 2017. If you were fooled by the graphic, why were you? Was it deliberate misrepresentation, or is something else going on here?

Alone, in pairs, or in groups, discuss in what other ways graphics can deceive, either intentionally or not. Try to find examples. Report back to the class and see what examples or ideas other students have come up with.

Try to find graphics in the media (magazines, newspapers, online articles) that distort values to make a point or reveal a bias through presentation.

Exercise 10.3: Graphics in the Professional Workplace

Use your contacts in industry to discuss the importance of graphics in technical reports. Graphics look easy, but how much time actually goes into the creation of an effective graphic? Do writers in industry go through multiple editions of their graphics; that is, do they edit their graphics much as they edit their text, for maximum effect?

Chapter 11

Job Application Packages

> **In this chapter you will learn**
> · how to craft scannable, clear, descriptive résumés
> · how to write concise, persuasive application letters
> · how to find job openings to which to apply in the first place.

The job application package consists of the résumé and application letter, but we'll also discuss the job search. Before we start, however, let's dispel a myth.

The Myth of the Experience Trap

No doubt, you've heard about the experience trap: jobs always ask for experience, but how do you experience until you get your first job? You really don't need to worry about that.

The fact is that every year the economy absorbs hordes of fresh-faced young people just like you, with absolutely no experience in their field. It's perfectly normal, of course, for employers to prefer applicants with experience, even for entry-level jobs. But people with more qualifications will apply for higher-level jobs, leaving the entry-level jobs wide open for you, regardless of the employer's optimistic wish list.

So, don't worry about your lack of experience. Focus instead on portraying yourself as the sort of employee that employers would like to invest in, long term. This is really how résumés work. They pull together verifiable facts that tell the prospective employer a lot about who you are as a person and what sort of employee you would make. Your job application package should paint a picture of you as a reliable, diligent, responsible, hard-working, enthusiastic, dependable person who will make an excellent investment as a long-term hire.

Résumés

Prospective employers will not look at your résumé as a mere list of facts about you or as a one-off by a busy student. They will see it as defining your professionalism, attention to detail, and respect for your employer's time, and as a reflection of your ability to communicate; they will see it as the kind of document that you will produce in the workplace and, potentially, send to clients. This is why sloppy and thoughtless formatting, spelling errors, and unclear or confusing expressions pretty much always consign a résumé to the trash bin—fair enough, because other applicants with similar qualifications will have taken the time to make their résumés perfect.

> Here's how to create the "e" with the proper accent in "résumé." In Windows, hold down the ALT key and type 0233 on the numerical keypad; release. On a Mac, you first insert the accent, then slip the "e" under it. Hold down the Option key and hit the E key. The acute accent will appear. Then hit just the E key again and the "e" will appear under the accent.

Parts of a Résumé

All résumés have several standard parts. The order of these parts will vary depending on your level of experience, as described in the "Organization of a Résumé" section (below). Some sections may not be included at all depending on whether you have something to put in them or not. If not, don't worry about it.

Letterhead (Contact Information)
The top of the résumé should contain your name, address, and contact information such as your telephone number and email address. This information should appear in a neat block of text, either centred or left aligned.

Career Objective
The career objective (optional) lets your prospective employer know that you have clear goals for your future and that you have realistic expectations for your current job prospects. A proper career objective can help you look confident, ambitious, and competent. When you submit an application online, a career objective can also help bump up your résumé in the queue if it uses key words that the employer has set the filters to scan for. So it's good to include a few words from the job ad in the career objective.

However, if you're also sending a letter (or email) of application, your objective on the résumé will sound redundant. In that case, just omit it.

Skills/Qualifications Summary
Skills summaries provide brief, bulleted lists of your chief qualifications. They are intended to whet the employer's appetite and are unabashedly self-promoting. The employer will look for proof in the rest of the résumé, so make sure your claims are backed up there. You might consider modifying this list slightly depending on the employer, to better match the expectations listed in the job description.

Include professional licences and fluency in languages other than English in this list. If you have a lot of each, as you might later on in your career, you could put them in separate sections further down in the résumé.

Education

The education section of the résumé lists the educational programs and institutions you have attended, as shown in the sample résumés below. List your grades or grade point average only if it is impressive. It's often better to list the skills you've acquired than the courses you've taken, as that makes it easier for prospective employers to visualize you doing things for them.

List educational accomplishments in reverse chronological order—that is, starting with the most recent. And don't omit programs that you chose not to complete. There are many good reasons to leave school temporarily or to change your major. What you learned there will continue to be useful, even if unrelated. Also, by including this information, you don't leave any unexplained gaps in the résumé timeline.

Experience

The experience section lists the full-time and part-time jobs you have had. You can also include volunteer experience because many volunteer positions teach valuable leadership, organizational, and management skills, thereby providing transferrable skills that are valuable in any job.

List these experiences in reverse chronological order, just like your educational qualifications.

Honours/Awards

Use an honours section if you have a series of honours to list. If you have only one or two, you can include them in the description of the job or the school at which you won the honour.

Activities and Interests

Employers like to get a complete picture of their prospective employees. Your education section will provide them with an idea of what skills you've acquired scholastically, but it won't tell them what you are like as a person.

By listing your activities, such as community involvement, and your hobbies and sports, you demonstrate that you are well-rounded. Your continued participation in team sports, for instance, may reassure the employer that you know how to work on a team and that you are fit and healthy. Fit people have longer attention spans, get sick less often, and have fewer accidents on the job. Employers are aware of these statistics. Employers are also increasingly interested in good corporate citizenship, so your prior community involvement will assure them that you share their values and will represent them well in the community.

If you pursued these activities and interests while going to school and holding down a part-time job, your prospective employer can't help but form a favourable impression of your time-management skills, your energy, and your maturity.

Memberships

The memberships section is optional. You'll use one only if you belong to a number of professional or volunteer associations; otherwise consider listing your memberships in the activities and interests section or some other appropriate place in the résumé.

Your membership in professional associations will assure the employer that you have met that association's professional standards and that you are keeping up with developments in your field. Your membership in the student branch of your future professional organization will tell the employer about your commitment to the field and hint at your enthusiasm for ongoing education.

Be sure to include any notable positions you have held within the association as well as any significant contributions you have made.

References

The references section does one of two things. It either lists references or simply states that "references are available upon request." If you provide references, include the name and title of the reference so the prospective employer knows how the reference fits into your life. Is the reference your manager at Tim Hortons or your basketball coach, for instance? You don't, however, need to provide the full mailing address. Just a phone number and an email address will do.

Employers won't call your references until after you have impressed them sufficiently at the interview. Then they'll ask your permission to contact your references. For this reason, more and more résumés simply promise excellent references instead of actually listing them. This strategy saves space. But if you choose it, be sure to bring a list of references to the interview.

Whether you include references in your résumé or provide them on a separate sheet at an interview, always list (at least) three references. Three seems to be a magic number. Provide three and the reader assumes you've selected a mere three from the throngs of people eager to say good things about you. Provide only two references and the impression is that you have fallen short, that you can find only two people in the whole wide world willing to speak well of you.

Organization of a Résumé

Broadly speaking, there are two types of résumés: standard (chronological) résumés and focused (functional) résumés. For both, the guiding principle is that the information that is most impressive for the prospective employer should be listed first.

The standard résumé focuses on your education and your experience. It often begins with a brief skills summary section followed by more detailed education and experience sections. This is the résumé most frequently used by recent or near-graduates because it focuses on recognized educational qualifications for entry-level jobs. This is the résumé we'll concentrate on in this chapter.

The focused résumé focuses on specific skills, projects, or achievements, and it leaves the more general educational qualifications and job titles for later. This is the résumé most frequently used by professionals with a few years in the field (and sometimes recent graduates) who are applying for higher-level positions where specific and related job experience and a proven track record count.

Formatting of a Résumé

Attractive formatting with plenty of white space is vital in a résumé. It shows your level of professionalism, your attention to detail, and your understanding of the importance of visual presentation. It suggests that you can produce professional, attractive, and effective documents on the job. And it shows that you respect the process.

Effective formatting also directs the employer's eyes to the most impressive and important information in the résumé, so that even with a quick once-over, which may be all you'll get on first reading, you can hope to impress.

In a job competition in which a company may receive a hundred applications for a single position, employers are forced to use a brutal elimination method to narrow the field. This means that résumés are merely skimmed the first time to determine whether they go in the No pile or the Maybe pile. So only those that convey the most important and impressive information in just a few seconds and make it into the Maybe pile will get a closer reading.

From this springs the chief layout principle of résumés. Because we read from top to bottom and left to right, you should sequence the résumé sections and items from most to least impressive and always format items to put the most important information at the top and on the left. In terms of sections, this will mean that you will probably put your education section ahead of the experience section when applying for your first career job.

Wording of a Résumé

Résumés that pass the scan test are shortlisted and read quite carefully. At this stage of the hiring process, employers want to get a clear picture of who you are and what you have done. They also want to know whether you are the kind of person they want working for them, whether you will fit into their corporate culture, and whether you have potential for long-term employment and promotion.

Let's take a look at Figure 11.1, which provides an excerpt from one of the sample résumés in this chapter.

This item paints a clear picture of what the applicant has done and what the applicant is like. The prospective employer may not be looking for someone to brew coffee (at least not primarily), but he or she will definitely be looking for someone who works "effectively" and "efficiently," who has strong interpersonal and teamwork skills, who

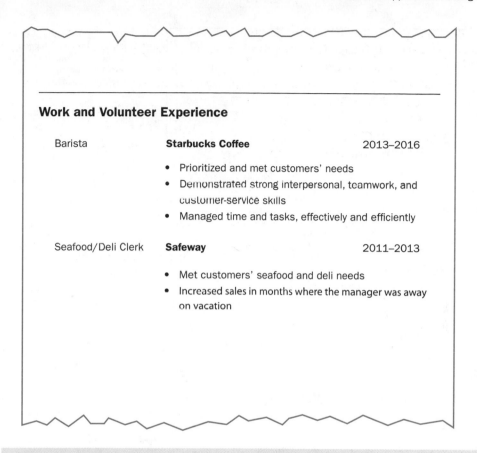

Work and Volunteer Experience

| Barista | **Starbucks Coffee** | 2013–2016 |

- Prioritized and met customers' needs
- Demonstrated strong interpersonal, teamwork, and customer-service skills
- Managed time and tasks, effectively and efficiently

| Seafood/Deli Clerk | **Safeway** | 2011–2013 |

- Met customers' seafood and deli needs
- Increased sales in months where the manager was away on vacation

FIGURE 11.1 A well-worded résumé item. These job descriptions paint a picture of a well-rounded, effective, efficient, pleasant, hard-working team player. Who wouldn't want to hire someone like this, regardless of the industry?

manages time well, and who is well organized. You need to find a way to demonstrate that you possess these sorts of attributes even if you've demonstrated them in another, completely unrelated job. These sorts of skills, learned in one industry, transfer easily to any other. Human resources professionals call them transferrable skills.

To paint a vivid, positive picture of yourself, use strong, active verbs to describe your activities and successes: "built," "served," "developed," "coordinated," "managed," "initiated." Use the present tense for current jobs and activities, the past tense for jobs and activities you no longer perform.

Support those strong verbs with strong modifiers: "effective," "efficiently," "dependable," "excellent," "strong," "supervisory," "advanced," "actively."

When you use such strong, vivid language, readers can't help but visualize you doing similarly wonderful things and being similarly effective at their place of work.

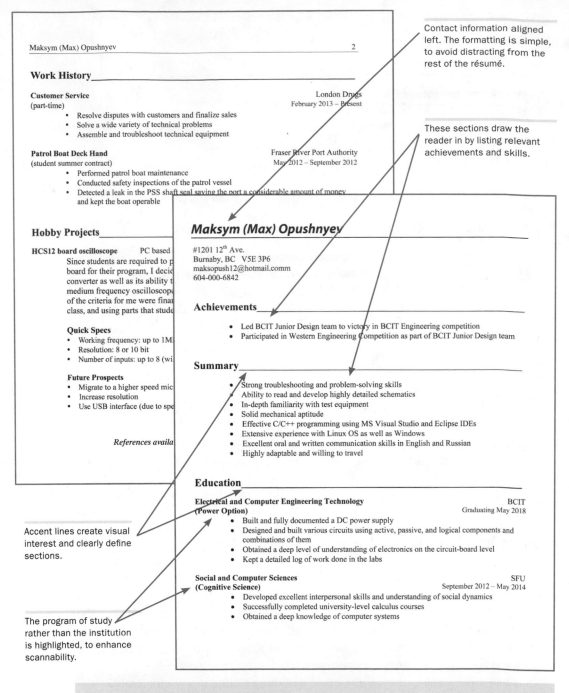

Contact information aligned left. The formatting is simple, to avoid distracting from the rest of the résumé.

Maksym (Max) Opushnyev   2

Work History

Customer Service   London Drugs
(part-time)   February 2013 – Present
  • Resolve disputes with customers and finalize sales
  • Solve a wide variety of technical problems
  • Assemble and troubleshoot technical equipment

Patrol Boat Deck Hand   Fraser River Port Authority
(student summer contract)   May 2012 – September 2012
  • Performed patrol boat maintenance
  • Conducted safety inspections of the patrol vessel
  • Detected a leak in the PSS shaft seal saving the port a considerable amount of money
    and kept the boat operable

These sections draw the reader in by listing relevant achievements and skills.

Hobby Projects

HCS12 board oscilloscope   PC based
  Since students are required to p
  board for their program, I decid
  converter as well as its ability t
  medium frequency oscilloscop
  of the criteria for me were fina
  class, and using parts that stude

Quick Specs
  • Working frequency: up to 1M
  • Resolution: 8 or 10 bit
  • Number of inputs: up to 8 (wi

Future Prospects
  • Migrate to a higher speed mic
  • Increase resolution
  • Use USB interface (due to spe

            References availa

Maksym (Max) Opushnyev

#1201 12th Ave.
Burnaby, BC   V5E 3P6
maksopush12@hotmail.comm
604-000-6842

Achievements

  • Led BCIT Junior Design team to victory in BCIT Engineering competition
  • Participated in Western Engineering Competition as part of BCIT Junior Design team

Summary

  • Strong troubleshooting and problem-solving skills
  • Ability to read and develop highly detailed schematics
  • In-depth familiarity with test equipment
  • Solid mechanical aptitude
  • Effective C/C++ programming using MS Visual Studio and Eclipse IDEs
  • Extensive experience with Linux OS as well as Windows
  • Excellent oral and written communication skills in English and Russian
  • Highly adaptable and willing to travel

Education

Electrical and Computer Engineering Technology   BCIT
(Power Option)   Graduating May 2018
  • Built and fully documented a DC power supply
  • Designed and built various circuits using active, passive, and logical components and
    combinations of them
  • Obtained a deep level of understanding of electronics on the circuit-board level
  • Kept a detailed log of work done in the labs

Social and Computer Sciences   SFU
(Cognitive Science)   September 2012 – May 2014
  • Developed excellent interpersonal skills and understanding of social dynamics
  • Successfully completed university-level calculus courses
  • Obtained a deep knowledge of computer systems

Accent lines create visual interest and clearly define sections.

The program of study rather than the institution is highlighted, to enhance scannability.

FIGURE 11.2 Sample résumé in vertical format. Variations are, of course, acceptable, even encouraged. Make your résumé look unlike those of others to help it stand out and to demonstrate your eye for and attention to detail and the sincerity of your effort. Anyone can put in an 80 per cent effort. It's those who put in the last 20 per cent who get hired.

Source: Maksym Opushnyef, student

Scott Bird 2

Babysitting **Neighbours and Friends** 2009–2012
- Made sure children were safe, fed, entertained, and put to bed

Worker **Western Campus Resources** Summer 2010
- Boxed, sorted out, and cleaned used textbooks for high schools and post-secondary schools

Newspaper **North Shore News** 2006 2011
Deliverer
- Delivered newspapers door to door on Wednesdays, Fridays, and Sundays

Interests
- Actively participate in North Sh
- Self-taught guitarist and pianis
- Avid tennis player
- Occasional soccer player
- Past president of the Argyle Stu

References

Brenda Chang
Former Starbucks Store Manager
b.chang34@gmail.com
250-000-9387

Jason Siu
BCIT Instructor
Jason_Sui@bcit.ca
605-000-7015

Russell Sanghera
Western Campus Resources Supervisor
Russell.sanghera@Wescampus.bc.ca
604-000-2564

Contact information centred. Again, the contact information is scaled modestly and unobtrusively. The reader is supposed to go directly from the name to the first heading.

Scott Bird

1189 Lynx Rd.
North Delta, BC V5M 5T2
s_bird12@hotmail.com
778-000-9571

Skills and Qualifications

- Electrical and Computer Engineering Technologist – Graduating 2017
- Extensive experience building and testing various kinds of electrical circuits
- Proven ability to repair electrical circuits quickly and efficiently
- Advanced training in computer programming (C, assembly language, VHDL)
- In-depth knowledge of computer drafting techniques (AutoCAD)
- Strong results manufacturing and testing power supplies

Education

Electrical and Computer **British Columbia Institute of Technology** Graduating 2017
Engineering Technology
Diploma
Electrical Circuit Design and Analysis, Computer Programming, AutoCAD Drafting, Math and Applied Physics, Technical Communication

Science Courses **Capilano University** 2013–2014
First-year Math, Biology, Geography, and Physics

Grade 12 Diploma **Argyle Secondary School** 2008–2013
Successfully completed high school graduating with honours

Work and Volunteer Experience

Barista **Starbucks Coffee** 2013–2016
- Prioritized and met customers' needs
- Demonstrated strong interpersonal, teamwork, and customer-service skills
- Managed time and tasks, effectively and efficiently

Seafood/Deli Clerk **Safeway** 2011–2013
- Met customers' seafood and deli needs
- Increased sales in months where the manager was away on vacation

Note the parallel format of these items. This provides a quick list of Scott's education and jobs in the left margin. The schools and places of work are bolded for visual appeal and to draw attention.

The education and experience sections are formatted identically. The dates in the right margin help to balance the margins.

FIGURE 11.3 Sample résumé in parallel format. Set up the parallel format by inserting a table with two columns, one for the job title and one for the rest. Use one row per item to keep title and description aligned as you edit. When you're done, hide the cell borders, using the cell border drop-down menu on the Home ribbon (MS Word).

Source: Scott Bird, student

Note the use of specific, technical jargon. It's okay that only a technical insider will understand these terms. Those are the only people who would read this résumé.

This résumé focuses on the skills that Eric can bring to an exploration program, first in a brief summary list and then in more detail in the Experience section, which organizes his work history by the type of exploration he is skilled in, rather than chronologically.

Education

- B.Sc. Geoscience, University of Manitoba, 1998. Thesis: Geology of the Albert Lake Gold Prospect, Manitoba

Courses–minerals

- *Drilling Techniques*. Johannesburg, RSA, 1992, sponsored by the South African Drillers Ass'n
- *Geochemistry of Tropical Environments*. Mineral Deposits Research Unit (MDRU), Vancouver, Canada, 1997
- *Uranium Exploration and Exploitation in Africa*. Professional Program of the GSSA, Johannesburg, RSA, 2007
- *ArcGIS 9.2 Short Course*. Windhoek, Namibia, 2007
- *Uranium Exploration Course* (4 weeks). World Nuclear University, Straz Pod Ralskem, Czech Republic, 2009
- *Namibian Uranium Deposits Field Trip*. Various locations, 2009
- *MapInfo GIS Course*. Santiago, Chile, 2013

Courses–petroleum

- *Sample Examination Techniques*. Calgar
- *H2S Alive*. Calgary, Alta, 2000 and 2004
- *Open Hole Logging*. Calgary, Alta, 2000
- *Estimating Permeability and Porosity*. Ca
- *Interpretations, Implications, and Fractu*
- *Carbonate Review and Porosity Classific*

Refere

Even though some of this education is quite recent, it's the least important to a reader. The fact that Eric has successfully done the work proves that he has the skills. This list of courses is impressive, but really just to prove that Eric is committed to ongoing professional development and that he stays current in his field.

The Experience section is entirely skills based. First it is grouped by the type of exploration skill (metals or petroleum), then by specific metals. In each case, it's the skill and duration that matters, not the chronology. Eric has, for instance, six years of experience looking for copper, spread over four locations and probably not consecutive. But it gives an employer an idea of what Eric is capable of.

This is a fairly text-based résumé, but the skills are easy to find because they are bolded. The text focuses on specific achievements.

Eric Hanson, P.Geo.

Cell: +56-9-9268-5898   ehansongeo@gmail.com
Canadian citizen and permanent resident of Chile

Skills & Qualifications

- 16 years' experience in mineral exploration and mining on four continents
- 4 years' experience managing a geochemical sample preparation laboratory
- Petroleum well-site geology: conventional oil and gas, and tar sands
- Professional Geoscientist (P.Geo.) registered in the province of Manitoba
- Qualified Person (QP), able to write NI 43-101 and JORC compliant reports
- Fluent English and Spanish, conversational Portuguese

Experience

Metals Exploration and Mining

Gold exploration and mining: various projects for junior and major mining and exploration companies in locations including Manitoba, South Africa, Namibia, Argentina, Senegal, Brazil, Chile, Bolivia, and British Columbia. Well-known companies include Anglo-American (Angola) and Randgold (Senegal). Approximately 6 years' experience.

Copper exploration (+/- gold): various projects for junior mining and exploration companies in locations including Manitoba, Portugal, Namibia, and Chile. Approximately 6 years' total.

Uranium exploration: participate in uranium exploration in Argentina and Namibia during the 2005 to 2008 price spike. Nearly 3 years' experience.

Silver exploration: worked in Bolivia on behalf of Silver Standard Resources. 4 months' experience.

Cobalt exploration: worked on a cobalt project in Uganda. 7 months' experience.

Petroleum Geology

Petroleum well-site geology: well-site geology for conventional oil and gas as well as oilsands in Alberta. 1 year, 4 months' experience.

Geochemistry Laboratory Management

Laboratory management: country manager for Bondar-Clegg/ALS Chemex Brazil. Duties included management, marketing, and QA/QC. 3 years' experience.

Set-up and business development: set up initial lab for ALS Global in Khazakhstan developed the business by travelling the region and marketing the testing services directly to mining operations; coordinated activities between management in Spain, technical experts in Ireland, and two additional labs, in Moscow and Chita. Grew the business to $15 million in annual testing fees.

FIGURE 11.4 Sample functional résumé. Notice that it leads with the applicants' impressive list of specific accomplishments. After you've got a few years in the field, your professional accomplishments will impress an employer more than your education and will be more relevant for the positions for which you are applying.

Source: Eric Hanson, Geologist

IN THE FIELD

Heidi Carson, P.Eng.

At an early age I discovered the key to excelling in school. Listen to what the teacher is telling you, and then tell the teacher what he or she told you. As a by-product of my strategy I also picked up several gems of advice from my teachers regarding effective communication. Later, when it came to sending out résumés, I learned to spend hours in careful editing and asked as many people as I could to proofread for me. I also learned how to properly highlight my skills and accomplishments. Because of this, I rarely applied for a job without being chosen for an interview. These skills also proved helpful during performance reviews and negotiations about pay increases.

When I graduated from engineering school I started working as a design engineer. At that time I noticed that how you communicate on paper is often the only impression people in a large organization have of you. You rarely get a chance to have a one-on-one conversation with everyone. But at some point everyone in an organization will read something you have written. Being able to properly document what you do goes hand in hand with everything you do in an engineering firm. And it really is true that most people who find a spelling or grammar mistake will discredit the entire message of a document.

Now, as a technical writer, I am responsible for communicating the ideas of engineers in a way that others can understand and implement. Often engineers do not understand how critical communication is. They tend to get a bit lost in their world and forget that the rest of the world doesn't speak "engineer." However, an uncommunicated idea is the same as no idea at all.

Once you get into it, you might be like me and enjoy playing with the English language to find the best word, or working with word order to make a sentence that flows well. But either way, learning the basic tools for effectively crafting the English language is the first step towards accomplishing whatever goals you have in life.

Application Letters

An application letter (sometimes referred to as a cover letter) is more than a brief note letting the reader know that you are applying for a job and that your résumé is enclosed or, in the case of an email, attached.

An application letter (or email) is a sales document tailored very specifically to the job for which you are applying. It expands on the two or three items from your résumé that will most convince the prospective employer that you are a suitable candidate.

The application letter should be no longer than a single page and should be formatted like a proper business letter. For details about letter-writing strategies and professional letter format, please review Chapter 5.

In general, an application letter has the following four-part structure:

1. introductory paragraph
2. education paragraph
3. experience paragraph
4. concluding paragraph.

In addition, you should also note, either in one of these paragraphs or in a separate paragraph, why you want to work for the company and what you think you could contribute to the company.

1. Introductory Paragraph

The introductory paragraph should do a number of purely perfunctory things:

- **Identify your source of information** so that employers know how you heard about them. More and more employers, particularly large ones, advertise exclusively on their own websites, but HR departments always want to know where their best applicants are coming from.
- **Identify the position for which you are applying.** Large companies might be advertising for several positions at once and will need to know how to file your application. Putting the position and reference number in your subject line/title will help. In your letter, restate that you are applying for the position.
- **Demonstrate your knowledge of and interest in the company.**
- **Indicate what points you'll be developing in the rest of the letter.** For instance, Scott starts his application letter (Figure 11.6) by mentioning his diploma and his interest in the company; he then expands on these points in the subsequent paragraphs.

The introductory paragraph also sets the tone for the rest of the letter. It should convey quiet confidence and professionalism. Remember that you are writing to someone who is your professional superior. Be confident, but don't sound overbearing or arrogant. Let your friends read your letter to check the tone for you.

2. Education Paragraph

The education paragraph describes your relevant educational background, not your entire educational history. It selects those parts of your education that will be of particular interest to the prospective employer and develops them in detail.

For instance, the job ad may indicate that you'll have to do quantity take-offs and estimating. The résumé might already have cited the relevant courses as part of your program of studies, but in your application letter you'd draw attention to those courses, describe particular projects you completed in them, and talk up your excellent marks, for instance. The idea is that the letter buffs up the most relevant parts of your education to help put your résumé over the top.

The education paragraph may refer the reader to the résumé for additional detail.

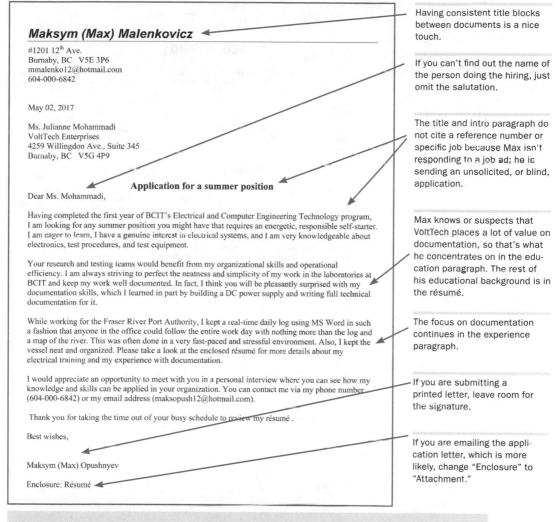

FIGURE 11.5 Sample unsolicited application letter. The content is no different than when responding to a job ad, except that you cannot cite a posting for which you are applying. However, you know the kind of position for which you are applying and you have seen job descriptions for those kinds of positions from other firms. Now just send out unsolicited applications in case you get lucky and for employers to keep on file.
Source: Maksym Opushnyev, student

3. Experience Paragraph

Please note that if you do not have a lot of experience, you do not have to include an experience paragraph. You could instead have two or three education paragraphs. By the same token, after a few years in the field, you'll probably dispense with the education paragraph and write a series of experience paragraphs instead. The key is to ask yourself what two or three things you could tell prospective employers that would

A consistent title block is not necessary, but it is a nice design element.

Because those doing the hiring don't want to be contacted by potentially hundreds of applicants, they often omit their names from the job ads. In such cases, don't use a saluta-tion; save the space to sell yourself better.

Scott is applying for a posted job, so he cites the reference number in the title and mentions how he found out about it in the intro paragraph.

The education paragraph provides a quick overview of the many skills that Scott could bring to TRK, taking its cue from the job ad and maybe from a bit of Google research on the company.

Because his current project will impress TRK more than his jobs would, Scott employs a second educa-tion paragraph, this time focusing on a specific and relevant project.

If you leave space for a signature, be sure to sign.

Scott Brady

1189 Lynx Rd.
North Delta, BC   V58 5T2
S_brady12@hotmail.com
778-258-9571

February 15, 2017

TRK Inc.
1050 West Hastings St., Suite 320
Vancouver, BC   V6E 3S7

Application for Electrical Engineering Technologist Position (File No. 2011-525-0853)

I am applying for the Electrical Engineering Technologist position for your growing Vancouver office as advertised on the eJobs website. I will be receiving my diploma from BCIT in Electrical and Computer Engineering in the Electrical Power and Industrial Control option in May, and I will be looking for a new challenge and a career job. While visiting your website, I became immediately interested in your company mission and projects.

BCIT's intensive diploma program has provided me with industry-specific skills that can be applied immediately at your company. The program has included courses in three-phase power systems analysis, power system relay applications, PLC and HMI programming, electrical equipment, technical communication, industry codes and standards, and much more. Although much of the work in these courses was completed independently, many labs and other projects included teamwork. Problem solving, troubleshooting, and the design of electrical power circuits are a normal part of most courses as well.

At the moment I am part of a group project that I feel may be a great example of the type of work your company is looking for. The project involves two automatic/manual water pump motors for a reservoir which have to be designed using both PLC and HMI programming. We have to devise solutions for tracking various conditions and fixing potential problems that could arise with the pump motors. The project also involves an oral presentation to the class, which I feel is an important skill for communicating information to coworkers and/or customers.

As a self-motivated person with strong technical and communication skills, with an interest in career growth and development, I believe I am a very strong candidate for this position. I would greatly appreciate the chance to meet with you. Please contact me any time by phone (778-000-9571) or email (s_bird12@hotmail.com).

Sincerely,

Scott Bird

Enclosure: Résumé

FIGURE 11.6 Sample solicited application letter.

Source: Scott Bird, student

make them take a closer look at your application. Write about those in the order of most to least persuasive.

The experience paragraph, should you find yourself using one, describes your rel-evant work experience, not your entire work history. Focus on those parts of your experience that will prove to the prospective employer that you can do the job. If the position for which you are applying requires supervisory skills, describe how you led a team to success at some other job, during a time of high stress. If you managed it then, you can do it again for a different employer, even in a different industry.

The experience paragraph may refer the reader to the résumé for additional detail if the education paragraph hasn't already done so. Avoid repetition.

4. Concluding Paragraph

Remember that the introductory letter is a sales document. So, in your concluding paragraph, ask for an interview and provide your phone number and email address so that, theoretically, the reader will pick up the phone right then and there. Does this always work? Obviously not. But ending confidently and with a standard, professional close makes a good impression, so just follow the formula.

If you have not yet referred the reader to your résumé, you should do so here.

Tone

Tone is a difficult thing to describe and a difficult thing to get right. You want to sound confident, but not overbearing, and you don't want to seem like you're bragging. So make your claims as neutral as possible and as factual as possible, and, when possible, rely on third-party endorsement.

For instance, don't say, "I am extremely good at math and have an excellent eye for detail," if you can instead say, quite provably, "I have consistently achieved first-class marks in all my math courses and was complimented on my attention to detail in my estimating and quantity take-off assignments." Don't just say, "I have excellent team leadership skills," if you can say, "Within six months of being hired, I was promoted to team lead and was able to complete the project on time and under budget." The fact that another employer promoted you is a third-party endorsement. It's almost as good as a personal reference.

Also don't be afraid to use technical terminology from another discipline with which the reader may not be familiar. One of the hallmarks of a professional is the mastery of professional language. Your prospective employer doesn't have to specifically understand what you mean to get the sense that you've done some technically interesting things. He or she will naturally assume that if you were able to do so in a prior job, you will do so again in your new job.

Finding Job Openings

There are two kinds of job openings: those that are advertised and those that are not. Most jobs in Canada are filled without ever being advertised.

Advertised Openings

Most companies advertise first on their websites, so google companies working in your field and check the Opportunities or Jobs page on their websites regularly. Some firms will allow you to subscribe to alerts so that you'll be notified when an opportunity comes along.

You can find other opportunities on job search sites such as monster.ca, find-a-job-canada.com, bcjobs.ca, wowjobs.ca, indeedjobs.com, eluta.ca, Craigslist, and many more. Some educational institutions offer student employment services and post jobs for employers looking for graduates from specific programs or with specific qualifications. BCIT's Student Employment Services is one example: www.bcit.ca/ses/ejobs. These sites will also often permit you to sign up for notifications when jobs with search parameters that you have defined become available.

Most professional and trade journals also offer access to job listings through their websites.

When you find a job in which you are interested, submit a résumé and application letter (or email) and wait for a response. Follow-up is generally discouraged, sometimes explicitly so, to protect the hiring committee from being badgered by potentially hundreds of applicants.

Unadvertised Job Openings

Most positions are filled either by word of mouth or more often through an existing pool of qualified job application packages kept on file. These jobs are never advertised. For companies, the advantage is speed and convenience. For you, if you can get in the pool, the advantage is limited competition. The trick is to get into that pool. Here's how.

When you find companies where you might like to work, write them an unsolicited application. The only difference between an unsolicited application letter and a solicited application letter is that you don't have a specific job number to quote and you can't cite in your intro paragraph where you found the job listed. But that's really it.

So apply for, say, "an entry-level civil engineering position" and write the rest of the letter as you would for any other entry-level civil engineering position in the industry. If, while browsing the company website, you find something specific to which you can tailor your application letter, do so. If you're qualified, they'll keep you in the pool for up to six months.

Unsolicited applications also offer a few other advantages. For one, you can follow up. When potential employers expect to receive lots of replies to a job ad, they don't like to give out the names of individuals doing the hiring (see the annotation in Figure 11.6). However, if no position has been advertised, you can call and ask for a name. You still might not get one, but it's worth trying.

If you do get a name, you can personalize the application and you can follow up. If you haven't heard back after a few days, feel free to send a follow-up email or make a call. When you get in touch, ask how long they keep résumés on file, ask if you can send another résumé when that time period expires, ask if they know of anyone else who might be hiring, and ask for an information interview (see below).

Social Media and the Job Hunt

Use Facebook and LinkedIn (which is Facebook for professionals) to make contacts and post queries about job openings. LinkedIn, especially, is a good way to network and establish contacts with professionals in your field. Once you've made a contact, ask for advice, ask whether they have heard of a potential opening, and ask for an information interview.

Continually keep your LinkedIn profile updated much like you would your résumé, for instance by describing projects on which you are working and listing projects you've completed successfully. This may open up an opportunity to discuss similar projects with some of your contacts, to share experiences, and to get advice. It may even get you headhunted if someone out there is looking for an employee with your skill set and experience. Just remember not to break nondisclosure requirements.

If you are unemployed, update your status on LinkedIn; most of your contacts will be notified, just as in Facebook, and you can begin to leverage those contacts to start looking for opportunities for you. If you are looking for a new job while still employed, however, you might not want to post your intentions. If your current employer were to find out, you might end up having an uncomfortable discussion about your commitment to the company. Take those inquiries off line.

However, you should be aware that prospective employers will always check you out on social media. So be careful about your online image and remember that it's not just the pictures and comments on your own Facebook page that matter, but also those on your friends' pages, if you appear in them. Alternatively, adjust your security settings.

Information Interviews

An information interview is a conversation between you and a more knowledgeable, experienced person in your field to get information from that person. Another important reason for participating in these sorts of professional interactions, though never mentioned during the interview, is to build contacts in the industry.

Be friendly, professional, and interesting. Bring intelligent questions about the industry, the direction it's going, and up and coming trends and technologies; ask how you can improve your odds of getting a job, for instance through ongoing education.

Say please and thank you, listen politely when the interviewee answers your questions, and generally strive to make a good impression. Ask if the interviewee knows anyone who might be hiring. When you send those firms your unsolicited application, mention the interviewee's name; your prospective employer will probably call the interviewee, so dropping his or her name functions as a sort of reference. For that reason, be sure to ask the interviewee if it would be okay to mention him or her.

In the future, the interviewee will have a face and a favourable impression to place with your name, so your résumé will be at the top of the list when his or her firm starts to think about hiring someone (with your level of qualifications, that is).

A word of caution: when you ask for an information interview on the phone, the interviewee may say something along the lines of, "Sure, why don't we just do it on the phone though? I've got a few minutes. What do you want to know?"

So make sure you have intelligent questions prepared beforehand.

After the information interview, send a polite thank-you note or email.

Editing Job Application Packages

When you edit your job application package, check for the following.

Résumés

☐ Is the contact information as small as or smaller than the body text of the résumé? But make sure your name is the largest thing on the page; it functions as the title of the document.

☐ Are the résumé sections sequenced from most to least relevant? Generally, for students this means that the education section comes before the experience section.

☐ Within each section have you used a reverse chronological order, that is, beginning with the current or most recent item?

☐ For each item within the sections, have you placed the most important information (the program of study or the job title) in the most prominent position to make the sections easier to scan?

☐ Have you described your educational attainments or learned skills in the education section and your job responsibilities in the experience section in active language to help readers visualize you doing similar things in their workplace?

☐ Have you asked someone to read over your résumé to see if he or she can spot any inconsistencies in the formatting, any spelling mistakes, or any errors in grammar?

Job application letters

☐ If you are making an unsolicited application, have you tried to get the name of the person to whom you should be addressing your application?

☐ Have you researched the company to which you are applying to find out about its culture, business, and projects?

☐ Have you chosen the two or three elements from your résumé that will be most impressive to the employer?

☐ Have you sequenced these elements from most to least impressive?

☐ Have you crafted a tone that is confident and professional, but still personable and lively?

☐ Have you asked someone to read over your application letter to check for any spelling or grammatical errors and to provide feedback on the tone and flow?

Exercises: Job Application Packages

Exercise 11.1: Research

Try to find an appropriate job opening in your field. Use some of the job search sites mentioned in the chapter, and try different search parameters until appropriate jobs come up. If you can't find a current listing in your location, broaden your search geographically.

When you've found some ads, take note of the qualifications and personal attributes for which the employer is looking and the tasks and duties for which the successful applicant will be responsible.

With your partner or group, draw up a profile of the sort of employee that your industry is looking for. Report your findings to the class. Your job in the application process will be to present yourself as exactly that kind of employee.

Exercise 11.2: Résumé

Create a résumé appropriate for the types of positions for which you are likely to apply, given your current qualifications. Your résumé will not change from application to application, except perhaps for minor adjustments to your skills list. So the résumé responds to the profile you created in Exercise 11.1.

Exercise 11.3: Application Letter

Choose a job application you found in Exercise 11.1 or take possession of one handed out by your instructor. Remembering that application letters expand on the two or three qualifications that will most impress a specific prospective employer, write an application letter tailored to that specific job ad.

Exercise 11.4: Comparing Applicants

At this point you get to play-act a little. Form pairs or small groups and pretend that you are the hiring committee tasked with scanning applications and making a first assessment.

As you review the résumés provided by your classmates or provided by your instructor, note your initial responses when you look at a résumé. Does it look well formatted and inviting or not? What works to make some résumés look better and scan better than others?

Does the wording work? Are the descriptions of skills or responsibilities at work or skills learned at school written in active language? Do the descriptions paint a clear and favourable picture of what the applicant would be like at work?

Does the writing of the application letter convey a sense of liveliness, enthusiasm, and personality?

If the application packages are from your classmates, be sure to provide useful feedback to help them improve. If you're not sure you want the competition, read Appendix C on ethics.

Chapter 12

Technical Definitions and Descriptions

> **In this chapter you will learn**
> - the functions of technical definitions and descriptions in technical writing
> - the three different kinds of technical definitions: parenthetical, formal, and extended
> - how to craft clear and properly structured mechanism descriptions
> - how to craft clear and properly structured process descriptions.

A considerable part of your writing responsibilities will consist not merely in recording information accurately, but also in translating it for those who might not otherwise understand—those in the field who are less knowledgeable than you and those outside the field who barely understand first principles. If it is your purpose to convey information to them, you must find a way. Technical definitions and descriptions help you to do so.

Technical Definitions

Whenever you use a term with which you think your readers may not be familiar, or when you are using a generally understood term in a very specific way, you'll need to define that term. You have three options, depending on the information requirements of your readers:

- parenthetical definitions (phrases)
- formal definitions (sentences)
- extended definitions (paragraphs).

Parenthetical Definitions

A parenthetical definition is generally a phrase squeezed into a sentence with parentheses, commas, or dashes. The idea is simply to provide a quick explanation for readers who may not be familiar with the term.

> The anode (positively charged electrode) is attached to the . . .
>
> The island chain has several haul-out sites for Steller sea lions, but only one rookery, a haul-out site reserved for breeding.
>
> Loss of ice cover in the Arctic is reducing the region's albedo—the proportion of incident sunlight that is reflected back into space—and thereby increasing global warming.

If you have a lot of terms to define or if you use a term frequently in longer documents, you can choose to define your terms in a glossary, as described in Chapter 7. That way, you won't have to provide the same definition at the beginning of each section.

Also use parenthetical definitions when you first introduce an acronym that you intend to use throughout the rest of a document:

> The fuel cell stack uses a proton exchange membrane (PEM) to strip protons off hydrogen atoms.

or when you want to define an acronym with which you suspect a less knowledgeable audience won't be familiar:

> Our tests showed high levels of rBGH (recombinant bovine growth hormone) in the samples.

Of course, if you feel that the reader will need more than a reminder about what rBGH stands for, you'll want to provide a formal or even extended definition.

Formal Definitions

Formal definitions are also known as sentence definitions. You'd use a formal definition for one of two reasons: if the term cannot be defined by a short phrase, or if the situation is more formal—for instance when you first introduce a term or object in an extended definition or in a manual.

Formal definitions have a standard (formal, if you like) structure consisting of three parts: the term being defined, the general class to which it belongs (group term), and the distinctions that set the defined term apart from all the other members of the class.

Term = class + distinctions

The trick is to make the class description as narrow as possible. That way, the distinctions—the differences that distinguish the term from the rest in the class—are fewer and easier to establish. For instance, in the sentence

> The ScanPen 150 is a hand-held, battery-operated scanning device about the size of a pen, capable of scanning bar and QR codes, as well as text.

the term is *The ScanPen 150*, while the class is *a hand-held, battery-operated scanning device*. Note that the writer has narrowed the class considerably by indicating that it is hand held (not a desktop scanner, for instance) and battery powered (not wired as at the checkout counter or like a computer peripheral). By narrowing the group in this way, the author doesn't have to include *hand-held* and *battery-operated* in the distinctions.

The distinctions that set the ScanPen 150 apart from all other hand-held and battery-operated scanners are that it has the dimensions of a pen (very portable indeed) and that it is capable of scanning text, not just codes.

This definition would make an excellent opening to a product manual for the device, though this made-up product would be quite out of date in the age of scanning cellphones.

Let's take a look at another example:

> The Weimaraner is a gun dog of German origin known for its mouse-grey to silver-grey fur and eyes that are blue in puppies and turn grey or amber in adulthood.

Term: *Weimaraner*
Class: *a gun dog of German origin;* that is, it's not a lapdog, a sheepherding dog, or a coursing hound, and it's not a gun dog of Hungarian origin, such as a Vizsla. This is a narrowly defined group of about six or seven breeds of dog.
Distinctions: what sets the Weimaraner apart from other German gun dogs is its *mouse-grey to silver-grey fur and eyes that are blue in puppies and turn grey or amber in adulthood.* No other German gun dog looks quite like it.

A few more quick examples and you should have the idea.

TERM	CLASS	DISTINCTIONS
Zoonosis	is an infectious disease	that can be transferred between species.
A cycle	is a complete process or series of processes	that ends in the same state or condition as it began.
Hydrogen embrittlement	is the process	by which metals become brittle and prone to fracture through hydrogen infiltration.
An impeller	is a rotating component within a tube, conduit, or housing	whose purpose is to increase or decrease the flow and pressure of a fluid.
Conservation of energy	is the principle	that energy can neither be destroyed nor created.

Admittedly, as in some of these examples, the class cannot always be narrowed down all that much.

Another useful hint: avoid circular definitions—that is, don't repeat the term in the class description, yielding no new or useful information:

> An electrical <u>insulator</u> is a material for <u>insulating</u> often made of rubber, glass, or ceramics. (Circular)

> An electrical <u>insulator</u> is a <u>non-conductive material</u> such as rubber, glass, or ceramics used to inhibit the flow of electrons. (A class description that narrows membership).[1]

Qualifiers

Often, terms have different meanings in different disciplines or are used in very specific ways for particular documents or situations. In those instances, add a qualifier.

> <u>In automotive applications</u>, mechanical efficiency is the ratio of the brake horsepower to the indicated horsepower.

> <u>In this report</u>, the XM12-32BA Transition Project will be referred to as the Project.

Audience-Appropriate Definitions

Definitions are useful only if they are clear and helpful to their intended audiences.

> Wind power density (WPD) is a calculation of the mean annual power available per square metre of swept area, taking into consideration wind velocity and air density.

This definition works for the more technically savvy who understand terms like *mean* and *swept area* and the influence of air density on potential power. For a less technically sophisticated reader, the following definition might be more appropriate:

> Wind power density (WPD) is a measure of how much wind energy is available per square metre of the circular area that a wind turbine's vanes sweep while turning.

This definition helps the reader understand the concept of swept area, but it leaves air density out of consideration entirely. The particular readers at whom the document was aimed, general readers with a mild interest in wind power, don't need to understand air density to get a sense that wind turbines can't be placed just anywhere.

Extended Definitions

Sometimes a sentence definition is not enough to suit your needs. In these situations, extend that definition using one or a combination of some of the following devices. They are listed in alphabetical order, not in order of relevance, preference, or recommendation. Use whatever means best suits your purposes and the readers' requirements.

---

1   Source: David Hamilton, BCIT Communication Dept., retired.

Appearance

The physical characteristics of something, what it looks like, is often an excellent way to define it. It is generally the best way to identify it.

> A hydrometer consists of a clear glass tube with a rubber bulb on one end, a thin rubber tube on the other, and a calibrated float inside the tube. Typical dimensions . . .
>
> A hydrometer weighs . . .[1]

Comparison/Contrast

Comparison and contrast helps readers understand your term in relation to something with which they are already familiar.

> "A Canadian is merely an unarmed American with health care."—John Wing
>
> An electron microscope is a microscope that uses a beam of electrons, which have a far shorter wavelength, to magnify an image instead of light.
>
> Because of its rotary cycle, the Wankel engine has lower vibration than a reciprocating engine and is more free-revving, allowing for higher redlines.

Etymology (Linguistic Derivation of Terms)

Etymological extensions help the reader understand the origins of a term.

> The Wankel, or rotary, engine is named after its inventor, Dr. Felix Wankel.
>
> Encephalitis is an inflammation of the brain. The term is derived from the ancient Greek *cephalus*, meaning head; the prefix *en-* for internal is added to refer to the brain, and the common medical suffix *-itis* indicates an inflammation.

Exemplification

One of the best ways to help readers visualize or understand something is to provide examples of it, some of which they are likely to be familiar with.

> A zoonosis is an infectious disease that can be transmitted between species. Rabies, for example, can be contracted by humans when bitten by infected animals. Hantaviruses, which cause hemorrhagic fever, among other potentially fatal diseases, are generally transmitted to humans through contact with mouse excrement.

Function/Purpose

The function, purpose, or *raison d'être* of your term makes for an excellent definition. Many things are known primarily for what they do because objects are generally created for a specific purpose.

> A sphygmomanometer is used to measure blood pressure.

History

The story of how something came to be developed or how it evolved will give readers a fuller understanding of what you are describing.

> Development of the Wankel engine began in 1951, with a first working engine produced in 1957 by Hanns Dieter Paschke. While initially embraced by the automotive industry, the technology had a number of problems, particularly high gas consumption, which made Wankel engines much less attractive after the oil crisis in 1973.

Operating Principles

Describing what makes something work is an excellent way to define it. Operating principles work hand in hand with descriptions of purpose. This is how something achieves its purpose.

> A mercury thermometer operates on the principle that mercury expands noticeably when heated and contracts when cooled. Thus the top of a mercury column rises and falls with temperature when it is confined in a cylinder.[1]

Sample Extended Definition

The following extended definition employs some of the extension methods described above. The example comes from the website of General Fusion, a Canadian company developing a small-scale fusion reactor for power generation. While there is obviously much more that can be said about nuclear fusion and while a different emphasis of material is possible, this definition suits the purposes of General Fusion specifically, because it focuses on the safety and other advantages of civilian nuclear fusion reactors over fission reactors.

Nuclear Fusion

Nuclear fusion involves fusing small atoms together and occurs when two light nuclei collide to form a heavier nucleus. Like nuclear fission, the reaction is accompanied by a significant energy release. Unlike nuclear fission, there is no potential for meltdown, there are no radioactive by-products, and fuel is virtually unlimited. Nuclear fusion is the mechanism that fuels the sun, which is the solar system's largest fusion energy source.

A variety of atoms can be used as possible fusion fuels, but the most practical involve isotopes of hydrogen. Hydrogen normally consists of one proton and one electron with no neutrons (denoted as 1H). Two other isotopes of hydrogen include one and two neutrons respectively. These are denoted as 2H and 3H, but

This is not a circular definition because "fusing" is the best verb to describe what fusion does. Rather this is an identification of the basic operational principle.

Comparison and contrast

Exemplification

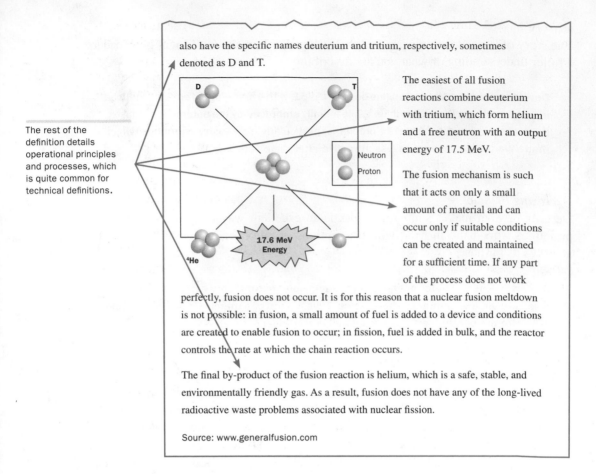

also have the specific names deuterium and tritium, respectively, sometimes denoted as D and T.

The rest of the definition details operational principles and processes, which is quite common for technical definitions.

The easiest of all fusion reactions combine deuterium with tritium, which form helium and a free neutron with an output energy of 17.5 MeV.

The fusion mechanism is such that it acts on only a small amount of material and can occur only if suitable conditions can be created and maintained for a sufficient time. If any part of the process does not work perfectly, fusion does not occur. It is for this reason that a nuclear fusion meltdown is not possible: in fusion, a small amount of fuel is added to a device and conditions are created to enable fusion to occur; in fission, fuel is added in bulk, and the reactor controls the rate at which the chain reaction occurs.

The final by-product of the fusion reaction is helium, which is a safe, stable, and environmentally friendly gas. As a result, fusion does not have any of the long-lived radioactive waste problems associated with nuclear fission.

Source: www.generalfusion.com

Technical Descriptions

Technical descriptions are necessary to give readers a clear idea about objects, mechanisms, or processes for which you are writing proposals, manuals, technical articles for publication, patent applications, specifications, requests for proposals, and the like. Sometimes the descriptions are an end in themselves, as in a patent application; sometimes they provide background to help the reader better understand the rest of a document, as in a user manual.

Mechanism and process descriptions are fairly closely related.

Mechanism Description

A mechanism is, for the purposes of technical descriptions, a system of parts (moving or not) designed to work together for a common purpose. A toothpick is as much a mechanism as is a Bombardier passenger jet. The latter, obviously, is more complicated.

When asked to describe a mechanism, we generally start with a sentence definition. After providing this general overview, we add a description of the mechanism's purpose and component parts. If the mechanism is very complicated, as in a passenger jet, we'd break its description into component systems, each of which would have to be broken down into further components, until we got down to individual parts—if the purposes of our description required such precision and detail.

When we break complex mechanisms into components, we have to create a logical structure and sequence for them. For instance, we might work from front to back, outside to inside, input to output, or first action to last (a version of cause and effect). This organization cannot be random. It can't jump around. The discussion on manuals in Chapter 13 describes how to properly partition a discussion of complex mechanisms, in that case, a mountain bike and its component systems.

We end a mechanism description by taking the reader through an operating cycle of the mechanism, to show how all the pieces work together. Strictly speaking, a mechanism description restricts itself to physical characteristic: location, dimensions, materials, textures and finishes, colour, weight, smell, and the like. Once we describe how something operates, we have a technical explanation, no longer just a description. For the most part, however, these two terms are conflated in common usage, even by technical people.

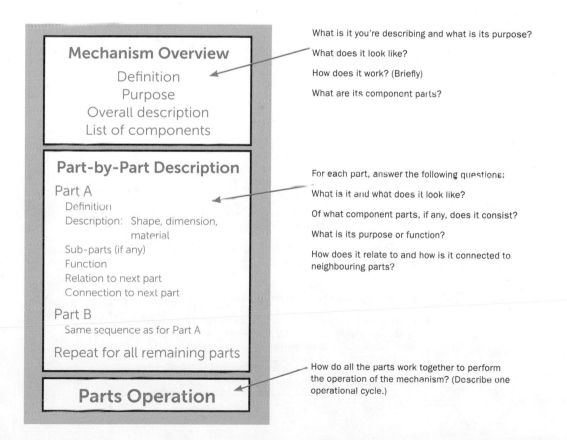

Mechanism Overview

Definition
Purpose
Overall description
List of components

What is it you're describing and what is its purpose?

What does it look like?

How does it work? (Briefly)

What are its component parts?

Part-by-Part Description

Part A
  Definition
  Description: Shape, dimension,
                material
  Sub-parts (if any)
  Function
  Relation to next part
  Connection to next part

Part B
  Same sequence as for Part A

Repeat for all remaining parts

For each part, answer the following questions:

What is it and what does it look like?

Of what component parts, if any, does it consist?

What is its purpose or function?

How does it relate to and how is it connected to neighbouring parts?

Parts Operation

How do all the parts work together to perform the operation of the mechanism? (Describe one operational cycle.)

The best way to illustrate this pattern in action is to look at an example.

Definition identifies the mechanism. It begins with purpose and function . . .

. . . and continues with appearance. Other methods of extensions could have been employed, if relevant.

List of component parts. Note that the part-by-part description that follows uses the same sequence (and numbers).

Graphics are always useful for helping readers understand what mechanisms look like and how the parts fit together.

Part-by-part list reprised to provide a proper introduction to the section.

Description of assemblies helps the reader to visualize how the parts fit together.

Description of a controlled temperature soldering iron

Overall Description

A soldering iron is an electrical device that applies heat to melt solder and make sound electrical and mechanical connections. In a controlled-temperature iron, a thermostat-like mechanism keeps the tip of the iron at a reasonably constant temperature. These kinds of soldering irons are commonly used in electronics labs.

In general terms the soldering iron consists of a tapered handle with a heated tip at one end, as shown in Figure 1. A power cord connected to the other end supplies the iron with low voltage power (e.g. 24 V) from a transformer in the soldering iron's docking stand.

In overall shape the soldering iron resembles a screwdriver. The user grips the handle like a pencil and uses the tip to make the solder joint.

Typical dimensions for a soldering iron are 18 cm long, with a diameter that tapers from about 3.5 cm to 1.5 cm. The iron without the cord weighs about 200 g.

The iron consists of six main working parts (see Figure 1):

1. barrel nut assembly
2. tip
3. heating assembly
4. switch assembly
5. handle
6. power cord and plug.

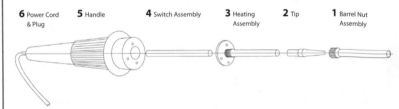

6 Power Cord & Plug   **5** Handle   **4** Switch Assembly   **3** Heating Assembly   **2** Tip   **1** Barrel Nut Assembly

Figure 1: An exploded, simplified view of the major components of a controlled-temperature soldering iron, showing the six main parts: barrel nut assembly, tip, heating assembly, switch assembly, handle, and cord and plug.

Part-by-Part Description

As shown in Figure 1, the soldering iron has six major working components: barrel nut assembly, tip, heating assembly, switch assembly, handle, and cord and plug.

Both the heating assembly and the switch assembly are long, thin tubes; the heating assembly is slightly wider so that it fits like a sleeve over the switch assembly. Both are secured to the larger end of the handle with three screws.

The tip is held on the end of the heating assembly by the barrel nut assembly, which screws onto the base of the heating assembly.

1. Barrel Nut Assembly

The barrel nut assembly is a thin metal tube, 8.5 mm in diameter, wide enough at one end to fit over the heating assembly and tip. This wider end has an externally knurled, internally threaded ring which mates with an external thread on the heating assembly.

The other end has an opening with a slightly smaller internal diameter, so that it allows the shaped end of the tip to protrude, but clamps onto the rim of the tip. When the barrel nut assembly is tightened it holds the tip securely in place on the heating assembly.

2. Tip

The tip is basically a solid metal cylinder with a tapered end. Measuring about 6 mm in diameter and 4 cm in length, it is made of high-conductivity copper, plated with iron and then with nickel to prevent oxidation. One end, which is used to make the solder joint, is shaped to make contact with the joint to be soldered. Many different tip shapes are available, to fit various kinds of soldering requirements, for example, screwdriver, bevelled, conical, or single flat.

The tip's other end is always a round cross-section so as to make good thermal contact with the heating element.

About 2.5 cm from the shaped end, the cylinder's diameter is enlarged slightly to form a narrow rim. The barrel nut assembly is screwed down onto this rim to hold the tip securely in place and can be unscrewed to change the tip when required.

On the shank of the tip is mounted a cylindrical ferromagnetic temperature sensor. When heated to a temperature above its Curie point, the material loses its magnetism. The sensor is coded with a number that indicates its idle temperature in hundreds of degrees F.

3. Heating Assembly

The heating assembly is housed in a stainless steel tube with a flange at one end that is secured onto the larger end of the handle. This tube fits over the switch assembly. The heating element is a stainless steel wire coiled around the inside of the heater tube. It is supplied with power by three wires that pass from the power cord and through the hollow handle.

4. Switch Assembly

The switch assembly fits within the heating assembly. It contains three major components inside a stainless steel tube – a permanent magnet with an attached shorting bar, a magnetic bushing, and switching contacts.

(a) The cylindrical permanent magnet can slide inside the tube. The magnet is attached to a long metal strip whose other end is attached to a set of switching contacts (the shorting bar). When the iron is cold this magnet is pulled towards the sensor mounted on the tip (see Operation, below). When the iron is hot the magnet is pulled the other way by the magnetic bushing.

(b) The magnetic bushing is made of a magnetic material and attracts the magnet in opposition to the temperature sensor.

(c) The switching contacts are metal strips and lugs that bring power from the power cord to the heating element. They are opened and closed by the magnet's movement.

The description of parts focuses on each part's appearance, function, and relation to other parts.

This part has sub-parts, each of which is also fully described—after being introduced in a list.

5. Handle

The handle is a hollow, plastic cone, slightly tapered from a diameter of 2.5 cm at one end (where it is connected to the switch assembly and heating assembly) to 1.5 cm at the other end (where the power cord is connected).

The wires from the power cord pass through inside the handle and are connected to the switch assembly and heating element.

A protective cover, made of a grooved plastic material, fits over the larger end of the handle. It insulates the user's hand from the heat generated by the heating element.

6. Power Cord and Plug

The power cord is a three-wire, round, flexible cord with a non-burning outer silicone rubber sheath. It is 1 m long and is attached to the iron with a strain relief at the end of the handle. The other end is fitted with a special three-pin plug that is inserted into the transformer outlet on the soldering iron stand.

Operation

Description of the operating principle of the mechanism . . .

When the soldering tip is cold, the temperature sensor attached to the tip attracts the permanent magnet (see Figure 2). The magnet in this position pulls the shorting bar into a position where it connects the electrical contacts to supply power to the heating element.

Switching Contacts　　Shorting Bar　　Magnetic Bushing　　Permanent Magnet　　Temperature Sensor　　Tip

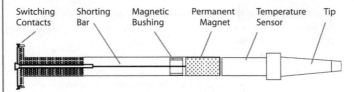

Figure 2: Simplified cross-sectional view of the switch assembly showing the main components used to control the temperature.

When the tip reaches its "idle" temperature (the Curie point) the sensor becomes nonmagnetic and no longer attracts the magnet. The magnet is then pulled towards the magnetic bushing, causing the shorting bar to move and disconnecting power to the heating element.

. . . through one full operational cycle.

Once the tip cools down, the sensor becomes magnetic again, attracting the magnet and completing the heater circuit, and the cycle begins again. In this manner, power to the heating element is turned on and off automatically so that the temperature of the tip remains constant.

Source: David Hamilton, BCIT Communication Dept., retired.

Process Description

A process description is in some ways very similar to a mechanism description. However, process descriptions are broken down into chronological steps, rather than into component parts.

A process description, however, should not be mistaken for a procedure (see Chapter 13). A procedure is a set of instructions that a user (reader) is intended to follow step by step to personally accomplish a task. Procedures are broken into bite-sized instruction steps, written in the active voice. They provide no explanations but contain plenty of cautions and warnings to make sure the user follows the procedure correctly and to prevent injury, damage to components, and failure of the procedure.

Process descriptions, on the other hand, are read for information only. They are there for readers to learn about and come to understand a process, not necessarily to follow it. If readers were to attempt the task, they should find appropriate instructions to help them.

Of course, some processes can't be attempted by a reader—for instance, the life cycle of salmon or the process by which stalactites and stalagmites are formed. Even human-driven processes, such as the manufacture of silicone wafers, are unlikely to be attempted by an individual reader, but that reader might be quite interested in how it is done.

Both types of process description have similar structures, though a process that an individual might follow would include a list of tools and materials (not appropriate for a natural or manufacturing process). Natural processes that follow cause-and-effect sequences will often be written in the active voice. Task-oriented processes that an individual could conceivably follow are generally written in the passive voice, so that they cannot be mistaken for instructions: the reader is emphatically not expected to follow the steps.

Process descriptions generally just end at the last step; there's no operating cycle to review at the end. When describing a cyclical process (such as a life cycle), the ending may briefly refer the reader back to the beginning: *"and then the cycle begins*

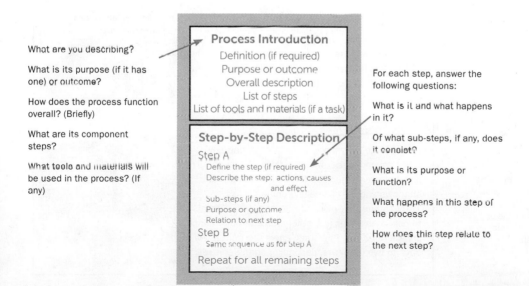

What are you describing?

What is its purpose (if it has one) or outcome?

How does the process function overall? (Briefly)

What are its component steps?

What tools and materials will be used in the process? (If any)

Process Introduction
Definition (if required)
Purpose or outcome
Overall description
List of steps
List of tools and materials (if a task)

Step-by-Step Description
Step A
 Define the step (if required)
 Describe the step: actions, causes
  and effect
 Sub-steps (if any)
 Purpose or outcome
 Relation to next step
Step B
 Same sequence as for Step A
Repeat for all remaining steps

For each step, answer the following questions:

What is it and what happens in it?

Of what sub-steps, if any, does it consist?

What is its purpose or function?

What happens in this step of the process?

How does this step relate to the next step?

anew." A brief overview of the cycle would, however, be part of the definition at the beginning of the description.

The following is a process description of the life cycle of salmon—an example of a process no reader could ever hope to attempt, but about which many might be curious. It's written for the general reader, not scientists.

The Life Cycle of Pacific Salmon

General overview including an informal list of steps: a formal, bulleted list might not have set the right tone for an informal description aimed at a general audience. The purpose, reproduction, is clearly implied. Salmon don't use tools, so no tools list was required.

While different species of Pacific salmon are somewhat different in the timing of their life stages, they all share common stages: they are anadramous, which means that they hatch in fresh water, where they will remain for days or years, depending on the species. At a time determined by instinct and development, they make their way to the saltwater of the ocean, where they will stay throughout their adulthood, for two to eight years, again, depending on the species. When they are ready to spawn, they will return to their natal waters, which could be as much as 1,000 km inland.

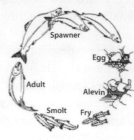

The different stages of the salmon life cycle are described below.

This is the first sub-step in the life cycle of salmon. Note that "redd" is defined parenthetically, as was "anadramous" above.

Eggs

The eggs are deposited by the female in a redd (a depression scoured out by the adults with their tails). The male then deposits milt (sperm) onto the eggs and the adults then cover the eggs with the scoured-out gravel to protect the eggs from predators, current, and other hazards. The eggs hatch 6 to 12 weeks later, depending on water temperature.

Relation to next step is stated or implied in each step.

Alevin

Alevin are newly hatched fish, with the remainder of their yolk sac from the egg still attached. They generally stay hidden in the gravel at the river or lake bottom for protection, until they've absorbed all the nourishment in their egg sacs and are forced to emerge and forage, at which point they are called fry.

Figure references and captions aren't necessary because of the informality of the writing scenario and because the pictures line up so perfectly and consistently with the headings and text.

Fry

Fry swim freely, feeding on tiny invertebrates, the carcasses of the spawned-out adults, and any other organic matter they can find. They generally stay hidden as much as possible, moving in the shadows and staying behind and under cover. At this stage they also learn to deal with currents, to school together, and other vital survival instincts. Fry will remain at this stage anywhere from a few days to two full years, depending on the species.

Each section describes clearly what happens in this step of the process: actions, purpose or outcome, and relation to the next step.

Smolts

In preparation for their journey to the saltwater, fry undergo a process called smolting, a series of physiological changes that enable them to live in saltwater without absorbing the salt into their bloodstreams. Once a fish turns into a smolt, at which point it will have a silvery covering over its scales, it is ready to begin its migration down the river, through estuaries and into the ocean, where it will spend its adulthood.

Adults

Once the salmon reach the ocean, as young adults, they range widely throughout the North Pacific and into the Bering Sea, migrating regularly, feeding voraciously, and growing rapidly for one to eight years, depending on the species. Little is known about this stage of the salmon life cycle, because their range and mobility make them hard to study.

Spawning

Spawning salmon are still adults, of course, but they go through physiological changes that make them quite distinct. Most notably, their colour changes, depending on the species, to become much darker, to turn a bright silver, or even to turn a bright red. Some species also change their body shapes noticeably. Note the humped back and hooked jaws on the male Coho salmon depicted on the right.

They return to their natal (place of birth) water, often as far as 1,000 km inland, where their changed colour and shape signals that they are ready to mate. Once paired, salmon will scour out a redd in which they can deposit their eggs.

This is, in a sense, a summary description of the circularity of the life cycle. Such end summaries are not necessary, but they do tie things up nicely at the end.

Having expended all their energy in the production of eggs and milt and in the physiological changes to their bodies, the exhausted salmon die, leaving behind their carcasses to nourish other animals and their own fry.

Atlantic salmon, which do not expend as much energy on physiological changes, have enough energy remaining to make a return journey to the ocean.

This is a general interest point (comparison and contrast) that like the paragraph above softens the ending. Again, it's not necessary, but not inappropriate in a piece of general interest writing.

The following is a process description for soldering. Its audience is electronics students.

Explicit statements of purpose are common in manuals and teaching aids. Note that this process description is meant to help the reader "understand" the process, not to perform it. That's what procedures are for (Chapter 13).

A brief and functional definition of soldering appropriate to the intended readers: electronics students.

A list of steps mirrored in the subheading structure that follows.

A list of tools and materials because this is a work process normally performed by people using tools and materials.

In this case the sub-steps don't require further description because they will be obvious to the intended reader.

This step, however, provides a full description: a definition and purpose statement and a clear idea of the actions that take place.

How Electronic Components Are Soldered

Introduction

This description will enable you to understand how electronic components are soldered in such units as circuit boards. Soldering is necessary in such devices to ensure permanent electrical connections.

The soldering process has four steps:
1. preparing the wire
2. tinning
3. connecting the leads manually
4. making the permanent connection.

The following tools and materials are required:
- electric soldering iron
- good grade electrical solder heat sinks
- wire cutter and stripper.

Description

1. Preparing the wire

Preparing the wire involves three main steps:

a) Cutting the wire to the required length.
b) Stripping the insulation from the ends of the wire. (Mechanical or thermal wire strippers are used to do this.)
c) Cleaning the wires before they are soldered because any grease or dirt will result in a poor connection.

2. Tinning

Tinning is the melting of a very small amount of solder onto the tip of the iron. The tip of the iron is tinned to provide maximum transfer of heat from the iron to the surface to be soldered (Figure 1). After tinning, the tip will look clean and shiny. The surfaces that are to be soldered together should also be tinned.

Figure 1: tip of a soldering iron that has been tinned. Note the shiny tip.

3. Connecting the leads manually

Before the two surfaces can be soldered, they must be connected mechanically. The connection is made by wrapping a wire or component lead around a terminal post or by inserting the ends of the component leads through holes in the circuit board and bending the leads to secure the component (see Figure 2).

Figure 2: Component leads being inserted into the holes in a printed-circuit board.

Note the use of the passive voice. The reader is not invited to perform these actions.

At this point, heat sinks can also be installed. Heat sinks are used to protect sensitive components such as diodes from heat damage during soldering. The heat sink is clipped between the component and the connection to be soldered. It is removed after the joint is soldered and cooled.

Note the consistently chronological development.

4. Making the permanent connection

The last step involves melting solder onto the joint and takes only a few seconds. The tip of the soldering iron is placed against the connection (Figure 3). Then the solder is placed against the tip of the soldering iron and the connection. Some solder will melt and flow onto the connection. At this point, the solder is removed. Next, the iron is removed from the connection.

Figure 3: Soldering involves holding the heated iron to the joint and touching the solder so that it flows into the joint.

The process description ends with the last step.

A good soldered connection looks smooth and bright and has a smooth, conical shape.

Source: David Hamilton, BCIT Communication Dept., retired.

Editing Technical Definitions

Is your definition

☐ necessary for the intended reader of your document?

☐ pitched at a level of diction and technical understanding appropriate to the intended reader?

Does your definition

☐ contain the right amount of information to suit your reader's needs and the purposes of your document? (Parenthetical, formal, extended)

Does your formal definition

☐ have a class as narrowly defined as possible?

☐ describe distinctions clearly and sufficiently narrowly that no other term or item could fit the same definition?

Does your extended definition

☐ begin with a formal definition?

☐ extend the formal definition by one or more extension strategies?

☐ focus on the information needs of the reader? (While history lessons, for instance, may be interesting, they should also be to the point.)

Editing Mechanism Descriptions

Does your mechanism description

☐ begin with a formal definition of the mechanism?

☐ extend that definition to include at least function and appearance?

☐ end with a logically organized list of component parts?

☐ include an illustration of the mechanism? (Optional, but particularly helpful)

Does your part-by-part description

☐ provide a clear description/definition of each part:

   ☐ appearance and materials

   ☐ function

   ☐ connection to and relation to other parts?

☐ identify any sub-parts (in a list) and describe those sub-parts in the same level of detail as all other parts?

☐ include an illustration of all the parts, properly integrated into the text? (Unless you already have one in the overview)

Does the parts operation section

☐ describe how all the parts work together?

☐ take the reader through one full operational cycle of the mechanism?

☐ include a graphic illustrating the operational cycle, if appropriate?

Editing Process Description

Does your process introduction

☐ define the process or indicate what the process is?

☐ include a statement about the purpose of the process (if it has been created for a specific purpose) or its outcome?

☐ list the steps in the process in chronological order, ideally using the same wording as in the subheadings for the sections that describe these steps?

☐ include a list of tools and materials, if you are describing a process that requires tools and materials?

Does your step-by-step description

☐ use a strictly chronological order throughout?

☐ describe the purpose or outcome of each step?

☐ define all terms where necessary?

☐ clearly describe the actions or processes that take place?

☐ define and describe all sub-steps (if any) clearly?

☐ indicate how the steps relate to one another?

Exercises: Technical Definitions and Descriptions

Exercise 12.1: Formal Definitions

Individually, in pairs, or in groups, write a formal definition for one of the following or for some other term approved by your instructor. Your audience and intended readers are your classmates. Display your completed definition on the whiteboard or projector, and discuss as a group whether the class of the definition is sufficiently narrow, whether the definition is sufficiently inclusive and exclusive. Do this without referring to a dictionary or Wikipedia; you'll find it more challenging than you might think.

- Van (motor vehicle)
- Corkscrew
- Whiteout (for error correction)
- Diode
- Paper clip
- Calculus
- Thermodynamics
- Transit
- Conduction
- Flagellum

Exercise 12.2: Mechanism Descriptions

Individually, in pairs, or in groups, write a mechanism description for one of the common objects listed below or some other object approved by your instructor, perhaps a mechanism commonly used in your field. Begin dividing the mechanism into a logical part-by-part partition.

Exchange your description with another person, pair, or group, or put it on a projector and discuss its effectiveness and accuracy. Check it against the checklist.

- Scissors
- Tweezers
- Tire iron
- Kettle
- French press coffee maker
- Compact mirror
- Kickstand for a bicycle
- Incandescent light bulb
- Hypodermic needle
- Ballpoint pen (non-retractable)

Exercise 12.3: Process Descriptions

Individually, in pairs, or in groups, write a process description for one of the common activities listed below or some other activity approved by your instructor, perhaps a process common in your field. Begin by dividing the process into a logical step-by-step sequence.

Exchange your description with another person, pair, or group, or put it on a projector and discuss its effectiveness and accuracy. Check it against the checklist. Remember that you are not writing instructions. You are describing what happens or needs to happen.

- Applying makeup
- Washing hair
- Cleaning pots and pans
- Changing tires on a car
- Patching a leak on an inner tube

- Giving an injection with a hypodermic needle
- Teaching a dog to sit on command
- Seasonal cycle of deciduous trees
- Life stages of human development
- Formation of mountain ranges or inland salt flats

Chapter 13

Instructions, Procedures, and Manuals

In this chapter you will learn
- the purpose, format, and organization of instructions
- the tone and wording of instruction steps
- the importance of notes, cautions, warnings, and danger alerts
- the use and placement of graphics in instructions
- strategies for designing and testing instructions for usability
- the combining of sets of instructions into manuals.

The purpose of procedures is to enable users to complete tasks with which they are not familiar. Thus the primary function of instruction steps is to describe for readers the actions that their hands must perform.

Users will refer back and forth to the individual instruction steps while performing the procedure, so procedures use a strictly chronological order: one step at a time. This means that procedures place notes, cautions, warnings, and danger alerts precisely where they are most needed.

Procedures do not, however, explain underlying concepts or physical principles unless the user needs to understand these concepts or principles in order to perform the necessary actions. Notes, cautions, and warnings perform that function but only in a very limited way in that they provide just enough explanation to ensure understanding and compliance. For a thorough understanding of a procedure, a reader would have to turn to a process description (Chapter 12). In addition, a procedure will include an overview in the introduction to provide some context and to help readers determine whether they should apply the procedure or not.

Fundamentally, however, the function of instructions is not to educate readers, but to guide them through a task.

You may find yourself writing end-user manuals for consumer products or software you are developing; installation, maintenance, and repair procedures for equipment you have designed; or simply instructions you want a colleague to follow while you're away on a business trip. The writing of instructions will form a considerable part of your technical workday.

Unsurprisingly, procedures, like many of the other documents we've looked at, are structured in three parts.

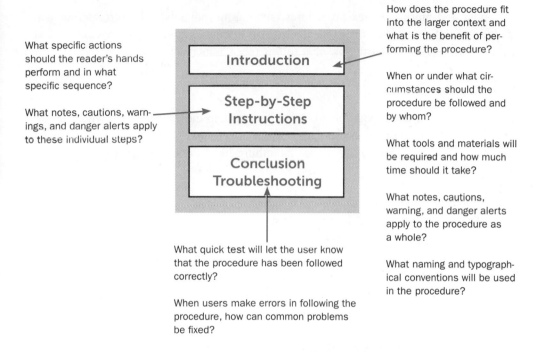

What specific actions should the reader's hands perform and in what specific sequence?

What notes, cautions, warnings, and danger alerts apply to these individual steps?

Introduction

Step-by-Step Instructions

Conclusion Troubleshooting

How does the procedure fit into the larger context and what is the benefit of performing the procedure?

When or under what circumstances should the procedure be followed and by whom?

What tools and materials will be required and how much time should it take?

What notes, cautions, warning, and danger alerts apply to the procedure as a whole?

What naming and typographical conventions will be used in the procedure?

What quick test will let the user know that the procedure has been followed correctly?

When users make errors in following the procedure, how can common problems be fixed?

The subsequent sections describe this organization in greater detail.

The Introduction

The introduction provides the basic information that the reader will need in order to follow the instructions easily and safely.

Purpose, Authorization, and Schedule

To motivate people to carry out difficult and time-consuming procedures, it is generally wise to explain why the procedure is necessary. So this is often how instructions open.

The user may also need to know whether this is the correct time to apply the procedure. For instance, a catalytic gas converter may have to be checked and cleaned every 2,000 hours of operation to prevent residue build-up and ensure operational efficiency; the reader may be referred to a running time meter.

In addition, some tasks should be carried out only by those certified, ticketed, insured, or otherwise authorized to do so. The reader will obviously need to know this. To provide proper emphasis, this information is frequently presented as a caution or warning (see below).

As always, the contents of a document depend on its audience and its purpose. You'll need to make some judgment calls.

Brief Process or Mechanism Description

In longer and more complex procedures (such as in manuals), the introduction will include a brief description of the mechanism or process as a whole, to provide context for the subsections of instructions that follow (see Chapter 12).

Typographic Conventions

Instructions often use typographic conventions to help the user identify when the instructions refer to parts or components. The conventions below, for instance, mean that the instructions don't have to say something like "Press the Return key on your keyboard." They can simply say "Press **Return**."

These instructions use the following typographic conventions:

Commands and Keyboard Keys	**Copy, Paste, Save As, Return**
Menu Selection Sequences	[Start] > [Programs] > [Adobe]
	> [Adobe Photoshop CS]
Dialog Windows	"New File Dialog Window"

Tools and Materials List(s)

Provide a list of all the tools and all the materials that the reader will require for the procedure and sort that list into these two types. If necessary or helpful, include parts numbers or brand names to help the reader; parts numbers might prevent misuse of very similar-looking parts, while brand names might be a warranty requirement.

Lists of tools and materials allow readers to pull together the required tools and to purchase the required materials before they begin following the instructions, thus preventing the nuisance of having to interrupt a procedure to go hunting for a tool or shopping for a replacement part.

Tools and Materials
Replacement filter, type FRDFF 2354
19 mm wrench
17 mm wrench

If the list is longer, break it into two lists, one for materials and one for tools:

Materials
Air filter, type FTWR786-23Q
Gasket, type XR-23PDR2017
Top seal, type XR-34PRC2013

1 L 1-Octanol Anhydrous Ammonia ≥99%
Somatech R23 test strip

Tools
gas mask
safety gloves
19 mm wrench
17 mm wrench
torque wrench
funnel

Time Required

If the procedure will take only a few minutes, don't bother citing a time. Otherwise, give users an idea of how long it should take them to complete the procedure, taking into account that users are generally performing the procedure for the first time and that they will be referring to the instructions every step along the way. It's common for writers of instructions to base these time estimates on their own experience and level of expertise, but readers may require two or three times as long.

A realistic time estimate will permit readers to schedule the procedure appropriately, so they won't be forced to abandon an unfinished procedure and leave behind disassembled equipment because, say, the shift is ending, daylight is fading, or they have an important meeting to attend.

General Cautions and Safety Measures

Any warnings or safety notices that apply to the whole procedure, and not just to individual steps, should be listed in the introduction. For instance, if readers should wear safety goggles throughout the procedure, tell them to do so here. But if you need to caution them against over-tightening a bolt in step 17, do so just before step 17. Otherwise readers will have forgotten about your caution by the time they get to the step.

The Step-by-Step Instructions

As with all documents, users don't really want to read the instructions; they just want to benefit from the information in them. Therefore, no matter how strongly you urge them to read the entire instructions before getting down to work, they won't. They just want to get started and get the job done, assuming that their common sense and general technical know-how will see them through. From this follows the cardinal rule of instruction writing: use a strictly chronological order—a just-in-time information delivery system. The following points describe what this looks like in practice:

- **Number all steps.** Users will read a step and then leave the page to do as instructed. Immediately after, they will return to the page for more instruction.

The numbers help users find their place. To avoid potential confusion, number only the steps. Never number the notes, cautions, warnings, or danger alerts.

- **Begin every step with a verb in the imperative mood (command voice).** You are commanding the user's hands to perform necessary actions in pared-down language in a setting where politeness is irrelevant. The imperative mood does this best because it is direct and clear.

17. Attach a hose to the drain valve.

Using the imperative mood consistently also helps to make the steps parallel and thereby speeds up comprehension.

- **Write simply and don't double up on steps**. Make each step easy to understand by using simple language and by putting only a single logical action in each step. Otherwise users won't be able to remember the entire step when they turn from the page. On the other hand, don't make the steps overly simple, as this will merely frustrate readers and slow them down. Use your judgment, based on what you know about the user's likely level of expertise.
- **Begin a step with an adverb if it is important how the reader performs an action**. "Carefully remove the detonator . . ."; "Calmly and slowly back away from the bear sow and her cubs."

IN THE FIELD

Behnaz Mortazavi

Written communication is an inseparable part of an engineer's job. Regardless of what engineering discipline you are pursuing, it is almost guaranteed that at some point during your career you will start writing technical data in the form of design specifications, data analysis reports, test procedures, assembly instructions, business proposals, etc. Depending on your role in the company, you may spend as little as one hour a day or as much as a few days a week creating technical records for your managers, team members, business partners, or customers.

To communicate accurately, clearly, and effectively with the outside world on the subject of your technical work, you have to be equipped with the right skills. You need to be able to analyze your audience and write in a way that is right for them. You need to design and lay out the technical information such that it is understandable and keeps your readers interested. And finally, you need to format the document so that it looks professional and presentable. Having such skills in your toolbox will be beneficial for the company you work for, will advance your career, and will certainly come in handy in other areas of your life.

I worked as an electronic engineer for eight years in the telecommunication, manufacturing, hydro, and printing industries. I have a master of engineering in microelectronics from Simon Fraser University and a technical communication certificate from the British Columbia Institute of Technology. I am currently working as a technical writer in the software industry in Vancouver, Canada.

- **Include graphics whenever you can**. Locations of components and physical actions and the direction in which those actions should be performed are usually best conveyed through graphics. In fact, graphics are so effective, and so universally understood, that some instructions use only illustrations so that they don't have to be translated into multiple languages. If you've ever assembled IKEA furniture or glanced at the quick start guides for installing computer peripherals, you'll be familiar with this concept.
- **Use "locate" steps for components that are difficult to find when you cannot generate a graphic**. It's no good telling readers to manipulate a component they can't find. By the time they do find it, they may well have forgotten what to do with it. So provide a locate step:

13. Locate the fuel filter on the fuel line inside the frame rail on the passenger side, immediately behind the tire well.
14. Loosen the nuts holding the filter in place. Begin with the nut closer to . . .

However, to avoid cluttering up the instructions with unnecessary steps, do so only if you anticipate that the user will have a hard time finding the component.
- **Subdivide long sets of instructions into several sections with clear, descriptive headings.** If all the steps are necessary to complete a single procedure, number the steps consecutively. For instance, if you are writing instructions on how to clean the parts of a mechanism, you might divide the procedure into several separate tasks: disassembly, cleaning, and re-assembly. However, the job isn't done until the mechanism is fully re-assembled and functioning normally, so number the steps consecutively. They are part of a single procedure.

   On the other hand, a manual compiles separate procedures—for instance, how to change the tire on your car, how to perform an oil change, how to change a fan belt, and so on. Each of these are completely separate undertakings, performed at different times. Restart the numbering at 1 for each.
- **Use "if-then" constructions when users have to check a condition and choose between two actions.** The following steps for adjusting the tank pressure on a fire suppression system demonstrate how much instructions function like a computer program for the reader's hands and eyes.

7. Shut the backflow valve.
8. Check the pressure readout on the gauge for the fire suppression tank. It should be between 30 and 35 psi.
   If the pressure is below 30 psi
   a) briefly press the fire retardant hose nozzle onto the tank valve to pump more retardant into the tank
   b) recheck the tank pressure (step 8).

If the air pressure is above 35 psi

    a) briefly press your key into the air valve to let a bit of air escape

    b) recheck the tank pressure (step 8).

9. Open the backflow valve.[1]

In this case, if neither condition applies, that is, if the pressure is between 30 and 35 psi, where it should be, the reader simply moves on to step 9.

It's never good enough to tell users to check for a condition without telling them how to do so and what to do if the condition isn't met.

The Conclusion

Instructions do not always require conclusions, but at a minimum and when appropriate, do try to include a brief check so users can be sure that they have followed the instructions correctly.

All three status lights on the modem should be steady green.

Sometimes, however, the instructions conclude with maintenance tips or with a trouble-shooter's checklist (for an example, see Figure 13.2). What, for instance, should the reader do if the status lights on the modem are not all green?

This checklist, often in the form of a table, identifies and indicates how to solve common problems associated with the mechanism or how to fix common errors made during the procedure.

If one of the status lights is flashing amber or red, check that the . . .

Of course, your notes, cautions, and warnings should prevent those errors in the first place.

Notes, Cautions, Warnings, and Danger Alerts

Place notes, cautions, warnings, and danger alerts immediately before the steps to which they apply.

Note: Leave the screws loose at this point so that the frame remains flexible. This will make it easier to fit in the cross brace in step 19.

14. Screw the support bracket to the back brace.

This is part of the just-in-time information delivery strategy. If you place a warning after the step to which it applies, users won't actually read it until after performing the step, which would be too late. On the other hand, if you place it in the introduction, users will have forgotten it by the time they get to the step.

---

1 Source: Andre Lanz

Notes, because they provide merely useful or helpful information rather than safety information, can be incorporated into the action step. If you find yourself doing this for many or most of your steps, it's a good idea to distinguish the action step from the note, perhaps by bolding the action. That way, knowledgeable users can just read the bolded action statement. More novice users can read the entire step for helpful and reassuring information.

14. **Screw the support bracket to the back brace.** Leave the screws loose at this point to make it easier to fit in the cross brace in step 19.

Most instructions employ four levels of special notes, presented in increasingly emphatic formatting, generally with increasingly emphatic graphics to draw attention to them.

Notes provide hints to help users perform the instructions more easily.

Note: Two different-sized screws are provided. Be sure to use the 3/8 in. screw here.

Cautions provide information that prevents the instructions from failing and prevents damage to the equipment.

Caution: Do not use non-rechargeable batteries in this charging unit or the charging unit could be damaged.

Warnings advise against potential harm to the user.

Warning: Put on safety goggles and a breathing mask before removing the battery caps. Make sure the workspace is well ventilated.

Danger alerts are particularly strong warnings, alerting the reader not just to potential harm, but to very likely harm or even the risk of death.

DANGER: EXTREME ELECTROCUTION HAZARD. DO NOT ATTEMPT THIS STEP WITHOUT VERIFYING THAT PROPER LOCKOUT PROCEDURES HAVE BEEN FOLLOWED.

Note that notes, cautions, and warnings are the only places within the instructions that provide explanations for actions, telling users why something should be done. This is a concession to human nature; explanations help people understand, remember, and comply. They motivate readers to follow the instructions precisely, instead of relying on their "common sense," as they are wont to do.

This brief introduction identifies the situation to which these instructions apply. Time estimates, tools and equipment lists, and general warnings are not necessary in this case.

The steps are numbered, matched by the numbers in the graphics on the left, making it clear which button is meant in each step. Note that the instructions are bolded to stand out and written in the imperative mood. The notes (additional information) are not bolded and not in the imperative mood.

Title announces the purpose of the instructions.

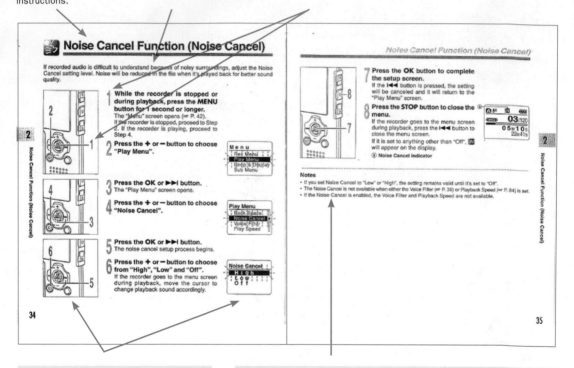

Note the extensive use of graphics to show the locations of buttons (on the left) and the results on the device's screen (on the right). This way, users are shown exactly what to do and know immediately whether they've done it correctly.

The conclusion is formatted as a set of notes telling the user the consequences that setting the noise cancel function might have for other functions, such as the voice filter not being available, and why the procedure might have failed, such as when the voice filter has been enabled previously. The page reference helps users find the instructions for correcting the problem. This is a mini troubleshooting guide.

FIGURE 13.1 Instructions from the Panasonic Digital Voice Recorder Manual

Source: © Olympus. Used with permission.

The following example comes from some in-class instructions for changing the resolution of graphics downloaded off the Internet. In this case, the introduction offers a more extensive explanation of the purpose of the instructions. However, time estimates and equipment lists are not relevant here, except for the assumption that the students are using specific graphics software.

The "How to" heading identifies the purpose of the instructions.

How to Change the Size or Resolution of Internet Graphics for Print Resolution

The introduction clarifies the purpose and explains why it's necessary to follow the instructions, to create comprehension and motivate compliance.

The following instructions show you how to change an Internet graphic from screen resolution to print resolution.

Internet graphics are optimized for quick download by having their resolution reduced to 72 dpi (dots per inch), which is the resolution at which monitors display information. However, when you download Internet graphics and print them (for instance in a report) the 72 dpi resolution will look very pixilated. You, therefore, need to change the resolution of Internet graphics to 150 dpi before inserting these graphics into documents you intend to print.

This description of assumptions specifies the equipment (in this case software) to which these instructions apply. The users are now ready to follow the instructions, even should they not have precisely the same software. The user requires no specific qualifications, so none are stipulated.

By establishing these conventions, the writer is able to refer to selection sequences and keyboard and mouse commands without creating confusion.

These instructions assume that you will be using Adobe Photoshop CS, the digital editing software available in your computer labs in NE1. Other digital editing software packages offer the same functions but call them by different names and sort them differently in their menu systems.

Conventions
These instructions use the following typographic conventions:

Dialog Window Buttons and Keyboard Commands:	**Copy, Paste, Save As, Okay**
Menu selection sequences:	[Start] > [Programs] > [Adobe] > [Adobe Photoshop CS]
Dialog Windows	"New File Dialog Window"

Notice how the conventions defined in the introduction allow the writer to identify commands like Copy and components like dialogue boxes instantly.

This heading starts the actual instructions.

Changing the resolution of a graphic
When you find an Internet graphic you want to use in your report, please do the following:

1. Right click on the graphic and select **Copy** from the "Windows Pop-up Menu."

The graphics allow the user to follow the instructions more easily and identify the locations of commands and dialogue boxes. Arguably, for something as simple as this, graphics might not be absolutely necessary, but they are always welcome and cost so little.

2. Open Adobe Photoshop CS: [Start] > [Programs] > [Adobe] > [Adobe Photoshop CS].

   Adobe Photoshop is a memory intensive program and will take some time to load. Once in Photoshop,

The instruction steps are not bolded because bolding identifies software commands. So the writer chose to present the notes in a separate paragraph. Choose a look that works for you; then apply it consistently.

3. Open a new Photoshop file: [File] > [New].

    At this point, the Photoshop "New File Dialog Window" will open. Please note that Photoshop will automatically create a file that matches the size and resolution of the graphic in the Windows Pasteboard.

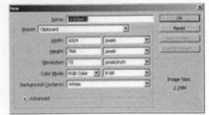

Note the consistent use of "At this point" to introduce the results of an action. This makes it easier for users to scan and comprehend the instructions. Always look for ways to make your writing more consistent.

4. Change the default file name to a file name that will make it easy for you to identify the contents of the file.

5. Click **Okay**.

    At this point, you will see a blank file. Photoshop is waiting for you to input content.

6. Paste the contents of your Windows Pasteboard into the Photoshop file: **Ctrl + V** (paste command).

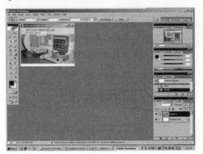

    At this point, you should see your image in the file window. You now need to change the resolution of this image.

Usability

If instructions are not comprehensible to or usable by your intended reader, they are essentially useless. Usability begins at the planning stage, but it is best supplemented with usability testing.

Planning for Usability

When you first sit down to plan your procedure, form a clear picture of your intended audience. Are they a generally educated but non-technical audience, as is the case with most end-user documentation for standard consumer software? Or are they technically competent people merely unfamiliar with the particular software or equipment you are documenting—for instance, machinists or mechanics tasked with performing maintenance on new industrial equipment or trained lab technicians requiring standard operating procedures to ensure they follow safety protocols perfectly every time?

Troubleshooting

Symptom	Probable cause	Action
Nothing appears on the display	The battery is not loaded properly.	Verify polarity is correct.
	The battery is dead.	Replace with new battery (☞ P. 12).
	The recorder is in HOLD mode.	Release the recorder from HOLD (☞ P. 75).
Won't start	The recorder is in HOLD mode.	Release the recorder from HOLD (☞ P. 75).
	The battery is dead.	Replace with new battery (☞ P. 12).
Unable to record	Low remaining internal flash memory.	Erase unnecessary files (☞ P. 72).
	The maximum number of files has been reached.	Check another folder.
	MUSIC mode is active.	Switch to VOICE mode (☞ P. 14)
No playback tone heard	The earphone is connected.	Unplug the earphones to use the internal speaker.
	The VOL(+ or -) button is set to 0.	Adjust the VOL(+ or -) button (☞ P. 30).
Unable to erase	The file is locked.	Unlock the file (☞ P. 40).
	The file is read-only.	Cancel the read-only setting of the file on the PC.
Noise heard during playback	The recorder was shaken during recording.	—
	The recorder was placed near a cell phone or fluorescent light while recording or during playback.	Move the recorder.
Recording level, too low	The microphone sensitivity is too low.	Set the microphone sensitivity to "Conf" mode and try again (☞ P. 25).
Unable to set index marks, tempmarks	The maximum number of marks has been reached.	Erase unnecessary marks (☞ P. 76).
	The file is locked.	Unlock the file (☞ P. 40).
	The file is read-only.	Cancel the read-only setting of the file on the PC.
Cannot find the recorded voice	Wrong folder.	Switch to the right folder.

7

Troubleshooting

96

FIGURE 13.2 Troubleshooting guide from Panasonic Digital Voice Recorder Manual. Note the table format for easy reference and the reader-friendly organization. The user looks for a symptom, is told a probable cause, and is directed to a solution, in that order. Nicely done.

Ask yourself what specific tasks your readers will need to perform. For example, end-users of standard office software are interested only in performing specific actions, such as opening, saving, and closing files, or creating databases and using them for specific work tasks. They don't want or need to know anything about the coding of the software or its specifications.

Once you've determined what tasks you need to describe, determine what level of detail to include. When writing an in-house maintenance manual for some equipment that you know will be serviced by specially trained technologists or machinists, it might be enough to write the following:

- Replace the fuel filter.
- Replace the oil filter.
- Check the belts.
- Lube the pulley system.

These tasks are bulleted because they don't need to be performed in any particular order. See Chapter 4 for details on numbered vs. bulleted lists.

But if you are writing a car engine maintenance manual for the curious DIY weekend amateur, you will probably have to provide a detailed procedure for each of these tasks. The reader may not know how to replace a fuel filter, for instance, or even where to find it:

Replacing the Fuel Filter

The fuel filter stops particulates in the gasoline from entering the fuel injection system and fouling it. The fuel filter should be replaced every 50,000 km to prevent a plugged fuel filter from impeding the flow of gasoline to the engine, which will hamper performance and fuel economy. In serious cases, it could cause the engine to stall.

This procedure will take approximately 15 minutes.

You will need the following:
• Replacement filter, type FRDFF 2354
• 19 mm wrench
• 17 mm wrench

Caution: The engine needs to be off during this procedure. If the engine is running, it will pressurize the fuel system, causing fuel to spray when you loosen the filter connections.

1. **Locate the fuel filter on the fuel line inside the frame rail on the passenger side.** Its location is identified in Fig. 1.
2. **Loosen the nuts holding the filter in place.** Begin with the nut on the filter outflow side (closer to the engine). You'll need to use two wrenches: one to hold the nut on the filter (19 mm), the other to turn the nut on the fuel line (17 mm).
3. **Loosen the nut holding the filter bracket to the frame rail.** This nut does not need to be removed, merely loosened sufficiently to permit the filter to slide out.

Note: Take note of the orientation of the filter so you can install the new one in the same way. Fuel filters are designed to work with fuel flowing in a specific direction.

4. **Push the fuel filter out of its clamp towards the engine side.** The fuel line is flexible on that side and will give.

Clearly, trained technicians would be frustrated by the level of detail provided in the second sample. You'd be telling them the obvious and slowing them down. Just as clearly, first-time amateurs would have no idea what to do with the first version of the instructions.

As always, the contents of a document depend on its audience and its purpose. You'll need to make some judgment calls.

Testing for Usability

The best way to test the usability of your instructions is to find someone as close to the intended reader as possible and to get that person to perform the actual procedure. Take note of where your tester hesitates and looks puzzled, but don't help your tester either by explaining an instruction step or, even worse, by performing it for them—unless of course your tester is totally stuck.

Debrief your tester afterward to get his or her feedback, and then tweak your instructions. If your first version failed miserably, you might want to test your revised instructions as well. If you got reasonably close the first time, you may not have to.

If you cannot find an actual intended user, at least find someone with a similar level of technical understanding or, at the very least, a first-time reader, someone who is coming to the instructions for the first time—not someone on your work team who has been helping you along the way. If your first-time readers can successfully put themselves in the place of the intended user, they should be able to tell you at least whether the individual instruction steps are clear.

The most common problem with instructions is that the writer assumes that the readers have more knowledge than they actually do. This causes the writer to write instructions that frustrate readers.

As a rule, it is better to provide a little too much information than too little. Too much information will bore readers, but too little will cause them to fail.

Manuals

A manual brings together numerous procedures for a common purpose. A software user manual, for example, brings together instructions for all the various tasks that the software enables the user to perform. A standard operating manual for a fuel refinery might describe the maintenance, safety, and emergency-response procedures in force at the refinery. It will obviously run to many volumes.

Increasingly, manuals are provided in electronic form or hosted on the Internet to provide superior search functions, to allow the manual to be continually updated, and to link the manual to databases that keep track of when procedures have been performed, that maintain parts inventories, and that perform other functions.

In all cases, however, you must begin by performing a clear analysis of who the user will be (as described above) and of all the tasks that the user will have to, or want to, perform.

Step 1, then, is a thorough task analysis.

Step 2 is to group and sequence those tasks into a logical order, generally chronologically—for instance, installing the software before opening it, or opening files before saving them. In the case of a maintenance manual, the procedures performed after 1,000 hours of operation would be placed before the procedures performed after 5,000 hours of operation. Another sequence might be from least to most complex.

In most cases, some logical sequence will present itself. Figure 13.3 shows what might, for instance, be the sequence of procedures for a mountain bike maintenance manual.

Step 3 is to write each procedure in a manner appropriate to the intended audience, as described earlier in this chapter. Again, a manual is a series of procedures. Write each one up as a separate, complete set of instructions for a reader to follow.

Step 4 is to provide a thorough introduction to the manual as a whole. Like the summaries of reports, it's best to write these introductions last, even though we place them first. The introduction will contain an overall description of the mechanism or software for which the manual is written.

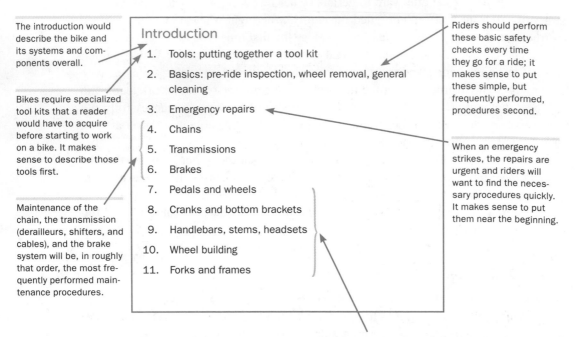

The introduction would describe the bike and its systems and components overall.

Bikes require specialized tool kits that a reader would have to acquire before starting to work on a bike. It makes sense to describe those tools first.

Maintenance of the chain, the transmission (derailleurs, shifters, and cables), and the brake system will be, in roughly that order, the most frequently performed maintenance procedures.

Introduction

1. Tools: putting together a tool kit
2. Basics: pre-ride inspection, wheel removal, general cleaning
3. Emergency repairs
4. Chains
5. Transmissions
6. Brakes
7. Pedals and wheels
8. Cranks and bottom brackets
9. Handlebars, stems, headsets
10. Wheel building
11. Forks and frames

Riders should perform these basic safety checks every time they go for a ride; it makes sense to put these simple, but frequently performed, procedures second.

When an emergency strikes, the repairs are urgent and riders will want to find the necessary procedures quickly. It makes sense to put them near the beginning.

The rest of a bike's components are less frequently adjusted, fixed, and replaced. These procedures are placed later in the book. If there's no compelling reason to think that one procedure is more frequent or more complex than another, there's no compelling reason to place one procedure before another. The sequence of these last few procedures could probably be rearranged without marring the effectiveness of the manual.

FIGURE 13.3 Task sequence for a mountain bike maintenance manual. Note that the sequence goes from the basics (assembling a tool kit and performing simple maintenance tasks) to what readers might want to know first or look up in a hurry (emergency repairs to get them home). The rest of the manual is devoted to regular maintenance, proceeding from what is simplest and most frequently maintained (the chain) to what least often requires repair and requires the greatest technical know-how (wheel building and spot welding forks and frames). The idea for this sequence came from the excellent *Zinn & the Art of Mountain Bike Maintenance*, 4th ed.

Editing Instructions, Procedures, and Manuals

Does the introduction to the instructions

☐ state the purpose of the task and, if appropriate, when and by whom it should be performed?

☐ describe safety measures or other concerns the reader should understand?

☐ clarify the naming and typographic conventions employed in the instructions?

☐ list the necessary tools, materials, and time?

☐ include any notes, cautions, and warnings that apply to the whole procedure?

Are the step-by-step instructions

☐ numbered?

☐ expressed in the imperative mood?

☐ simple and direct, yet written in complete sentences?

☐ accompanied by helpful graphics?

Does the conclusion include

☐ a quick check that the instructions have been completed correctly?

☐ follow-up or maintenance advice (where appropriate)?

☐ a troubleshooter's guide (if appropriate)?

Are the notes, cautions, warnings, and danger alerts

☐ placed before the steps to which they apply (or in the introduction if they apply to the entire procedure)?

☐ descriptive to help the reader understand their necessity, purpose, and urgency?

☐ formatted to draw the necessary attention?

Have you

☐ used the same terms and names to refer to the same parts and steps?

☐ tested your instructions by having someone perform them to see where you might have to clarify or expand?

Exercises: Editing Instructions and Writing Instructions

The following are exercises in writing, editing, and interpreting instructions.

Exercise 13.1: Paragraphs into Instructions

Turn the following paragraph description on how to plant a tree into a proper set of planting instructions.

Trees are a great way to improve the looks of a garden, to create shade, and to establish blinds to prevent neighbours from looking into your yard. It's generally best to plant trees in spring or fall to reduce stress on them and it's always wise to investigate what kinds of trees do well in the local climate.

Once you've got your tree at home, dig a hole for it. When you fill the dirt back in, gently, it might be a good idea to mix in some compost or manure to build up the nutrients in the soil. Of course, you really only need to do this if the soil in your yard is not very fertile.

Then you'll have to place the tree in the centre of the hole, which should be about four to five times the diameter of the root ball. Make sure the top of the root ball sits level with the ground. But you want to give the water a place to drain, so leave a pedestal in the middle of the hole but dig deeper around the edges.

When the dirt is back in the hole, the tree needs a thorough watering. This will settle the dirt and also has the benefit of removing air pockets. About an hour after this first watering, the tree should be watered again, but with less water this time. In future, the tree will need regular watering during its first year to help establish its root system.

Of course, before you can put the tree in the hole you'll have to remove the covering of the root ball. You can simply tip smaller trees on their side and remove the plastic pot in which the root ball sits.

The new, soft soil, once backfilled, should be covered with mulch. Mulch prevents weeds from taking root and keeps in moisture. But it's best not to put the mulch right up against the trunk of the tree. You should leave a small circle free.

Root rot is a major cause of death in newly planted trees, which is why you want to have a pedestal in your hole in the ground.

Larger trees tend to have their root balls covered in burlap. You'll want to cut that off carefully. Do this as close to the hole as possible so you don't have to carry the trees too far once the covering is off.

After the first big watering, when the dirt has settled, you will want to fill the hole with more dirt, back to level, but it's a good idea to leave a small depression around the base of the trunk.

When you remove the root ball from its covering, either a plastic pot or the burlap, it's important that the root ball not be left exposed to the elements too long. If it's sunny, the root ball could dry out and if it's raining, for instance, the root ball could dissolve.

Exercise 13.2: Editing a Set of Instructions

Edit the following instructions, making any changes you think would improve them and would make them comply more closely with the rules we set out in class. It doesn't matter if it's messy. Cross out words, circle stuff, draw arrows, renumber steps. Do whatever you have to do, but do not rewrite these instructions. It will take too long.

How to Change a Flat Tire

If you are ever stuck on the side of the road with a flat tire, you don't need to wait or pay for roadside service. You can change the tire yourself.

Equipment and Supplies
To get started, you will need

- a spare tire (check to make sure it's inflated)
- a tire jack and wrench (usually found with the spare tire)

Getting set up

1. First pull the car over in a stable, safe place to change your tire. Avoid hills or soft ground and pull as far away from traffic as you can.
2. Then put the car in park and engage the handbrake. This will prevent the car from rolling.

CAUTION:
Turn on your emergency flashers (hazard lights) to alert other drivers.

3. Place a heavy object in front of the front and back tire to prevent the car from rolling. If you are parked on a slight slope, place the object on the downslope side of the tire.
4. Locate the lift point on the frame near the flat tire. It will often be a flattened area on a rounded or peaked frame, generally within a foot of the tire well. Place the jack directly under the lift point.
5. Raise the jack until it is supporting, but not lifting, the car.

Removing the flat

6. Using the chisel-tip end of the tire wrench, pry off the hubcap.
7. Loosen the lugnuts using the tire wrench.
8. Now raise the jack until the tire is off the ground.
9. Unscrew the lugnuts the rest of the way. You should be able to do this by hand.
10. Pull the flat tire off the hub and put it in the trunk.

CAUTION:

The tire may not come off easily if the bolts are rusty. In this case it is best to work the tire off by rocking it side to side and walking it off the bolts. If you pull too hard and the tire comes off suddenly, you may lose your balance, fall, and injure yourself.

Putting on the spare

1. Place the spare tire on the hub.

CAUTION:

Most spare tires (the undersized "donut" tires) are not designed for speeds of more than 50 MPH or for long distances. Exceeding this speed can cause problems, including failure of the spare tire. It is best to drive slowly and carefully to a shop and have your tire repaired or replaced.

2. Then just tighten the lugs back into place by hand until they are snug.
3. Lower the car without putting full weight on the tire.
4. Tighten the lugs fully with the tire wrench as much as possible.

CAUTION:

If you use full force to tighten the lugnuts while the car is still raised, you could rock the car off the jack, causing it to drop suddenly.

5. Lower the car fully and remove the jack from under the car.

Congratulations! You're done!

CAUTION:

Be aware of your surroundings. If you're on a busy road, be particularly wary of vehicles driving by that might get too close. Hundreds of people are killed each year while changing a tire on the side of the road.

Exercise 13.3: Writing Procedures

Write instructions for one of the simple tasks listed below. Do not use the Internet. Do include an introduction; a tools list if appropriate; necessary notes, cautions, and warnings; and so on.

- Brushing your teeth
- Feeding a pet
- Filling up your car
- Some other task approved by your instructor

Hand the instructions to a classmate and ask the classmate to visualize performing the instructions. Obtain feedback, edit your instructions, and exchange them with a different classmate for more feedback:

Alternatively, have a volunteer act out the instructions as you read them out. The volunteer will attempt to deliberately misinterpret your instructions wherever possible.

Exercise 13.4: Instructions for Random Creations

Using whatever art and building supplies you can access, draw a simple picture or put together a simple (or even random) object. This should be done quite quickly. Then write instructions for duplicating the drawing or the object.

Find a partner and exchange instructions. Try to duplicate the drawing or object with fresh materials, following only the instructions provided. Consider this an instant usability test and a lesson in the difficulty of writing unambiguous instructions.

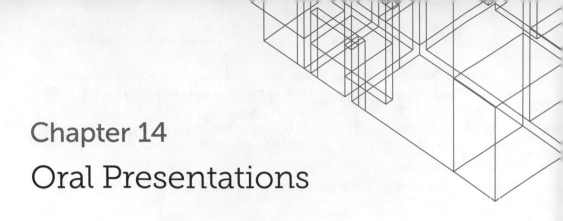

Chapter 14

Oral Presentations

> **In this chapter you will learn**
> - why presentations matter in a technical career
> - how to plan and practise a presentation
> - how to deliver a presentation
> - how to create slides and graphics to get your point across.

You'll frequently have to present information orally in the workplace, often in conjunction with the presentation of a report or proposal, in the latter case, often competitively. This is not a chapter to skip or to gloss over.

While speakers seldom enjoy giving presentations, audiences who hear them and bosses who assign them love oral presentations. Orally presented materials, with proper graphic support, have much more impact, are much more persuasive, and convey impressions far better than written reports. They are in real time and they are personal, which is the way we evolved to communicate.

So, whatever industry and role you end up settling into, you will be required to present information orally, whether it be an impromptu 1-minute project update at a team meeting or a formal 40-minute proposal presentation to a potential client, a government agency, or the public.

While it can be intimidating, public speaking is a vital and recurring demand. And it's one that will grow with your career; the more responsibility you have, the more people you manage, and the more you represent your organization, the more public speaking you will have to do. Do it well and you will progress. Do it poorly and your career may stall because public speaking is vital to team building and leadership and, as such, is viewed as a key test of managerial ability.

But don't let this scare you. Public speaking, like any other communication skill, follows simple, logical guidelines and can be mastered with practice. Practice, in fact, is key. So, throw yourself into the oral presentation assigned by your instructor and seek out opportunities to speak in public as often as you can. Then get feedback. Don't ask, "How'd I do?" because everyone will assure you that you did well. Ask instead, "What specifically can I improve?" That way you'll get concrete advice on what to work on, as well as the usual assurances that you did well. Make your mistakes and learn from them now when the stakes are relatively small, before you give that important first presentation on the job.

In this chapter we will cover the steps involved in preparing and delivering an oral presentation, breaking our discussion into the following parts:

- planning the presentation
- making speech notes
- designing and using slides
- practising the presentation
- overcoming stage fright and answering questions.

Planning the Presentation

Just as with a written document, you need to consider your audience, and you need to focus on the purpose of your oral presentation. What is it you want the audience to understand that they didn't before, or what is it you want them to do that they weren't prepared to do or expecting to do before?

However, you also need to keep in mind that while oral presentations have a much more immediate impact than written reports, they don't convey specific facts as well as reports do. Presentations lend themselves to conveying a strong impression on a topic, but the audience won't retain as much specific information. This is because readers have a couple of advantages. They can always pause to allow information to sink in or take a break when their heads get full. They can reread sections of particular interest to them. They can skip back and forth to confirm information or jog their memory. An audience can do none of those things. This is why an audience can generally retain no more than a few facts and a handful of opinions from a 15-minute presentation.

That's fine. It's not the purpose of a presentation to fill the audience's heads with specific numbers and minute details. Leave the specifics for the accompanying report. The purpose of a presentation is to give a clear overview, to leave a clear impression of ideas and broader issues.

Keep this in mind while preparing the content of your presentation's three parts:

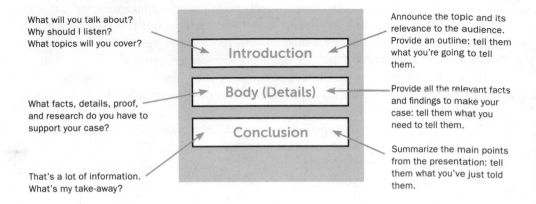

What will you talk about?
Why should I listen?
What topics will you cover?

Introduction

Announce the topic and its relevance to the audience. Provide an outline: tell them what you're going to tell them.

Body (Details)

Provide all the relevant facts and findings to make your case: tell them what you need to tell them.

What facts, details, proof, and research do you have to support your case?

Conclusion

That's a lot of information. What's my take-away?

Summarize the main points from the presentation: tell them what you've just told them.

Introduction

You'll want to open with a strong and attention-grabbing statement to make sure you have the audience's full attention from the start. But this does not mean capering about like you're hosting a late-night show. It means letting the audience know what you'll be talking about and why they should listen, and doing so in an engaging manner.

Place yourself in the audience's shoes and see if you can spot the difference between the following two opening statements:

"Hi, my name is . . . and I'm going to talk about wind turbines. . . ." (Pretty standard opening—Yawn.)

"Good evening, ladies and gentlemen. The discussion about wind turbines is fraught with misperceptions and exaggerations on both sides, and if we are going to make sensible decisions about whether to build them, we need to establish the facts of the matter. My name is . . . ; I have worked with wind turbines since the 1980s in both Europe and North America, and I want to examine the claims made about wind turbines with facts from the field and refocus the discussion on what really matters." (An attention-grabbing opening that promises to reward the audience for investing their time.)

This is an opening that provides context and relevance for the topic. If you have a lot of credibility on a subject, try to work that into the opening as well.

One way of drawing in an audience is to ask an opening question: "Have you ever wondered why . . .?" or "Did you know that . . .?" Interesting and surprising facts always gain attention—and explain the popularity of games like Trivial Pursuit. Of course, those interesting facts should clarify the benefit of listening to the presentation.

Some texts on presentations recommend opening with a joke, but that's a risky strategy as not everyone shares the same sense of humour, particularly if there's a political dimension to your subject matter—as is the case even with wind turbines. Also, ask yourself how confident you feel in your stand-up material. An opening joke that falls flat risks losing the audience and deflating your confidence. Until you've become a much more experienced public speaker, leave the joke openings to the late-night hosts.

At the end of your introduction, do one more thing: provide an outline. Tell the audience how you've organized your presentation, what topics you'll cover. Audiences don't have a table of contents to refer to; they can't leaf through your presentation to see how you've organized information and what you'll talk about. But they'll want to know. Satisfy this natural curiosity in the opening so that the audience isn't left to wonder where you're taking them. See Figure 14.1 for a sample outline slide.

Body

Create a logical sequence of topics that helps to achieve your purpose and provides good, factual information with lots of objective, verifiable support. The body of the presentation makes your argument. Structure and support it well, as you would in a report. Select a level of detail that is both appropriate to the audience and to your time limit. Exceeding your time limit imposes on the audience's workday and, if your presentation is one in a series being given that day, robs the other presenters of their presentation time. It's rude. It is also a clear sign that you are not in control of your material, which will cost you professionalism points.

Use transition phrases and, ideally, transition slides to indicate when you are moving from one section to the next so that the audience knows exactly where you are in your presentation.

Remember that the purpose of a presentation is to give an overview. An audience cannot, for instance, wrap their minds around specific numbers if they cannot read them; they cannot apprehend lists of test results, so just summarize them. For the specifics, refer the audience to the report that generally accompanies a presentation.

Note the difference in the following two presentations of the same information:

"So, while our overall billing for our engineering services grew by over 10% last year, our billing in facilities consulting, where we'd hoped also to grow our business, actually declined slightly. We are obviously doing something wrong." (Presentation)

Last year our total billable hours for the engineering department increased by 10.7% to a total of $12,342,765.98. While this seems a promising trend, closer analysis revealed that our billing in an area that we had specifically targeted for growth, that is, facilities consulting, actually declined by 3.5% year to year, from $1,324,743.65 to $1,278,377.62. (Report)

Introductions   vs.   Conclusions

The discussion about wind turbines is fraught with misperceptions and exaggerations on both sides, and if we are going to make sensible decisions about whether to build them, we need to stick with facts . . .

First I want to discuss some of the criticisms made by both sides about wind turbines: that they kill birds in large numbers, that they cause illness in people living near them, that they take more energy to create than they generate; that the energy they produce is not competitively priced. When we've established the facts, I want to discuss the importance of sticking with facts when discussing technical topics if we are to make good decisions. At the end, I'd like to suggest what our next step in this ongoing discussion should be.

Wind Turbines: Outline

☐ Claims both for and against wind turbines
   ☐ Bird Strikes
   ☐ Wind Turbine Syndrome
   ☐ Excessive Embodied Energy
   ☐ Cost of Energy Generation

☐ Separating facts from politics
☐ Where do we go from here?

[Notes: Outlines are like a table of contents. They list topics. Conclusions reprise main ideas that arise from the discussion of those topics. They function as end-summaries of the important information provided during the presentation, to make sure that the audience takes away exactly this information. This is an example of constructive repetition. Notice that conclusions are generally longer than the outline part of the presentation.]

So, in conclusion, what do the facts reveal about wind turbines? That many of the claims made against them are false. They do not, according to all reliable evidence, kill birds in large numbers. They do not, in any measurable way, affect human health. And they clearly do not take more energy to produce than they generate.

They do, however, produce electricity at a cost twice as high as that generated by coal and natural gas. And while this cost is coming down with every generation of wind turbines, it'll be some time before the costs are comparable, at least as long as there's no carbon tax to push up the price of coal and natural gas.

These are the facts; there is no clear, overall winner. Instead, we are left with a trade-off. Are we willing to pay more for cleaner energy? In fact, considerably more? Or do we continue to produce energy cheaply but uncleanly and wait for the cost to come down? But this is a decision that we need to make with our eyes open. It's a decision that needs to be based on facts and a discussion of fundamental values.

Thank you, ladies and gentlemen. Are there any questions?

Wind Turbines Conclusion

☐ Claims of naysayers and enthusiasts both false
   ☐ No evidence of bird kills
   ☐ No scientific or medical basis for wind turbine syndrome
   ☐ Embodied energy is not greater than energy production
   ☐ Wind turbines do not provide cheap energy

☐ Exaggerated claims don't get us anywhere
☐ Need a sensible discussion of trade-offs
☐ Pricey but clean vs. cheap and dirty

FIGURE 14.1 **The difference between a presentation intro and conclusion.** The column on the left provides the text for an intro to a presentation on wind turbines; the slide provides the outline, the list of topics to be discussed, like a table of contents in a report. The column on the right provides the text for the conclusion to that same presentation. You'll note that it doesn't repeat the outline, but instead repeats the most important information that the presenter wants the audience to take away. The constructive repetition will help the audience remember the information, and the context provided by the presentation will help the repeated facts make sense.

Conclusion

Because an audience will remember little specific information from your presentation, you need to make sure that what they do remember is the stuff that you consider important rather than whatever happened to capture their attention. So, reprise your main points at the end. The context provided by the preceding presentation will help those points make sense; the constructive repetition will help them stick. If appropriate, point to future action.

In effect, the conclusion to a presentation functions like the summary of a report, but it is placed at the end.

Making Speech Notes

Once you've got your presentation planned out and know what to say, you'll have something very close to a speech written out. However, if you take a full speech up to a lectern, you'll end up reading it, which always turns a potentially dynamic, interactive, and interesting presentation into a droning bore, entirely devoid of eye contact and audience engagement.

Instead, turn your written speech into speech notes on cue cards or on PowerPoint notes pages for use in Presenter View. The idea is that you simply glance down at your notes from time to time to find your place, look back up at your audience, and speak extemporaneously: naturally and normally from your knowledge of the subject.

Make sure that your lettering is large enough to be read at a glance and that your notes are brief enough and spaced well enough that you can find your place at a glance. Use just enough information to jog your memory, as shown in the sample notes (Figure 14.2).

Some speakers jot the timing allotted to each topic with their speech notes. Consider whether this will just clutter the notes and create stress if you find yourself straying slightly from the timeline. If you do choose to jot times against the topics, do so cumulatively so that you don't have to do any math while presenting. That is, if, for instance, you've assigned 30 seconds for introducing the first topic, 45 seconds for introducing the second topic, and 40 seconds for introducing the third topic, write "0:30," "1:15," and "1:55" on your notes. Then use the stopwatch app on your smartphone to keep track of time. It's larger and easier to see at a glance than the stopwatch function in PowerPoint.

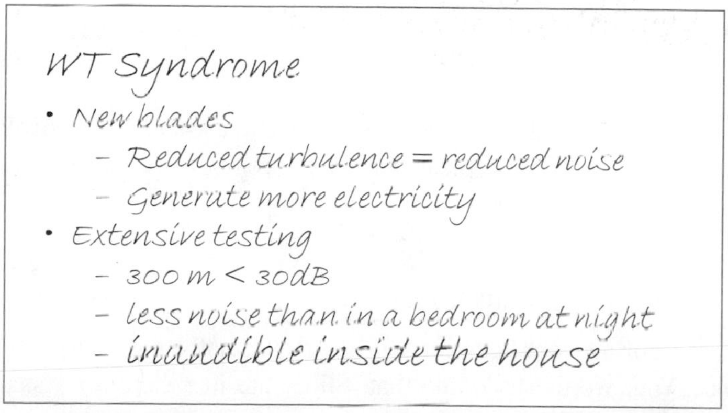

WT Syndrome
- New blades
    - Reduced turbulence = reduced noise
    - Generate more electricity
- Extensive testing
    - 300 m < 30dB
    - less noise than in a bedroom at night
    - inaudible inside the house

FIGURE 14.2 Functional speech notes. The text is large and well organized so it's easy for the speaker to find the next topic at a glance. Make your writing large enough that you can read them with a single glance at the monitor (or have hard copy lying on your lectern) while standing and delivering the presentation.

Do not use PowerPoint to automatically advance slides at preset times unless you are absolutely sure of your timing. Otherwise, you may end up waiting awkwardly for a slide to advance or rushing to catch up.

Using Presenter View

PowerPoint has a Presenter View function that allows presenters to see on the monitor not just the slide that the audience is seeing on the screen, but also the coming slide (or next animation) and the notes for the slide. These three discrete bits of information are shown in three separate panes, the margins of which you can slide around to suit yourself. However, unless your eyes are excellent, you will need a reasonably sized monitor to use Presenter View effectively; a 15-inch laptop screen may not be large enough when you are standing at some distance from the lectern. So be sure that you know precisely how the presentation room will be set up before committing to Presenter View. Or just make sure you have cue cards as backup.

Presenter View includes a timer as well, but it, too, could be quite small. You don't want to be bending forward and squinting at it, so you would still be well advised to use a smartphone setup to keep track of the time.

Designing and Using Slides

Please consult Chapter 10 ("Technical Graphics") for information on how graphics work, what graphics to put to what uses, and how to construct graphics properly. This section will focus on how to adapt graphics for use in oral presentations.

Visuals such as outline slides, lists of talking points, graphs, charts, and technical illustrations are vital to oral presentations because graphics make complex information easier to understand and more likely to be remembered. Text slides help the audience keep track of where you are in your presentation, especially if their attention has temporarily wandered.

The following sections describe how to design and use slides effectively in presentations. Figure 14.3 shows what a typical slide sequence might look like (without graphics) and provides some tips on delivery.

Simplified Text and Illustrations

The slides used during your presentation are not actually meant to explain things to your audience. Your words should do that. Slides are just there for visual support and confirmation.

Text-based slides are there to help the audience keep track of where you are in your presentation. You'll have an outline slide that indicates how you've organized your topic into sections. For each section you'll have a separate slide listing your main talking points. None of this will help your audience understand what you say; it will just help them keep track of where you are in the presentation.

The Truth about Wind Turbines

Debunking myths and making sensible choices

Wind Turbines: Outline

☐ Claims both for and against wind turbines
  ☐ Bird Strikes
  ☐ Wind Turbine Syndrome
  ☐ Excessive Embodied Energy
  ☐ Cost of Energy Generation
☐ Separating facts from politics
☐ Where do we go from here?

Outline

☐ Claims both for and against wind turbines
  ☐ Bird strikes
  ☐ Wind Turbine Syndrome
  ☐ Excessive Embodied energy
  ☐ Cost of energy generation
☐ Separating facts from Politics
☐ Where do we go from here?

A cover slide for the audience to look at before you speak and during your intro. Set-up photos or illustrations can help identify the topic and make good backgrounds to create cohesion between slides.

An outline slide is an absolute requirement to put your audience in the picture. Don't leave them wondering where you're taking them.

Use a transition slide to announce the next topic and help the audience to see how it fits into the presentation outline as a whole. Don't let the audience get lost.

The Wind Turbine Syndrome Myth

☐ Residents complained about being kept awake and driven mad by noises
☐ Residents complained about headaches and nausea
☐ New, quiet blade designs
☐ Extensive testing of noise loads and electromagnetic fields at various distances
☐ Noises too low to register. Insignificant or no electromagnetic fields

---

The Bird-Kill Myth

☐ Claims of migratory devastation
☐ Extensive bird-kill studies in Europe
☐ No proof that birds are killed in great numbers
☐ Birds can avoid stationary objects that move predictably

References

☐ Suzuki, David. "Whirling for Energy." Straight Goods News [Online magazine] 2011 July 11 [cited 2011 July 18]. Available at www.straightgoods.ca/2011/ViewArticle.cfm&Ref=589
☐ Nova Scotia Wind Integration Study. Report to Nova Scotia Dept. of Energy: 2008 [cited 2011 Oct. 15]. Available at www.govns.ca/energy/resources/EM/NS-Wind-Integration-Study-Final.pd

---

Place the rest of your presentation graphics here, to develop your argument step by step . . . .

Highlight your main points while you speak. Use a progressive reveal to stop the audience from reading ahead of your presentation.

Wind Turbines Conclusion

☐ Claims of naysayers and enthusiasts both false
☐ No evidence of bird kills
☐ No scientific or medical basis for wind turbine syndrome
☐ Embodied energy is not greater than energy production
☐ Wind turbines to do not provide cheap energy
☐ Exaggerated claims can't get us anywhere
☐ Need a sensible discussion of trade-offs
☐ Pricey but clean vs. cheap and dirty

Aim for a consistent look across all slides. Use consistent, modest slide transitions and animations as well. Surprises will distract from your content.

Reprise your main points at the end to remind your audience of what was most important in your presentation. It's like a report summary, except that it goes at the end.

Just as in a report, end with your references. They give your claims credibility and show your intellectual honesty. If there is to be a Q & A session, use another slide to announce it.

FIGURE 14.3 A typical slide sequence with graphics omitted. Graphics to help illustrate key points, or as thematic backgrounds, help to create clarity and aesthetic appeal. They've been omitted from these examples, however, because of scale. When you do include graphics and animations, make sure they don't distract from the presentation of your information.

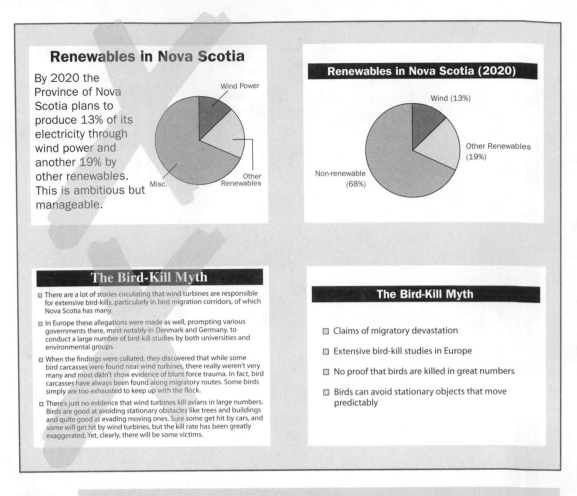

FIGURE 14.4 The bad and ugly, and the good. Don't create cluttered slides as on the left. Aim for clear, clean slides. Slides are just there to help the audience keep track of what you're talking about and where you are in your presentation. They confirm what you say; they should not take the place of what you say. If the audience is reading, they aren't listening to you.

Therefore the text on slides should be simple. Use bulleted items instead of paragraphs; phrases instead of sentences. Limit text to 6 bullets per slide and 10 words per bullet, roughly. If the audience is reading your slides, they aren't listening to you.

Lettering on slides must be large enough that it can be read easily from the back of the room in which you are presenting. It helps to know in advance what the room will look like and how it will be set up. Generally speaking, though, the PowerPoint defaults will work well.

Similarly, illustrations simply serve to verify the concepts you've already described in words. They're there for visual clarification and confirmation, but not to make your main points. So, as with text: simplify, simplify, simplify. Focus the audience's attention on the important details by eliminating the rest. Every second they spend interpreting your graphic is a second they're not listening to you.

Introduce Graphics before Showing Them

Because graphics to some extent compete with the speaker for attention, you should do two things:

- Before showing the graphic, tell the audience what the graphic is about.
- When you've revealed the graphic, give the audience a second to absorb the information on the graphic before continuing to speak.

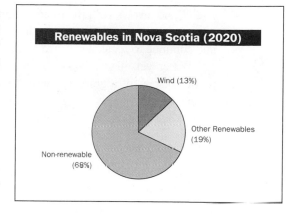

FIGURE 14.5 **A simple and properly introduced graphic.** See the text for the introduction.

For instance, say something like the following just before you reveal the graphic: "As you'll see in the following graphic, Nova Scotia has set an ambitious renewable energy target for itself. By 2020 it plans to produce 13% of its electricity through wind power and another 19% through other renewables." Then show the graphic (Figure 14.5).

With this introduction, the audience doesn't have to spend time interpreting the graphic. They can glance at it, see that it confirms your claims, get a visual sense of the proportions of the power-generation mix, and turn their attention back to you.

It is important, however, that you give the audience a chance to glance at the graphic. So, after you've advanced to the slide, pause briefly. Take a breath and let it out slowly to help you relax. Then continue.

Drawing the Audience's Attention to Parts of your Graphics

If you need to direct the audience's attention to a particular part of a graphic, use the mouse pointer on the screen. If you assign Power-Point's pen function to the mouse, you can draw

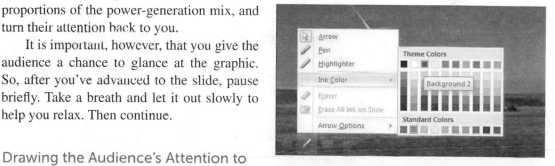

FIGURE 14.6 **PowerPoint's pen function turns the mouse pointer into a pen.** In presentation mode, click on the greyed-out pen icon in the bottom left corner of the screen. The pointer will turn into a dot; click and draw right on your slides.

circles and arrows with the mouse, clumsily to be sure, but effectively nonetheless. The advantage of using the mouse in this way is that you can mark your location, step away, and continue to speak and move naturally.

Better yet, if you know that you are going to draw the audience's attention to a particular part of a graphic, use animations to do so, either creating annotations, as in Figure 14.8, or simply using arrows to point at components or circles and ovals to isolate areas. That way you don't have to turn and point at the screen; you can keep facing and looking at your audience.

Always make sure you stand to the side of the screen so you don't block your audience's view and don't get blinded by the projector's light beam. Never get stuck talking into the screen.

Hints about Using PowerPoint

A progressive reveal prevents the audience from reading ahead of your presentation instead of listening to you. So use an animation to set up PowerPoint to advance the slide one bullet item at a time with each mouse click.

This technique can also be applied to graphics. Sometimes the best time to add detail to a graphic is while you're speaking. In that way, you can initially use a graphic that is very basic and easy to comprehend. The audience will glance at it, understand it, and return their attention to you. Then, as you discuss the graphic, you can fill in the missing details.

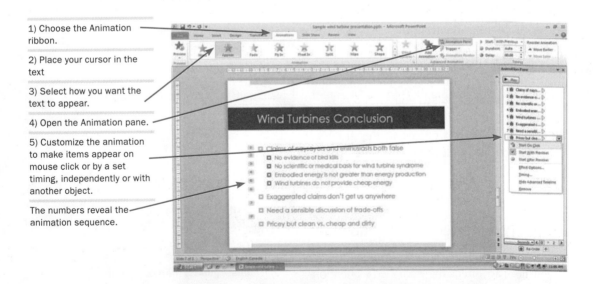

FIGURE 14.7 Animating text to create a progressive reveal. You'll most frequently be using the Start On Click option so that you can control the pace at which text items appear—right after, not before, you start to speak about them.

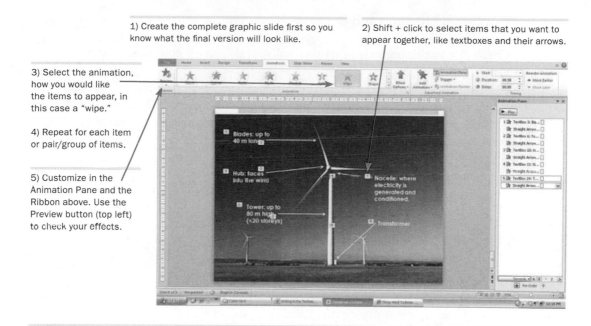

1) Create the complete graphic slide first so you know what the final version will look like.

2) Shift + click to select items that you want to appear together, like textboxes and their arrows.

3) Select the animation, how you would like the items to appear, in this case a "wipe."

4) Repeat for each item or pair/group of items.

5) Customize in the Animation Pane and the Ribbon above. Use the Preview button (top left) to check your effects.

FIGURE 14.8 Animating graphics for a progressive reveal. This works much like with text animation (see instructions above), but you'll select items individually or in specific pairs/groups instead of highlighting all the text at once.

Source: Kratochvil, Vera. Three Wind Turbines. Photo [downloaded 2010 July 12]. Available at www.publicdomainpictures.net/Vera Kratochvil

This prevents the audience from being confused by an overabundance of unexplained details at the beginning of your discussion of the graphic.

Practising the Presentation

At this stage of your public speaking career, practice is the key to success. So, now that you have your speech notes and your PowerPoint slides, practise the presentation until you are thoroughly familiar and comfortable with the material. Set up your laptop, put your speech notes on the desk, and run through your presentation. At the end of each session, check that you are within the time limit and that your speech notes work for you. Make adjustments to your materials, your notes, and your slides as necessary.

It's best if you video-record yourself and watch your performance. You'd be surprised how incredibly awkward it will feel to speak and look into your smartphone's camera eye, but actually watching and listening to your performance is the best way to check for the following important points.

Confident Opening and Delivery

Check that you've begun strongly and that your delivery is confident, relaxed, and conversational throughout.

Beginnings are always hard, so memorize your opening to make sure it turns out as attention-grabbing and effective as you've crafted it to be. Once you have uttered a couple of well-constructed sentences, you'll be more relaxed and should be able to continue smoothly. Faltering at the beginning of a talk can be fatal to your confidence. Instead, make this an opportunity to create a good first impression. You will not only seem more confident, you'll feel that way too.

Throughout your presentation, speak slowly and clearly. Keep the delivery slightly slower than ordinary speech. Cast your voice, if you can, slightly lower. This will not only make your delivery much clearer, but also prevent your chest from tightening and your throat from constricting. It's a little kinesthetic trick that always works; simply by forcing yourself to speak like someone who is relaxed, you will find yourself relaxing.

Vocal Pauses

Check that you've not resorted to vocal pauses. Speakers tend to use vocal pauses, the painfully embarrassing "ahm," as a sort of placeholder to indicate that they are thinking of what to say next. Here's how to stop yourself from doing so.

If you practise a lot and your speech notes work for you, you shouldn't be at a loss as to what to say next. This is a matter of preparation. If you remember to speak slowly, your words won't run ahead of your thoughts, and hence you won't find yourself needing to pause to catch up with yourself. This is a matter of proper delivery. And finally, should you still at any point be at a temporary loss for the proper word or fact, just pause silently and think of it. This is a matter of discipline.

Vocalizing won't help you think any better and a short pause won't make your audience get up and head for the doors. If anything, it will give them a moment to process the information that you've been providing.

Eye Contact

Check that you're merely glancing at your notes to find your place. If you're speaking down at your notes, you're not allowing enough eye contact.

Different cultures have different expectations about eye contact, but in the Western business and personal context, it's vital. We tend to see someone's willingness to look us in the eye as a sign of confidence and truthfulness. People who won't hold a forthright gaze are often described as "shifty," a term denoting nervousness and guilt. And a shifty person is not someone to trust. So, always talk to the audience, not at them or past them. Look them in the eye.

Make eye contact with an audience member for a few seconds, then smoothly move on to someone a few seats and rows over, scanning back and forth across the whole room.

Occasionally, you'll have to look at your monitor or at your notes. That's fine. Take your time and find your place, pause before continuing. But the general rule is, if your lips are moving, you should be looking at the audience.

Body Language and Posture

Check that your body language is comfortable and relaxed.

Stand with your feet, hips, chest, and shoulders squarely facing the audience. That way there's no place to hide, no place to look but at your audience.

While presenting, strive to speak as naturally and conversationally as possible. Make your movements just as natural. Use your hands to make expressive gestures, both large and small. Don't stand rock still and don't jerk about like some tinpot dictator, but anything between these extremes will probably work. If you caught a big fish, feel free to extend your arms to show how big it was. If you were netting minnows, use your thumb and forefinger to show how small they were. If it's a gesture you'd use in conversation, it's a gesture you can use in front of a larger audience as well—rude gestures excepted, of course.

Just make sure that you don't do anything too repetitively or it will seem like a nervous twitch. If your nose itches, by all means scratch it—briefly and once. Do it repeatedly and it becomes an obvious sign of nervousness that draws attention to itself and distracts from what you are saying. The same goes for your feet. Feel free to shift your weight and to move around a bit. But if you are constantly shifting your weight side to side, for instance, you'll look like a dancing bear, and the audience will be watching your performance instead of listening to it.

Overcoming Stage Fright and Answering Questions

You've prepared your materials and you've practised diligently, so you should feel pretty confident. The only two things that might still concern you are stage fright and the question and answer session at the end of the presentation. They needn't.

Overcoming Stage Fright

Some people are natural, fearless performers irresistibly drawn to the limelight. They generally choose a career on the stage or in sales where they hope to get by on dash and charm. Most of you, however, would rather not draw attention to yourselves. You are modest, and that's probably to your credit. For you, a little anxiety is a perfectly normal reaction to the prospect of presenting before a group.

You are not alone, so it might be worth following a ritual that other presenters find calming:

- **Check out the venue ahead of time.** It's a good idea to check out the room a few days ahead of time to familiarize yourself with the layout and to imagine yourself presenting there. This will help you prepare your delivery. How loudly will you have to speak? How far will you have to project your voice? You'll also find out about the technology that you'll be using.

    As a student, you'll probably be presenting in your usual classroom, but you may never have stood at the front. Do so one lunch hour before your presentation to get a feel for the perspective.
- **Arrive early to set up.** Arriving early on the day of the presentation does two things. It allows you to set up and test the equipment and, if necessary, resolve any technical issues before you actually have to start speaking. It will also permit you to take another look at the room from the perspective of the lectern and to visualize yourself presenting there. Preparation is the key to calm nerves.
- **Withdraw for some quiet time.** While people are filing into the room, withdraw to a corner or a neighbouring room for a little quiet time. Breathe deeply, think about your presentation. Get comfortable. Relax.
- **Remind yourself that you've practised** and are as prepared as you can be. You've delivered this very presentation flawlessly several times. You have mastered the material and honed its delivery. You are as ready as you can be.
- **Remind yourself also that you know more about the topic than the audience does.** They're there to learn from you. If you've gathered information carefully, there's no way for you to get tripped up or found out.
- **Remember that the audience is on your side.** They are hoping that you'll give a great presentation because they want to learn from it; they are grateful that it's not them up there; and they will cheerfully overlook any small glitches in your delivery because they are colleagues, friends, or associates who bear no ill will. Just talk to them as you would one on one, except that you have slides and have to project your voice a bit more.

It may not help if this is your first presentation, but know also that the more presentations you give, the better you'll get and the less anxiety you'll feel. As with all skills, public speaking is something you get better at with practice.

Answering Questions

Most presentations are followed by question and answer sessions. When you are asked a question, repeat it to make sure everyone has heard it; the person asking the question is always facing you, so the people behind that person may not have heard the question. Often you'll also find yourself having to clarify the audience member's question.

In addition, and quite deviously, repeating a question buys you a few seconds to compose your answer, even if only subconsciously. It'll help you to stay calm and to provide a better, more thoughtful response.

Continue to stand square to the audience and address your answer to the whole audience, with the requisite eye contact. It's safe to assume that if the question was intelligent, others share it. You also don't want to get into a two-way conversation, which excludes the rest of the audience and invites debate. When you're done, ask, "Does this answer your question?"

If you cannot answer the question, don't guess or sidestep to save face. If you do, the audience will catch on, your honesty will be put into question, and then your entire presentation will lose credibility. If you don't know, say so. But then offer to take personal contact information so that you can get in touch when you do have an answer.

When the last question has been asked—generally there's a time limit or a limit to the number of questions—thank your audience for attending and tell them how much you've enjoyed the experience. This is one of those times when it is okay not to tell the full truth.

Editing Your Presentation

The introduction

- ☐ grabs audience attention
- ☐ makes the presentation relevant to the audience
- ☐ provides an outline (oral and graphical).

The body

- ☐ provides an amount and level of detail appropriate to the topic, the audience, and the time limit
- ☐ follows the outline and provides clear transitions between sections
- ☐ provides a slide with text or illustration to support each point.

The conclusion

- ☐ repeats the main ideas, not the outline
- ☐ opens the discussion up or points to the future (where appropriate); ties the presentation together
- ☐ invites questions (where format permits).

Visuals

- ☐ use a progressive reveal to prevent the audience from getting ahead of the presentation
- ☐ are clear, clean, uncluttered, easy to read, and free of errors in grammar, spelling, and fact.

Exercises: Oral Presentations

Exercise 14.1: The Importance of Oral Presentation in the Technical Workplace

Ask a professional in your field how often he or she gives presentations, both formal and informal; how important presentation skills are in his or her career; and the kinds of presentations that are given in his or her field.

Exercise 14.2: Observing a Professional Presentation

Watch a presentation by a professional in your or any field. Track your reaction to the presentation and take note of what made the presentation work well and what wasn't as successful. Imagine advising the speaker on how to improve. Incorporate the speaker's strengths and your suggested improvements into your own presentation techniques.

If you do not know a professional whose presentations you could attend, you can find plenty on YouTube. An excellent resource for technical presentations is www.bcit.ca/idol which makes available sample presentations given by engineering students at the British Columbia Institute of Technology's Presentation Idol competition.

Exercise 14.3: Performing an Impromptu Presentation

Do an impromptu presentation on a topic in your field. Come up with a list of topics, such as basic concepts or current environmental, technological, ethical, or legislative trends. Choose a topic from your list. Then take 15 minutes to prepare a one- or two-minute presentation on your chosen topic. Give your presentation in front of the class and collect feedback.

Exercise 14.4: Prepare a Presentation

Give a 10-minute presentation on a topic in your field. Your instructor will help you with a list of appropriate topics. You'll have a week to prepare and practise, so your materials and delivery should be fairly polished.

Exercise 14.5: Prepare a Presentation on Your Research

If you are writing a report as a term assignment, prepare a presentation on it for the class. Consider your audience's technical knowledge. It's quite common for professionals to do a presentation on a major report they are submitting.

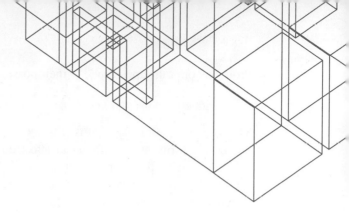

Appendix A

Punctuation and Grammar

The following subsections describe in alphabetical order some frequent points of grammar confusion, with an emphasis not on the most egregious errors, but on the most common. This appendix is not intended to provide a full compendium of potential grammar problems. For that, please check out some of the excellent book-length grammar texts available.

Apostrophes

Many writers omit apostrophes where they should be and add them where they shouldn't be.

An apostrophe indicates a contraction with the following verb "is" or "has" or "are" or "were." This is fine in informal correspondence, but it is considered unprofessional in formal correspondence and in reports.

He's meeting me at the pub after work.

How come there's so much grammar in engineering?

An apostrophe also indicates that a noun is possessive: add an apostrophe and an "s" to the end of a noun to show possession. For words ending in an "s" (or the "s" sound, such as in "Hertz"), you can choose to add the "s" or not (most commonly not)—unless it is pronounced as a separate "s," in which case the "s" must be added after the apostrophe (as in "Iris's house").

The core sample's assay results were positive.

The power supply for the city's streetlighting system is separate from the transit authority's lighting system.

The class's performance was dismal. (The final "s" pronounced separately)

The ladies' room is on the right, the gentlemen's is on the left. (No additional "s" sound added for the possessive)

The firm is doing the statics on a new seniors' centre.

The City of Toronto has short-listed four companies' proposals.

Pronouns omit the apostrophe in their possessive form.

> Theirs are not the only centrifuges on the market. In fact, ours are better.

This is most commonly confused when applied to the pronoun "it," which takes the possessive form "its" (without an apostrophe). "It's" (with an apostrophe) is used only as a contraction to mean "it is" (or "it has") where the apostrophe indicates the missing "i." Note, however, that such contractions are discouraged in business and technical documents.

> It's occurred to me that the current government has lost its mandate.

An apostrophe is never used as a separator for non-possessive plurals of initialisms, acronyms, or numerical expressions.

> The Internet gained prominence in the 1990s.
>
> The store advertised DVDs for sale. (Simple plural of "DVD")
>
> The DVD's label was scratched. (Possessive form; the label "belongs to" the DVD)
>
> The DVD's broken. (Contraction of "DVD is")

An apostrophe is also used to indicate other missing letters or missing numbers. Note the direction the apostrophe takes in the following examples.

> The Internet gained prominence in the '90s.
>
> The contract called for the construction of two Kiss 'n' Ride facilities.
>
> It's seven o'clock. (Contraction of "of the clock")

Colons

Colons have two main grammatical applications.

Colons are used to introduce lists of items when the lead-in is a complete sentence. But a colon indicates the end of a sentence, so don't use it when the lead-in is not a complete sentence. (The one exception is the "shopping list"; see Chapter 4.)

> The metallurgical test results are in: 16% of the bolts had defects, 32% had fractures, and 52% were suitable for use.
>
> According to the metallurgical test results, 16% of the bolts had defects, 32% had fractures, and 52% were suitable for use.
>
> The new proposal submission procedure offers a number of benefits: companies will be treated equally, questions will be seen by all proponents, and the evaluation criteria will be obvious.
>
> The new proposal submission procedure offers a number of benefits including that companies will be treated equally, that questions will be seen by all proponents, and

that the evaluation criteria will be obvious. (Note that "including" indicates that this is a partial, not a complete, list.)

Colons can also be used to express a clarification, to underscore a point, or to introduce a formal question or a long quote (Chapter 9). The first word following a colon generally doesn't begin with a capital letter, unless the word is being quoted and is capitalized in the original source, if the word is a proper noun, or if you want to provide emphasis.

> There was no turning back: he had submitted his resignation in writing.
>
> Let there be no doubt: proposals received after April 12 will not be reviewed.
>
> The association's verdict after the disciplinary hearing was unexpected: Not guilty.

Commas

Commas are frequently used punctuation marks whose omission or unnecessary insertion can change or confuse the reading of a sentence. Some uses, of course, are strictly conventional. In many cases, you'll find that commas mark locations where a speaker either pauses or changes intonation.

Commas with Addresses

Use commas to separate geographic units. Use a comma at the end of such series when they appear in the middle of a sentence:

> My address will be 12 Mountain View Cr., Whistler, BC, during Christmas break.
>
> London, England, is quite different from London, Ontario.

Do not use a comma before a postal code, but add an extra space, and don't use a hyphen to separate the code groups:

> Toronto, Ontario M4B 2W8

Commas with Dates

Use commas to separate days from years in the month-day-year format. Place another comma after the year if the date appears in the middle of a sentence:

> The project completion date is June 15, 2017.
>
> I was born on March 15, 1994, under a bad alignment of the stars and with ill omens in the sky.

Do not use commas if they're not necessary to separate number groups:

> I was born on 15 March 1994 in exotic Porcupine Plain, Saskatchewan.
>
> I was born in March 1994.

Commas with Introductory Elements

Use a comma to separate introductory elements from the main clause.

> Yesterday, I went to the store.
>
> This being a Saturday, we worked only until 8 p.m.
>
> When you embarked on your career in engineering, you probably thought you'd seen the last of English teachers.

The lack of a comma could confuse readers because they won't know where to pause.

> In the office filing cabinets were in disarray.
>
> In the office, filing cabinets were in disarray.

Commas with Non-restrictive Modifiers

Use commas with non-restrictive modifiers, but not with restrictive ones. A restrictive modifier defines the object being described; that is, it answers the question, "Which one?" A non-restrictive modifier is essentially a parenthetical element (see below) nonessential to the meaning of the sentence. You'll find yourself pausing and changing intonation when you read a non-restrictive element aloud. Mark those locations with commas.

> Our technologist, Susan, is a crackerjack poker player.

The company has only one technologist. The name is an additional, parenthetical, detail and doesn't clarify which technologist is meant.

> Our technologist Susan is a crackerjack poker player.

In this sentence, "Susan" is a restrictive modifier that defines which technologist is meant. The company has several technologists, but only the one named Susan is likely to take your money in a poker game.

> One of our technologists, Susan, is a crackerjack poker player.

The company has several technologists; it's not important which one is the exceptional poker player, just that there is one.

The engineer who is supposed to do the statics this weekend has had to go to Toronto because of a family emergency. (One specific engineer of many)

The engineer, who does our statics, likes to take three-martini lunches. (There is only one engineer; he does the statics.)

The porta-potties with the separate urinals have been placed throughout the site for your convenience. (Which particular type of porta-potties?)

Porta-potties, portable non-flush toilets made of easy-to-clean plastics, have been placed throughout the site for your convenience. (Parenthetical definition answering the question, "What's a porta-pottie?")

Commas in Parallel Constructions

In parallel constructions, use commas to indicate omitted words, much as apostrophes mark missing letters in a contraction. Again, the comma marks a pause:

Jim was recording the measurements; Dave, the locations.

Commas with Parenthetical Elements

Parenthetical elements are words and phrases that are not essential to the fundamental meaning of the sentence, although they may clarify it or create the proper emphasis. These parenthetical elements should be separated from the main sentence with commas. For greater emphasis, they can also be separated with en or em dashes (explained below).

An easy test to determine whether something is functioning parenthetically is whether you find yourself pausing, dropping your voice, or changing your intonation when you read the sentence aloud. Commas denote these pauses and changes of intonation typographically.

Porta-potties, <u>however</u>, mean never having to go far when you have to go.

Framing hammers, <u>on the whole</u>, have a longer handle than regular hammers.

It was the supplier, <u>not the contractor</u>, who damaged the material.

Tell me, <u>Bill</u>, what is this symbol on the drawing supposed to mean?

<u>Sure</u>, porta-potties are easy to clean, but chlorine pucks would help keep down the smell.

You're not serious, <u>are you</u>?

This proposal, <u>for example</u>, was laid out in inDesign.

The portable sanitary facilities, <u>that is, porta-potties</u>, were badly damaged by the backhoe.

Commas with Quotes

Use commas to introduce direct quotations:

> Agnes Macphail, the first woman elected to Canada's House of Commons, once said, "Patriotism is not dying for one's country, it is living for one's country. And for humanity. Perhaps that is not as romantic, but it's better."

But do not use a comma when you introduce a quote with "that":

> Agnes Macphail stated that "patriotism is not dying for one's country, it is living for one's country."

Nor should you use one when you weave parts of quotes into the structure of your own sentence so that "that" is unnecessary:

> Agnes Macphail defined patriotism as "living for one's country. And for humanity."

Commas in Series

Use a serial comma (before the "and" or "or") to separate three or more items in a series:

> He is an experienced, well-educated, and eager candidate.
>
> Frank will make the coffee, I will provide the doughnuts, and Jean will write the report.

Omitting the serial comma can lead to confusion:

> I went to lunch with Dave, my best friend, and my favourite client (Three guests for lunch)
>
> I went to lunch with Dave, my best friend and my favourite client (One guest for lunch)

In the latter case, Dave is both best friend and favourite client.

Commas with Titles

Use commas when titles follow names (to match intonation), but not when the titles precede the names, in which case the titles are treated like part of the name:

> Mr. Bean, P.Eng.
>
> Justin Trudeau, prime minister
>
> Prime Minister Justin Trudeau

Dashes (En Dash and Em Dash)

Two types of dashes are used typographically: en dashes (–), and em dashes (—). (Hyphens are described in the section below.) En and em dashes take their names from their lengths, which in each font match the widths of the letters "n" and "m," respectively.

Em dashes are traditionally used to separate parenthetical clauses and phrases. In Word (both PC and Mac versions), simply type a double hyphen between two words, without spaces, and the two hyphens will change to an em dash as you keep typing.

> Greasy fast food—if you're into that sort of thing—can cause heartburn. (Clause)
>
> I'll be finished—with a little luck—by the deadline. (Phrase)

In certain (particularly informal) contexts, en dashes with intervening spaces before and after have begun to take over the role of em dashes surrounding subordinate clauses and phrases. In Word (both PC and Mac versions), simply type a double hyphen and it will change to an en dash as you keep typing, as long as you've inserted a space before the first and after the second hyphen.

> I'll be finished – with a little luck – by the deadline.

Note that commas can also be used to set off parenthetical elements, but en and em dashes provide more emphasis because they indicate a longer pause.

> I'll be finished, with a little luck, by the deadline.

Also, en and em dashes are less confusing than commas when used with parenthetical lists and longer parenthetical elements.

> Engineers from across North America, civil, mechanical, and electrical, convened in Ottawa. (Unclear)
>
> Engineers from across North America—civil, mechanical, and electrical—convened in Ottawa. (Revised)

Use an en dash for negative signs. This is a convention, so just do it.

> The temperature in Winnipeg varies from –40°C to +40°C, at 30% to 100% relative humidity.

Use an en dash, not hyphens, without intervening spaces to connect ranges from one number or word to another—except when preceded by "from" or "between."

> I read the encyclopedia Aardvark-Xylophone.
>
> Dates in question cover the years 1992–99.

The period the investigators examined ran from January 1992 to June 1999.

Use a spaced en dash to attribute a quote.

"A Canadian is merely an unarmed American with health care." – John Wing.

Use an em dash or a spaced en dash to provide a degree of emphasis. A colon would work just as well; see above.

This much is certain – the exam results will tell all.

Use an en dash to add a prefix to an already hyphenated word.

The activist attended the pre–anti-pipeline rally.

Hyphens

A hyphen is the typographical symbol corresponding to the minus key on your keyboard (-). It performs a number of useful functions that aid clarity and readability.

Compound Adjectives

Hyphens combine multiple words into compound words that function as single adjectives. Without hyphens, the sentence meaning may be unclear or ambiguous:

ten foot lengths of fuel rods (Unclear)

ten foot-lengths of fuel rods (Ten individual fuel rods, each one foot long)

ten-foot lengths of fuel rods (An unspecified number of fuel rods that are each ten feet long; compound adjective describing "lengths")

Other examples of compound adjectives:

We engaged a third-party testing agency.

The hedge fund is investing in a 70-storey casino hotel.

The pump uses a state-of-the-art impeller.

The paint is delivered in 50-gallon barrels. (Note that metric measurements are not hyphenated, only imperial ones.)

Do not use hyphens when these same word combinations follow instead of precede a noun. In such cases, the combinations don't function as single modifiers.

The barrels contain 50 gallons of paint. (Standard measurement: two words)

The high-pressure system is under high pressure.

Adverb-adjective pairings are not connected by hyphens. They do not function as single words.

The newly elected president has made a statement. (Not newly-elected)

Compound Nouns

Use hyphens to combine multiple words into compound words that function as single nouns. In each of the following sentences, the hyphenated words form a compound noun.

The 18-year-old proved with his presentation that he has the makings of a future researcher.

My father-in-law will pick up the lumber.

Electrical energy is often stated in units of kilowatt-hours. (But kWh, no hyphen, the proper metric unit)

It's time for me to conduct a self-analysis of why I entered engineering.

By convention, some compound nouns no longer require a hyphen to provide clarity. For example, "ice cream" was originally hyphenated because no one was familiar with this newfangled combination of dairy with ice. Once everyone grew to know and love the idea, the hyphen was dropped.

Other Uses

Use a hyphen to distinguish words with different meanings but similar spellings.

Resign (quit); re-sign (sign again).

Use a hyphen to avoid awkward letter combinations that might make the reading or pronunciation unclear.

The engineers had to <u>re-evaluate</u> their statics after the <u>cave-in.</u> (Not "reevaluate" and not "cavein")

Use a hyphen to avoid tripling a consonant or duplicating a prefix.

He ran the construction site with a drill-like efficiency.

The proposal review committee contained a sub-subcommittee for budget review.

Use a hyphen to indicate joint titles and between nouns that together name one thing:

She is the secretary-treasurer of the engineering alumni club.

Walkie-talkies are effective communication tools for geologists in the field.

Use a hyphen with stand-alone fractions and written numbers between 21 and 99.

Two-thirds of respondents to the survey strongly agreed that service could be improved.

Thirty-seven of her closest friends attended her surprise birthday dinner.

When you omit the second part of a hyphenated compound in a parallel construction, retain the hyphen.

Depending on the institution, nursing degrees can be obtained in two-, three-, or four-year programs.

Modifiers

Dangling Modifiers

When a modifier has no specific subject to modify, it's kind of left hanging. We say that the modifier is dangling. The same is true if the wrong subject is suggested. Make sure that every action and description in your sentences has a clear subject:

Rechecking the calculations, some transposed figures were found. (Who is rechecking the calculations?)

While rechecking the calculations, the engineer found some transposed figures.

Jumping and snapping at flies playfully, Tom spotted the fox pup. (Tom was snapping at flies?)

Tom spotted the fox pup as it playfully jumped and snapped at flies. (Revised)

Rife with calculation errors, the lead engineer rejected the EIT's statics. (The lead engineer was rife with calculation errors?)

Rife with calculation errors, the EIT's statics were rejected by the lead engineer.

The lead engineer rejected the EIT's statics because they were rife with calculation errors.

Misplaced Modifiers

Modifiers must be placed directly before or after the word they modify, depending on common usage. If they are placed elsewhere (misplaced), they will modify the wrong word and change or muddle the meaning of the sentence.

The company won in <u>nearly every category</u> at the industrial design award luncheon. (They won in most of the categories.)

The company <u>nearly won</u> in every category at the industrial design award luncheon. (They didn't win in any category, but they got close in all.)

The lab supervisor instructed the technicians frequently to sterilize the equipment. ("Frequently instructed" or "frequently sterilize"?)

The lab supervisor <u>frequently instructed</u> the technicians to sterilize the equipment. (Revised)

The lab supervisor instructed the technicians <u>to sterilize</u> the equipment <u>frequently</u>. (Revised)

Pronouns

Incorrect Pronoun Selection

Words such as "I," "he," "she," and "it" are pronouns; they replace nouns in sentences, making those sentences flow better because we don't have to keep repeating the proper names of the people and things we're writing about. Pronouns take other forms, such as "me," "myself," "him," "himself," and "them," depending on function. Many writers use the incorrect form of pronouns, especially when a sentence involves multiple subjects or multiple indirect objects. Consider the following examples:

With the new software, he can do the task more quickly than me. (Incorrect; you wouldn't say ". . . more quickly than me can do the task.")

With the new software, he can do the task more quickly than I. (Correct: "more quickly than I can do the task")

Me and him worked on the proposal together. (Incorrect)

I (not me) worked on the proposal. He (not him) worked on the proposal also. (Correct; two sentences)

I and he worked on the proposal. (Grammatically correct)

He and I worked on the proposal. (Grammatically correct and socially proper)

Consider the difference between the following two sentences, both of which are correct but mean different things:

Mary likes calculus more than me. (Mary likes calculus more than she likes <u>me</u>.)

Mary likes calculus more than I. (Mary likes calculus more than I like calculus.)

These sorts of errors are particularly common with the reflexive pronouns (i.e., "myself," "himself," etc.). Reserve reflexive pronouns for self-inflicted actions; that is, only you can feed yourself, only you can dress yourself, and only you can touch yourself. Consider the following examples:

> Myself am four days ahead of schedule. (Obviously incorrect)
>
> Edgar, Bram, and myself are four days ahead of schedule. (Just as incorrect)
>
> I am four days ahead of schedule. (Correct)
>
> Edgar, Bram, and I are four days ahead of schedule. (Correct)
>
> Please give the report to myself. (Obviously incorrect; only you can give the report to yourself.)
>
> Please give the report to Bill or myself. (Just as incorrect)
>
> Please give the report to me. (Correct)
>
> Please give the report to Bill or me. (Correct)

The word "whom" is confusing to many people and is often erroneously replaced with "who." However, "who" is the subject of a verb; it performs the action. "Whom" is the object of a verb; the action gets performed to it, on it, for it, or with it. Hence, when the (interrogative) pronoun follows a preposition, use "whom."

> She gave the report to whom? (Not "She gave the report to who?")
>
> To whom did she give the report?
>
> She can give the report to whomever she likes. (Not "whoever")
>
> On whom are we operating today?
>
> From whom did you get these flowers? (But "Who gave you these flowers?")

Unclear Pronoun References

Pronouns must clearly identify to what they are referring.

> When John met with his manager at the year-end review meeting, <u>he</u> got a bad evaluation. (Does "he" refer to John or to John's manager?)
>
> When John met with his manager at the year-end review meeting, <u>the manager</u> gave him a bad evaluation.
>
> John gave <u>his manager</u> a poor evaluation at the year-end review meeting. (Less likely, admittedly, but some places ask employees to evaluate their managers.)
>
> Jack knew that the proposal contained the calculation he needed for the meeting, but he couldn't find <u>it</u> in time. (Couldn't find the report or the calculation in the report?)
>
> Ours was the lowest bid, but <u>that</u>'s not what they were hoping for. (They weren't looking for the lowest bid or they were hoping it wouldn't be yours?)

Ours was the lowest bid, but unfortunately, price was not their only criterion. (Revised)

Ours was the lowest bid, but unfortunately, they didn't want to work with us. (Revised)

Quotation Marks

Quotation marks ("/") are not the same as inch marks ("). Quotation marks are curled or slanted, depending on the typeface, whereas inch marks are always straight, vertical strokes. The same is true for apostrophes (') versus imperial foot marks (').

Use quotation marks when you are using someone else's words verbatim.

According to the client's feedback, the engineer's assistance was "greatly appreciated" and "delivered with a genuine desire to help."

Quotations longer than two lines should be indented rather than enclosed in quotation marks (see Chapter 9).

The North American typographical style is for periods and commas to go inside quotation marks (the reverse is true with British writing guidelines).

The presentation was entitled "2010 and Beyond: Infrastructure in Ontario."

The DB contractor shall ensure that fill material brought on site meets the criteria outlined in the document entitled "Alberta Tier 1 Soil and Groundwater Remediation Guidelines."*

Question mark and exclamation point placement depends on whether the punctuation is part of the quote or part of the sentence that contains the quote.

Have you never heard the expression, "Red sky in morning, sailors take warning"? (The question mark is not part of the original expression and therefore is placed outside of the quotation mark.)

The riot police shouted, "Clear the streets!" at the G20 protestors. (The exclamation mark is part of the quote and therefore appears within the quotation mark.)

Quotation marks are used to define custom terminology upon first use.

The end-of-track device shall include an "anti-climber" to engage the vehicle symmetrically about the coupler at bumper height.

Machine the tongue rails from "Zu2-49" rail or approved equivalent.

For the purpose of this proposal, "long-term" shall be defined as 25 years.*

---

* Examples on the following pages are provided by Andre Lanz.

Quotation marks are used when defining legal terminology upon first use.

Any reference to "Contractor," "General Contractor," "Manufacturer," "Tenderer," "Supplier," or "Consultant" shall be interpreted to mean the "DB Contractor."

These Terms and Conditions form a binding contract (the "Contract") between Bachman Kellogg Easton Ltd. (the "Company") and the City of Vancouver (the "City").*

Quotation marks are never used for emphasis; when used this way, they give the impression of dishonesty or insincerity. Use italics or bolding for emphasis.

Push the "button" and then turn the "crank." (Incorrect, unless the words "button" and "crank" refer to something other than a button and a crank)

Push the button and then turn the crank. (Revised)

Push the button and then turn the crank. (Revised—no emphasis necessary)

Semi-colons

Semi-colons between Sentences

A semi-colon can be used in place of a period when two sentences are closely related logically. A semi-colon better expresses this logical relationship because it introduces a shorter pause than a period.

Yesterday's inquiry hearing began on time. All members of the disciplinary committee attended.

Yesterday's inquiry hearing began on time; all members of the disciplinary committee attended.

Yesterday's inquiry hearing began on time, and all the members of the disciplinary committee attended.

Note that a comma cannot link two sentences unless you also employ a coordinating conjunction: and, but, or, nor, for, so, yet.

Note also that conjunctive adverbs—such as "however" and "therefore"—cannot join two sentences with a comma. Logically they may function like coordinating conjunctions, but they do not function in the same way grammatically. Often semi-colons are used to indicate that sentences linked with conjunctive adverbs are closely linked logically.

The concrete will not reach full strength for 28 days; however, the forms can be stripped within three.

The concrete will not reach full strength for 28 days. However, the forms can be stripped within three.

The concrete will not reach full strength for 28 days. The forms, however, can be stripped within three.

Semi-colons in Series

A semi-colon should be used in place of a comma to separate listed items that themselves contain commas.

Station security can be maintained in a number of ways: closed-circuit video cameras; security guards, around the clock; anti-shoplifting programs, including "undercover passengers"; and doors, windows, and access panels fitted with appropriate locks and alarms.*

When such a sentence is stacked in list form (see Chapter 4), the semi-colons can be maintained as long as the final conjunction ("and" in this case) is also maintained. Or you can omit "and" as well as the semi-colons. Either way, as the following list will make clear, complex lists are generally clearer when stacked.

Station security can be maintained in a number of ways:
- closed-circuit video cameras;
- security guards, around the clock;
- anti-shoplifting programs, including "undercover passengers"; and
- doors, windows, and access panels fitted with appropriate locks and alarms.*

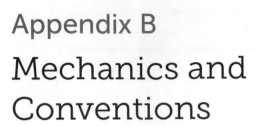

Appendix B

Mechanics and Conventions

Aside from being subject to rules of grammar, English is also subject to mechanics and conventions. Mechanics are rules that don't actually affect the sequencing of words (syntax), the selection of words (diction), or their conjugation, but that may affect meaning. Mechanics overlap with conventions, which are one-off rules for which there may not even be a good reason, but which should be followed for the sake of clarity.

Failure to follow any of the mechanics and conventions of English also constitutes an error. While not everyone will notice such errors, those who do will view them as indicating a lack of know-how, professionalism, and attention to detail.

The following sections describe some of these mechanics and conventions.

Acronyms and Abbreviations

Use of Acronyms and Abbreviations

Writers often create acronyms or abbreviations as a form of personal shorthand for common words or phrases that pertain to their topic, area of interest, or expertise. But, obviously, such idiosyncratic references will not be clear to most readers, especially readers outside the writer's field of expertise.

Words or phrases should be abbreviated only if they are used frequently in a given document and if it is too onerous or repetitive to repeat them in full. Abbreviations should not be used as shorthand for the convenience of the writer. Abbreviations are appropriate only if they improve flow for the reader, and they must not leave the reader wondering what the abbreviation means.

In general, reduce the number of unnecessary acronyms and abbreviations in your writing. Any term or phrase that is used less than 10 times (in a longer document) should probably not be abbreviated.

Note that some acronyms and abbreviations are widely understood and can be used without prior definition, such as USA, NASA, Ltd., Mr., St., Ave.

Some acronyms and abbreviations are widely understood within a specific industry or technology. When writing for one of these audiences, you may use these without prior definition if it would seem patronizing to define them. Some examples could include OEM, UNC, UNF, NPT, SAE, ASTM, and SCADA.

Introduction of Acronyms and Abbreviations

For the most part, an abbreviation or acronym must be spelled out in full followed by its short form in parentheses the first time you use the abbreviated form. In large documents, the term should be re-defined at the first use in each major section. The term should not be re-defined randomly throughout the document. Acronyms are generally written without periods between the letters.

> Mechanically stabilized earth (MSE) walls with dry-cast concrete block facings are not approved for use in the bridge structure.

> Traction power shall be supplied to the overhead contact system (OCS) via positive feeder cables that provide a nominal positive voltage of 660 VDC.*

Parenthetical definitions also apply to difficult or obscure terminology, not just abbreviations and acronyms.

> The milk sold locally contains high levels of recombinant bovine growth hormone (rBGH). These high levels of rBGH are of considerable concern as rBGH is a known carcinogen (cancer-causing agent) and a suspected teratogen (birth-defect-causing agent).

An alternative to supplying parenthetical definitions is placing definitions in a glossary. A glossary is appropriate when

- the definition is too long and will break up the flow of reading too much, or
- not all readers will require the definition and you want to save the knowledgeable readers some time.

Read the section titled Glossary in Chapter 7 to see how glossary items are identified and how glossaries are set up.

Acronyms are typically capitalized, but the non-abbreviated forms generally will not be, unless they are, or include, proper nouns (see Capitals below).

> Run the signal wires through a 2-in. high-density polyethylene (HDPE) duct.

> A closed circuit television (CCTV) system shall provide remote video surveillance of all public spaces within the station. The CCTV camera video stream shall be transmitted to the Operations Control Centre (OCC) where it will be recorded.*

Acronym definitions are not pluralized even if the non-abbreviated reference is.

> Of the nine traction power sub-stations (TPSS), five shall be equipped with four DC feeders and four shall be equipped with six DC feeders.

---

* Examples provided on the following pages are by Andre Lanz.

When pluralizing an acronym, do not capitalize the "s." (And don't add an apostrophe!)

> The light rail system will include nine TPSSs.

Do not abbreviate the name of an organization that does not normally shorten its own name.

> The Ministry of Transportation should not be abbreviated to MOT or MoT.

Do not abbreviate "Street," "Avenue," "Road," "Boulevard," "Trail," and similar words within sentences, in order to avoid the awkward period that accompanies these abbreviations.

> The interchange is at 45th Avenue and Granville Street.

Provinces that are not commonly referred to by their abbreviations in speech should not be abbreviated in writing. For provinces that are known by their abbreviations, include periods when abbreviating them.

> Ontario is Canada's most populous province.
>
> B.C. has 24,000 registered engineers.
>
> There is one engineering school in P.E.I.

Province names can be abbreviated in the following ways, depending on usage:

FOR GENERAL REFERENCE	FOR MAILING ADDRESSES
British Columbia – B.C.	British Columbia – BC
Alberta – Alta.	Alberta – AB
Saskatchewan – Sask.	Saskatchewan – SK
Manitoba – Man.	Manitoba – MB
Ontario – Ont.	Ontario – ON
Quebec – Que.	Quebec – QC
New Brunswick – N.B.	New Brunswick – NB
Nova Scotia – N.S.	Nova Scotia – NS
Prince Edward Island – P.E.I.	Prince Edward Island – PE
Newfoundland and Labrador – Nfld. (or N.L.)	Newfoundland and Labrador – NL
Yukon – Y. T.	Yukon – YT
Northwest Territories – N. W. T.	Northwest Territories – NT
Nunavut – Nun. (or Nvt.)	Nunavut – NU

Generally, use the following Latin abbreviations only in source citations and comments in parentheses. Otherwise, use the English equivalent. Do not italicize them.

ABBREVIATION	LATIN	ENGLISH EQUIVALENT
i.e.	id est	that is
cf.	confer	compare
e.g.	exempli gratia	for example
et al.	et alll	and others
etc.	et cetera	and so forth
NB	nota bene	note well

The portable sanitary facilities, that is, porta-potties, were badly damaged by the backhoe.

The portable sanitary facilities (i.e., porta-potties) were badly damaged by the backhoe.

One of our contractors, namely Choir of Angles Drywalling Ltd., billed us $80/h for his workmen, whereas the industry standard is $50/h (cf. attached invoice from White Walls Drywalling Ltd.).

Capitals

Writers often erroneously capitalize general nouns, particularly nouns that pertain to their topic, area of interest, or expertise, or to create unwarranted emphasis. For example,

The Market Street Station is one of six new <u>Stations</u> along the South LRT expansion.

The Market Street Station is one of six new <u>stations</u> along the South LRT expansion. (Revised)

In case of <u>Fire</u>, do not use elevators.

In case of <u>fire</u>, do not use elevators. (Revised)*

However, capitalization is restricted to proper nouns: people, places, specifically named features and things, organizations, companies, acronyms, religions, awards, government departments, languages, nationalities, the days of the week, months, and explicitly defined legal terms. Refer to online dictionaries (www.onelook.com provides access to several dictionaries simultaneously) and style guides for guidance, and if in doubt, use lower case.

Capitalize specific names, but use lower case for nouns that refer to several specific names and for nouns used in a general way.

The Port Mann Bridge crosses the Fraser River. The Pattullo Bridge crosses the Fraser River. The Port Mann and Pattullo <u>bridges</u> cross the Fraser River. The <u>bridges</u> are inadequate and need to be replaced.

Refer to the City of Calgary's Temporary Traffic Control Manual 2011. This <u>manual</u> will answer any questions you may have.

The track follows 42nd Street. This <u>street</u> has four lanes.

In legal documents (e.g., contracts), capitalize legal terms that are explicitly defined in the document you are writing, even if the terms would not normally be capitalized in a non-legal document. (These sorts of legal terms should be defined either in a definitions section of the document or individually.) For example, in a legal contract in which "design-build (DB) contractor," "quality management plan," "project," "owner," and "work" have been explicitly defined, the following treatment would be correct.

> The DB Contractor shall develop and implement a Quality Management Plan for the delivery of the Project.

> The DB Contractor shall provide monthly progress reports of the Work, as defined, to the Owner.

But in a letter, report, proposal, résumé, project sheet, or any other document wherein legal terms have not been explicitly defined, the following would be correct:

> The project was completed on time.

> The work was completed satisfactorily.

> BKE completed the detailed design to the owner's satisfaction.

> BKE was the owner's engineer for the Elm Street Overpass project. (Where "Elm Street Overpass" is a proper name)

> BKE's quality management system provides for peer reviews.

Capitalize professional or honorific titles only when they come before a specific person's name or if they are explicitly defined legal terms in a contract (as above). Use lower case if the titles are not used as part of an individual's title, or if they are used in a general sense. Don't capitalize titles just because they have a generally understood or specific meaning, or because they are capitalized in legal documents elsewhere.

> Prime Minister Justin Trudeau met with Bachman Kellogg Easton President Michael Scott.

> Michael Scott, president of Bachman Kellogg Easton, met with Prime Minister Justin Trudeau.

> The Bachman Kellogg Easton Board of Directors meets quarterly. At the last meeting, the board of directors voted on several important issues. The board will meet next in September.

> Dr. Tyseer Aboulnasr is the dean of the faculty of applied science at the University of British Columbia.

> On Monday, Dean Tyseer Aboulnasr travelled to UBC's Kelowna campus.

Capitalize certain honorific titles (such as "President of the United States" or "Queen of England") regardless of use. These are conventions and represent exceptions to the rules.

The President, in his State of the Union Address, acknowledged that the economic crisis is deepening.

Capitalize the proper titles of reference documents.

Refer to the City of Calgary's Snow and Ice Control Policy, Temporary Traffic Control Manual 2011, and bylaws 20M88, 26M96, and 29M97. (Where "Policy" and "Manual" are part of the proper titles.)*

Use lower case for "website," "email," "log on," "login," and "online"; "Internet" is most often capitalized.

Association registrants use the Internet and email to keep up to date on information.

The information was collected from various online sources.

Capitalize specific geographical and regional names, but use lower case for general geographic, location, and direction references.

Lower Mainland (region surrounding Vancouver), Vancouver Island, the Bay of Fundy, the Interior (of B.C.), Georgia Strait, the Rocky Mountains, the Maritimes

Engineers from northern B.C. have to travel south to the Lower Mainland or east to Alberta for professional development opportunities.

Capitalize names of organizations but use lower case for general references or common parts of an organization.

The Association of Professional Engineers and Geoscientists of British Columbia (APEGBC)

APEGBC is the association responsible for regulating B.C.'s engineers and geoscientists.

The National Fire Protection Association

The faculty of applied science at McGill University (Not faculty's official name)

Capitalize names of specific government ministries and authorities, but not when they are used in a general sense.

The B.C. Ministry of Transportation is located in Victoria. The ministry regulates the transportation of dangerous goods according to the Transportation of Dangerous Goods Act.

The ministry representative will attend an Association of Professional Engineers and Geoscientists of British Columbia meeting.

APEGBC is one of 10 provincial engineering regulatory bodies.

Capitalize specific section references in a report but use lower case for general references.

> Refer to Section 3.4 for structural loads.
>
> Dynamic loads are defined in the following sections.

Capitalize abbreviated university degrees or professional designations, except when the abbreviation is a combination of capital and lower case letters; in this case, include periods between the abbreviations. An exception to the use of periods in a combination of capital and lower case letters is a doctor of philosophy (PhD) degree.

> He has a B.A.Sc. from UBC.
>
> She received her P.Eng. after five years.
>
> Some engineers cross to the dark side and earn an MBA.

Do not capitalize a university degree or professional designation when you spell it out.

> She has a bachelor of applied science degree in civil engineering from UBC.

Do not capitalize the second part of a hyphenated word. Technically, the same rule applies to section headings, but it can look odd, so it is up to you in those instances.

> Use T-head bolts and spring clips.
>
> Section 10.2: Multi-person Writing Process

Numbers

Numbers between zero and nine are generally spelled out, while those 10 and above are written numerically.

> The controller has two input modules, each with 16 channels.

If a number is not a measurement and is less than 10, write it in words.

> The office was furnished with three desks and one phone.

Regardless of its value, a number should always be spelled out at the beginning of a sentence.

> Two thousand five hundred and ten new condos went on the market in October.
>
> In October, 2,510 new condos went on the market.

Numbers with four digits or more contain commas as separators.

The control group in the study's first phase contained 4,335 people.

Numbers between 21 and 99 that are spelled out include a hyphen, as do fractions where the numerator and denominator are under 10.

Ninety-three of 120 stanchions need replacement.
One-fifth of the engineers worked the weekend.

For rough approximations, write the number in words. If the number is over a million and is approximate, spell out "million." A numeral is always expected to be accurate to the exact digit.

This building is fifty years old. (More or less)
This building is 50 years old. (Exactly)
The company's revenue is over nine million dollars.
Last year, Toyota sold more than 10 million cars worldwide.

Write out numerically numbers that include decimals.

The company estimates 1.5 million air bags will be replaced after the recall.

When whole numbers and fractions are mixed, use numbers.

The exam will take 1½ days to write.

When fractions are used alone, use the "nine or less, 10 or more" rule.

Only two-thirds of the students passed the exam.

When writing about money, use the "nine or less, 10 or more" rule as a guideline, although this changes with large amounts of money.

A two-dollar toll is unheard of today: nine dollars is closer to the current amount.
The company received a $1 million grant to develop a carbon sequestration prototype.
The $29 million engineering campus opens at the end of this year.

When one number appears immediately after another as part of a phrase, one should be in words and the other in numerals. If one of the numbers is a measurement, that number should be expressed as a numeral. Otherwise, choose the one that would be more difficult to write out as a word.

Four 7-member crews

Twelve 6-in. timbers

Two 10-storey buildings

If the number is a reference or identity number, use numerals. This rule includes addresses and dates.

Page 3, figure 2, Chapter 13, week 4, question 7, exercise 5

In a series of numbers, all numbers should be in the same form.

The staff consists of 12 clerks, 4 engineers, and 2 supervisors.

or

The staff consists of twelve clerks, four engineers, and two supervisors.

Don't add numerals in parentheses after a number as is done in some legal documents. If a lawyer wants to add these in a legal contract, let the lawyer do it.

The bridge includes two (2) piers.

Units of Measurement

Engineering unit syntax is defined by international standards and is not subjective. The metric system uses the following case-sensitive prefixes without variation:

SYMBOL	PREFIX	FACTOR
E	exa	10^{18}
P	peta	10^{15}
T	tera	10^{12}
G	giga	10^{9}
M	mega	10^{6}
k	kilo	10^{3}
h	hecto	10^{2}
da	deca	10^{1}
—	—	1
d	deci	10^{-1}
c	centi	10^{-2}
m	milli	10^{-3}
µ	micro	10^{-6}
n	nano	10^{-9}
p	pico	10^{-12}
f	femto	10^{-15}
a	atto	10^{-18}

Common case-sensitive metric and imperial units include the following (note that a period is used in the abbreviation for "inch"):

CATEGORY	COMMON UNITS
Time	s, min, h, d, yr
Pressure	Pa, kPa
	psi, psig, psia
Temperature	°C, K (note: no degree symbol for K)
	°F, °R
Distance	mm, cm, m, km
	in., ft, mi
Area	mm², m²
	in², ft²
Volume	mL, L, mm³, m³
	gal, US gal, Imp. gal, in³, ft³
Mass, weight, and force	g, kg, t (metric tonne)
	oz, lb, ton (imperial ton)
	N, kN, MN
Energy and power	J, kJ, MJ, kWh, mW, W, kW, MW
	Btu, Btu/h, HP
Electrical	A, ADC, AAC
	V, VDC, VAC
	Ω, Hz
Luminosity	lx
Sound level	dB
Currency	$, $US, $CDN

An easy way to add a superscript in Microsoft Word is to select the character and then type Ctrl + Shift + plus sign (PC) or Command + Shift + Spacebar + plus sign (Mac).

Do not spell out units of measurement when you are referring to a specific measurement.

Replace all water mains within 6.0 metres of the train track.

Replace all water mains within 6.0 m of the train track. (Revised)

The foreman purchased 25 km of wire and 280 m of pipe.

Conductors carrying 50 VAC or more shall not be bundled with any lower voltage conductors.

Leave a single space between the last digit of the number and the symbol except when using the % symbol. When written out, "per cent" is spelled as two words, but "percentage" is one word.

Impedance to all audio frequencies 500 Hz and above shall be greater than 5 Ω.

Fuel may not be stored withln 30 m of a watercourse.

The structure must withstand wind loads of 100 km/h with a 30% gust factor.*

Thirty per cent of the students achieved a percentage of 80 or above.

Do not leave spaces between combined units.

One m3 of natural gas contains 11.06 kWh of energy.

The maximum long-term tunnel leakage is 2 L/min per 100 m of tunnel.

The catalyst costs $0.78/mL.

Do not leave a space between a currency symbol and the number, unless the symbol has been modified to indicate a specific currency.

The project cost $178 million.

The baseplate cost $US 320.

With units of temperature, keep the degree symbol with the symbol letter. You'll find the degree symbol under Insert > Symbol in Word. Scroll down until you find the proper one. Note that the unit for Kelvin (K) does not include a degree symbol.

The temperature in Calgary varies from −40°C to +40°C, at 30% to 100% relative humidity including condensation.

The liquefaction temperature of hydrogen is 20 K (36°R).

Hyphenate imperial units that are used as adjectives, but not metric ones.

Maintain a 1 m separation between topsoil and subsoil stockpiles.

Topsoil and subsoil stockpiles must be separated by 1 m.

Maintain a 50-ft distance behind this vehicle.

Stay 50 ft behind this vehicle.

Add a zero before numeric values that start with a decimal point.

At 20°C, track-terminal-to-track-terminal DC resistance shall not be greater than 0.00085 Ω.*

Do not pluralize units, even if the number is plural.

Calculate the stress using a live load of 500 lb at the end of the arm.
(Not 500 lbs)

Write symbols without a period, except at the end of a sentence, or in the midst of confusing combinations of imperial units (like in.lb or ft.lb, but not Nm or kWh). An exception to this is the problematic abbreviation for inch (in) since it is also the preposition "in." To distinguish it within a sentence, add a period after the unit unless it is combined with other symbols that make its context clear. Do not substitute the " and ' symbols for inches and feet. (Note that the " and ' symbols are not quotation marks ("") or apostrophes ('), which are curvy or slanted, depending on the typeface. You can find the proper symbols under Insert > Symbol in Word.)

The pipe is 3 in. in diameter.

The pipe is 76.2 mm (3 in) in diameter. (Revised)

The pipe diameter is 3 in. (Revised)

Use a ¾-in wrench to tighten the nut.

Torque the bolts to 200 in.lb after installation.

Use consistent units throughout a document (i.e., use metric, imperial, or both consistently). When stating both metric and imperial units, use a consistent order and format throughout the document, with the second unit in parentheses.

Water freezes at 0°C (32°F)

or

Water freezes at 32°F (0°C).

Flow rates can be expressed in shorthand form as cfs, cfm, gpm, and so on, and speeds can be expressed in shorthand form as kph, mph, and so on. Use these short forms sparingly, and opt instead to write out the units fully for consistency.

The compressor transfers 32 cfm and uses 0.43 gpm of diesel fuel.

The compressor transfers 32 ft^3/min and uses 0.43 gal/min of diesel fuel. (Revised)*

Clarify mixed fractions.

The screw is 2 3/8 cm long. (Unclear)

The screw is 2-3/8 cm long. (Revised)

The screw is 2.375 cm long. (Revised)

Clarify compound units. Here are some suggestions, although these are not rules. Just be consistent so your reader learns what to expect and can read these constructions effortlessly.

Use four eight foot two by fours and eight four foot two by eights. (Unclear)

Use four 8-ft 2x4s and eight 4-ft 2x8s. (Revised)

Use 4 @ 8-ft 2x4s and 8 @ 4-ft 2x8s. (Revised)

The dimensions are 50 mm x 25 mm x 0.5 mm.
The dimensions are 50 x 25 x 0.5 mm. (Revised)

The dimensions are 50 x 25 x 0.5 mm (LxWxH). (Revised)

The dimensions are 50 (1.9) x 25 (.95) x 0.5 (0.2) mm (in).

The dimensions are 50 x 25 x 0.5 mm (1.9 x 0.95 x 0.2 in). (Revised)

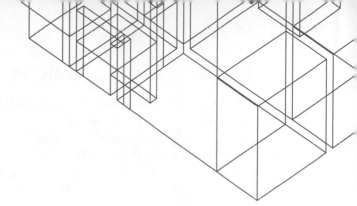

Appendix C
Ethics

Whole libraries have been written on the subject of ethics, with some texts dating back millennia. In Canada alone, there are probably dozens of book-length philosophy dissertations being written right now on the subject, and several non-academic books.

Obviously it's a rich, complex, thorny, and potentially unresolvable issue. But in the end and for our purposes, it's kind of simple if we come at it from the other direction. Let's talk about what isn't ethical.

Unethical behaviour is any act of selfish advantage-taking. It's any act that deliberately harms, misrepresents, or deceives; or abuses power, position, or superior knowledge for personal or professional gain. And this harm needn't be physical or financial. The harm could, for instance, be emotional: a slight to someone's dignity or humanity or an erosion in their trust in others.

And, of course, the harm can easily spread beyond the initial victim. Breach the ethics of your professional organization and you harm the entire organization if the public begins to lose faith in it. Look at the harm that an unethical police officer can do to the public's trust in police forces as a whole. So, a slip in ethics will affect not only your own reputation, but potentially that of your employer and your entire profession.

Now, this does not necessarily mean that if you tell a white lie to a friend or colleague you are single-handedly causing society to unravel. But it does mean that every act that you perform is part of the ongoing opinion-forming conversation that society has about the trust that we can place in one another or, conversely, the cautions we must take against one another (1). The less trust there is, the more constrained we are, the less freely we can act, the more afraid and paranoid we must be about each other—though, to adapt the old saw, it's not paranoia if there is a reason to be suspicious.

The fundamental question, then, is the one that springs from the golden rule: Would you want others to treat you as you are treating them (2)? It sounds trite, of course, because it sounds so simple. But in a sense, it is that simple. Everything else is elaboration and exemplification or an effort to balance harm when neither choice is ideal—the old lesser-of-two-evils dilemma. These are valid discussions, but even in these cases, given enough information, reasonable people can for the most part agree on what an ethical choice would be in a given situation.

> "Do unto others as you would have others do unto you."
> —Matthew 7:12

Ethics in the Professions

You need to understand that you are not just working for your own benefit or promotion or for your company's benefit and profitability. You are an integral part of creating a technical legacy and of building a better knowledge base, a better infrastructure, and a better society (1). Others will rely on these bases and will use them as a foundation for further developments for the betterment and advantage of all. Such improvements cannot be built on lies or half-truths.

A lack of ethics destroys trust, which makes business less adaptable, flexible, and efficient. If you cannot trust other professionals, you'll view their ideas and suggestions with skepticism. If you cannot assume the honesty of bidders, how can you make a good decision between proposals? If you cannot rely on the accuracy of test results or product specifications, how can you move forward with your research, project, or product design? If a selection process is biased or otherwise compromised, how can you be sure that the best proposal will win, that the most appropriate technology, solution, or applicant will be employed?

The vast majority of professionals are ethical, or try to be, and see the value in it, which means that if you develop a reputation for not being ethical, you will suffer for it. So, while a lack of ethics may provide short-term gain, once you or your company is found out, there will be consequences. Misrepresentation in a proposal may get you a project once, but if your accomplishments don't match your promises, you'll soon lose out on opportunities.

We are all and always responsible for acting ethically, but it's a responsibility that is easy to abdicate when working in large groups, following established procedure, or submitting to someone in a position of authority (3). But while that may get us off the hook legally, it doesn't morally. Of course, there may be repercussions for speaking out. If you feel that your organization or a colleague is acting unethically, you'll need to weigh the seriousness of the transgression against your convictions and against the potential risk to you. Speaking up or, in extreme cases, whistleblowing, is not without consequence.

You are, however, protected from wrongful dismissal by law if you end up losing your job as a result of taking an ethical stance. Even milder consequences, such as being frozen out or harassed at the workplace and being denied promotion—if you document them carefully—are actionable in law. It's best, however, to discuss your concerns with someone, just in case there are considerations you hadn't taken into account in your initial interpretation (3).

Unions and larger organizations will have shop stewards, advisors, mentors, or counsellors to whom you can turn. Many organizations have ethics counsellors or advisors or an anonymous helpline where you can report your concerns. These can provide support and legal protection (3).

In the end though, after all discussion, do a quick check to see whether you are being true to your ethics or are giving in to group think, peer pressure, or career anxiety. Ask yourself whether you would still defend your action, would have made the same decision, if you were to be solely responsible and had to defend it before a judge or an ethics committee.

Ethics for Students

The main academic concern when it comes to ethics is, of course, plagiarism: taking someone else's ideas or words and passing them off as your own. The temptation to plagiarize can be strong. On the one hand, there's the pressure to do well in spite of a crushing study schedule; on the other, there's the Internet with its easy access to information that you can simply cut and paste into your own work. There are even sites that will sell whole essays and research papers.

But aside from the very personal cost of getting caught—something else the Internet is making easier and easier, so consider yourself warned—there are wider consequences to plagiarism. First of all, because you haven't actually done the work, you are unfairly getting marks for something that you did not do, which means that you are unfairly competing with other students who have actually put in the effort. How do you imagine other students will feel about that?

In addition, by gaining undeserved marks by misrepresenting your abilities to your professors and instructors, you are also misrepresenting your abilities to your future employers. This means you'll be unfairly competing against the students who have gotten through on their own merit and you will probably disappoint your employers to some extent after you unfairly secure your position. This affects your school's reputation and cheapens its brand for any future students who graduate from your program.

Finally, and this is the reason you'll hear most often, it's intellectual property theft to take someone else's work without giving credit. When someone has used his or her ingenuity and put in the effort to produce something, it belongs to that person. For you to use it and pass it off as your own is dishonest and illegal. In the workplace it can get you sued for damages and fired. In academia it can get you kicked out of a course or even a school. Chapter 9 describes how to acknowledge other people's ideas and information properly.

By the way, submitting a friend's paper, even with your friend's permission, is still plagiarism if you're passing it off as your own. And if you buy a paper online, though it might technically be yours because you've paid for it, you're still practising deception and committing academic fraud because you're passing it off as your own work and genius.

You need to understand that your reputation will prove very important to you in your career and in your social life. And you are starting to build that reputation now, in school. The people who go to school with you will form a large part of your contact list in industry, and they will be connected, by however many degrees of separation, to the rest of your industry, particularly in today's highly connected world. Take the wrong step here at school, be found to be a cheat and a fraud now, and that taint will haunt you for a very long time (4).

What it boils down to, really, is honesty and character.

Ethics in Technical Writing

In technical writing, as in points of law, intent largely determines whether your behaviour is ethical. It is your job, as a technical writer, to present information as accurately and objectively as possible. You must not omit or alter information that runs counter to your preferences or is likely to lead a reader to a conclusion or a decision other than the one you hope for.

For instance, you shouldn't change the specifications of your product to better match the requirements of a potential client. You shouldn't omit or bury information that potentially weakens your proposal; nor should you phrase this information so vaguely that the reader is likely not to understand its real meaning. The intention of all these little manoeuvres is to deceive for personal or professional gain, to take advantage of your greater knowledge of a subject, project, product, or what have you, to manipulate others into doing something that isn't to their advantage, but to your own. Do anything like that and you are writing unethically.

Perhaps a short list of guidelines will help:

- Treat all persons fairly and equally, regardless of race, gender, orientation, profession, level of technical understanding, or wealth.

- Always tell the absolute truth about matters where ethics are in play, where a form of abuse is possible. Little white lies about whether you enjoy someone's cooking or whether the tie matches the suit are fine, unless, in the case of the tie, you are hoping the person will embarrass themselves, because that would be to your advantage.

- Acknowledge all sources of information or ideas; give credit for the work, ideas, and efforts of others when you are writing. See Chapter 9 for details. If the material is copyrighted, make sure you obtain permission before using it. If that means you have to pay for the privilege, do so. Anything less is theft. Along the same lines, always give credit to colleagues who have helped.

- Make your work as accurate as you can; indicate where your numbers are approximate. Don't hide disadvantageous information through vague, unclear writing, and don't lie with statistics or alter graphics to convey a false impression of what the numbers actually mean. See Chapter 10 for details.

- Clearly distinguish between established facts and personal opinions or hunches. The reader has the right to verify for themselves information that isn't 100 per cent verified by you. Of course, you should try to verify these things for yourself, both for the reader's sake and for your own ongoing education.

- Alert readers to all potential drawbacks, detriments, or dangers of your ideas, suggestions, or recommendations so that they can make informed decisions for themselves.

- Know that you will be found out; the consequences will be costly both personally and professionally, and it's possible that the consequences will affect your employer and colleagues and even ripple out into society as a whole.

- Be honest about whether you can meet a deadline or not. That applies not just to writing projects.

Exercises

The following exercises are for class discussion, moderated by the instructor. Consider the details of the ethical dilemmas described; discuss them in pairs or groups and then present your thoughts to the class. Listen carefully to the positions of others in case your classmates raise factors you haven't considered. Students could be divided to represent both sides of a debate.

Exercise C.1

Within Canada, asbestos is recognized as a cancer-causing substance and has been banned in most applications. However, until late in 2012, Canada not only continued to sell asbestos abroad, but actively blocked an effort by the UN World Health Organization to label chrysotile asbestos a cancer-causing substance. This reduced the likelihood that authorities or the public abroad would ask for its use to be restricted. This was clearly good for exports. But was it ethical considering the potential health consequences abroad?

Exercise C.2

Tobacco companies are marketing heavily in newly opened markets in the developing world. This is not only because the markets are available and the potential customers are increasingly affluent, but also because knowledge of the consequences of smoking are less well known in these areas. Is this ethical? Is it ethical to sell cigarettes at all, given what we know about how addictive they are and how dangerous to a smoker's health? If the sale of tobacco is not ethical, are there ethical considerations to prohibiting it? (Think of the prohibition of alcohol in Canada from 1918 to the 1920s, depending on the province; P.E.I. had prohibition from 1907 to 1948. The horror!)

Exercise C.3

What are the consequences of plagiarism on your campus? What is the reason for your institution's policy on plagiarism? And if plagiarism went unchecked, what would the consequences be for the student who plagiarizes, for students who don't, for the institution, for future employers, for the originator of the plagiarized material, and for society as a whole?

Exercise C.4

At a meeting, an engineer repeats an idea he had earlier been told by a colleague. Everyone loves the idea and compliments the engineer for it. He fails to mention that the idea was not his own, thereby tacitly taking credit. What consequences might arise from this little lapse in ethics? What might happen if the colleague who had the idea finds out? What about the rest of the company or the bosses if they find out? What might the immediate consequences be and what might be the long-term consequences?

Glossary of Commonly Misused Words and Phrases

Many words are frequently used incorrectly, especially when they are easily confused with similar words. Professional writers need to be aware of these subtleties and use words carefully. For example,

a lot "A lot" is always spelled as two words: there is no compound form.

> In a lot of cases, engineers are blamed for the mistakes of others.

a vs. an Use "a" before a consonant sound. Use "an" before a vowel sound. Note that words beginning with the same letter may be preceded by "a" or "an" depending on how that letter is pronounced.

> I think we should have a follow-up meeting about the Pinnacle Manufacturing draft proposal this Wednesday at 3 p.m., in my office.

> It was a historic day for the company.

> An hour passed quickly during the professional practice exam.

> We wonder whether an LRT extension in that area would have enough of a passenger catchment.

> Have you been to a library lately?

acute vs. chronic "Acute" means sudden, intense, and requiring immediate attention. "Chronic" means of long standing and not easily overcome. A project may, for instance, be chronically underfunded. If a source of funding is suddenly lost and the payroll can no longer be met, the funding problem is acute.

affect vs. effect "Affect" is generally used as a verb meaning "to influence." "Effect" is generally used as a noun meaning "result" or "outcome."

> The company was affected immediately by the recession.

> Heat treatment increases strength but also has the effect of increasing brittleness.

all ready vs. already "All ready" means completely prepared. "Already" means "previously."

> The alumni committee is all ready for tonight's wine and cheese reception.

> Ministry officials were already aware of the problem when the association called.

among vs. between vs. amid "Among" is generally used for three or more items; "between" is usually restricted to two items. "Amid" is used for items that cannot be counted or separated.

> Conference delegates chose among various technical and business sessions.

> The banter between the engineer and the receptionist stopped when her boyfriend arrived.

> The rescuers searched for survivors amid the rubble.

amoral vs. immoral Things that are "immoral" are, essentially, "evil"; when notions of morality don't apply, neither for the good nor for the bad, you're dealing with something that is amoral.

analysis vs. analyses "Analysis" is singular and "analyses" is plural.

> The soil analysis shows that extensive shoring is required.

> The data analyses gave conflicting results.

any one vs. anyone "Any one" means any single person or thing. "Anyone" means "anybody," as in "any person whatever."

> Is there anyone here who can tell me what happened?

> Go ahead, choose any one of those puppies.

See also "every one vs. everyone" below.

appraise vs. apprise "Appraise" means to evaluate or to assess the worth of something, as in jewels; "apprise" means to inform, most commonly used in the expression "keep me apprised."

because vs. as "As" is commonly used to show causation, but it is better used to show simultaneity or coincidence in time. Use "because" to show causation.

> I struck him as I was backing out of the garage because I could not see him.

because (of) vs. due to Although many people think these two phrases are interchangeable, they are not. "Because of" usually answers the question, "Why?" "Due to" means "caused by." "Due to" is usually preceded by a form of the verb "to be" (be, is, are, was, were, etc.). It should be used only if it can be replaced with "caused by." "Because" should never be preceded by any form of the verb "to be." Confused yet? The following examples should clarify the point:

> The province banned asbestos use because of a federal government order.

> The province's ban on asbestos use was due to a federal government order.

complement vs. compliment "Complement" means to enhance or complete. "Compliment" means to praise or flatter.

> The new writing course complements the association's professional decelopment requirements.

> The manager complimented his staff on a job well done.

continual vs. continuous "Continual" means regular repetition, and "continuous" means extending for a period without interruption.

> Civil engineers must continually refer to codes and standards as part of their work.

> Media coverage of the bridge collapse was continual for several weeks.

> The stresses act upon the bearing member continuously. (never ceases for a moment)

convince vs. persuade You convince someone to believe; you persuade them to act. This is a useful distinction, as you can persuade someone to do something without convincing them that it is the correct thing to do.

> He persuaded me to invest in Nortel last year, but I'm not convinced it was a good idea.

council vs. counsel A "council" is an advisory or deliberative body; "counsel" means advice or to advise, depending on whether it is used as a noun or a verb.

criterion vs. criteria "Criterion" is singular and "criteria" is plural.

> The deflection criterion is 5 mm.

> The track-design criteria specify the maximum vertical, longitudinal, and lateral loads.

> This criterion shall apply to at-grade, underground, elevated, and trenched stations.

> These criteria shall apply to at-grade, underground, elevated, and trenched stations.

definite vs. definitive "Definite" means clear, precise, or unmistakable; "definitive" means authoritative, final, or conclusive. A definite opinion leaves no room for ambiguity. A definitive opinion leaves no room for argument.

discrete vs. discreet "Discrete" means distinct, as in discrete mathematics, or separate, as in discrete categories. "Discreet" means to be careful and circumspect. Use "discreet" when you refer to discretion.

disinterested vs. uninterested "Disinterested" means "neutral" or "objective"; "uninterested" means not giving a damn. A good judge is interested (as opposed to uninterested) in the case, but disinterested in the outcome.

e.g., vs. i.e., These abbreviations for two Latin terms have different meanings: "e.g." means "for example," and "i.e." means "that is." "E.g." introduces a partial list of instances or applications; "i.e." introduces a definition or clarification. Spelling these phrases out in English is preferable to abbreviating them in Latin, but if the abbreviations are used, they should have periods between both letters and be followed by a comma.

> Work interruptions, e.g., phone calls and emails, delay project progress.

> If this occurs, i.e., the project is a success, the managers will take the credit.

ensure vs. insure "Ensure" means to make sure, and "insure" means to provide insurance.

> Can we ensure the engineers' concerns are being heard?

> High liability exposure forces engineering firms to insure their work.

every one vs. everyone "Every one" means each individual person or thing. "Everyone" means "everybody" or "all persons."

> Everyone knows you have to complete every one of the assigned exercises every week.

exacerbate vs. exasperate vs. aggravate "Exacerbate" means to make worse. "Exasperate" means to irritate or frustrate intensely. It's a much stronger word than "irritate." Colloquially, people often use "aggravate" to mean "exasperate," but it actually means to make worse, like "exacerbate."

> All of these grammar rules exasperate me.

> His stubborn attitude exacerbated the conflict with his boss.

farther vs. further "Farther" describes actual, measurable, physical distances, while "further" explains quantity or degree; "further" is used figuratively.

> After construction, the train tracks are located farther from the road.

> The new company procedures further impede worker efficiency.

> The screaming children further aggravated his headache.

fewer vs. less "Fewer" is used for items that can be counted individually. "Less" is used to describe amounts, that is, things that cannot be individually counted.

> Our company has fewer worksite accidents than our competitors.

> Fewer people are eating out in these financially uncertain times.

> Engineers make less money than lawyers.

> There is less water in a pond than in a lake.

flotsam vs. jetsam The two are usually used in conjunction but are not redundant as many people suspect. Flotsam is what floats off a boat on its own accord as the boat sinks. Jetsam is what has been thrown overboard (jettisoned). The distinction used to have insurance and salvage implications, but today it is merely interesting, and relevant only when you're playing Trivial Pursuit. You're welcome.

flout vs. flaunt "Flout" means to disregard, as in laws or convention; "flaunt" means to show off, as in bling or fancy cars.

forceful vs. forcible vs. forced "Forceful," like "strong," implies the potential for force; hence we speak of forceful personalities or forceful arguments. "Forcible" means the application of force, as in "forcible entry." "Forced" is usually used when something is done under coercion, as in "forced laughter" at the boss's jokes and "forced marches" to the department meeting.

former vs. latter "Former" refers to the first of two; "latter" refers to the second of two. If more than two referents are in play, use "first," "second," "third," "last," and so on, instead.

infer vs. imply To "infer" means to deduce logically; to "imply" means to suggest.

> After three unsuccessful attempts I inferred that I would not get the position. In fact, the interviewer implied that I should leave the industry entirely.

irregardless vs. regardless vs. irrespective There's no such word as "irregardless." It's an unfortunate cross-pollination of "regardless" and "irrespective," on par with George W. Bush's "misunderestimate." Lose this word from your vocabulary. "Regardless" means "in spite of obstacles or objections"; "irrespective" means virtually the same thing, "not taking something into account." The two words can be used almost interchangeably, but "regardless" is more common.

> I specified the stainless steel support beams regardless of their cost.

> I specified the stainless steel support beams irrespective of their cost.

is vs. are "Is" is singular and "are" is plural. "Is" is often erroneously used instead of "are" in conjunction with plural quantities, especially in contractions. "None" (as a quantity) can be singular or plural depending on context.

> There is no milk left in the fridge.

> None of the candidates are to my liking.

> There's one train every 15 minutes.

> There are six new stations along the proposed LRT right-of-way.

> There're 24 alarm signals entering the controller.

it's vs. its "It's" is a contraction of "it is" or "it has"; "its" is a possessive pronoun that generally replaces "of it" or "belonging to it." If your sentence makes sense using "it is," use it's.

> Thank God it's Friday.

> Engineering has lost its appeal now that I have to write so much.

licence vs. license "Licence" is a noun, and "license" is a verb.

> She received her licence from the association on her birthday.

> The association has licensed her to do this kind of work.

lie vs. lay "Lie" and "lay" have several meanings and represent different tenses.

MEANING	PRESENT TENSE	PAST TENSE
To be prone	lie	lay
To place	lay	laid
To tell a falsehood	lie	lied

"Lie" and "lay" are also used in the expression "the lay of the land" (American/Canadian) or "the lie of the land" (British) to mean "the general appearance or state of an area" or "the existing circumstances or state of affairs." Of course, "lay" and "laid" have another meaning too.

> This book is so boring I need to lie down before I fall asleep.

> Yesterday, I lay down after getting home from work.

> Lay the concrete in the form.

> I laid the flowers on Susan's desk during her lunch break, and I saw them in the garbage in the afternoon.

> I cannot tell a lie; James did it.

> I lied about James. It was Harry.

many vs. much "Many" is used for items that can be counted individually. "Much" is used to describe amounts, that is, things that are not individually counted.

Too many people use words carelessly.

How much time is left before this meeting is over?

obsolete vs. obsolescent "Obsolete" means defunct, no longer relevant or pertinent; think "dead." Use "obsolescent" for something that is becoming obsolete; think "dying" or as the adjective "sunset" in the phrase "sunset industry."

off of vs. off "Off of" is redundant and should never be used but is, unfortunately, becoming more common—a bad habit moving north from the States. "Off" already contains the sense of direction supplied by "of" in colloquial speech.

Get off of my lawn. (Redundant)

Get off my lawn. (Correct)

peak vs. peek vs. pique A "peak" is an apex, as in the peak of a mountain; a "peek" is a quick or stolen glance; "pique" means to arouse and is generally reserved for expressions to do with curiosity or interest: "he piqued my curiosity."

practice vs. practise "Practice" is a noun and "practise" is a verb in Canadian English. American English tends to use "practice" for both noun and verb.

The engineer's practice has been in the same building for 20 years.

A career in engineering gives ample opportunities to practise English.

principle vs. principal "Principle" is used only as a noun and means "rule," "law," "doctrine," or "concept." "Principal" can be used as a noun to mean "capital" in finance or the head of a school or other organization, or it can be used as an adjective to mean "chief" or "primary."

The guiding principle of universal health care is social justice. The principal reason insurance companies oppose it is profit.

"Thorsten Ewald, please report to the principal's office."

purposely vs. purposefully "Purposely" means "on purpose," but "on purpose" is more commonly used and sounds better; "purposefully" means "for a specific reason."

He bumped into me on purpose. (It was no accident.)

His wife kicked him on the shin purposefully. (Her purpose was to stop him from continuing to embarrass her.)

Of course, there are circumstances in which either meaning applies.

shear vs. sheer To "shear" is to remove, as in shearing sheep, or to want to or to cause to break, as in shearing forces in a structure. "Sheer" means transparent, as in negligees; perpendicular, that is, more than steep, as in cliffs; and pure or unmitigated, as in madness.

take vs. bring "Take" indicates direction away and "bring" indicates direction towards. The same duality exists with the words "going" (away from you) and "coming" (towards you).

I am going somewhere, so I need to take something with me.

Someone is coming here, so they can bring me something.

Take your lunch to work.

I will need to take this work home with me; I will bring it back tomorrow.

than vs. then Use "than" to make comparisons; use "then" to establish a sequence in time or to establish causation and consequence.

Mine is bigger than yours.

I would rather travel by train than fly in a plane.

First he said he'd come, then he said he couldn't.

He pushed, then I shoved.

that vs. which "That" should be used to introduce subordinate clauses. This use of "that" is not controversial but is often overlooked.

It is widely believed that the earth is round.

The confusion between "that" and "which" arises in their use with modifying phrases. A modifying phrase can be either restrictive, meaning that it helps to define the subject (i.e., provides a necessary piece of information—use "that"), or non-restrictive, meaning that it merely describes the subject but does not define (restrict) which subject is being described (i.e., provides a non-essential piece of information—use "which").

Writers (especially Canadians and Britons, but not so much Americans) often use "which" when they should use "that." As a rule of thumb, read your sentence over. If you can use "that" instead of "which," use "that."

"Which" phrases are separated by commas. "That" phrases are not. This is because "that" phrases are necessary to the sentence, whereas "which" phrases are more or less parenthetical.

The contract that you need to sign is on your desk. (You're looking for one specific contract only, the one you need to sign.)

This contract, which Bill signed yesterday, is too long. (You already know which contract you are talking about; the fact that Bill signed it yesterday is additional, but not defining, or restricting, information.)

The porta-potties that you delivered had not been cleaned.

Porta-potties, which are sanitary, cheap, and plentiful, have done much to improve morale on the site.

Statics, which have to be signed off by a professional engineer, involve a lot of complex calculations.

try and vs. try to It's never "try and" do something; it's "try to" do something. "And" connects two grammatical elements of the same kind: two clauses, two verbs, two nouns in a series, for instance. But when you are talking about an attempt to do something, you are creating a verb phrase. Use the infinitive. You'd never say, "Attempt and" do something, would you?

Try to text and call more often.

until vs. till Both forms are correct, but "till" is much less common. 'Til is an informal contraction and not acceptable in formal writing. It's, therefore, best to use "until."

was vs. were "Was" is singular and "were" is plural.

> The catch basin was installed at the tunnel's low point.

> The test results were inconclusive.

"Were" (not "was") is also used for the past subjunctive mood, which means for conditional "if" phrases that include "would" or "could":

> If I were in charge, I'd give everyone in my department a raise.

> I could reach the top shelf if I were taller.

Statements starting with "as if" or "though" follow the same rules.

> He acts as if he were infallible.

> She behaves as though money were scarce.

The subjunctive "were" also comes into phrases that include "wish."

> I wish I were home.

Similar Words

Be aware of the differences between the following similar words:

> their (possessive of "they")

> there (positional)

> they're (contraction of "they are")

> where (positional)

> wear (pertains to clothing, deterioration, etc.)

> were (past tense of "are")

> we're (contraction of "we are")

> whose (possessive of "who" or "which")

> who's (contraction of "who is" or "who has")

> your (possessive of "you")

> you're (contraction of "you are")

> to (directional)

> too (also)

> two (the number 2)

References

Chapter 1

1   "Survey: Poor Communication Causes Most IT Project Failures." www.computerworld.com/action/articles. Downloaded June 7, 2011.
2   Maggiani, Rich. "The Costs of Poor Communication." thecontentwrangler.com/2008/12/30/the_costs_of_poor_communication. Downloaded June 9, 2011.
3   Olsen, Keith. "How Does Poor Communication Cost Money?" www.eHow.com. Updated May 12, 2011. Downloaded June 9, 2011.

Chapter 2

1   Williams, Joseph M. *Style: Lessons in Clarity and Grace*, 9th ed. New York: Pearson Longman, 2007.

Chapter 8

1   Beamer, Linda, and Iris Varner. *Intercultural Communication in the Global Workplace*, 4th ed. New York: McGraw-Hill Irwin, 2008.
2   Schmidt, Wallace V., et al. *Communication Globally: Intercultural Communication and International Business*. Los Angeles: Sage Publications, 2007.

Appendix C

1   Finkelstein, Leo Jr. *Pocket Book of Technical Writing for Engineers and Scientists*, 2nd ed. New York: McGraw-Hill, 2005.
2   Maxwell, John C. *There's No Such Thing as Business Ethics: There's Only One Rule for Making Decisions.* New York: Warner Books, 2003.
3   Audi, Robert. *Business Ethics and Ethical Business*. New York: Oxford University Press, 2009.
4   Peterson, James. Comm 5105 class lecture. Topic: References, Plagiarism, and Professionalism. Burnaby, BC: BCIT, Nov. 26, 2010.

Bibliography

Aaron, Jane E. and Elaine Bander. *The Little Brown Essential Handbook for Writers*, 1st Cdn. ed. Don Mills, ON: Addison-Wesley, 1999.

Anderson, Paul V. *Technical Communication A Reader-Centered Approach*, 5th ed. Boston, MA: Thomson Heinle, 2003.

"Appendectomy." Available at http://emedicine.medscape.com/article/195778-overview.

"Appendectomy." Available at www.medicinenet.com/appendectomy/page5.htm.

"Appendectomy." Wikipedia [modified 12 Mar. 2012 at 01:48]. Available at en.wikipedia.org/wiki/Appendectomy.

Athienitis, Andreas, and Rémi Charron. "Design and Optimization of Net Zero Energy Solar Homes." *ASHRAE Transactions* 112, part 2 (2006): 285–95.

Athienitis, Andreas, Matt Doiron, and William O'Brien. "Energy Performance, Comfort, and Lessons Learned from a Near Net Zero Energy Solar House." *ASHRAE Transactions* 117, no. 2 (2011): 585–96.

Atteberry, Jonathan. "How to Change a Fuel Filter." HowStuffWorks. Available at howstuffworks.com/under-the-hood/vehicle-maintenance/change-fuel-filter.htm

Audi, Robert. *Business Ethics and Ethical Business*. New York: Oxford University Press, 2009.

Barton, Matthews D., and James R. Heiman. "Process, Product, and Potential: The Archeological Assessment of Collaborative, Wiki-Based Student Projects in the Technical Communication Classroom." *Technical Communication Quarterly* 21, no. 1 (Jan.–March 2012): 46–60.

Beamer, Linda, and Iris Varner. *Intercultural Communication in the Global Workplace*, 4th ed. New York: McGraw-Hill Irwin, 2008.

Beer, David, and David McMurrey. *A Guide to Writing as an Engineer*, 3rd ed. John Wiley & Sons, 2009.

Blackberry Curve 8350i Specs at a glance. Available at http://us.blackberry.com/smartphones/blackberrycurve8300/#!phone-specifications.

Blake, Gary, and Robert W. Bly. *The Elements of Technical Writing*. New York: MacMillan General Reference, 1993.

Blicq, Ron, and Lisa Moretto. *Technically-Write!* 7th Cdn ed. Toronto, ON: Pearson Prentice Hall, 2008.

Boone, Louis E., et al. *Contemporary Business Communication*, Cdn. ed. Scarborough, ON: Prentice Hall Canada, 1999.

Bovee, Courtland L., John V. Thill, and Jean A. Scribner. *Business Communication Essentials*, 2nd Cdn. ed. Toronto: Pearson Canada, 2005.

Burnett, Rebecca E. and Jan Shepherd McKee. *Technical Communication*, 1st Cdn ed. Scarborough, ON: Thomson Nelson, 2003

Byrne, Dan. "Writing Government Policies and Procedures in Plain Language." *Business Communication Quarterly* 71, no. 1 (Mar. 2008): 88–92.

Canadian Electricity Association. *Power Generation in Canada: A Guide. Canadian Electricity Association*. Ottawa, 2006. Available at www.electricity.ca/media/pdfs/backgrounders/HandBook.pdf.

Canadian Mortgage and Housing Corporation. *Wood-Frame Envelopes in the Coastal Climate of British Columbia—Best Practices Guide Building Technology*. Canadian Mortgage and Housing Corporation, 2001.

DeGagne, David C., Anita Lewis, and Chris May. "Evaluation of Wind Turbine Noise." Alberta Energy & Utilities Board. Available at www.noisesolutions.com/upoads/images/resoucres/pdfs/Wind%20Turbine%20Noise.pdf.

Dieken, Connie. *Talk Less, Say More: The Habits to Influence Others and Make Things Happen*. Hoboken, NJ: John Wiley & Sons, 2009.

Dobrin, Arthur. *Ethics for Everyone: How to Increase Your Moral Intelligence*. New York: John Wiley & Sons, 2002.

Doumont, Jean-Luc. *Effective Oral Presentations*. Brochure. JL Consulting, 2004.

Edelman, Mark. "SOPs and the Technical Writer." *Intercom* 50, no. 4 (Apr. 2003): 8–11.

Engineering Specifications and Standard Drawings. Capital Region District Water Services Dept. Victoria, BC. Revision July 2009. Available at www. Crd.bc.ca/water/engineering/documents/engineering_specs2009.pdf.

Evans, Mark. "How to Change your Fuel Filter." CarMD.com. Available at www.youtube.com/watch?v=S0bWLUA2IQ4

Ewald, Thorsten, and Andre Lanz. *Writing Write: A Practical Writing Guide for Practical People*. 2009.

Finkelstein, Leo Jr. *Pocket Book of Technical Writing for Engineers and Scientists*, 2nd ed. New York: McGraw-Hill, 2005.

Flick, Jane, and Celia Millward. *Handbook for Writers*, 3rd Cdn. ed. Scarborough, ON: Nelson Thomson Learning, 1999.

Goban, Stephen B. and Nathan M. Greenfield. *Canadian Business Writing: A Structural Approach*. Toronto: Thomson Nelson, 2002.

Goguen, Claude, P.E., LEED AP. Thermal Mass. Precast Inc., Jul/Aug. 2011, p.6. Available at http://precast.org/precast-magazines/precast-inc/july-august-2011/

Golder, Katherine. "Unit 11: Process Descriptions." Handout for Comm 1143. BCIT. Emailed 27 Sept. 2012.

———. "Unit 13: Technical Definitions & Descriptions." Handout for Comm 1143. BCIT. Emailed 27 Sept. 2012.

Goldman, Lynda. "The Ten Best Rules for Email Etiquette." Available at http://ezinearticles.com/?Netiquette-Rules---10-Best-Rules-for-Email-Etiquette&id=785177.

Grigg, Darry, and Newman, Jennifer. "Goal-oriented Teams More Likely to Break the Rules." *Vancouver Sun*. Saturday, May 28, 2011, p. C4.

Guffey, Mary Ellen, Kathleen Rhodes, and Patricia Rogin. *Business Communication Process and Product*, 5th Cdn. ed. Toronto: Nelson Thomson, 2008.

Gurak, Laura J., John M. Lannon, and Jana Seijts. *A Concise Guide to Technical Communication*, Cdn. ed. Toronto: Pearson Canada, 2010.

Holtzclaw, Theresa K. "Lab Bench Activity: Transpiration." Pearson Education: Available at www.phschool.com/science/biology_place/labbench/lab9/intro.html.

Howard, Ronald A., and Clinton D. Korver. *Ethics [for the Real World]: Creating a Personal Code to Guide Decisions in Work and Life*. Boston: Harvard Business Press, 2008.

Hypergrammar. University of Ottawa Writing Centre. Available at www.writingcentre.uottawa.ca/hypergrammar/grammar.html.

IEEE Citation Reference. IEEE Org. Available at www.ieee.org/documents/ieeecitationref.pdf.

Immen, Wallace. "First Things First: Getting a Foot in the Door." *The Globe and Mail*. Friday, March 23, 2012, p. B18.s

Lannon, John M., and Don Klepp. *Technical Communication*, 3rd Cdn. ed. Toronto: Pearson Longman, 2006.

Lee, Jeff. "Wood to Reach New Heights." *The Vancouver Sun*. Thursday, March 22, 2012, p. C5.

Lee, Mary et al. *The Handbook of Technical Writing Form and Style*. Toronto, ON: Harcourt, Brace, Jovanovich, 1990.

Life Cycle of a Salmon, The. Seymour Salmonid Society. Available at http://seymoursalmon.com/lifecycle.php.

Locker, Kitty O. "Will Professional Communication Be the Death of Business Communication?" *Business Communication Quarterly* 66, no. 3 (Sept. 2003): 118–32.

MacLennan, Jennifer. *Effective Communication for the Technical Professions*. Toronto: Prentice Hall, 2003.

Maggiani, Rich. *The Cost of Poor Communication*. Available at thecontentwrangler.com/2008/12/30/the_cost_of_poor_communication.

Makecitation.com.

Maxtor 7131 A 131 Mbyte Integrated AT Controller Hard Disk Drive Installation Guide. Maxtor Corporation. Available at www.schematicsforfree.

Maxwell, John C. *There's No Such Thing as Business Ethics: There's Only One Rule for Making Decisions*. Warner Books, 2003.

McTighe, Tom. "Moving the World with Collaborative Writing." *Intercom* 52, no. 4 (Apr. 2005): 22–4.

Mousten, Birthe, Bruce Maylath, Sonia Vandepitte, and John Humbley. "Learning Localization through Trans-Atlantic Collaboration: Bridging the Gap." *IEEE Transactions on Professional Communication* 53, no. 4 (1 Dec. 2010): 401–11.

NAPA Auto Parts. "Fuel Filter Change." NAPA Auto Parts. Available at www.napacanada.com/en/NAPA-Know-How/Fuel-Filter-Change.aspx

Netiquette. Wikipedia.org. Available at http://en.wikipedia.org/wiki/Netiquette.

Newell, Ben, and Ty Newell. "Thermal Mass Design." *ASHRAE Journal* 53, no. 3 (Mar. 2011): 70–6.

Nice, Karim. "How Rotary Engines Work." Available at www.howstuffworks.com/rotary-engine.htm.

Nova Scotia Wind Integration Study. Report for Nova Scotia Dept. of Energy, 2008. Available at www.gov.ns.ca/energy/resources/EM/NS-Wind-Integration-Study-Final.pdf.

O'Connor, Patricia T. *Woe is I*. New York: Grosset/Putnam, 1996.

Olsen, Keith. "How Does Poor Communication Cost Money?" eHow.com. Updated May 12, 2011.

Otte, Michael. Communication Course Manual. British Columbia Institute of Technology, 1997/8

Perlin, Neil. "Shifts in Technical Communication." *Intercom* 57, no. 1 (Jan. 2010): 17–19.

Peterson, James. Comm 5105 class lecture. Topic: References, Plagiarism, and Professionalism. Burnaby, BC: BCIT, Nov. 26, 2010.

Pfeiffer, William S., and Jan Boogerd. *Technical Writing: A Practical Approach*, Cdn. ed. Toronto: Prentice Hall Canada, 1997.

Pfeiffer, William S. *Pocket Guide to Technical Writing*. Upper Saddle River, NJ: Prentice Hall, 1998.

Prohibition in Canada. Wikipedia.org. Available at www.wikipedia.org/wiki/Prohibition_in_ Canada.

Prohibition. Wikipedia.org. Available at www .wikipedia.org/wiki/Prohibition.

Quick and Dirty Tricks for Better Writing. Available at http://grammar.quickanddirtytips.com.

Rice, J.A. "Bridging the Gap: Contextualizing Professional Ethics in Collaborative Writing Projects." *Business Communication Quarterly* 70, no. 4 (Dec. 2007): 470–5.

RIM Blackberry Curve 8310 Specifications. Available at www.wireless.att.com/support_static_files/ KB/KB84956.html.

Royal Architectural Institute of Canada. *Climate Change and Architecture.* Available at www .raic.org/architecture_architects/green_ architecture/2030/2030factsheet_e.pdf.

Rukmini, S. "Quality Standard Document: A Practical Application of Scientific and Technical Writing for English Language Professionals." *IUP Journal of Soft Skills* 5, no. 3 (Sept. 2011): 46–9.

Salmon. Wikipedia [modified 16 Oct. 2012 at 23:13]. Available at http://en.wikipedia.org/wiki/ Salmon.

Salmon Life Cycle Egg and Onward: Think Salmon. Available at www.thinksalmon.com/learn/ life_cycle/salmon_life_cycle.

Samovar, Larry A., Richard E. Porter, and Edwin R. McDaniel. *Intercultural Communication: A Reader*, 13th ed. Boston: Wadsworth Cengage Learning, 2012.

Schmidt, Wallace V., et al. *Communication Globally: Intercultural Communication and International Business.* Los Angeles: Sage Publications, 2007.

Schmutz, L.E. "Transistor Gain Boosts Capacitor Value." *Electronics*, 25 July 1974. Available at www.schematicsforfree.com.

Sharp, Helen M. "Challenging Students to Respond to Multicultural Issues." *Business Communication Quarterly* 58 (June 1995): 28–31.

Smith, Deborah A. Lab Report: Transpiration. February 27, 1990. Available at http://water. me.vccs.edu/report_example.htm.

Snair, Scott. *Stop the Meeting I Want to Get Off!* New York: McGraw-Hill, 2003.

Suagee, Dean B. "Solar Energy: Let's Get Passive!" *Natural Resources & Environment* 26, no. 2 (Fall 2011): 54–6.

"Survey: Poor Communication Causes Most IT Project Failures." Available at www .computerworld.com/action/articles.

Suzuki, David. "Whirling for Energy." *StraightGoodsNews* [online magazine], 11 July 2011. Available at www.straitgoods.ca/2011/ ViewArticles.cfm?Ref=589.

Thermal Mass. Wikipedia.org. May 2008 [modified 14 Feb. 2012]. Available at http://en.wikipedia. org/wiki/Thermal_mass.

Torchinsky, Jason. "The Last Mazda Wankel Engine Has Been Built." Jalopnik.com. Available at jalopnik.com/5921410/the-last-mazda-wankel-engine-has-been-built.

Wankel engine. Wikipedia.org. Available at www .wikipedia.org/wiki/Wankel_engine.

Weis, Tim. *Wind Power Realities: Fact Sheet.* Pembina Institute. Available at www.pembina. org/docs/re/revised-final-wind-fastsheet.pdf.

Whiteside, James D. "How to Present a Technical Paper." *AACE International Transactions*, 2009, pp. Dev06.1–Dev06.9.

———. "How to Write a Technical Paper." *AACE International Transactions*, 2009, pp. Dev01.1– Dev01.9.

Wild Salmon Spotlight: Gold Seal. Available at www.goldseal.ca/wildsalmon/life_cycle. asp#adults.

Williams, Joseph M. *Style: Lessons in Clarity and Grace*, 9th ed. New York: Pearson Longman, 2007.

Worley, Peter. "Writing Skills Essential in Tech Ed Today." *Tech Directions* 68, no. 2 (Sept. 2008): 17–19.

Writer's Handbook, The. The Writing Center at the University of Wisconsin, Madison. Available at http://writing.wisc.edu/ Handbook.

Xu, Peng, P.E., Phd. "Case Study of Demand Shifting with Thermal Mass in Two Large Commercial Buildings." *ASHRAE Transactions* 115, part 2 (2009): 586–98.

Yu, Han. "Intercultural Competence in Technical Communication: A Working Definition and Review of Assessment Methods." *Technical Writing Quarterly* [serial online] 21, no. 2 (April 2012): 168–86. Available from Academic Search Complete, Ipswich, MA.

Zinn, Lennard. *Zinn & the Art of Mountain Bike Maintenance*, 4th ed. Boulder, CO: Velo Press, 2005.

Zoonosis. Wikipedia. Available at en.wikipedia.org/ wiki/Zoonosis.

Zoonosis. The Free Dictionary. Available at medical-dictionary.thefreedictionary.com/Zoonosis

Index